A HISTORY

OF THE EXPEDITION

TO JERUSALEM

1095–1127

· FULCHER OF CHARTRES ·

A HISTORY
OF THE EXPEDITION
TO JERUSALEM
1095-1127

Translated by Frances Rita Ryan
(Sisters of St. Joseph)

· EDITED WITH AN INTRODUCTION BY HAROLD S. FINK ·

THE UNIVERSITY OF TENNESSEE PRESS
KNOXVILLE

LIBRARY OF CONGRESS CATALOG CARD NUMBER: 78–77847

STANDARD BOOK NUMBER: 87049–097–4

Copyright © 1969 by The University of Tennessee Press. All Rights Reserved.
Manufactured in the United States of America. First Edition.

To

· A<small>UGUST</small> C<small>HARLES</small> K<small>REY</small> ·

Late Professor of Medieval History
At the University of Minnesota

PREFACE

✝

IN 1913 Heinrich Hagenmeyer published his definitive edition of the *Historia Hierosolymitana* of Fulcher of Chartres,[1] a chronicle of the First Crusade and a history of the Latin states in the East during their formative years. In 1916 Frances Rita Ryan (Sisters of St. Joseph) submitted an English translation of Hagenmeyer's text to the Faculty of the Graduate School of the University of Minnesota as a master's thesis prepared under the direction of August Charles Krey.[2] Much of Book I of her version was published in 1921 in Krey's *First Crusade,* a collection of translations from chronicles and letters by western writers dealing with the principal incidents of that crusade,[3] but Sister Frances' complete translation of Fulcher's work, including Books II and III, was never published. Later, in 1941, Martha Evelyn McGinty independently translated Book I of Fulcher.[4] This book ends with an account of the capture of Bohemond of Antioch by the Turks in the middle of August, 1100, and a report of the subse-

---

[1] Heinrich Hagenmeyer (ed.), *Fulcheri Carnotensis historia Hierosolymitana* (1095-1127), mit Erläuterungen und einem Anhange (Heidelberg: Carl Winters Universitätsbuchhandlung, 1913). Future references to this volume will be to *HF,* with page and footnote numbers. In the case of Fulcher's text, whether to Hagenmeyer's Latin text or to the Ryan translation, reference will be to book, chapter, and paragraph, or if within the book, to chapter and paragraph.

[2] Sister Frances Rita Ryan (trans.), "History of the Expedition to Jerusalem by Fulcher of Chartres" (Master's thesis, University of Minnesota, 1916).

[3] August C. Krey (ed.), *The First Crusade: The Accounts of Eye-Witnesses and Participants* (Princeton: Princeton University Press; London: Humphrey Milford, Oxford University Press, 1921), vi.

[4] Martha Evelyn McGinty (trans.), *Fulcher of Chartres, Chronicle of the First Crusade* ("Translations and Reprints from the Original Sources of History," third series, Vol. I [Philadelphia: University of Pennsylvania Press; London: Humphrey Milford, Oxford University Press, 1941]).

quent arrival in Edessa of the news of the death of Godfrey of Bouillon in Jerusalem on July 18, 1100.

Professor Krey, before his death in 1961, sent his personal copy of Sister Frances' manuscript to me with the suggestion that it be edited and published in its entirety. He pointed out that Books II and III, never published in English translation, are in many respects the most important because they cover a period largely neglected by other eyewitness chroniclers. Further, he suggested that Sister Frances' text, almost completely unannotated, needed references pointing to new developments in scholarship since the time of Hagenmeyer.

These two tasks I have undertaken to perform. I have carefully compared Sister Frances' translation with Hagenmeyer's Latin text in order to insure accuracy in the former. Not many changes have been necessary, and I gladly assume responsibility for any inaccuracies that remain in the translation as I have altered it or for any clumsy changes in English that I have introduced. One would be bold to undertake to improve upon Hagenmeyer's exhaustive annotation. I do not claim to have done this. Nevertheless, I have attempted to reduce the footnotes to more manageable compass as well as to take note of more recent studies of the crusades. For the most part I have been content to refer the reader to the principal corroboratory or variant medieval sources so that he may judge the reliability of Fulcher's testimony and to suggest to him one or two modern authorities for further reference.

H. S. F.

ACKNOWLEDGMENTS

✝

IN EDITING and annotating the accompanying translation by Frances Rita Ryan of the *Historia Hierosolymitana* of Fulcher of Chartres, I have become intensely aware of her beautiful Latin scholarship and of her instinct for choosing precisely the right word or expression in rendering this chronicle into English. For these reasons I wish to pay tribute to her, and also to the Christian devotion manifest throughout her work. In addition, I want to extend my sincere thanks to Mrs. Nelle Ryan Freeman of St. Paul, Minnesota, sister of Sister Frances, for her gracious permission to publish this translation, and for the *vita* of Sister Frances.

At the same time I wish to acknowledge my deep personal indebtedness to August Charles Krey, who originally introduced me to the study of the crusades and who was a source of kindly help and inspiration to me for many years. My thanks are also due to Dr. LeRoy P. Graf, chairman of the Department of History at The University of Tennessee, for much support and encouragement in this project; to Miss Olive Branch and many others of the staff of the University Library for generous assistance that has never failed; to Mrs. Eileen Cave for her patience and skill in typing; and finally to my wife Magnhild, whose loyalty and affection have made possible this work.

H. S. F.

CONTENTS

✝

ABBREVIATIONS

✝

AHR   *The American Historical Review,* I (1895 ff).

AOL   *Archives de l'Orient latin.* 2 vols. Paris: Pub.
             sous le patronage de la Société de l'Orient lat-
             in, 1881–84.

Crusades-Munro   Louis J. Paetow (ed.). *The Crusades and Other
             Historical Essays Presented to Dana C. Munro.*
             New York: F. S. Crofts and Co., 1928.

HChr   Heinrich Hagenmeyer. "Chronologie de la pre-
             mière croisade (1094–1100)," ROL, VI–VIII
             (1898–1901); and "Chronologie de l'histoire
             du royaume de Jérusalem, règne de Baudouin
             I (1101–1118)," ROL, IX–XII (1902–11).

HEp   ———— (ed.). *Epistulae et chartae ad historiam
             primi belli sacri spectantes.* Innsbruck, 1901.

HF   ————. *Fulcheri Carnotensis historia Hieroso-
             lymitana (1095–1127).* Heidelberg, 1913.

HG   ————. *Anonymi gesta Francorum et aliorum
             Hierosolymitanorum.* Heidelberg, 1890.

MPL   J. P. Migne (ed.). *Patrologiae cursus comple-
             tus,* series latina. 221 vols. Paris, 1844 ff.

RHC   *Recueil des historiens des croisades,* Académie
             des inscriptions et belles-lettres. 16 vols. in fol.
             Paris, 1841–1906.
             Arm.   *Documents arméniens.* 2 vols. 1869–
             1906.

	Occ. *Historiens occidentaux.* 5 vols. 1841–95.
	Or. *Historiens orientaux.* 5 vols. 1872–1906.
ROL	*Revue de l'Orient latin.* 12 vols. Paris, 1893–1911.
Rolls Series	William Stubbs (ed.). *Rerum Britannicarum medii aevi scriptores*: or *Chronicles and Memorials of Great Britain and Ireland during the Middle Ages,* pub. by the authority of Her Majesty's Treasury under the direction of the Master of the Rolls. 99 works in 244 vols. London: Her Majesty's Stationery Office, 1858–96.
Setton (ed.), Crusades	Kenneth M. Setton (editor-in-chief). *A History of the Crusades.* Vol. I, Marshall W. Baldwin (ed.), *The First Hundred Years.* Philadelphia, 1955.

A HISTORY

OF THE EXPEDITION

TO JERUSALEM

1095–1127

INTRODUCTION

✝

IDENTITY OF FULCHER

INITIATED BY POPE URBAN II and blessed by the Holy Roman Catholic Church, the First Crusade (1095–99) invited all of the men of European Christendom to take up the cross of their religion and free the holy city of Jerusalem and the Holy Sepulcher from the infidels' grasp. One of the many who answered the call was Fulcher of Chartres, the chaplain of Baldwin I, lord of Edessa from 1098 to 1100 and first of the crusader kings at Jerusalem from 1100 to 1118. Fulcher was a resident of Jerusalem from the end of 1100 at least until 1127, when he disappears from view, and was the author of one of the three full-length Latin chronicles of the First Crusade to be written by participants. His account of the important Council of Clermont and the progress of the contingent of crusaders with which he started, that of Duke Robert of Normandy and Count Stephen of Blois and Chartres, is entirely free of dependence upon other writers. This is also true of Fulcher's report of the establishment of the county of Edessa by Baldwin I early in 1098. But his account in Book I of the progress of the main army of crusaders during the period from May, 1097, to August, 1099, while Fulcher was absent with Baldwin at Edessa, relies largely on the two other eyewitness chronicles of the First Crusade, the anonymous *Gesta Francorum et aliorum Hierosolymitanorum* and the *Historia Francorum qui ceperunt Iherusalem* of Raymond of Aguilers.[1] The events of this

---

[1] The *Gesta* has been several times edited, viz., by Jacques Bongars in the *Gesta Dei per Francos* (2 vols. in 1; Hannov.: Typis Wechelianis, 1611), 1–29; Philippe Le Bas in the *Recueil des historiens des croisades, Historiens occidentaux*, pub. by

latter period include the siege of Nicaea in May and June, 1097, the march thereafter across Anatolia, and, particularly, the progress of the crusaders from the siege of Antioch beginning on October 20–21, 1097, to the capture of Jerusalem, July 15, 1099, and the resultant battle of Ascalon on August 12, 1099.

Unlike the other two writers, Fulcher continued his work, the *Historia Hierosolymitana,*[2] for another generation until 1127, when it abruptly ends. He covered the reign of King Baldwin I in Jerusalem from 1100 to 1118 in Book II and the reign of King Baldwin II until 1127 in Book III. Although his record is centered around the affairs of Jerusalem, Fulcher often touched upon the city's relations with the Turkish rulers of Damascus, Aleppo, and Mosul, who were Sunnites, with the powerful Shī 'ite Arab caliphate of Cairo, which operated from its advanced base at Ascalon, and with the other crusader states of Antioch, Edessa, and Tripoli. In fact, during the reign of Baldwin II, Fulcher's account is practically a history of all four crusader states. This is true because Baldwin was the regent of Antioch from 1119 to 1126 and also the protector of all the Franks—the crusaders in the East.

Fulcher's history is the only one by a local Frankish resident

---

the Académie des inscriptions et belles-lettres, III (Paris: Imprimerie Impériale, 1866), 119–63 (this set hereinafter cited *RHC, Occ.*); Heinrich Hagenmeyer (Heidelberg: Carl Winter's Universitätsbuchhandlung, 1890); Beatrice A. Lees (Oxford: Clarendon Press, 1924); Louis Bréhier (ed. and trans.), *Histoire anonyme de la première croisade* (Paris: Librairie ancienne Honoré Champion, 1924); and Rosalind Hill (ed. and trans.) (London, Edinburgh, Paris, Melbourne, Toronto, and New York: Thomas Nelson and Sons, Ltd., 1962). Reference to the *Gesta*, unless otherwise indicated, will be to Hagenmeyer's edition as *HG*. This has a valuable preface and footnotes and also permits citation of text by chapter and paragraph. The *Historia Francorum* of Raymond of Aguilers may be found in *RHC, Occ.*, III, 231–309. John Hugh Hill and Laurita L. Hill have just finished *Raymond d'Aguilers Historia Francorum qui ceperunt Iherusalem* (Philadelphia: The American Philosophical Society, 1968), an annotated translation, and are also preparing a new edition of the Latin text. I do not regard the *Historia de Hierosolymitano itinere* of Tudebode of Civray as a fourth Latin source of independent value because it is very dependent upon the anonymous *Gesta*. See text in *RHC, Occ.*, III, 1–117; *HG* 80–92; and Hill, *Gesta*, x.

[2] Apparently Fulcher's chronicle was first known by the name of his first book, which was something like the *Gesta Francorum Hierusalem peregrinantium*, and then as the *Historia Hierosolymitana* when the second redaction was made (*HF* 19–20; 119, note a).

covering all of this early formative period following the First Crusade. The one Latin account that can be compared with it in extent is the *Liber Christianae expeditionis* of Albert of Aix. This work reports events until 1120, but was written in Germany and hence lacks eyewitness value.[3] Indeed, the Franks in the Holy Land were not to produce another local historian such as Fulcher until William, Archbishop of Tyre, wrote his famous *Historia rerum in partibus transmarinis gestarum*. The work is partly dependent on Fulcher in its early stages and was written late in the twelfth century (1167–84).[4] Consequently, the work of Fulcher, in view of his status as an eyewitness, his long residence in the capital city of Jerusalem, his closeness to Baldwin I, his learning, and his zeal for accuracy, is of unusual importance.

Our chronicler identifies himself as "Fulcher" three times and as "Fulcher of Chartres" three other times.[5] He is referred to as "frater Fulcherius Carnotensis" by an anonymous contemporary chronicler commonly called Bartolf of Nangis, who probably knew Fulcher personally and who wrote the *Gesta Francorum Iherusalem expugnantium*, an epitome of as much of the *Historia Hierosolymitana* as Fulcher had finished in the winter of 1105–1106.[6] Fulcher is also mentioned by three well-known Occidental contemporaries, Guibert of Nogent (d. 1124), William of

[3] Albert's chronicle has been published in *RHC, Occ.*, IV (Paris: Imprimerie Nationale, 1879), 265–713. It will be cited by book and chapter. Two other contemporary chronicles, but not Latin, are those of Ibn-al-Qalānisī, an Arab savant (trans. H. A. R. Gibb as *The Damascus Chronicle of the Crusades* [London: Luzac and Co., 1932]), and Matthew of Edessa, an Armenian (ed. and trans. Édouard Dulaurier as *Extraits de la Chronique de Matthieu d'Édesse* in the *Recueil des historiens des croisades, Documents Arméniens*, I [Paris: Imprimerie Impériale, 1869], 1–150). The *Documents* will be hereinafter cited as *RHC, Arm.*

[4] Text in *RHC, Occ.*, I (Paris: Imprimerie Royale, 1844). There is an English translation by Emily A. Babcock annotated by August C. Krey, *A History of Deeds Done Beyond the Sea* ("Records of Civilization: Sources and Studies," ed. Austin P. Evans, No. 35 [2 vols.; New York: Columbia University Press, 1943]). Reference to either edition will be by book and chapter.

[5] As "Fulcher": I, xiv, 2; II, v, 1 (in first redaction, "Fulcher of Chartres," see *HF* 377, note f); xxxiv, 1; as "Fulcher of Chartres": I, v, 12; xiv, 15; xxxiii, 12.

[6] *Gesta Francorum Iherusalem expugnantium*, *RHC, Occ.*, III (Paris: Imprimerie Impériale, 1866), 487–543, esp. 492. For comments on the author see *HF* 1, 45–46, 71–73.

Malmesbury (d. after 1142), and Ordericus Vitalis (d. *ca.* 1142).[7]
He may be the Fulcher named as a witness in three contemporary
Palestinean documents—in one of them, dated 1112, as Prior of
the Mount of Olives.[8]

That Fulcher came from the area of Chartres in the *départe-
ment* of Eure-et-Loire is indicated in three or possibly four ways.
First, he is commonly called Fulcher of Chartres. Second, he
began the crusade in the following of Robert of Normandy and
Stephen of Blois and Chartres, in whom he manifested a peculiar
interest until the latter's death in 1102.[9] Third, when caught in
an ambush at Nahr al-Kalb north of Beirut in the fall of 1100,
Fulcher plaintively said he wished he were back at Chartres or
Orléans,[10] a clear indication that he came from this region. Finally,
he often quoted classical authors. This point is significant because Bishop Fulbert (d. 1028), Chancellor Bernard (d. *ca.*
1130), and a later local bishop, John of Salisbury (d. 1180), had
maintained a tradition of classical studies at Chartres. However,
it should be added that Fulcher displayed more interest than
skill in such subjects. Fulcher also revealed his French origin in
other ways. He called himself a "western Frank," he said he could
not understand a Briton or a German, and at one point he used
an old French word, *standarz*, meaning "banner."[11]

Our author says that he left the main army of the crusaders a
day's journey south of Marash (October 17, 1097) to go as the

---

[7] Guibert of Nogent, *Historia quae dicitur Gesta Dei per Francos, RHC, Occ.*,
IV (Paris: Imprimerie Nationale, 1879), 250, 252, 256; William of Malmesbury,
De gestis regum Anglorum libri quinque (ed. William Stubbs in *Rerum Britanni-
carum medii aevi scriptores: or Chronicles and Memorials of Great Britain and
Ireland during the Middle Ages* [2 vols.; London: Her Majesty's Stationery Office,
1887–89], II, 434); and Ordericus Vitalis, *Historiae ecclesiasticae libri XIII*, in
J. P. Migne (ed.), *Patrologiae cursus completus*, series latina, CLXXXVIII
(Paris: Garnier fratres, 1890), col. 648. Albert of Aix refers to a Fulcher or
Fulbert of Chartres, probably a knight, however (V, xv, xxii). Future reference
to Stubbs's *Chronicles and Memorials of Great Britain* will be to the *Rolls Series*,
and Migne's *Patrologiae*, series latina, will be noted as *MPL*.

[8] Reinhold Röhricht (ed.), *Regesta regni Hierosolymitani* (MXCVII–
MCCXCI) (Oeniponti: Libraria academica Wagneriana, 1893), Nos. 52, 68 (as
Prior), and 101. Consult *HF* 2.

[9] I, vi, 8; vii, 1; viii, 1; x, 1; xi, 10; xvi, 7; II, xvi, 1; xix, 4.

[10] II, ii, 4.   [11] I, vii, 1; xiii, 4; III, xviii, 5.

chaplain of Baldwin I into the country of Tell Bashir and Edessa.[12] This statement indicates that he was probably a priest and that he was close to Baldwin. Throughout Fulcher's chronicle we find him attentive to religious devotions but never taking part in the fighting, although he was often present with Baldwin on campaigns, at least until 1111. He frequently quotes the Bible, takes clerical license to admonish others, adores the relic of the Holy Cross, and displays the simple piety and the interests to be expected of a priest. Guibert of Nogent calls him a "presbyter," and the same word is used in the title of one of Fulcher's own manuscript texts.[13] There can be little doubt of his clerical status.

Fulcher wrote in 1123 that he was sixty-five years of age and in 1125 that he was sixty-six years old.[14] This indicates, in the absence of knowledge of the month and day of his birth, that he was born in 1058 or 1059 and that he was a mature man throughout all the years that he chronicled. Unfortunately, we know nothing about his early life in France.

Fulcher as an Eyewitness

That Fulcher participated in the First Crusade, thereafter lived in the East, and was an eyewitness to much that he related is shown throughout most of his chronicle. A tantalizing question is whether he was present at the Council of Clermont, where the crusade was initiated in November, 1095, and which he describes in considerable detail. Henri Wallon believes that Fulcher's intimate knowledge of the Council indicates that he was there, but

---

[12] I, xiv, 2–15. Fulcher does not say how long he was the chaplain of Baldwin I. The last time he says he was with Baldwin on a campaign was in 1111 (II, xlv, 9); he says "we" were in and out of the *Templum Domini* for almost fifteen years after its capture (I, xxvi, 7), which was in 1099; and he disapproved of Baldwin's bigamous marriage to Adelaide of Sicily in 1113 (II, lix, 3; cf. lxiii, 4). All of this seems to indicate that Fulcher had a more distant relationship with Baldwin after 1112 or 1113. There is no indication that he was ever the chaplain of Baldwin II.

[13] Guibert, RHC, Occ., IV, 250. Ms. K, HF 16; 115, note b; 119, note a; 642, note e.

[14] III, xxiv, 17; xliv, 4.

Hagenmeyer is not certain.[1] Fulcher does not say definitely that he attended, but it would seem that if he had been present at that stirring gathering, he would have indicated it. He is certainly one of the major authorities for the event and must have at least known some of those who were in attendance.

Fulcher began the crusade in October, 1096, in the army led by Duke Robert of Normandy, Count Robert of Flanders, and Count Stephen of Blois and Chartres. He crossed into Italy with them and writes as if he shared the audience they had with Pope Urban at Lucca early in the next year. In Rome he noted with dismay the disorders created in St. Peter's Basilica by the partisans of the antipope, Guibert of Ravenna. The army reached Bari late in 1096 as winter was approaching, but only Robert of Flanders crossed immediately to Albania.[2] The remainder of the force, including Fulcher, spent the winter in southern Italy and embarked at Brindisi on April 5, 1097, where Fulcher wrote of his horror when one ship foundered, causing a loss of four hundred lives. He crossed to Durazzo, Albania, and with Robert and Stephen traveled the old Roman road, the *Via Egnatia*, across Albania and Thrace to Constantinople. Fulcher says that only five or six Franks were allowed to enter the city per hour to pray in the churches, and he apparently was one of these. He admired Constantinople tremendously, describing it as noble and beautiful, filled with monasteries and palaces, and teeming with wealth and commerce. One can see that this great metropolis made a deep impression upon Fulcher, a comparatively unsophisticated westerner who had never seen such a large and wealthy city.[3]

Still in the contingent of Robert and Stephen, Fulcher went

[1] Henri Wallon (ed.), *Historia Iherosolymitana*, in *RHC, Occ.*, III (Paris: Imprimerie Impériale, 1866), xxvii; and *HF* 3, note 5. D. C. Munro once listed Fulcher as among those "probably present" at Clermont ("Urban and the Crusaders," *Translations and Reprints from the Original Sources of European History*, Vol. I [Revised; Philadelphia: History Department, University of Pennsylvania, 1902], No. 1, p. 2), and Martha E. McGinty has stated that Fulcher was present (*Fulcher of Chartres*, 3).

[2] I, vi, 8; vii. Hagenmeyer estimates that Fulcher reached Bari in November, 1096 (*HF* 167, note 16).

[3] I, viii; ix, 1.

on to Nicomedia, where he viewed with pity the bones of the followers of Peter the Hermit who had been slain by the Turks during the previous autumn. Later, he witnessed the siege operations around Nicaea and its surrender to the officers of Alexius, the Roman Emperor in the East and the crusaders' Byzantine ally, on June 19, 1097. Like most Franks, Fulcher seemed to feel that the Byzantines deprived them of the spoils of victory.[4] The army marched on to Dorylaeum (Eskishehir), and Fulcher, still with Robert and Stephen, described the desperate plight of the Franks in the battle and their victory over the Turks on July 1.[5] Then he told of the hardships he and others endured in crossing the hot, dry Anatolian highlands that summer by way of Antioch (Yalvach) in Pisidia, Iconium (Konya), Heraclea (Eregli), and Marash.[6]

A day's journey south of Marash on October 17, 1097, Fulcher took leave of the main force of the crusaders to go with Baldwin I inland into the area of Tell Bashir and Edessa. He says nothing of any previous connection with Baldwin nor why he joined him. Presumably, he went to serve an able master in a responsible capacity, or perhaps he was responding to the challenge of adventure, or both. Fulcher describes briefly the journey to Tell Bashir, which he says Baldwin secured by peace and war, and to the city of Edessa, which Baldwin soon acquired by rather guiltily countenancing the murder of the governor he had been invited to defend.[7]

The center of Fulcher's interest, however, was the main crusade, and he says little more of Edessa. Rather, he reports the progress of the crusaders' main force from its arrival before Antioch on October 20–21, 1097, to the capture of Jerusalem, July 15, 1099, and the battle of Ascalon, which followed on August 12.[8] Because Fulcher was with Baldwin and did not witness these events, he used other sources to fill the gaps in his knowledge, particularly the anonymous *Gesta* and Raymond of Aguilers.

[4] I, ix–x.
[5] I, xi–xii.
[6] I, xii, 6; xiii.

[7] I, xiv.
[8] I, xv–xxxi.

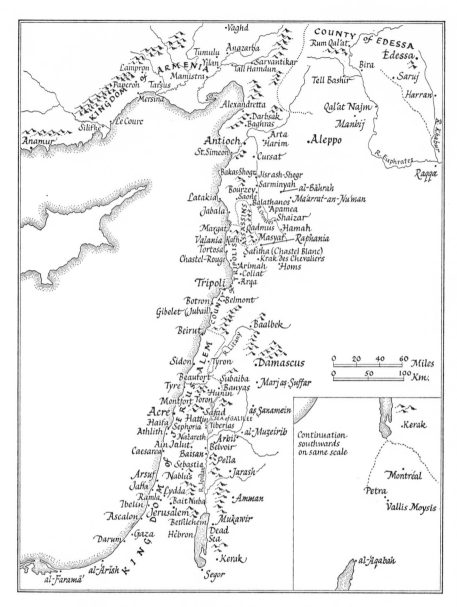

The map contains the following labels:

County of Edessa
Rum Qal'at. Edessa
Vaghd
Tumulu Anazarba
Lampron Yilan Sarvantikar Bira Saruj
Armenia Tall Hamdun
Mamistra Tell Bashir Harran.
Kingdom Tarsus
of Paperon
Mersina Qal'at Najm R. Khabur
Silifke Le Courc Alexandretta Manbij
Anamur Darbsak
Baghras Arta
Antioch Harim Aleppo
St.Simeon Cursat R. Euphrates
Raqqa
Bakas Shogr Jisr ash-Shogr
Bourzey Sarminyah al-Bahrah
Latakia Saone Ma'arrat-an-Nu'man
Jabala Balathanos Apamea
Shaizar
Margat Qadmus Hamah
Valania Kafr Masyaf Raphania
Tortosa Safitha (Chastel Blanc)
Chastel-Rouge Krak des Chevaliers
Arimah Homs
Coliat
Tripoli Arqa
Botron Belmont
Gibelet (Jubail)
Beirut Baalbek
Sidon Tyron Damascus
Beaufort Subaiba Marj as-Suffar
Tyre Banyas
Hunin
Montfort Toron
Acre Safad as-Sanamein
Haifa Hattin Sea of Galilee Kerak
Athlith Sephoria Tiberias al-Muzeirib
Ain Jalut Nazareth
Caesarea Arbil Continuation
Baisan Belvoir southwards
Sebastia Pella on same scale
Arsuf Nablus Jarash
Jaffa Lydda
Ramla Bait Nuba Amman Montréal
Ibelin Jerusalem Petra
Ascalon Bethlehem Mukawir Vallis Moysis
Darum Gaza Hebron Dead Sea
al-Arish Kerak al-Aqabah
al-Farama' Segor

0 20 40 60 Miles
0   50   100 Km.

SYRIA DURING THE PERIOD OF THE CRUSADES, 1096–1291

This map is based on one appearing in *Castles and Churches of the Crusading Kingdom*, by T. S. R. Boase. By permission of the Oxford University Press.

Late in 1099, however, Fulcher again becomes a personal witness when he describes the pilgrimage that Bohemond, now holding possession of Antioch, and Baldwin of Edessa made through Syria to Jerusalem to perform their Christmas devotions at the Holy Sepulcher. Fulcher accompanied them and mentions the route—Laodicea, past Tripoli and Caesarea, and on to Jerusalem and Bethlehem, and the return journey via the Jordan Valley, Lake Tiberias, Banyas, Baalbek, Tortosa, and Laodicea.[9]

Fulcher starts Book II by telling of his second journey with his master Baldwin from Edessa to Jerusalem when Baldwin went south to succeed his brother Godfrey. On this trip, from October 2 to about November 9, 1100, Fulcher tells of the ambush near Beirut (*ca.* October 24–25), the one that caused him to wish he were back at Chartres or Orléans. The route south was via Antioch, Laodicea, the environs of the Arab towns of Gibellum (Jabala), Maraclea, Tortosa, Archas ('Arqah), Tripoli, Beirut, Tyre, and Haifa, and through Caesarea, Arsuf, and Joppa to Jerusalem.[10] Here Fulcher made his home and observed events, took part in many of them, inquired from eyewitnesses, and recorded happenings soon after they occurred.

The first event that Fulcher records after coming to Jerusalem was a reconnaissance trip on which he accompanied Baldwin to Hebron, then down to the Dead Sea, south to Petra, and back to the Dead Sea, Hebron, and via Bethlehem to Jerusalem, from mid-November to December 21. Fulcher had a curious and inquisitive disposition, and his description of the area and its flora, fauna, and people is highly interesting. After the return, Baldwin was crowned king at Bethlehem on December 25. Fulcher, because he was Baldwin's chaplain, very likely was present at the ceremony, and although he does not mention his attendance, his description of the desperate condition of Jerusalem in the winter of 1101 indicates that he probably was there.[11]

Early in 1101 Fulcher may have gone with Baldwin to welcome the Genoese fleet, which arrived at Laodicea before Easter, 1101.

[9] I, xxxiii–xxxiv.
[10] II, i–iii *passim*, esp. ii, 4.
[11] II, iv–v; vi, 1, 4–12.

He was in Jerusalem for Easter, however, and mentions the excitement caused by the nonappearance of the Holy Fire on Easter Sabbath, a matter that he dismissed in one sentence, probably because he was skeptical. We cannot be sure that he witnessed the siege and capture of Arsuf by Baldwin and the Genoese on April 29, but his knowledge of the treaty between the allies and of the details of the siege seems to indicate that he was present.[12] He says he saw the capture of Caesarea on May 17, and in his religious fanaticism he gives many gruesome details about the looting and burning of the Saracen dead.[13] Possibly, he was with Baldwin during the events that followed—the establishment of an archbishopric at Caesarea and the vigils of twenty-four days at Ramla and seventy at Joppa against the Egyptians at Ascalon.[14] At the battle of Ramla on September 7, 1101, Fulcher says he was near Baldwin when the latter drove his lance into the abdomen of an enemy and then pulled it out to carry it ready for the next foe. Fulcher glories in the victory but momentarily discloses his personal fears in eloquently describing the horrors of battle. He then says that the next day he heard mass in Baldwin's tent and that the Franks returned via Joppa to Jerusalem, where they remained safe from war for eight months.[15]

Fulcher's exact whereabouts during the years 1102–1103 are not known, but his voluminous knowledge of Jerusalem implies that he was in or near that city.[16] At Easter, 1102, he probably saw the arrival of the survivors of the Crusade of 1101 in the holy city, among them Count Stephen of Blois. Fulcher could not have been with Baldwin when the king was defeated at Ramla on May 17, 1102, in spite of his use of the first-person plural pronoun; otherwise Fulcher would have named himself as one of the six survivors. Furthermore, he does not describe Baldwin's subsequent victory near Joppa on May 27 as if he had been present.[17]

[12] II, viii.

[13] II, ix, esp. pars. 5–9.

[14] II, x, 1; xi, 1.

[15] II, xi, 11; xii, 1; xiii, 1; xiv, 8.

[16] II, xv–xxi.

[17] For the Crusade of 1101, see II, xvi–xvii; for Stephen of Blois: xvi, 1; xviii, 3; xix, 4; for the survivors of Ramla: xix, 5; xx, 1; and for the two battles: xviii, 5–9; xxi, 9–13.

Fulcher mentions Baldwin's futile siege of Acre, *ca.* April 6–
May 16, 1103, but does not indicate his own presence. He says
Baldwin was wounded by an enemy assassin during that year. Because Fulcher knew the location of the wound, in the back near
the heart, and how the missile was taken out, by excision, he must
have had the close access to Baldwin that would be his chaplain's
prerogative.[18] Perhaps he celebrated Easter, 1104, in Jerusalem,
for he mentions the event. Whether he was with Baldwin at the
subsequent siege and capture of Acre, May 26, is undetermined,
but he knew some valuable details.[19] However, he was absent
from the battle near Joppa in which Baldwin defeated a force
of Turkish archers and Egyptians from Damascus on August 27,
1105: he says he stayed behind to pray in barefoot procession,
probably in Jerusalem.[20] Fulcher reports that he witnessed the
Vigils of the Lord's Nativity in Jerusalem on December 24, 1105.
He also writes that those present in the city that Christmas Eve
experienced an earthquake. In addition, he says, they saw a comet
and two parahelia or sun dogs in February, 1106, and another
comet and some meteors in March.[21]

Fulcher seems to have stopped writing in 1106 and drops from
sight until he reports observing a comet that was visible from
May to July, 1110.[22] When he resumes his chronicle, his entries
recalling the events of 1106 and 1107 are sparse: one item concerns the death of Hugh of Tiberias in 1106; another refers to a
skirmish near Joppa in 1107. For 1107–1108 Fulcher retraces the
events of the war that Bohemond waged and lost against Alexius.
A report of the siege and capture of Tripoli in the early summer
of 1109 ends Fulcher's review of the four-year period during which
he was apparently not writing as events occurred.[23]

In describing three events of the next year (1110)—the capture of Beirut in the spring, Baldwin's Edessan campaign in the
summer, and the capture of Sidon in December—Fulcher does
not indicate that he was a witness to any of them. We may pre-

---

[18] II, xxiv.
[19] II, xxv.
[20] II, xxxi, 12.

[21] II, xxxiv, 3; xxxv.
[22] II, xliii, 2.
[23] II, xxxvi; xxxvii, 2–5; xxxviii–xxxix; xl–xli.

sume that he saw King Sigurd of Norway in Jerusalem prior to the siege of Sidon, for he mentions the youthfulness and handsome appearance of this prince, though not his name. Fulcher says that he traveled with Baldwin on the latter's Edessan campaign in 1111, the last clear statement that he accompanied the king in the field. Whether he was present at the futile four-month siege of Tyre in the winter of 1111–12 is not certain, although Hagenmeyer, judging from Fulcher's intimate knowledge, thinks he was.[24]

The men of Jerusalem were free of war in the year 1112, according to Fulcher, probably meaning from the end of the siege of Tyre in April, 1112, to the invasion by Sharaf-ad-Dīn Maudūd of Mosul and Tughtigin of Damascus in June, 1113. Very likely, Fulcher was in the city during most of this time. He seems to have been in Jerusalem when Maudūd and Tughtigin made their dangerous invasion of Palestine in the summer of 1113, for he says that it was difficult to get messages through to the king, who was near Tiberias, during this period. He experienced two earthquakes in 1113, on July 18 and August 9, another on August 10, 1114, and a plague of locusts in April and May of the latter year. He conceivably could have accompanied Baldwin on his march to aid Roger of Antioch in September, 1115, but this does not seem probable because Fulcher describes the defense of Jerusalem against the men of Ascalon in too much detail not to have been present.[25]

There is no indication that Fulcher went with King Baldwin to ash-Shaubak when the latter built the castle of Montréal in 1115. We know that Fulcher remained at Jerusalem in 1116 when Baldwin made a visit to the Red Sea Gulf of 'Aqabah at Elath because he says he questioned Baldwin's men closely about the nature of this sea upon their return. He mentions the departure of Adelaide of Sicily, Baldwin's discarded queen, from Acre in 1117 and gives some descriptive details about the singing of the

[24] II, xlii–xlvi, esp. xliv, 1; xlv, 9; and HF 14.
[25] II, xlvii; xlviii; l; li, 1; lii, 1, 2; liii, 4–7.

litany and the number of ships (seven) that Adelaide used, causing one to wonder if he, a sympathizer of Adelaide, were present.[26]

In 1117 Fulcher witnessed a locust invasion, in May, lunar
eclipses on June 16 and December 11, an earthquake on June 26,
and a display of the aurora borealis on December 16.[27] Apparently
he did not accompany Baldwin on the latter's fatal journey to
al-Faramā' on the delta coast of Egypt in the spring of 1118, but
we may assume that he was present at the king's funeral in Jerusalem soon after Palm Sunday (April 7) of that year.[28]

Fulcher's third book concerns the reign of King Baldwin II.
There is no evidence that he served as chaplain for this king, as
he did for Baldwin I, and little that he traveled with him on
military campaigns. That Fulcher was a sexagenarian by this time
makes it probable that he did not venture far from home. Although he uses the first-person plural pronoun to describe some
of Baldwin's expeditions, Fulcher occasionally states that he himself was in Jerusalem during those times, indicating that such
usage was probably rhetorical. If his knowledge of distant events
is sometimes detailed, it may be that he learned from witnesses; indeed, he sometimes says that this was the case. Thus, it is reason-
able to assume that except in rare instances Fulcher probably
stayed in or near Jerusalem during the time of Baldwin II and
wrote Book III there. This location had advantages, for Jerusalem
was the capital city, the center of comings and goings, the place
where important decisions were made, and a choice spot for ob-
taining accurate information. Jerusalem also offered library facili-
ties, which Fulcher seems to have used.[29]

Baldwin II was consecrated on Easter Sunday, April 14, 1118,
and his coronation was held in Bethlehem on Christmas Day in
1119; Fulcher probably attended both ceremonies. He was, in
addition, well informed about the military stalemate in Palestine
in the summer of 1118, about Baldwin's decisive victory at Tell
Dānīth, Syria, on August 14, 1119, and about Baldwin's assump-

[26] II, lv; lvi, 4; iv–v; lx, 1.
[27] II, lx, 2; lxi; lxiii, 1–2.
[28] II, lxiv.
[29] HF 598, notes g, 11.

tion of the regency of Antioch following the defeat and death of
Roger on June 28 that year; but he does not reveal his own whereabouts.[30]

Fulcher says he spent the first six months of 1120 in Jerusalem
and was there when word came that Il-Ghāzī ibn-Artuk of Aleppo
was launching a campaign in the lands of Antioch. He records
Baldwin's march to the north but does not write as if he had accompanied him. Similarly, he describes the king's expedition to
Jarash (Gerasa) against Tughtigin of Damascus in 1121 and his
attempt to relieve the town of Zardanā in the summer of 1122
but does not indicate his own presence.[31]

In the spring of 1123 Fulcher says that he and others at Jerusalem learned of the approaching arrival of a Venetian fleet. About
the same time they heard that King Baldwin had been captured
by Il-Ghāzī's nephew and successor, Nūr-ad-Daulah Belek of
Aleppo, and imprisoned in the distant castle of Kharput in eastern
Anatolia. Also, they learned that the Egyptians from Ascalon had
advanced to attack Joppa by land and sea. Fulcher tells how
an army was sent to defeat the Egyptians, near Ramla, on May
29, 1123; but he says he remained at Jerusalem with the Latins,
Greeks, and Syrians, that is, with the clergy, to pray in barefoot
procession and to receive the Holy Cross upon its return to the
Holy Sepulcher.[32]

In mid-September, 1123, Fulcher and the residents of Jerusalem witnessed the arrival of Count Joscelin of Edessa, who had
recently escaped from Turkish captivity at Kharput. Joscelin reported that Baldwin had stayed behind to defend the castle, which
the Christians had captured by surprise from within just prior
to Joscelin's escape and which was now beleaguered by a fresh
Turkish force under Nūr-ad-Daulah Belek of Aleppo. Fulcher
then tells of the futile expedition to relieve Baldwin, which got as
far as Tell Bashir; but Fulcher had apparently remained in Jerusalem, for he says he learned of Belek's recapture of Kharput
through others.[33]

30 III, i; vii, 4; ii, 3; iv–v; vii, 1.   32 III, xiv–xix.
31 III, ix; x; xi, 3–6.   33 III, xxiv, 2, 14; xxv, 1; xxvi, 5.

Presumably, Fulcher was still in Jerusalem at Christmas, 1123, when the Doge of Venice (Domenico Michiel) came to perform his devotions, to seek an alliance with Patriarch Gormond (who was regent in Jerusalem during Baldwin's incarceration), and to demand subsidies that required the pledging of the sacred ornaments of the church at Jerusalem. Fulcher relates the latter reason for the doge's visit without comment, but his silence might be presumed to mean disapproval. He tells of the resulting siege of Tyre in 1124 with surprising brevity; but in spite of an occasional use of the pronoun "we," Fulcher was in Jerusalem during this time, for he relates how three messengers arrived from the patriarch with the news of the capture of Tyre on July 7, and he vividly describes the resultant jubilation at Jerusalem. He also includes an account of a raid from Ascalon against the weakened defenses of Jerusalem, which implies that Fulcher was in that city rather than with the army before Tyre.[34]

Fulcher gives no indication that he was with Baldwin, ransomed in August, 1124, on the campaign against Aleppo in the fall of 1124 and winter of 1125, but he does mention that he was in Jerusalem when Baldwin returned on April 3, 1125. He writes of Baldwin's victory over Aksungur al-Bursukī of Mosul and Tughtigin of Damascus at ʿAzāz (Hasar) on June 11, saying that he learned of this through eyewitnesses.[35]

Our author writes in detail of Baldwin's spectacular raid in the north to the outskirts of Damascus in January, 1126, and of the capture of Raphania in March but does not say that he was present at either event. Indeed, his account suggests that he was in Jerusalem when Baldwin returned from the former campaign. He does say that he was in the holy city at Easter, April 11, 1126, when news arrived of the death of Emperor Henry V in Germany, an event of May 23 in the previous year.[36] Probably, Fulcher was in Jerusalem throughout most of the year 1126, for he reports that many times pilgrims and travelers came to the city with rumors that Bohemond II, heir to Antioch, was coming to take

[34] III, xxvii; xxxviii, 1; xxxii; xxxiv, 5–6; xxxiii.
[35] III, xxxviii, 1, 2; xl; xliii, 2.   [36] III, l; liii; liv, note 2.

possession of his inheritance. Finally he states that Baldwin, who was then in Antioch as regent, informed those in Jerusalem of his reception of Bohemond at Antioch.[37] Bohemond arrived at Antioch in the latter part of October; therefore Fulcher must have heard the news during the next month.

Fulcher's last entry concerns a plague of rats in 1127, whose rotting bodies lasted into the summer. There the chronicle suddenly stops, as if arrested in mid-course by a sudden illness or even the death of the elderly author. If Fulcher had remained alive or well, he doubtless would have mentioned Baldwin's expedition into the Wādī Mūsâ in September, 1127, or the arrival of Count Fulk of Anjou in the spring of 1128 to become Baldwin's son-in-law and heir.

TIME OF COMPOSITION

Information about the time when Fulcher wrote his chronicle must be gleaned from the work itself. Almost at the start, after discussing the Council of Clermont, he says that he is going to write the history of the march to Jerusalem and its glorious success.[1] In his Prologue, written years later, perhaps in 1118 or 1119,[2] he makes the same declaration—that he is going to write the history of those who made the pilgrimage to Jerusalem. These statements indicate that Fulcher began his chronicle after the First Crusade had been completed at Jerusalem (1099) and not before.

But exactly how early did Fulcher begin to write? We have seen that he left the main army of the crusaders a day's journey south of Marash in 1097 and therefore did not witness its trials and triumphs, which culminated in the capture of Jerusalem in 1099. Yet he wrote about these events in considerable detail by using the anonymous *Gesta* and the *Historia Francorum* of Raymond of Aguilers. Both of these chronicles seem to have been completed around Jerusalem after the battle of Ascalon, August 12,

---

[37] III, lvii, 1, 4; lxi, 2.   [2] HF 42; 115, note 1.
[1] I, v, 12.

1099, the last event they mention; but precisely how soon afterward, we do not know. However, the chronicler Ekkehard of Aura, who came to Palestine originally as a member of the Crusade of 1101, mentions that he saw a *libellus* that seems to have been the *Gesta*, and textual comparison indicates that this was the case.[3] Hagenmeyer has shown that Raymond's work was completed after the *Gesta* because Raymond used the *Gesta*, and both were complete before Fulcher of Chartres began writing because he used both of them.[4]

Fulcher first went to Jerusalem on December 21, 1099, when Bohemond of Antioch and Baldwin I of Edessa went to perform their Christmas devotions, and he began his return with them on January 2, 1100.[5] Consequently, Fulcher had no time to start writing on this trip. He came back about November 9, 1100,[6] with Baldwin, this time to reside permanently. In describing the second journey to Jerusalem, he referred to the time "when we first entered the land of Palestine,"[7] *i.e.*, 1099, a sure indication that he wrote not after his first trip to Jerusalem in 1099 but after his second trip, late in 1100.

How late did Fulcher start writing? At one point early in his chronicle he speaks of "the year in which the Franks first passed through Rome on their way to Jerusalem," a reference, probably, to the beginning of the First Crusade in 1096.[8] The next such passage by crusaders through Rome occurred probably early in 1101 and was made by some members of the Crusade of 1101, called "Secunda peregrinatio" by Fulcher in the heading of chap-

---

[3] Ekkehard of Aura, *Hierosolymita*, RHC, Occ., V (Paris: Imprimerie Nationale, 1895), 21 and *passim*; and HF 75.

[4] HG 50–58, 58–60; and HF 66–67.   [5] I, xxxiii, 16; xxxiv, 1.

[6] II, iii, 13. For the date, see Heinrich Hagenmeyer, "Chronologie de la première croisade (1094–1100)," *Revue de l'Orient latin*, VI–VIII (1898–1901), item No. 514. Future reference to the *Revue* will be to ROL. For the continuation of the "Chronologie," see "Chronologie de l'histoire du royaume de Jérusalem, règne de Baudouin I (1101–1118)," ROL, IX–XII (1902–11); further reference to Hagenmeyer's "Chronologie" will be to HChr by item, as above.

[7] This statement is in Fulcher's original text, the first redaction (HF 274, note 1).

[8] I, v, 5.

ter xvi of Book II. This would indicate that Fulcher probably started writing after the news of the Crusade of 1101 had reached him. He could easily have heard rumors of its approach early in 1101, and he certainly heard of its failure after refugees reached Antioch in October or November, 1101.

A more definite indication of when Fulcher began his history may be inferred from his treatment of Stephen of Blois. Fulcher first calls Stephen's flight from Antioch in 1098 a disgrace and adds that "a good beginning does not profit if one does not end well." Later Stephen "ended well" by suffering martyrdom at Ramla on May 19, 1102. In telling of this crusader's death Fulcher praised him as "a prudent and noble man."[9] Obviously, Fulcher wrote the first statement before he knew that Stephen had redeemed his reputation by death at Ramla in the spring of 1102.

Therefore, we may conclude that Fulcher began writing after he came to live in Jerusalem, late in 1100, and before he heard of the death of Stephen of Blois in May, 1102. Also, he had started or was writing when the news of the Crusade of 1101 reached him, probably in 1101. As a corollary, this conclusion implies that the anonymous *Gesta* and Raymond's *Historia Francorum* had been finished by the period from late 1100 to late 1101, before Fulcher started using them.

Fulcher seems to have continued writing until he brought his chronicle to a climax in chapter xxxiii of Book II, an account of Baldwin's great victory over the Egyptians at Ramla on August 27, 1105. Then Fulcher added another chapter, giving his name, pleading lack of skill, granting permission to someone to read his chronicle to improve his diction if necessary, but begging such a person not to sacrifice truth for eloquence. All of this sounds as if Fulcher were preparing to end his work. But then he wanders on into still another chapter and mentions an earthquake of December 24, 1105, and various astronomical events of 1106.

It so happens that at this time two anonymous persons were busy rewriting the chronicle of Fulcher, adding some details, changing emphasis, and polishing Fulcher's diction. One, the

[9] I, xvi, 7; II, xix, 4.

author of the *Gesta Francorum Iherusalem expugnantium*, commonly called Bartolf of Nangis, wrote "Atque finis hic est" at the point marked by the end of chapter xxxiii of Fulcher's second book, then added details of the astronomical phenomena as found in chapters xxxiv–xxxv of Fulcher, and ended with "Explicit hystoria." This indicates that Fulcher probably first stopped with chapter xxxiii, added his precautionary warnings in chapter xxxiv, and stopped again with chapter xxxv, perhaps in March, 1106, or a little later, and that the author of the *Gesta Francorum Iherusalem expugnantium* was probably working along with Fulcher at the time.[10]

The other anonymous writer produced a version known as Codex L. It purports to be a text of Fulcher and has those characteristics in the beginning. However, in Book II the author of Codex L begins to show an independent point of view and, like "Bartolf," adds some extra details, including a long section about the Holy Fire of 1101, which Fulcher dismissed with a sentence. But beginning with his account of the events of 1103, near the point at which Fulcher asks someone not to sacrifice truth for eloquence, the writer of Codex L becomes a much more faithful copyist of Fulcher's text. This may have been a result of Fulcher's plea.[11]

It is probable that Fulcher and his two anonymous copyists were trying to finish their accounts of the deeds of the Franks in the Holy Land in time to circulate them in western Europe to stir up enthusiasm for Bohemond's drive (1105–1107) for what they hoped would be a new crusade. Bohemond, however, used his newly recruited army to wage war against Emperor Alexius in Albania (1107–1108). That a text of Fulcher or one of the revisions reached Europe at this time is shown by the *Gesta Dei*

[10] *Gesta Francorum Iherusalem expugnantium*, RHC, Occ., III, 541; HF 46, 71–73.

[11] The text of Codex L may be found among the footnotes of Wallon's edition of Fulcher of Chartres (*RHC, Occ.*, III, 321–418). See entry in Codex L for the year 1103 in *RHC, Occ.*, III, 406, where it corresponds to Fulcher, II, xxii. Codex L is the Cambridge University Library MS. K K, VI, 15 (No. 2079 in *RHC, Occ.*, III, p. xxxv). See HF 75–78.

per Francos of Guibert of Nogent, six books of which were in circulation by 1108 and which refer to Fulcher of Chartres several times. At one place Guibert says that Fulcher and the chaplain of the patriarch (Daimbert) ascended the Mount of Olives at the time of the Holy Fire of 1101. Codex L states that they ascended Calvary, but Fulcher says nothing of this. Possibly Guibert used a copy of Codex L and garbled it.[12] In any event, it seems evident that Fulcher stopped writing early in 1106 and that his two imitators brought their works to an end at about that time as well.

If Fulcher originally finished his work in 1106, he changed his mind and started writing again later. This may have been in 1109, the year when the news of Bohemond's defeat and the death of King Philip I of France, both events of 1108, probably reached the Holy Land. He recorded these two events, and also the fall of Tripoli to the Franks in 1109. His entries for the summer of 1106 and for 1107 are very brief, and there are none for affairs of 1108 in the Holy Land. Perhaps, therefore, he wrote nothing until he began to chronicle the incidents he learned of in 1109.[13]

One cannot tell how soon after the events occurred that Fulcher wrote the entries in his chronicle for the period 1109–13. He may have written more or less contemporaneously and then stopped for a while.[14] However, in speaking of the military crisis caused by the invasion of the *Atabeg* Maudūd of Mosul in 1113, he says, "Our men could not at that time [*tunc*] do any damage to the Turks,"[15] a statement that sounds as if it had been written after the invasion. In the preceding sentence, Fulcher had called Baldwin "imprudent, rash and disorderly" in military conduct, and one wonders if Fulcher had dared to make these statements while Baldwin, who died in 1118, was still alive? If Fulcher lost some enthusiasm for Baldwin in 1113 or later, the reason may have been in part the marriage of the king to Adelaide of Sicily in that

---

[12] See Guibert in *RHC, Occ.,* IV, 256 (excerpt in *HF* 837); Codex L, *RHC, Occ.,* III, 386 (excerpt in *HF* 832); and discussion in *HF* 73–74; 395, note 5.
[13] II, xxxix; xl–xli; *HF* 46.
[14] This is the opinion of Hagenmeyer (*HF* 46).
[15] II, xlix, 8.

year. Fulcher regarded the marriage as bigamous, and after Baldwin dismissed Adelaide, Fulcher said she had been "forsaken" [*dereliquerat*].[16] Clearly, he disapproved of the king's conduct in the matter. Also, it is probable that chapter liv, dealing with events of 1115, and perhaps the remainder of Book II were written in 1118 or later. This seems to be true because in chapter liv, Fulcher refers to Paschal II as "pope at that time [*tunc*],"[17] 1115. Since Paschal died in 1118, Fulcher obviously wrote the statement in 1118 or later. One concludes that Fulcher, after resuming work on his history in 1109 or 1110, stopped again as early as 1115, if not in 1113.

When Baldwin I died in 1118, Fulcher wrote an eloquent tribute to him, recognizing that Baldwin had accomplished great things for the kingdom and that his death was the end of an era. Apparently, this was enough to prompt Fulcher to start writing again, for next begins Book III, a chronicle of the reign of Baldwin II. The first thirty-six chapters cover the period from 1118 to the capture of Tyre in 1124. These chapters may have been written more or less contemporaneously. For example, in the latter part of 1123 Fulcher says, "I have now [*nunc*] completed my sixty-fifth year." Shortly thereafter he indicates that he is writing at the end of 1123.[18]

The manuscripts of Fulcher's first redaction end with chapter xxxvi.[19] He then seems to have begun a revision or second redaction,[20] going over his whole text from 1095 to 1124, making slight modifications in places, and considerably revising his description of Jerusalem. He added a chapter on the battle of Harran in 1104, another on the release of Baldwin of Edessa (whom he called the

---

[16] II, li, 3; lix, 3; lx, 1; lxiii, 4.
[17] This statement is in Fulcher's first redaction. See *HF* 591, note c.
[18] III, xxiv, 17; xxvi, 6. See *HF* 47.   [19] *HF* 47; 746, note h.
[20] For the list and description of the manuscripts of the first and second redactions, see *HF* 92–104. The chapter divisions and titles in Fulcher's chronicle are those of scribes or copyists, for they do not always fit the contents of the chapters. Fulcher apparently made no chapter divisions but was satisfied with the divisions and titles of his three books. See *HF* 20–21.

future king of Jerusalem) from Turkish captivity in 1109, and a third on Bohemond's journey to Gaul in 1106.[21] Finally, Fulcher listed the events of 1124–27, starting with chapter xxxviii of Book III.

Fulcher evidently recorded the occurrences of these last three years concurrently. He refers to the year 1125 as in the present time, later says that he is writing just as the year 1125 is passing into 1126, and still later mentions that 1126 is changing to 1127. On all three occasions as once before he uses the adverb "now" [*nunc*].[22] His last chapter gives every evidence of having been interrupted in mid-course in 1127.

FULCHER'S REASONS FOR WRITING

In several places Fulcher explains why he wrote. Very early, just after describing the Council of Clermont, he states, "Now therefore I must turn my pen to history in order clearly to tell the uninformed about the journey of those going to Jerusalem, what happened to them and how the undertaking and the labor gradually came to a successful conclusion with the help of God."[1] This passage, written probably in 1101, reflects Fulcher's desire that the crusade, a holy war, should be known of and generally supported in the West. Later, in the winter of 1105–1106, he says he is writing in order that the accomplishments of the crusaders should not be forgotten.[2] This was the time when the anonymous writers of the *Gesta Francorum Iherusalem expugnantium* and of Codex L, both epitomes of Fulcher's chronicle, and perhaps Fulcher himself, were bringing their works to a conclusion, probably in order to be used to inspire support for the call of Bohemond of Antioch for more European manpower in the East.

Much later Fulcher, in his Prologue, written perhaps in 1118 or 1119,[3] states his purpose at greater length. He says he wants

---

[21] I, xxvi; II, xxvii, esp. par. 4; xxviii; xxix. See *HF* 281, note n; 468, note a. Baldwin II was king from 1118 to 1131.

[22] III, xliv, 3; xlix, 18; lxi, 5. Cf. III, xxiv, 17.

[1] I, v, 12. [3] *HF* 42; 115, note 1.

[2] II, xxxiv, 1.

to recount the deeds of those fighting for God in order to inspire the worldly to leave parents, wives, and wealth and embrace God, *i.e.*, the crusade, even if it means the blessed death of martyrdom. He adds that he was moved by a former comrade[4] to write the deeds of the Franks, which he compares to the wars of the Israelites and the Maccabees, a veritable miracle of God.

But Fulcher's purpose by then was not only to call for more men to fight for the Cross in the Holy Land but also to persuade some of them to remain as permanent residents to strengthen the little kingdom around Jerusalem. In a remarkable passage written after the capture of Tyre in 1124 and somewhat contradictory in tone to the Prologue, he tells how easy it was for Westerners to become accustomed to the East, to forget old homes and old ties, to learn the idiom of the Holy Land, and to acquire homes, families, and even riches.[5]

ORIGINAL CONTRIBUTIONS TO KNOWLEDGE

The chronicle of Fulcher provides much that is unique, valuable, and interesting. In Book I the first ten chapters are composed entirely of original information. The first three relate the proceedings of the Council of Clermont. Rather surprisingly, we learn that most of the business seems to have dealt with decrees proposed by Pope Urban as the leader of the Cluny reform movement in the Church. Not until the third chapter does Fulcher set forth the call for the First Crusade and its enthusiastic reception. The fourth chapter deals with the organization of the crusade. The fifth describes Urban's quarrel with the antipope Guibert of Ravenna and mentions the help given Urban by the Countess Mathilda of Tuscany. Chapter vi speaks of the economic prosperity of the time, the various leaders of the crusade and their contingents, and the touching scenes as wives kissed husbands whom they felt they would never see again. Chapters

[4] Hagenmeyer conjectures that King Baldwin I might have been one of those who prompted Fulcher to write (*HF* 116, note 8). But Fulcher does not say this, and it is impossible to tell.
[5] III, xxxvii, 2–8.

vii–ix describe the trip made by Fulcher from France as far as Nicaea in the army of Robert of Normandy and Stephen of Blois. The tenth chapter reports the siege and capture of Nicaea in considerable detail.

The next three chapters, xi-xiii, deal with the battle of Dorylaeum, the resultant flight of the Turks, and the hardships of the march of the crusaders from Dorylaeum to Iconium. The details are based in part upon Fulcher's observations and experiences and in part upon the anonymous *Gesta*, which Fulcher must have had in mind for use again in chapters xv–xxxi. Chapter xiv describes the excursion of Baldwin I to Edessa in the winter of 1097–98, a valuable eyewitness account of a little-known event. We wish it were more complete.

Instead of giving details of the excursion with Baldwin, Fulcher continues with his principal theme, the progress of the main crusade. He reports the events from the siege of Antioch, which began late in 1097, to the capture of Jerusalem and the battle of Ascalon in the summer of 1099. This portion of the chronicle includes seventeen chapters, xv-xxxi, and is derived largely from secondary sources. However, not all is from the *Gesta* and Raymond. Chapter xxiv is the text of a famous letter from Bohemond and the princes of the crusade to Pope Urban II, dated at Antioch on September 11, 1098. Chapter xxvi is a personal description of Jerusalem by Fulcher; and in chapters xxvii, xxviii, and xxxi are details of the sack of Jerusalem and of the battle of Ascalon, gathered by Fulcher perhaps from eyewitnesses after he first came to Jerusalem soon afterwards in the fall of 1099.

The last chapters of Book I, xxxii–xxxvi, are based almost entirely upon Fulcher's own knowledge. He tells of the return of most of the crusader princes to Europe and then of the pilgrimage to Jerusalem made by Bohemond and Baldwin at the end of the year. He describes the suffering on the march caused by the chill winter rains and his revulsion at the stench in Jerusalem rising from the still unburied bodies of Egyptian defenders slain during the previous July; then he mentions the election of Daimbert as patriarch and briefly describes the journey back via Lake Tiberias and Baalbek. Fulcher notes that Bohemond was captured by Gümüshtigin ibn-Dānishmend of Sebastia near Malatiya in July, 1100, and that Baldwin's efforts to rescue Bohemond accomplished nothing. He closes Book I with the arrival of a messenger from Jerusalem announcing the death of Baldwin's brother, Godfrey of Jerusalem, on July 18, 1100.

Fulcher's second book is the story of a man and of the kingdom founded by that man, of Baldwin I and the compact military monarchy that he developed around Jerusalem in the years 1100–18. It is the story of a fearless and energetic lord who usually attacked first, gave his enemies little rest, and ended his career by invading Egypt, his most powerful and dangerous neighbor. Although Fulcher's account is primarily military history, it also describes the relationships of the king with the patriarchate, with the maritime cities of Genoa and Pisa, and with the other Frankish states and tells of Bohemond's efforts to maintain the Frankish position, in reality Bohemond's position, around Antioch, the northern pole of Frankish activity.

The first three chapters of Book II deal with Baldwin's succession to the throne in Jerusalem. We find that Baldwin ceded his holdings at Edessa to his cousin Baldwin, gathered nearly two hundred knights and seven hundred footmen, and started for Jerusalem on October 2, 1100. Many men were lost by desertion, and Baldwin's strength was further diminished by a dangerous ambush set by the troops of Dukak of Damascus at Nahr al-Kalb, a narrow pass between the sea and the cliffs north of Beirut. The new ruler reached Jerusalem *ca.* November 9.

Baldwin's active and resolute nature is revealed by Fulcher's account in chapters iv-v of his master's reconnaissance into the area of Hebron, the Dead Sea, and the Wādī Mūsâ south of it (*ca.* November 15–December 21). Fulcher accompanied Baldwin and took an immense interest in the nature of the Dead Sea, the people, the fruits of the land, and the Biblical history of the area.

Then we learn something of the relations between Baldwin and the patriarchate. Patriarch Daimbert, who had refused to meet

Baldwin upon the latter's arrival from Edessa, was now prevailed upon to crown Baldwin as king on Christmas Day, 1100; but the ceremony was held in Bethlehem, not Jerusalem.[1] However, Fulcher, the chaplain and partisan of Baldwin, does not explain that Patriarch Daimbert considered Jerusalem to be his city by right of his election as patriarch, not the king's, and that coronation in Bethlehem was tacit recognition of this fact.[2]

Chapter vi offers an eloquent statement of the initial weakness of the minuscule kingdom. Fulcher says it consisted of four towns —Jerusalem, Joppa, Ramla, and Haifa—and Baldwin had no more than three hundred knights and as many footmen to defend them all. The king's tiny force lacked enough horses for the knights and manpower of every kind because many soldiers chose to return to Europe rather than remain to defend the Holy Sepulcher. Aid was available only through the open roadstead to Joppa because Antioch was distant and far out of reach. In chapter vii we learn that Tiberias was added to the list of cities to be defended because Tancred, one of Baldwin's vassals, then held Haifa and Tiberias. However, in March, 1101, Tancred turned them over to Baldwin to assume the regency of Antioch for his kinsman Bohemond, then a prisoner of Gümüshtigin ibn-Dānishmend of Sebastia. The departure of Tancred, an able man but unfriendly to the king, undoubtedly strengthened Jerusalem, and Antioch as well.

Fulcher's account of the conquest of the seaport towns along the Mediterranean, although unconnected and scattered through nine chapters, forms the most important train of events in Book II.[3] Cut off at first from the sources of manpower and support in Europe except through the single port of Joppa, Baldwin conducted a steady and persistent campaign that in ten years added

---

[1] II, v, 12; vi, 1.

[2] For a description of the jealousies between the patriarch and king, see H. S. Fink, "The Foundation of the Latin States, 1099–1118," in Kenneth M. Setton (editor-in-chief), A History of the Crusades: I, Marshall W. Baldwin (ed.), The First Hundred Years (Philadelphia: University of Pennsylvania Press, 1955), 381–82. Future reference to this volume will be to Setton (ed.), Crusades, I.

[3] II, viii; ix; xxii; xxv; xl–xli; xlii; xliv; xlvi; lxii.

five more seaports to his kingdom and a sixth, Tripoli, as a feudal dependency. Arsuf and Caesarea were taken in 1101, Acre was unsuccessfully besieged in 1103 but fell after renewed onslaughts the next year, Tripoli was captured in 1109, and Beirut and Sidon were conquered in 1110. Baldwin laid an unsuccessful siege to Tyre for six months in 1111–12, but even without Tyre, his position was secure. He had re-established vital connections with Europe, broadened the revenue base of his kingdom through collection of tolls, and made the Muslims of the interior, particularly those of Damascus, dependent upon him as the master of their maritime outlets.

Included within the story of the conquest of the seaports is the record of other events. For example, fifteen chapters deal with the Frankish defeats of three major Egyptian invasions from Ascalon in 1101, 1102, and 1105, and three minor ones in 1107, 1113, and 1115.[4] The invasion of 1102 is of greatest interest because King Baldwin's force was wiped out near Ramla on May 17.[5] Baldwin's personal escape to Ramla and Arsuf, the arrival of reinforcements, and Baldwin's final victory near Joppa on May 27 are all described in a vivid, if not melodramatic, manner.[6] The disaster near Ramla involved some of the survivors of the Crusade of 1101 from an earlier disaster in Anatolia. Fulcher devotes a chapter to that crusade and those of its leaders who were French and three more chapters to the escape of some of them to Syria and Palestine and to the death of several of them at Ramla, including Stephen of Blois, in whom Fulcher always had a special interest.[7]

Also of value are the details Fulcher furnishes of Bohemond, Prince of Antioch, in six chapters. He says that Bohemond, captured by ibn-Dānishmend in 1100, was released in 1103, defeated by the Turks at Harran on May 7, 1104, and that he left for Apulia late in that year to recruit manpower there in 1105 and in France in 1106.[8] He brought his account of Bohemond to a

---

[4] II, xi–xiv; xv; xviii–xxi; xxxi–xxxiii; xxxvii; xlix, 12; liii.
[5] II, xviii.   [7] II, xvi; xvii–xix.
[6] II, xix–xxi.   [8] II, xxiii; xxvi; xxvii; xxix.

logical conclusion by telling of the latter's frustrating campaign against the Emperor Alexius in Albania in 1107–1108, of his humiliating treaty with the emperor, and of his return to Apulia in 1108.[9] Coupled with his story of Bohemond, Fulcher mentions the trip made by ex-Patriarch Daimbert to Rome in 1104–1105 to recover his office. We are told that Daimbert succeeded but died on the return journey.[10]

Five chapters deal with the attempts of Sharaf-ad-Dīn Maudūd, the Turkish *Atabeg* of Mosul and representative of the Sunnite Caliph of Bagdad, to unite the power of Mosul, Aleppo, and Damascus and conquer the Latin states in the East.[11] Fulcher does not report Maudūd's siege of Edessa in 1109, but he mentions the one of 1110 in which Baldwin marched to the relief of that place. The king made this march between the capture of Beirut in May and the beginning of the siege of Sidon in October. Fulcher next tells of the campaign of 1111 in which he says he accompanied Baldwin to Rugea, Apamea, and Shaizar but omits the one of 1112, which principally concerned Edessa again. Fulcher's account in chapter xlix of Maudūd's great effort of 1113 in conjunction with Tughtigin of Damascus, which nearly crushed Baldwin's kingdom, is extremely valuable and illuminating. He tells how Baldwin rashly engaged the Turkish advance guard at aṣ-Ṣinnabrah at the outlet of Lake Tiberias and how he and his troops were overwhelmed. The king managed to retire with the remnant of his force to a hill where he could not be attacked, and there Baldwin was marooned while his kingdom was plundered from one end to the other by the Turkish cavalry, assisted by the native Arab peasantry on the Frankish estates. But with the exception of Nablus the walled cities held out, Pons of Tripoli and Roger of Antioch brought aid, the arrival of pilgrims from Europe built up an additional manpower reserve, and eventually the Turks retired. This was followed by Maudūd's murder in Damascus, which gave Fulcher occasion to recognize frankly the Turk's very great ability.[12]

---

[9] II, xxxviii–xxxix.
[10] II, xxvi.

[11] II, xliii; xlv; xlix; l; li.
[12] II, li, 4–5.

Fulcher follows these events with an account of the Turkish invasion of 1115 led by Bursuk ibn-Bursuk, Maudūd's successor as *Atabeg* of Mosul and as leader of the forces of the caliph of Bagdad in the *jihād* against the Franks. Bursuk was fighting, however, a novel alliance between Tughtigin of Damascus (under suspicion for the murder of Maudūd) and two Frankish princes, Baldwin of Jerusalem and Roger of Antioch. According to Fulcher, Bursuk eventually was forced to retire, and Baldwin went home. Roger, however, pursued the Turks and succeeded in ambushing and killing Bursuk near Tell Dānīth on September 14 in a decisive battle that ended the threat of the holy war for some time.[13]

Following an interpolated account of Baldwin's marriage to Adelaide of Sicily, Fulcher ends Book II with a view of the growing strength of the kingdom. The Turkish menace from the north had been contained by Roger's defeat of Bursuk, and later in 1115 Baldwin constructed the important castle of Montréal at ash-Shaubak, south of the Dead Sea. In 1116 he marched from this base as far as the port of Elath to extend the influence of his kingdom to the Gulf of 'Aqabah. Always audacious, Baldwin dared in 1118 to invade the Egyptian delta itself as far as al-Faramā'. Here he became mortally ill from food poisoning and died on April 2 at al-'Arīsh on the homeward journey. Fulcher closes by quoting an epitaph that accurately and eloquently assesses Baldwin's achievements: a militant and successful defense of his people, the conquest of vital seaports, and the extension of his power to the Red Sea.[14]

Fulcher's third book, written in Palestine, has unique value as the only contemporary Latin account for the period from 1120 to 1127. It deals chiefly with four subjects: the second Baldwin's regency of Antioch and his defense of Edessa and Tripoli along with Antioch, his wars with Tughtigin of Damascus, the capture of Tyre in 1124, and the defense of Jerusalem against the Egyptians operating from Ascalon. Indeed, the first two of these subjects, because the wars with Tughtigin of Damascus were often

[13] II, liii, liv. [14] II, lv; lvi; lxiv.

connected with the defense of Antioch, Edessa, and Tripoli, are of such volume and importance that they tend to make Book III a history of all four Latin states rather than a history of the monarchy of Jerusalem alone, as was Book II. As Fulcher rhetorically said of Baldwin II, "God gave to him the land far and wide from Egypt to Mesopotamia."[15]

Baldwin's involvement in the affairs of Antioch and the defense of the north began when Roger, regent of Antioch since Tancred's death in 1112, was defeated and killed at Sarmadā on June 28, 1119. To protect the Frankish interests, the new king immediately marched north and won an important victory over Il-Ghāzī of Aleppo and Tughtigin at Tell-Dānīth. The victory assured Baldwin control of the area around Antioch, and as a result he became regent for Bohemond II, a youth still living in Apulia.[16] After this, Baldwin found that he had to march north almost annually to defend the lands of Antioch and Edessa,[17] and sometimes Tripoli as well,[18] and he spent perhaps half of his time in this pursuit. His difficulties were increased by the capture and imprisonment of his redoubtable successor as Count of Edessa, Joscelin I, from September, 1122, to August, 1123, and by his own capture and imprisonment from April, 1123, to August, 1124.[19] When Baldwin was released, however, we find that he mounted a formidable winter offensive against Aleppo and defeated his enemies, Aksungur al-Bursukī of Mosul and Aleppo and Tughtigin, decisively at 'Azāz on June 11, 1125.[20] Baldwin ended his regency by enthroning Bohemond II as Prince of Antioch and giving him his daughter Alice in marriage at the end of 1126.[21] Our chronicler recorded these events with obvious satisfaction.

Fulcher's account of Baldwin's relations with Tughtigin is scattered throughout Book III, but the thread is discernible. It starts with an alliance between Tughtigin and the Egyptian gar-

[15] III, vii, 3.   [16] III, iii; iv–v; vii.
[17] III, ix; xi; xvi; xxxviii–xxxix; xlii–xliii; lv. See also III, xxv; xxxi.
[18] III, li, liii.   [20] III, xxxviii–xxxix; xlii–xliii.
[19] III, xii and xxiv; xvi and xxxviii.   [21] III, lxi.

rison of Ascalon in 1118 that resulted in watchful waiting by both Egyptians and Franks; as Fulcher said, each side "preferred to live rather than to die."[22] The next year Baldwin won a victory over Tughtigin, now allied with Il-Ghāzī, in Syria at Tell-Dānīth. He skirmished with them in 1120 and with Tughtigin alone around Jarash in 1121.[23] Three years later, we find that the regency of Jerusalem, while Baldwin was a captive of the Turks, besieged Tyre, fought off Tughtigin, and then negotiated the surrender of the city with the Muslim leader.[24] Baldwin, after his release from captivity, took the offensive and defeated Tughtigin and Aksungur al-Bursukī at 'Azāz in the summer of 1125. He raided Tughtigin's lands in the fall of that year and then in January, 1126, initiated a formidable invasion of the Damascan state that carried him to the outskirts of the city before he had to turn back.[25] Fulcher's accounts of the battle of 'Azāz and the campaign of 1126 are particularly complete and valuable.

The capture of Tyre gave the Franks a decided advantage because the city was extremely important strategically and economically to Jerusalem as well as to the Muslims of the interior, especially those at Damascus. Tyre had successfully resisted a siege by Baldwin I in 1111–12. Hence, Fulcher gives much space to its final siege and capture, although he devotes more space to its legendary history and renown than to its actual siege in 1124. As a churchman of Jerusalem, Fulcher was very much interested in the transfer of ecclesiastical jurisdiction over Tyre from the patriarchate of Antioch to that of Jerusalem. He quotes in full a *privilegium* of Pope Paschal II, dating from 1111, in support of the claims of Jerusalem.[26] One further aspect of the siege claimed Fulcher's attention—the participation of the Venetian fleet. Fulcher reveals that the fleet wintered on Corfu, which was Byzantine territory, on coming out and that during the return the mariners committed depredations on several Byzantine islands,

22 III, ii, 3.
23 III, v; ix; x.
24 III, xxvii–xxviii; xxxii; xxxiv; xxxvi.

25 III, xlvi, 1–2; l.
26 III, xxxv.

the knowledge of which shocked Fulcher and, in turn, throws some light upon Venetian-Byzantine rivalry.

The history of Jerusalem's relations with the Egyptian advanced base at Ascalon may be regarded as a continuation of the story begun with the battle of Ascalon in August, 1099. Presumably, there were threats to Jerusalem from Ascalon every year thereafter, although only the most important seem to have been recorded. In Book III Fulcher speaks of hostilities in 1118, 1123, 1124, 1125, and 1126. The action in 1118 is important because it was a joint attack by the Turks of Damascus, who were Sunnites, and the Egyptian garrison at Ascalon, which was under the authority of the Shī'ite Caliph of Cairo.[27] Later, the Egyptians launched a giant land and sea offensive from Ascalon and Egypt in 1123[28] and attacked by land in 1124 and 1125 and by sea in 1126.[29] Fulcher also says, if we can believe him, that the Frankish counterattack of 1125 almost penetrated the gates of Ascalon.[30] If the Franks had succeeded, the later history of Jerusalem would have been far different, for Ascalon was not captured until 1153. The fields and orchards of Jerusalem were often raided by the Egyptians while Baldwin and his army were absent in the north, giving Fulcher cause to write of them with anguish. In chapter xlii he writes plaintively that the husbandman (of 1125) had scarcely a month's rest at home, that he lived attuned to the trumpet call of war, that on leaving home he went loaded with provisions and utensils, wondering whether he would ever return, and that many were captured or killed by Egyptian soldiers lurking in ambush.

Perhaps the most distinctive impression that emerges in Book III is of the inner strength of Jerusalem and the other three Latin states in the East. In the third decade of the twelfth century they were no longer feeble but solidly established. Jerusalem, the kingdom in the south, suffered no lack of order or leadership while King Baldwin II was absent for long periods defending the three states in the north, indeed, not even when he was a prisoner of the Turks. Patriarch Gormond and two successive constables,

27 III, ii.
28 III, xvii–xviii; xx.
29 III, xxxiii; xlvi, 3–7; lvi.
30 III, xlvi, 4.

Eustace Garnier and William of Bures,[31] governed the country. When the situation required it, they made an alliance with the doge of Venice; and later, they captured Tyre while the men left at home beat off raids from Ascalon.

Much the same might be said about the strength of Antioch, Edessa, and even Tripoli, although Fulcher writes less about them. These cities had an advantage in that their protector Baldwin II knew the area thoroughly because he had been count of Edessa from 1100 to 1118. Fulcher offers a significant glimpse of how Antioch was controlled and protected in telling us that when Baldwin became regent in 1119, he found vassals to defend the land by immediately finding husbands for widows in the fiefs that were left vacant by Roger's defeat and death at Sarmadā.[32] Thus, Antioch stood firm while the king was absent. He turned over the principality to the heir Bohemond II in 1126 and cemented their relationship by making Bohemond his son-in-law. Edessa likewise remained secure while Count Joscelin was a prisoner in 1122–23. Then in 1125 Baldwin and Joscelin's victory over the Turks gave the northern Franks more permanent security. Tripoli stood sheltered between Jerusalem and Antioch during the 1120's, although it had to be brought back to feudal obedience to Baldwin in 1122.[33]

The internal strength of Jerusalem, if not the other Latin states, is revealed in a significant way in chapter xxxvii of Book III. Here Fulcher tells how the Franks were beginning to feel at home in the land they had conquered a generation before. They were beginning to forget the lands of their birth, to think of themselves as Orientals, not Occidentals, to adopt a lingua franca in the East, to establish homes, to have children and grandchildren, to inherit property, and some to become wealthy. The former crusaders were a solidly established and native people. What they lacked and needed, although Fulcher was too unsophisticated to realize it, was a modus vivendi and a sense of community of interest with the local Arab and Turkish populations of the

---

[31] III, xvi, 2; xxii.   [33] III, xi, 2.
[32] III, vii, 1.

Near East, whose lands they had entered and with whom they now shared a common destiny.

Attitude of Fulcher

Fulcher of Chartres was a pious and devout man, thoroughly convinced of the righteousness of his cause. For him, the crusade was a holy war, similar to the ancient wars of the Israelites or of the Maccabees. He thought of the Frankish invaders of the Holy Land as weak, as on the defensive, and as beset by murderous and unrelenting foes. He regarded the crusade as a pilgrimage and the crusaders, armed or unarmed, as pilgrims. He equated death on the crusade with martyrdom; therefore it was something to be desired.[1] Hence, he was scornful of those who turned back from the crusade at Rome and Bari in 1096 or at Brindisi in 1097.

As would be expected, Fulcher had no charitable sentiments regarding either the Turks or Arabs. For example, when some Turkish women were captured in Kerbogha's tents before Antioch in 1098, he says the Franks "did them no evil but drove lances into their bellies."[2] In speaking of the Arabs slain at Jerusalem in 1099 or at Caesarea in 1101, he notes that their bodies were piled up and burned to recover the money they had swallowed.[3] At Jerusalem where ten thousand were beheaded in the Temple area, Fulcher says simply that the Franks were stained to the ankles by the blood of the slain and that not even women and children were spared.[4] That these people might have had rights in their own homelands did not occur to him. He regarded them as cruel and pitiless, as heathen, and as enemies of Christ. Rarely was he complimentary to his foes, though he called the Turks "a valiant race skilled with the bow" and later he paid tribute to Maudūd of Mosul as "rich, powerful, renowned, and astute" although a scourge of God.[5] He was indifferent to distinc-

---

[1] Prologue, 3; II, liv, 5; vi, 10; xxvii, 10–13.
[2] I, xxiii, 5.
[3] I, xxviii, 1; II, ix, 8. Years later he referred to the bodies of the enemy as food for wolves and hyenas (III, xviii, 7).
[4] I, xxvii, 13.   [5] I, ix, 4; II, li, 5.

tions between the Sunnite and Shī'ite Muslims or between the caliphs of Bagdad and Cairo, as indifferent indeed as were Muslim writers to religious distinctions among Christians. His contempt for or ignorance of Islam was such that once he spoke of an idol set up in the name of Mohammed.[6]

An intense admirer of Pope Urban II and of the Cluny reform movement in the Church, Fulcher was naturally hostile toward the antipope, Guibert of Ravenna,[7] and toward Emperor Henry IV, Urban's antagonist. He greatly admired Bishop Adhemar of Le Puy, the Pope's choice as legate for the crusade.[8]

We should expect to find that Fulcher was also loyal to Urban's plans for the First Crusade. The primary objectives seem to have been a rapprochement with the Byzantine emperor and the Orthodox Church after the so-called Schism of 1054, a recovery of much of Anatolia for the Byzantines from the Turks, and the reconquest of the Holy Sepulcher at Jerusalem.[9] Fulcher, in fact, admired the Emperor Alexius for his wealth and power and recognized the need for the oath of fealty that he required of the Frankish princes.[10] On the other hand, he seems to have accepted the common Frankish view that Alexius procured the surrender of Nicaea in 1097 by sharp practice and then cheated the Franks of their rightful spoils.[11]

After the crusaders reached Syria and Palestine, Fulcher's interest turned to the defense of these lands and away from the problems of the Byzantines, who wanted to recover their former

[6] In the great Mosque Qubbat aṣ-Ṣakhrah at Jerusalem, called the *Templum Domini* by the Franks (I, xxvi, 9).

[7] I, v, 1–8; vii, 1–3.　　　　　　　　　[8] I, iv, 1; xi, 9; xxii, 1; xxiv, 12.

[9] I, iii; iv, 6. Carl Erdmann, *Die Entstehung des Kreuzzugsgedankens* (Stuttgart: W. Kohlhammer Verlag, 1965 [Unveränderter reprografischer Nachdruck der Ausgabe Stuttgart, 1935]), 296–306; August C. Krey, "Urban's Crusade— Success or Failure," *American Historical Review*, LIII (1948), 235–50; Frederic Duncalf, "The Councils of Piacenza and Clermont," in Setton (ed.), *Crusades*, I, 220–52; and Alfons Becker, *Papst Urban II (1088–1099)*, 1: *Herkunft und kirchliche Laufbahn: Der Papst und die lateinische Christenheit* ("Schriften der Monumenta Germaniae historica" 19/1), Stuttgart: Anton Hiersemann, 1964. *The American Historical Review* will hereinafter be cited as *AHR*.

[10] I, ix, 1–3.　　　　　　　　　[11] I, x, 9–10.

territories as far as Antioch. He did not object when Bohemond occupied Antioch and Baldwin seized Edessa, although it was certainly not in Pope Urban's plans for the crusader princes to create personal principalities in former Byzantine territory. By the time Bohemond fought Alexius in 1107–1108, Fulcher had accepted Bohemond's propaganda at full value and accused Alexius of "using trickery and open violence" to obstruct the pilgrims' route by land and sea.[12] Fulcher conveniently forgot that the organization of Latin patriarchates and hierarchies in Syria and Palestine where there was or had been an Orthodox establishment was not consistent with Urban's hopes for reconciliation with the Greek Church.

In these years Fulcher was chiefly interested in popularizing the crusade and not in discussing past questions, such as Urban's plans for a rapprochement with the Byzantines, or subsequent political matters that might interest us. Thus, he mentions the oath of fealty that Alexius required of the crusader princes but does not explain what the oath implied nor why Bohemond, Godfrey, and Robert of Flanders took it and why Raymond of Saint-Gilles refused.[13] He speaks of the rivalry of Baldwin I and Tancred over Tarsus, but only in passing.[14] He says nothing of the ambition of Raymond to be the military leader of the crusade, nor does he explain why Raymond objected to Bohemond's plans for appropriating Antioch; he merely says that Bohemond later expelled the guards of Raymond from that city.[15] He does not mention the objection of Raymond to the establishment of a dominant secular state in Jerusalem or explain why Godfrey was chosen "prince of the realm," not king,[16] and why Baldwin I and Baldwin II subsequently took the royal title.

Fulcher, a cleric himself, says nothing about the debate as to whether Jerusalem should be controlled by a patriarch or a secular ruler. He fails to state that Arnulf of Chocques was chosen patriarch in July, 1099, and deposed in December; he merely says that

[12] II, xxxviii, 3.
[13] I, ix, 2.
[14] I, xiv, 3.

[15] I, xxv, 4.
[16] I, xxx, 1.

the decision about who should be patriarch was delayed for referral to Rome. He later writes that Daimbert of Pisa was chosen in December, 1099, but says nothing of papal approval. Nor does he mention Daimbert's far-reaching ambitions to be the ruler of a church state at Jerusalem. Fulcher does, however, reveal that Daimbert was jealous of Baldwin and notes that the patriarch agreed to crown Baldwin in 1100 only after "sensible men" intervened.[17] Still later, Fulcher very tersely states that Daimbert went to Italy in 1104 to recover the patriarchate from which Baldwin had deposed him and succeeded—but died on the return journey. This caused Evremar, the successor to Daimbert, to go to Rome in 1107 to ascertain his status; however, we are not told the outcome. Later we hear that Patriarch Arnulf was deposed in 1115, went to Rome to recover his seat, and succeeded.[18] But none of the questions about how or when Arnulf was elected a second time (in 1112), or why he was deposed in 1115 and restored, are answered. Although Fulcher's selection of detail is disappointing, we must remind ourselves that he was writing to popularize what seemed to him a holy war and was not inclined to discuss matters that might tarnish this cause.

Regarding the politics of friendly relations or cooperation with neighboring Muslim states, Fulcher is usually silent. There is one reference to a battle near Tell Bashir (1108) between Tancred on one side and Baldwin II and Joscelin on the other in which both groups have Turkish allies;[19] but Fulcher mentions only the allies of Baldwin and Joscelin, who lost, he would probably have us think, because they had such allies. Later, he writes of a similar alliance in 1115 between Baldwin I, Roger of Antioch, and Tughtigin of Damascus against Bursuk ibn-Bursuk of Hamadan; but that it exhibited the wisdom of permanent cooperation between the Franks and Turks of Syria against a growing pressure from Iraq did not occur to Fulcher. Likewise, neither Fulcher nor Baldwin II realized the folly of Baldwin's dangerous raid on Damascus in January of 1126.[20]

[17] I, xxx, 2; xxxiii, 20; II, iii, 14; v, 12. [19] II, xxviii, note 5.
[18] II, xxvi, 1–2; xxxvii, 1; liv, 8. [20] II, liii, 2–3; III, l.

Fulcher's attitude toward his master Baldwin I is very interesting. He says nothing of Baldwin before he became the latter's chaplain in 1097. Then, lamely and briefly, he reveals Baldwin's failure to protect the life of his host, Thoros of Edessa, and his succession to Thoros' place as ruler of Edessa.[21] But he has abundant praise for Baldwin's military ability around Tell Bashir and Edessa[22] and for his energy and valor in a long string of victories while king. An astonishing piece of frankness is Fulcher's statement that Baldwin, when he heard of Godfrey's death in 1100, "grieved somewhat at the death of his brother but rejoiced more over his inheritance."[23] Also, when Baldwin was defeated at Ramla in 1102 and at aṣ-Ṣinnabrah at the outlet of Lake Tiberias in 1113, Fulcher frankly upbraided him for rashness and sinfulness as well.[24] He disapproved of Baldwin's marriage to Adelaide of Sicily, and about that time our author seems to have had less close relations with the king. But he rallied to give Baldwin his due as a doughty warrior when the latter died in 1118.[25]

If Fulcher did not realize the value of Damascan friendship, he did at least know the value of having strong Frankish states at Antioch and Edessa to protect the Franks at Jerusalem. He pointed out that Baldwin I in holding Edessa and Bohemond in holding Antioch had protected the rest of the Franks as they marched south to conquer Jerusalem.[26] Hence, he was always interested in Antioch and Edessa and always wrote favorably of Bohemond and Tancred, who defended the area with great ability.

He was much concerned with Bohemond's subsequent career from his journey to Jerusalem in the fall of 1099 to his war upon the Byzantines in 1107–1108, as we have already learned. We have also seen that his sympathies were completely with Bohemond in this war.[27]

Our chronicler especially admired Tancred in spite of the fact that Tancred early in his career, in 1097 and 1099, had been at

21 I, xiv.
22 I, xxxiii, 2–6.
23 II, i, 1.
24 II, xviii, 5–7; xxi, 14–17; xlix, 4–7.
25 II, lxiv.
26 I, xxxiii, 2–4.
27 I, xxxiii–xxxiv; xxxv, 3; II, vii; xxiii, 1; xxvii, 2, 5; xxvi; xxix; xxxviii.

odds with Baldwin I, Fulcher's patron, over Tarsus and Haifa. Fulcher even took Tancred's side in a war with Baldwin of Edessa in 1108, although Baldwin was trying to recover his Edessan lands that were unjustly held by Tancred.[28]

Consistent with this concern for a strong Frankish bastion in the north, Fulcher was very proud of Baldwin II when the latter became regent of Antioch in 1119. He also took much satisfaction in the way Baldwin turned over Antioch to Bohemond II in 1126, giving the latter his daughter in marriage and thus, in Fulcher's hopeful mind, uniting the fortunes of the Franks from south to north.[29]

Fulcher was in most respects a very ordinary person whose attitudes present interesting contradictions. He said he wrote in a simple Latin style and usually did so. However, he often tried to embellish his prose with Biblical and classical quotations, imaginary speeches thrust into the mouths of participants, similes, and artificial plays upon words that are less successful.[30] He was interested in natural phenomena such as the peculiarities of the Dead Sea area. Yet he used Solinus' *Collectanea rerum memorabilium*, a revision of the *Historia Naturalis* of Pliny the Elder, for much mythical description of the animal life of the Near East when we wish he had relied upon personal observation, based upon a lifetime in that area.[31] He believed in miracles, attributing many hard-won victories to the presence of the Lord's Cross, yet was plainly worried when this relic was carried into battle and was relieved when it was returned to the safety of Jerusalem.[32] He felt that the crusade was a sacred cause, even while he pointed out that it enabled some Franks to become rich.[33] He believed himself to be a devout Christian; but by today's standards he ex-

[28] I, xiv, 3; II, iii, 10; xxviii.　　[29] III, vii, 1–3; lxi, 3–4.
[30] For examples of speeches see III, xxiv, 6–10; for similes, I, xi, 8; II, iii, 1; III, lv, 2; *HF* 50, note 6; for plays upon words, II, x, note 3; xii, note 1; *HF* 50, note 5.
[31] II, iv–v; lvi, 4; III, xlviii; xlix; lix; lx.
[32] III, v, 2, 4; vi; ix, 2–4, 7; xi, 6–7; xix.
[33] I, xxix, 1; xxxi, 10; II, ix, 7; III, xxxvii, 6.

hibited a most un-Christian attitude toward his fellow men who happened to be Muslims.

For one inconsistency we are decidedly grateful. Although Fulcher usually glorified the crusade as a holy cause, he once wrote, "Oh war, hateful to the innocent and horrible to the spectators! War is not beautiful although it is thus called . . . . I saw the battle, I wavered in my mind, I feared to be struck. . . . One struck, his enemy fell. The one knew no pity, the other asked none. One lost a hand, the other an eye. Human understanding recoils when it sees such misery."[34] Here Fulcher eloquently reveals the cruel nature of war, and his own inner humanity.

FULCHER'S SOURCES OF INFORMATION

The sources of information used by Fulcher were first, the knowledge that he gained as an eyewitness and participant, second, what he learned from others, sometimes from purposeful inquiry, and third, written sources. He says by way of introduction that he intended to write as exactly as possible what he had seen and remembered.[1] Because Fulcher several times expressed a concern for truth[2] and sometimes a skepticism of certain of his informants,[3] and because his statements where they can be checked usually correspond with those of others, we have gained increased confidence in his work. We are particularly pleased to find that his dates are usually reliable.[4]

Much that Fulcher recorded, particularly in Books I and II, came from his own observations. When he was not a witness, he often learned from those who were, or from documents. He must have gathered some details about the First Crusade during the years 1098 to 1099 from participants whom he met later in Jeru-

---

[34] II, xii, 1. For a somewhat similar passage see III, xliii, 3.

[1] Prologue, 2; I, v, 12.

[2] Prologue, 2; I, v, 12; II, xxxiv, 1–2; III, xliii, 1–2; lvii, 1, 4.

[3] II, xiv, 2; III, xxvi, 5; xliii, 1–2; lvii, 1, 4.

[4] Fulcher used different methods of chronology, such as the feast days of the church, the signs of the zodiac, or the Roman system of Ides and Kalends. He usually began the Christian year with December 25, the anniversary of the birth of Christ, rather than with January 1 following.

salem, for certainly he did not use the anonymous *Gesta* and the *Historia Francorum* of Raymond of Aguilers exclusively for this period. His information regarding the Crusade of 1101[5] and the disaster at Ramla[6] obviously came from survivors. So also must he have learned of the great defeat of Baldwin I at aṣ-Ṣinnabrah in 1113[7] and of the king's expedition to Egypt in 1118.[8]

Because Fulcher seems not to have been the chaplain of Baldwin II and probably stayed near Jerusalem during the reign of this king, he must have obtained from others the details, to be found in Book III, of Baldwin's activities away from Jerusalem. These would include Baldwin's defense of Antioch as its regent from 1119 to 1126,[9] his captivity at Kharput in 1123–24,[10] and his transfer of the regency to Bohemond II in 1126.[11] For example, Fulcher says he made careful inquiry concerning the imprisonment of King Baldwin in 1123[12] and that he learned of the death in the next year of Baldwin's erstwhile captor, Nūr-ad-Daulah Belek, from Baldwin's squire.[13] He heard of the surrender of Tyre in 1124 from messengers from the patriarch.[14] Amidst all of this Frankish detail, it is very interesting to find that Fulcher made use of Arab tradition on at least two occasions.[15]

Of written sources the two that were most important to Fulcher were the anonymous *Gesta* and the *Historia Francorum* of Raymond of Aguilers, which he drew upon for information in Book I. Another written source used in Book I was the text of a famous letter purporting to be from Bohemond and the crusader princes at Antioch to Pope Urban II, September 11, 1098, which Fulcher incorporated into the original text of his chronicle.[16] He also seems to have seen and made slight use of another document, known as the second letter of Count Stephen of Chartres

[5] II, xvi–xvii.
[6] II, xv; xviii–xxi.
[7] II, xlix.
[8] II, lxiv.
[9] III, iv–v; vii; ix; xi; xvi; xxv; xxxi; xxxix; xlii–xliii.
[10] III, xvi, 1–2; xxi, 2; xxiii; xxvi.
[11] III, lxi.
[12] III, xxvi, 5.
[13] III, xxxi, 6–7.
[14] III, xxxiv, 5.
[15] III, xxxviii, note 5; li, note 3.
[16] See I, xxiv, note 1. Fulcher omitted this letter in his second redaction. He may have thought that it was superfluous because Urban never came to Antioch as requested.

to his wife Adela, of March 29, 1098.[17] He may have found these and other written sources at a library or libraries in Jerusalem, for he refers once to his use of such a facility—"ut in bibliotheca legimus."[18]

Two minor classical works were also helpful sources of details for Fulcher. One was Rufinus' *Flavii Josephi Hebraei opera*,[19] a Latin translation of two Greek works by the Jewish historian Flavius Josephus, the *Bellum Judaicum* and the *Antiquitates Judaicae*. Possibly, Fulcher used the translations because he was unable to read Greek. There are evidences of the *Bellum Judaicum* in his description of Lake Tiberias,[20] the Dead Sea area,[21] the areas of Raphania and Acre,[22] and the history of Tyre.[23] The history of Tyre reveals also a dependence on the *Antiquitates*.[24] The second minor work used was Solinus' *Collectanea rerum memorabilium*,[25] an epitome of the *Historia Naturalis* of Pliny the Elder, which Fulcher drew upon chiefly for biological descriptions.[26] In addition he referred twice to a document known as the *Epistula Alexandri regis magni ad Aristotelem magistrum suum*[27] in support of Solinus. One wonders why Fulcher did not use Pliny in the original text. Perhaps it was not available.

[17] *Epistula II Stephani comitis Carnotensis ad Adelam uxorem*, in Heinrich Hagenmeyer (ed.), *Epistulae et chartae ad historiam primi belli sacri spectantes: Die Kreuzzugsbriefe aus den Jahren 1088–1100* (Innsbruck: Verlag der Wagner'schen Universitätsbuchhandlung, 1901), 150; future reference to this volume will be to HEp. HF 67; 219, note 23; 226, note 9.

[18] HF 598, note g.

[19] *Flav. Josephi Hebraei historiographi opera interprete Ruffino* (Colon., 1524). See HF 69, note 3; and 847. Because this translation is unavailable, direct reference will be made to Josephus.

[20] I, xxxiv, 3, note 4.

[21] II, v, notes 2, 4, 7, 12.

[22] III, li, 4–5; lii.

[23] III, xxx, notes 12, 14, 16.

[24] III, xxix, note 3; xxx, notes 1, 11, 12, 13.

[25] Claude de Saumaise (ed.), *Plinianae exercitationes in Caji Julii Solini Polyhistoria* (2 vols.; Trajecti ad Rhenum apud Johannem vande Water *et al.*, 1689), Vol. I of which has copious notes; and Theodor Mommsen (ed.), *C. Ivlii Solini Collectanea rervm memorabilivm* (Berolin apud Weidmannos, 1895). Reference will be to Mommsen's edition. Fulcher mentions Solinus twice (III, xlix, 17; lix, 5).

[26] III, xlviii–xlix; lix–lx.

[27] III, xlix, 17; lx, 9. Latin text in Alfons Hilka (ed.), "Zur Alexandersage. Zur Textkritik von Alexanders Brief an Aristoteles über Wunder Indiens,"

Other classical works that Fulcher drew from were Ennius' *Annales*, Sallust's *Bellum Jugurthinum*, Publius Syrus' *Mimi*, Vergil's *Aeneid* and *Georgics*, Horace's *Odes*, Ovid's *Metamorphoses* and *Fasti*, Lucan's *Pharsalia*, possibly either Livy's *Ab urbe condita* or Eutropius' *Breviarium ab urbe condita*,[28] and perhaps others to whom Hagenmeyer gives tenuous reference.[29] Christian works used, in addition to the Bible, were early ones: the *Hexaemeron* of St. Ambrose, the *Commentaria* and *Liber de situ et nominibus locorum Hebraicorum* of St. Jerome, the *Historiarum adversum paganos libri* VII of Orosius, the *De consolatione philosophiae* of Boëthius, the *Homiliae* of Gregory I, and the *Decretales pseudoisidorianae*.[30]

Documents that Fulcher may have found in the libraries at Jerusalem were a possible letter of the queen of Baldwin I to Tancred of September, 1101,[31] and the *privilegium* of Pope Paschal II to Patriarch Gibelin, dated July 11, 1111,[32] both of which Fulcher incorporated into his text. The *privilegium* may have been in the cartulary of the Holy Sepulcher. Fulcher may also have found there the decree concerning the remission of taxes in 1120. He mentions the remission, though not the decree.[33]

Jahresbericht über das königliche katholische St. Matthias-Gymnasium zu Breslau für das Schuljahr 1908–1909 (Breslau: Druck von R. Nischkowsky, 1909), i–xx; also in Stanley Rypins (ed.), *Three Old English Prose Texts in MS Cotton Vitellius A xv* ("Early English Text Society," CLXI; London: Humphrey Milford, Oxford University Press, 1924), 79–100. Reference will be to Rypins' text.

[28] *Annales*: II, xxxii, note 6; *Bellum Jugurthinum*: II, xl, note 6; *Mimi*: II, li, note 6; *Aeneid*: III, xxiv, note 3; xxix, note 9; xliii, note 4; *Georgics*: III, xi, note 8; *Odes*: III, li, note 1; *Metamorphoses*: I, xxviii, note 3; II, xxxii, note 2; III, xliii, note 3; *Fasti*: II, xxxii, note 3; III, xxviii, note 3; *Pharsalia*: II, xxvii, note 5; and *Ab urbe condita* or *Breviarium ab urbe condita*: III, xxix, note 13.

[29] See HF 425, note 6; 499, note 28; 554, note 18; 663, note 13; 713, note 48.

[30] *Hexaemeron*: III, lix, notes 3, 6; *Commentaria*: I, xxxiv, notes 5, 6; *Liber de situ et nominibus locorum Hebraicorum*: I, xv, note 2; III, x, note 3; xxx, note 10; *Historiarum adversum paganos libri* VII: III, xxix, 6, note 10; *De consolatione philosophiae*: II, xxi, 17, note 13; *Homiliae*: I, ii, 12, note 3; *Decretales pseudoisidorianae*: III, xxxiv, note 5.

[31] Fulcher quotes this letter very freely—if indeed he did not make it up as a rhetorical device. See II, xiv, 3–5, note 3.

[32] III, xxxv.   [33] III, viii.

Hagenmeyer suggests that Fulcher made use of the *Bella Anti-ochena* of Walter the Chancellor and the *Gesta Tancredi* of Ralph of Caen after 1118–19. Ironically, these authors had used Fulcher earlier.[34] He also suggests that Fulcher used a copy of the Concordat of Worms between Pope Calixtus II and Emperor Henry V of 1122 and a letter from Calixtus to Henry of December 13 of that year.[35]

ATTENTION GIVEN FULCHER BY OTHER WRITERS

It was inevitable that Fulcher's chronicle should have been used by other writers.[1] We have already noted that his text as it stood in the winter of 1105–1106 was worked over by two anonymous chroniclers, the authors of the *Gesta Francorum Iherusalem expugnantium* and of Codex L, which purports to be a text of Fulcher. This text of 1105–1106, whether Fulcher's own or Codex L, was used by at least three other writers. One, Guibert of Nogent, wrote in France (*ca.* 1108–1109) a history of the First Crusade covering the years 1095–1104. He used in part the testimony of returning participants, the anonymous *Gesta*, and, in his seventh and last book, possibly Codex L after it had arrived in France. Another, Ekkehard of Aura, went to Palestine in 1101 and later returned to Germany where he wrote (*ca.* 1112–15) a short account of the First Crusade from 1095 to 1105, making frequent use of the anonymous *Gesta* and Fulcher[2] in rather vague references, as well as of his own experiences. Finally, Ralph of Caen, who came to Syria (*ca.* 1107–1108) and entered the service of Tancred, wrote his *Gesta Tancredi* (1096–1105) between 1112 and 1118, making some use of Fulcher's work.[3]

---

[34] *HF* 68, 74. For Walter, see the text in *RHC, Occ.*, V (Paris: Imprimerie Nationale, 1895), 75–132, or in Heinrich Hagenmeyer (ed.), *Galterii cancellarii bella Antiochena* (Innsbruck: Verlag der Wagner'schen Universitäts-Buchhandlung, 1896); and for Ralph, see *Gesta Tancredi in expeditione Hierosolymitana* in *RHC, Occ.*, III (Paris: Imprimerie Nationale, 1866), 587–716.

[35] *HF* 68; III, xiii, note 1.

[1] For an elaborate discussion, see *HF* 71–91.

[2] Ekkehard, *Hierosolymita*, in *RHC, Occ.*, V, 11–40.

[3] *HF* 68.

A number of other writers, active after the first group, went to Fulcher's first redaction, which ended with the year 1124. Walter the Chancellor, a resident of Antioch who died after 1122, wrote a history of Antioch covering the years 1114–22. He seems to have made some use of Fulcher for details of the defeat of Roger of Antioch by Il-Ghāzī in 1119 and of the victory of Baldwin II over Il-Ghāzī near Zardanā later that year.[4] Albert of Aix, who never came to the East but whose account of Frankish history covering the years 1099–1120 is next in value to that of Fulcher, used Fulcher's work in a number of places as well as the anonymous *Gesta* and oral tradition. About the same time another German, who was anonymous, wrote in his own language the *Millstätter Exodus* in which he likened the invasion of Palestine by the crusaders to that of the Hebrews in ancient times, viewing both invasions as God's work. He made frequent quotations from Fulcher and other chroniclers of the First Crusade.[5] In Normandy, the monk Ordericus Vitalis wrote his *Historiae ecclesiasticae libri XIII*, which quotes Fulcher, often inaccurately, about events following the First Crusade. These citations appear mainly in Books X–XIII (written *ca.* 1135–42).[6] William of Malmesbury composed a famous history of the kings of England from 449 to 1125 using Fulcher, or possibly a text of Codex L, for his account of affairs in the Holy Land to 1102. However, what he wrote of events after 1102 cannot be definitely ascribed to Fulcher, for much of it may have been common knowledge.[7] About 1146 or 1147 an anonymous person in the Holy Land saw the need of bridging the gap between Fulcher and his own time, much as William of Tyre was later to do. The result was the *Historia Nicaena vel Antiochena*, which condensed Fulcher's text but added nothing of value; it stopped

---

[4] HF 74.

[5] HF 79–81; Peter Knoch, *Studien zu Albert von Aachen: Der erste Kreuzzug in der deutschen Chronistik* ("Stuttgarten Beiträge zur Geschichte und Politik," Band I [Stuttgart: Ernst Klett Verlag, 1966]), 71, note 4; D. H. Green, *The Millstätter Exodus, A Crusading Epic* (Cambridge: The University Press, 1966), *passim.*

[6] Ordericus, Books X–XIII; and HF 81–82.

[7] HF 82–83.

with events of 1123.[8] Another revision of Fulcher, called the
Secunda pars Historiae Hierosolymitanae (1099–1124) because
the earlier part (1095–99) seems to be missing, was attributed by
the seventeenth-century scholar Kaspar von Barth to Lisiard of
Tours, who was alive in Laon as late as 1168.[9] It adds as little of
value to knowledge of the period as the chronicle of Richard of
Cluny. The latter work was written in the last half of the twelfth
century, covers the years 800–1162, and makes some use of Fulcher's first redaction.[10]

Hagenmeyer suggests also that two other writers drew upon
Fulcher's history, but it is not clear which redaction of his text
they used. One was Matthew of Edessa, the celebrated Armenian
chronicler who wrote between 1124 and 1136. However, the
evidence that Hagenmeyer cites is not convincing, and he himself admits that further study is needed.[11] A little later, in the
mid-twelfth century, an unknown author wrote a sermon on the
capture of Jerusalem in 1099, attributing it to Fulcher. It is without value.[12]

About 1170 William of Tyre, a resident of Palestine and one
of the greatest historians of medieval times, began his work, a
history of the whole crusading movement up to his time.[13] A pains-
taking and usually accurate craftsman, he devoted one book to
the preliminaries of the First Crusade and included the legend
that it had been initiated by Peter the Hermit, a romantic story

[8] See text in *RHC, Occ.*, V (Paris, 1895), 133–85; and *HF* 83–84.
[9] See text of *Secunda pars* in *RHC, Occ.*, III (Paris, 1866), 545–85; (Jo.) Kaspar von Barth, "Animadversiones ad Bongarsianos scriptores historiae Palaestinae,"
in Petri a Ludewig, *Reliquiae manuscriptorum*, III (Lips., 1720), 523, quoted in
HF 84, note 3.
[10] Richard of Cluny, *Chronicon ab imperio Caroli magni 800–1162*, in L. A.
Muratori (ed.), *Antiquitates italicae medii aevi* (6 vols.; Milan, 1738–42), IV,
1079–1104, quoted in *HF* 85.
[11] *HF* 79. Cf. Fulcher, I, xxxv, 2–6, and Matthew of Edessa, *RHC, Arm.*,
I, 51–52.
[12] Charles Kohler (ed.), "Un sermon commémoratif de la prise de Jérusalem
par les croisés, attribué à Foucher de Chartres," *ROL*, VIII (1901), 158–64.
[13] See Hans Prutz, *Kulturgeschichte der Kreuzzüge* (Hildesheim: Georg Olms
Verlagsbuchhandlung, 1964; Reprografischer Nachdruck der Ausgabe Berlin,
1883), 458–69; Krey (ed.), *A History of Deeds Done Beyond the Sea, by William. Archbishop of Tyre*, I, 27–28; and *HF* 85–86.

that he unfortunately believed after reading the work of Albert of Aix. William covered the First Crusade itself in the next eight books, using the anonymous *Gesta*, Raymond of Aguilers, Fulcher of Chartres, and other sources of information. He wrote two books about the reign of Baldwin I and two about that of Baldwin II. For these four books he depended heavily upon Fulcher and in places slightly upon Walter the Chancellor. He continued his history to 1184 in ten final books, which are the most valuable part of his work because they are the most original.

The fame and reputation of William of Tyre soon crowded Fulcher and the other chroniclers of the early period of the crusades from attention. William's work was comprehensive, well balanced, and couched in excellent Latin; as a result, it seemed to be the authoritative account even for the early history of the crusades. This is why William's unfortunate inclusion of the legend of Peter the Hermit was accepted for six centuries without question.

In spite of the importance of William's chronicle, which tended to overshadow others, Fulcher's was used and cited from time to time, although usually in works of slight value. Hagenmeyer lists as examples the *Narratio profectionis Godefridi ducis ad Jerusalem*, written perhaps by Theodore of Kloster Pöhde, the anonymous *Estoire de Jerusalem et d'Antioche*, and the works of Sicard of Cremona, Oliver the Scholasticus of Cologne, and Alberic of Trois-Fontaines—all written during the thirteenth century. Another example was the *Vitae pontificum Romanorum* of Dietrich von Niem (d. 1418), who used a few excerpts from Fulcher's chronicle.[14]

14 *Theodori Palidensis narratio profectionis Godefridi ducis ad Jerusalem*, in *RHC, Occ.*, V (Paris: Imprimerie Nationale, 1895), 187–98; *Li Estoire de Jerusalem et d'Antioche*, in *RHC, Occ.*, V (Paris: Imprimerie Nationale, 1895), 621–48; Sicard of Cremona, *Chronicon*, in L. A. Muratori (ed.), *Rerum italicarum scriptores*, VII (Mediolani: Ex Typographia Societatis palatinae in regia curia, 1725), cols. 529–626; Oliver the Scholasticus, *Historia regum Terrae S.* (1096–1217), in *Die Schriften des Kölner Domscholastikus Oliverus*, ausg. v. Hoogeweg (Tübingen, 1894), 80–158; Alberic of Trois-Fontaines, *Chronicon*, ed. G. G. Leibnitius (Hannov., 1698), preceding works all listed in *HF* 86–88. Dietrich von Niem, *Vitae pontificum Romanorum*, excerpts quoted in Alph. Fritz, *Zur Quellenkritik der Schriften Dietrichs von Niem* (Paderborn und Münster: Druck und Verlag von Ferdinand Schöningh, 1886).

In 1611, in the early days of modern scholarship, Jacques Bongars published a collection of texts for the study of the crusades, collated from such manuscripts as he could find. One of these was a text of Fulcher, the first to be collated and printed.[15] Another text of Fulcher was published in 1641 in a collection of chronicles for the study of French history begun by André Duchesne, who died in 1640, and finished by his son François.[16] About the same time Barth wrote a series of "Animadversiones" or comments on Bongars' text of Fulcher, but these were not published until 1720.[17]

In the eighteenth century Edmond Martène and Ursin Durand, noting that Bongars and Duchesne had not included Fulcher's Prologue, published it themselves (1717).[18] J. A. Fabricius, who printed a bibliography of medieval Latin literature, remarked in 1734 that Fulcher was valuable for the period from the First Crusade to 1127.[19] Five years later, the French Benedictines of the Congregation of Saint-Maur began collecting materials for the study of the crusades. The famous scholar Dom Berthereau joined them about 1772, but their work was interrupted in 1794 both by his death and by the French Revolution. Fortunately, their collection was deposited in the Bibliothèque Impériale in 1813. Berthereau had made notes on Fulcher from the Bongars text and from some of the manuscript copies of Fulcher, but these notes were neglected until Paul Riant publicized them in 1884.[20]

[15] Bongars (ed.), *Gesta Dei per Francos*, I, 381–440. See *HF* 105–106.
[16] André Duchesne (ed.), *Historiae Francorum scriptores* (5 vols.; Paris, 1636–49), IV, 816–89. Reprinted in *MPL*, CLV (Paris, 1854), cols. 821–942; *ibid.* (Paris, 1880), cols. 821–940. See *HF* 106–108, 108–109.
[17] Barth, "Animadversiones," in Ludewig, *Reliquiae manuscriptorum*, III, 291–365 (quoted in *HF* 49 [291–369 in *HF* 111]).
[18] Edmond Martène and Ursin Durand (eds.), *Thesaurus novus anecdotorum* (5 vols.; Paris, 1717 ff), I, 364. Reprinted in *MPL*, CLV (Paris, 1880), cols. 823–24. See *HF* 108.
[19] Johann Albert Fabricius, *Bibliotheca latina mediae et infimae aetatis* (6 vols.; Hamburg, 1734–46), II, 643–46 (quoted in *HF* 111). The text of his statement may also be found in *MPL*, CLV (1880), cols. 821–22.
[20] Henri Dehérain, "Les origines du *Recueil des historiens des croisades*," *Journal des Savants* (Nouvelle série, 17e année; Paris: Hachette et Cie, Libraires-Éditeurs, 1919), 260–66; and Paul Riant, "Inventaire des matériaux rassemblés par les Bénédictines au XVIIIe siècle pour le publication des *Historiens des*

After the Napoleonic wars, Friedrich Wilkin and J. F. Michaud revived the study of the crusades, both quoting Fulcher in their histories. In addition, Michaud wrote a *Bibliothèque des croisades* in which he analyzed the chronicle of Fulcher.[21] F. P. G. Guizot published in 1825 a translation of Fulcher's chronicle amidst a vast collection of translations of sources for the history of France, including many of the chronicles of the crusades.[22] A little later, in 1837, Leopold von Ranke conducted a seminar for the study of the original sources of the First Crusade. The work was continued by one of his students, Heinrich von Sybel, who disproved the legend that Peter the Hermit started the First Crusade. Von Sybel analyzed the value of each of the chronicles of the First Crusade and pointed out that Fulcher of Chartres is one of the very few primary sources of information for that crusade but that he is of the highest value for the period thereafter to 1127.[23]

During the early nineteenth century the French Académie des Inscriptions et Belles-Lettres was planning its magnificent folio collection of texts of chronicles of the crusades, the *Recueil des historiens des croisades*. The project had been proposed originally in 1796, two years after the death of Dom Berthereau, but the first two volumes of the *Recueil* did not appear until 1841. The text of Fulcher, edited by Wallon with preface and footnotes, was published twenty-five years later.[24] In the meantime, J. P. Migne

---

croisades" (Collection dite de Dom Berthereau), *Archives de l'Orient latin* (2 vols.; Paris: Pub. sous le patronage de la Société de l'Orient latin, 1881–84), II, 105–30. The *Archives* will be hereinafter cited AOL.

21 Friedrich Wilken, *Geschichte der Kreuzzüge nach morgenländishchen und abendländischen Berichter* (7 vols. in 8; Leipzig, 1807–32), I–II, *passim*. J. F. Michaud, *Histoire des croisades* (3 vols.; Paris, 1812–17), I, *passim*; *Bibliographie des croisades* (2 vols.; Paris, 1822), I, 71–81; and *Bibliothèque des croisades* (2nd ed.; 4 vols. in 5; Paris, 1829–30), I, 82–96. The last two are quoted in *HF* 111–12.

22 *Histoire des croisades, par Foulcher de Chartres* in F. P. G. Guizot (ed.), *Collection des mémoires relatifs à l'histoire de France* (Paris: Chez J. L. J. Brière, Libraire, 1825), XXIV, 1–275.

23 Heinrich von Sybel, *Geschichte des ersten Kreuzzugs* (Dusseldorf, 1841), 51–56; second edition (Leipzig, 1881), 46–50 (both quoted in *HF* 112).

24 Fulcher of Chartres, *Historia Iherosolymitana*, in RHC, Occ., III, 311–485.

had anticipated Wallon, but not adequately, by reprinting the text of Fulcher from Duchesne's collection in 1854.[25] As a result of the publication of these texts, a vast amount of scholarship was accomplished in the field of the crusades in the latter half of the nineteenth century. Among the researchers were Paul Riant, Charles Kohler, E. G. Rey, Reinhold Röhricht, Bernhard Kugler, Hans Prutz, Heinrich Hagenmeyer, and Thomas Archer, to list only a few.

Interest in the crusades and in Fulcher continued. In 1900 Oliver J. Thatcher reviewed the progress made in the study of the First Crusade and indicated that much remained to be done, including a thorough commentary on Fulcher of Chartres.[26] Two years later Auguste Molinier in his *Sources de l'histoire de France* described Fulcher as a companion of Baldwin I, an eyewitness, a man of good sense, but a writer of obscure and affected style.[27] In 1910 Ernest Barker published a celebrated article entitled "The Crusades," which, kept up to date, remained a fixture in the *Encyclopaedia Britannica* until 1963. He wrote that Fulcher's account of the First Crusade itself is poor but that otherwise Fulcher is an excellent authority. He added that our author was "a kindly old pedant who interlards his history with much discourse on geography, zoology and sacred history."[28]

It remained for Hagenmeyer, who had already edited the chronicles of Ekkehard of Aura, the anonymous *Gesta*, and the *Bella Antiochena* of Walter the Chancellor, to publish in 1913 a new edition of the chronicle of Fulcher of Chartres. He used the second redaction of Fulcher's Latin text, establishing his base text by collating the manuscripts of the second redaction and then

[25] See note 16.
[26] Oliver J. Thatcher, "Critical Work on the Latin Sources of the First Crusade," *Annual Report of the American Historical Association for the Year* 1900 (2 vols.; Washington, D.C.: Government Printing Office, 1901), I, 501–509.
[27] Auguste Molinier, *Les sources de l'histoire de France* (6 vols.; Paris: A. Picard et fils, 1901–1906), II, 284.
[28] Ernest Barker, "The Crusades," *Encyclopaedia Britannica* (1910), VII, 550. Later reprinted as a separate volume, *The Crusades* (London: Humphrey Milford, Oxford University Press, 1923); see p. 106.

indicating in footnotes the variations from the first redaction and from Codex L. He analyzed Fulcher, his life, attitude, methods, sources of information, value, and the contents of the chronicle—all with a thoroughness and an exhaustiveness not possible or necessary in the present study.[29]

Soon followed Sister Frances Rita Ryan's translation of Hagenmeyer's text, in 1916. Book I of most of this translation was published five years later in Krey's *First Crusade*, an annotated collection of translations of the principal sources for the study of that crusade. Krey in his Introduction noted that Fulcher had an interest in the welfare of the common (Frankish) people and likened it "to the kindly concern of a simple French curé." Then he went on to say that Fulcher was undoubtedly the most important single source of information for the early history of the Latin kingdom at Jerusalem.[30]

In 1928 Nicolas Iorga published a valuable criticism of the primary sources for the study of the First Crusade. He made a comprehensive analysis of the contents of Fulcher's chronicle, of Fulcher's literary qualities, and of his attitude, the most complete such effort since the Introduction to Hagenmeyer's edition. He began by describing Fulcher as the official chronicler and advisor for both Baldwin I and Baldwin II, certainly an exaggeration in the case of the latter monarch, though Fulcher is the chief Latin authority for the years 1118–27 of Baldwin II. Iorga presented Fulcher as a participant, a cleric, a local resident, and a constant observer; as pious, superstitious, learned enough to quote classical authors, and interested in zoology and local geography; and as sympathetic to "the little people." Thus, like Barker and

[29] See particularly Hagenmeyer's Introduction (*HF* 1–112).
[30] Krey, *First Crusade*, 10. Krey's sponsorship of Sister Frances' thesis and the publication of a part of its first book and of parts of other chronicles of the First Crusade indicated the need for translations. This need was earlier recognized by D. C. Munro, one of the editors of the *Translations and Reprints from the Original Sources of European History* (Philadelphia: History Department, University of Pennsylvania, 1894–99), and later by John L. La Monte ("Some Problems in European Crusading Historiography," *Speculum*, XV [1940], 63–64) and James A. Brundage ("Recent Crusade Historiography: Some Observations and Suggestions," *Catholic Historical Review*, XLIX [1964], 502–503).

Krey, Professor Iorga noticed Fulcher's benevolent attitude—
toward the Frankish commoners.[31] Two years later Harold Lamb
published his popular history of the crusades, based upon research
in the original sources and often quoting them, including Fulcher.
He made a short analysis of Fulcher, calling him "less intelligent"
than Raymond of Aguilers but valuable for the years 1100–26
and able to give "almost the only clear picture of the crusaders
at home in their conquest."[32]

Dana C. Munro, upon becoming president of the Medieval
Academy of America in 1932, read a paper on Fulcher of Chartres
entitled "A Crusader," which was published in *Speculum* later in
that year. He stressed the importance of Fulcher for the study
of the Franks during their early years in the East following the
First Crusade. He regarded Fulcher as "above the average in
intellect and education, . . . a witness of stirring events and a keen
observer," and one "in a position to know the facts." He ended
by cautioning that the material for the period was scanty and
that much would have to be read between the lines.[33]

In 1940 Claude Cahen briefly analyzed the sources for the study
of the First Crusade and described Fulcher as "*sobre, intelligent,
curieux du choses du pays*" for the period up to 1127.[34] In 1941
Martha Evelyn McGinty, a student under the direction of John
L. La Monte, published a new translation of Book I of Fulcher
with an excellent introduction and brief annotation. She described Fulcher as well situated to obtain information up to 1127,
well educated for his time in spite of a self-admitted "rustic style,"
relatively impartial, pious but much less superstitious or gullible
than Raymond of Aguilers, and keenly interested in new places,
in novel experiences, and in history and geography.[35]

[31] Nicolas Iorga, *Les narrateurs de la première croisade* (Paris: J. Gamber, Éditeur, 1928), 38–61.
[32] Harold Lamb, *The Crusades: Iron Men and Saints* (New York: Doubleday,
Doran and Co., 1930), 354.
[33] D. C. Munro, "A Crusader," *Speculum*, VII (1932), 321–35, esp. 325.
[34] Claude Cahen, *La Syrie du Nord à l'époque des croisades* (Paris: Librairie
orientaliste Paul Geuthner, 1940), 10–11.
[35] McGinty (trans.), *Fulcher of Chartres*, 4–7.

A year later James Westfall Thompson analyzed the Latin historians of the crusades. He described Fulcher as a keen observer, careful with chronology, possessed of unusual descriptive power, especially in drawing word pictures of battles, and as the best source of information for the early years of the Franks at Jerusalem.[36] In 1951 Steven Runciman published the first number of his scholarly three-volume *History of the Crusades*. In an appendix he described the chroniclers of the First Crusade. He termed Fulcher "the best educated of the Latin chroniclers and the most reliable" and noted that he was remarkably objective except toward the Byzantines in his text written between 1124–27.[37]

Among modern authorities who have appraised Fulcher are Adolf Waas, Hans Eberhard Mayer, Jean B. Richard, and James A. Brundage. Waas was impressed by Fulcher as an authority on the Council of Clermont and on the zeal of the crusaders but also by occasional glimpses of him as a hater of war and as an Occidental turned Oriental by long residence in the East.[38] Mayer also noted that Fulcher was an authority on Clermont and, in addition, that he was a close associate of Stephen of Blois and Baldwin I and that toward the end Fulcher sounded a sympathetic note regarding the common people as residents of new homes in the Levant.[39] Richard observed that Fulcher offers the most valuable account of the foundation of the Frankish states in Syria and Palestine,[40] and Brundage wrote that Fulcher remains a "major and unusually reliable source" for this period.[41] Finally,

---

[36] James Westfall Thompson, "The Latin Historians of the Crusades," chap. XVIII in *A History of Historical Writing* (2 vols.; New York: Macmillan Co., 1942), I, 312.

[37] Steven Runciman, *A History of the Crusades* (3 vols.; Cambridge: University Press, 1951–54), I, 329.

[38] Adolf Waas, *Geschichte der Kreuzzüge* (2 vols.; Freiburg: Verlag Herder & Co., 1956), I, 7, 71–72, 83–84, 56, and II, 209.

[39] Hans Eberhard Mayer, *Geschichte der Kreuzzüge* (Stuttgart: W. Kohlhammer Verlag, 1965), 17, 53, 90.

[40] Jean B. Richard, "Fulcher of Chartres," *Encyclopaedia Britannica* (1966), IX, 994.

[41] James A. Brundage, "Fulcher of Chartres," *Catholic Encyclopedia* (1967), VI, 217.

Fulcher's value is amply attested to by frequent reference to him in the works of nearly all other modern historians of the First Crusade and of the early years of the four Latin states in the East.[42]

[42] For a detailed discussion of the manuscripts and printed editions of Fulcher, see *HF* 91–104 and 104–11.

PROLOGUE

✝

IT IS A JOY to the living and even profitable to the dead when the deeds of brave men, especially those fighting for God, are read from written records or, retained in the recesses of the memory, are solemnly recited among the faithful.[1] For those still living in this world, on hearing of the pious purposes of their predecessors, and how the latter following the precepts of the Gospels spurned the finest things of this world and abandoned parents, wives, and their possessions however great, are themselves inspired to follow God and embrace Him with enthusiasm [Matth. 12:29; Marc. 10:29; Luc. 18:29; Matth. 16:24; Marc. 8:34; Luc. 9:23]. It is very beneficial for those who have died in the Lord when the faithful who are still alive, hearing of the good and pious deeds of their forebears, bless the souls of the departed and in love bestow alms with prayers in their behalf whether they, the living, knew the departed or not.

2. For this reason, moved by the repeated requests of some of my comrades, I have related in a careful and orderly fashion the illustrious deeds of the Franks when by God's most express mandate they made a pilgrimage in arms to Jerusalem in honor of the Savior. I have recounted in a style homely but truthful what

---

[1] The Prologue appears in most manuscripts of the second redaction, which was begun in 1124, and, oddly enough, in MS I (Br. Museum, King's Library 5 B XV) of the first redaction. Hagenmeyer suggests that the Prologue was written between 1118–20, at about the same time as a reference to the Maccabees that occurs in Book II, chap. liv, and after the death of Baldwin I in 1118 but before 1120, the last date in MS K (*HF* 115, note 1).

I deemed worthy of remembrance as far as I was able or just as I saw things with my own eyes on the journey itself.[2]

3. Although I dare not compare the above-mentioned labor of the Franks with the great achievements of the Israelites or Maccabees or of many other privileged people whom God has honored by frequent and wonderful miracles, still I consider the deeds of the Franks scarcely less inferior since God's miracles often occurred among them. These I have taken care to commemorate in writing. In what way do the Franks differ from the Israelites or Maccabees? Indeed we have seen these Franks in the same regions, often right with us, or we have heard about them in places distant from us, suffering dismemberment, crucifixion, flaying, death by arrows or by being rent apart, or other kinds of martyrdom, all for the love of Christ. They could not be overcome by threats or temptations, nay rather if the butcher's sword had been at hand many of us would not have refused martyrdom for the love of Christ.

4. Oh how many thousands of martyrs died a blessed death on this expedition! But who is so hard of heart that he can hear of these deeds of God without being moved by the deepest piety to break forth in His praise? Who will not marvel how we, a few people in the midst of the lands of our enemies, were able not only to resist but even to survive? Who has ever heard of the like? On one side of us were Egypt and Ethiopia; on another, Arabia, Chaldea and Syria, Assyria and Media, Parthia and Mesopotamia, Persia and Scythia. Here a great sea[3] separated us from Christendom and by the will of God enclosed us in the hands of butchers. But His mighty arm mercifully protected us. "Blessed indeed is the nation whose God is the Lord" [Psalm. 32:12].

5. The history which follows will tell both how this work was

[2] Fulcher's characterization of his style as "homely" is a reminder that he came from Chartres, then famous for its classical studies. Fulcher must have been aware of this and indeed often quoted classical authors. He used medieval rather than classical Latin and apparently was a little sensitive about it. He also reveals at this point that he was an eyewitness to the First Crusade.
[3] The Mediterranean.

begun and how, in order to carry out the journey, all the people of the West freely devoted to it their hearts and hands.

Here Endeth the *Prologue*

BOOK I

✝

Here Beginneth the First Book Concerning the Deeds of the Franks, Pilgrims to Jerusalem

I

The Council Held at Clermont. 1. In the year 1095 after the Incarnation of Our Lord, while Henry the so-called emperor was reigning in Germany[1] and King Philip in France,[2] evils of all kinds multiplied throughout Europe because of vacillating faith. Pope Urban II[3] then ruled in the city of Rome. He was a man admirable in life and habits who strove prudently and vigorously to raise the status of Holy Church ever higher and higher.

2. Moreover he saw the faith of Christendom excessively trampled upon by all, by the clergy as well as by the laity, and peace totally disregarded, for the princes of the lands were incessantly at war quarreling with someone or other. He saw that people stole worldly goods from one another, that many captives were taken unjustly and were most barbarously cast into foul prisons and ransomed for excessive prices, or tormented there by three evils, namely hunger, thirst, and cold, and secretly put to death, that holy places were violated, monasteries and villas consumed by fire, nothing mortal spared, and things human and divine held in derision.

[1] Henry IV (1054–1106), German king and antagonist of the Cluny reform papacy, had been crowned Emperor of the Romans by antipope Clement III in 1084. Fulcher's sympathies with the reform party are apparent here and below.

[2] Philip I (1060–1108), already in trouble with the church for his bigamous relations with Bertrada of Montfort, was re-excommunicated at Clermont in November, 1095.

[3] Urban II (1088–99) was the friend and disciple of Gregory VII (1073–85), the great champion of the Cluny reform movement.

3. When he heard that the interior part of Romania had been occupied by the Turks and the Christians subdued by a ferociously destructive invasion,[4] Urban, greatly moved by compassionate piety and by the prompting of God's love, crossed the mountains and descended into Gaul and caused a council to be assembled in Auvergne at Clermont, as the city is called.[5] This council, appropriately announced by messengers in all directions, consisted of 310 members, bishops as well as abbots carrying the crozier.[6]

4. On the appointed day[7] Urban gathered them around himself and in an eloquent address carefully made known the purpose of the meeting. In the sorrowing voice of a suffering church he told of its great tribulation. He delivered an elaborate sermon concerning the many raging tempests of this world in which the faith had been degraded as was said above.

5. Then as a suppliant he exhorted all to resume the powers of their faith and arouse in themselves a fierce determination to overcome the machinations of the devil, and to try fully to restore Holy Church, cruelly weakened by the wicked, to its honorable status as of old.

II

The Decree of Urban in the Same Council. 1. "Dearest brethren," he said,[1] "I, Urban, supreme pontiff and by the permission

---

[4] Fulcher refers to the overrunning of the peninsula of Anatolia in the east Roman (Byzantine) empire by the Seljuk Turks in the generation following their defeat of the Emperor Romanus Diogenes at Manzikert on August 26, 1071.

[5] Fulcher's report is one of the very few extant accounts of the Council of Clermont. The others are by Robert the Monk, *Historia Iherosolimitana*, in *RHC, Occ.*, III (Paris: Imprimerie Impériale, 1866), 727–30; Baldric of Dol, *Historia de peregrinatione Jerosolimitana, ibid.*, IV (Paris: Imprimerie Nationale, 1879), 12–15; Guibert of Nogent, *Gesta Dei per Francos, ibid.*, IV, 137–40; and William of Malmesbury, *De gestis regum Anglorum*, ed. William Stubbs (*Rolls Series*), II, 393–98. For discussion, see D. C. Munro, "The Speech of Pope Urban II at Clermont, 1095," *AHR*, XI (1906), 231–42.

[6] The number of delegates is variously given and probably varied during the council. Most were Frenchmen. See *HF* 122, note 16.

[7] The council met November 18–28, 1095 (*HF* 122, note 19).

[1] According to D. C. Munro, Pope Urban made three speeches at Clermont: he called upon the clergy to support the Cluny reform movement, he appealed to the faithful to take the Cross, and he issued practical directions to insure the means of

of God prelate of the whole world, have come in this time of urgent necessity to you, the servants of God in these regions, as a messenger of divine admonition. I hope that those who are stewards of the ministry of God shall be found to be good and faithful, and free from hypocrisy [I Cor. 4:1–2].

2. "For if anyone is devious and dishonest, and far removed from the moderation of reason and justice, and obstructs the law of God, then I shall endeavor with divine help to correct him. For the Lord has made you stewards over His household so that when the time comes you may provide it with food of modest savor. You will be blessed indeed if the Lord of the stewardship shall find you faithful [Matth. 24:45–46].

3. "You are called shepherds; see that you do not do the work of hirelings. Be true shepherds always holding your crooks in your hands; and sleeping not, guard on every side of the flock entrusted to you [Joan. 10:12–13].

4. "For if through carelessness or neglect a wolf carries off a sheep you will certainly not only lose the reward prepared for you by our Lord, but after first having been beaten by the rods of the lictor you will be summarily hurled into the abode of the damned.

5. "In the words of the Gospel, 'You are the salt of the earth' [Matth. 5:13]. But if you fail how will the salting be accomplished? Oh how many men must be seasoned! [Matth. 5:13; Marc. 9:50; Luc. 14:34]. It is needful for you to salt with the corrective salt of your wisdom the ignorant who gape overmuch after the lusts of the world. Otherwise they will be putrefied by their transgression and be found unseasoned when the Lord speaks to them.

6. "For if He shall find in them worms, that is sins, because of your slothful performance of duty He will forthwith order them, despised, cast into the abyss of filth [Marc. 9:44–48]. And because you will not be able to restore such loss to Him He will

_____

the crusade. The first two are reflected clearly in Fulcher, chaps. ii–iii; the third is vaguely in chap. iv. See Munro, "Speech of Pope Urban," 232, note 16. Fulcher's precise knowledge of the decrees issued by the council led Hagenmeyer to suggest that he had a copy before him (*HF* 124, note 1).

straightway banish you, damned in His judgment, from the presence of His love.

7. "But one that salteth ought to be prudent, farseeing, modest, learned, peacemaking, truth-seeking, pious, just, equitable, and pure. For how can the unlearned make others learned, the immodest others modest, and the impure others pure? If one hates peace how can one bring about peace? Or if one has soiled hands how can he cleanse those who are soiled of other pollution? For it is read, 'If a blind man leads a blind man, both will fall into a pit' [Matth. 15:14; Luc. 6:39].

8. "Accordingly first correct yourself so that then without reproach you can correct those under your care. If you truly wish to be the friends of God then gladly do what you know is pleasing to Him.

9. "Especially see to it that the affairs of the church are maintained according to its law so that simoniacal heresy in no way takes root among you. Take care that sellers and buyers, scourged by the lash of the Lord [Matth. 21:12; Marc. 11:15; Luc. 19:45; Joan. 2:15], be miserably driven out through the narrow gates to utter destruction [Matth. 7:13; Luc. 13:24].

10. "Keep the church in all its ranks entirely free from secular power, cause a tithe of all the fruits of the earth to be given faithfully to God, and let them not be sold or retained.

11. "Whoever shall have seized a bishop, let him be accursed. Whoever shall have seized monks or priests or nuns, and their servants, or pilgrims and traders, and despoiled them, let him be accursed.[2] Let thieves and burners of houses, and their accomplices, be banished from the church and excommunicated.

12. " 'Thereafter we must consider especially,' said Gregory, 'how severely punished will be he who steals from another, if he is infernally damned for not being generous with his own possessions.'[3] For so it happened to the rich man in the familiar Gospel story [Luc. 16:19–31]. He was not punished for stealing from another, but because having received wealth he used it badly.

[2] Fulcher here refers to the Peace of God.
[3] S. Gregorii Magni Homil. ii, 40: 3.

13. "By these evils it has been said, dearest brethren, that you have seen the world disturbed for a long time and particularly in some parts of your own provinces as we have been told. Perhaps due to your own weakness in administering justice scarcely anyone dares to travel on the road with hope of safety for fear of seizure by robbers by day or thieves by night, by force or wicked craft, indoors or out.

14. "Wherefore the truce commonly so-called,[4] which was long ago established by the holy fathers, should be renewed. I earnestly admonish each of you to strictly enforce it in your own diocese. But if anyone, smitten by greed or pride, willingly infringes this truce, let him be anathema by virtue of the authority of God and by sanction of the decrees of this council."

III

Urban's Exhortation Concerning a Pilgrimage to Jerusalem[1]. 1. When these and many other matters were satisfactorily settled, all those present, clergy and people alike, spontaneously gave thanks to God for the words of the Lord Pope Urban and promised him faithfully that his decrees would be well kept. But the pope added at once that another tribulation not less but greater than that already mentioned, even of the worst nature, was besetting Christianity from another part of the world.[2]

2. He said, "Since, oh sons of God, you have promised Him to keep peace among yourselves and to faithfully sustain the rights of Holy Church more sincerely than before, there still remains for you, newly aroused by Godly correction, an urgent task which belongs to both you and God, in which you can show the strength of your good will. For you must hasten to carry aid to your breth-

[4] The Truce of God.
[1] This heading does not fit chap. iii because the chapter does not mention Jerusalem, the Holy Sepulcher, nor the Holy Land. The chapter is broad in scope and includes the rescue of the Byzantines as a large part of the purpose of the crusade. As this and some other chapter headings do not fit the chapters they entitle, it is probable that the divisions in the text were made and titled by a later scribe, not by Fulcher.
[2] This speech of Pope Urban was delivered on November 27, 1095 (*HChr* 9–10).

ren dwelling in the East, who need your help for which they have often entreated.[3]

3. "For the Turks, a Persian people, have attacked them, as many of you already know, and have advanced as far into Roman territory as that part of the Mediterranean which is called the Arm of St. George.[4] They have seized more and more of the lands of the Christians, have already defeated them in seven times as many battles, killed or captured many people, have destroyed churches, and have devastated the kingdom of God. If you allow them to continue much longer they will conquer God's faithful people much more extensively.

4. "Wherefore with earnest prayer I, not I, but God exhorts you as heralds of Christ to repeatedly urge men of all ranks whatsoever, knights as well as foot-soldiers, rich and poor, to hasten to exterminate this vile race from our lands[5] and to aid the Christian inhabitants in time.

5. "I address those present; I proclaim it to those absent; moreover Christ commands it. For all those going thither there will be remission of sins if they come to the end of this fettered life while either marching by land or crossing by sea, or in fighting the pagans. This I grant to all who go, through the power vested in me by God.

6. "Oh what a disgrace if a race so despicable, degenerate, and enslaved by demons should thus overcome a people endowed with faith in Almighty God and resplendent in the name of Christ! Oh what reproaches will be charged against you by the Lord Himself if you have not helped those who are counted like yourselves of the Christian faith!

7. "Let those," he said, "who are accustomed to wantonly wage

[3] The most recent appeal was made at the Council of Piacenza in March, 1095. Consult D. C. Munro, "Did the Emperor Alexius Ask for Aid at the Council of Piacenza?" AHR, XXVII (1922), 731–33.

[4] The Turks seemed to be a Persian people to Fulcher because they entered Anatolia and Syria through Iran and, indeed, adopted some Persian culture. The Arm of St. George refers to the Bosporus and the Sea of Marmora.

[5] The reference to "our lands" [regionibus nostrorum] shows that Urban regarded Christendom as a unity in spite of the so-called Schism of 1054 between the Latin and Greek churches.

private war against the faithful march upon the infidels in a war which should be begun now and be finished in victory. Let those who have long been robbers now be soldiers of Christ. Let those who once fought against brothers and relatives now rightfully fight against barbarians. Let those who have been hirelings for a few pieces of silver [Matth. 27:3] now attain an eternal reward. Let those who have been exhausting themselves to the detriment of body and soul now labor for a double glory. Yea on the one hand will be the sad and the poor, on the other the joyous and the wealthy; here the enemies of the Lord, there His friends.

8. "Let nothing delay those who are going to go. Let them settle their affairs, collect money, and when winter has ended and spring has come, zealously undertake the journey under the guidance of the Lord."

IV

Concerning the Bishop of Le Puy and Subsequent Events. 1. After these words were spoken and the audience inspired to enthusiasm, many of them, thinking that nothing could be more worthy, at once promised to go and to urge earnestly those who were not present to do likewise. Among them was a certain Bishop of Le Puy, Adhemar by name,[1] who afterwards acting as vicar apostolic prudently and wisely governed the entire army of God and vigorously inspired it to carry out the undertaking.

2. So when these matters which we have mentioned were de-

---

[1] Adhemar of Monteil, of the seigneurial family of Valentinois, became Bishop of Le Puy with the support of Pope Gregory VII. The diocese was directly subordinate to the papacy and was therefore a center of papal and Cluniac influence in its area. To Le Puy came Pope Urban on August 15, 1095, and from there he issued the summons for the Council of Clermont. Presumably, he consulted Adhemar at Le Puy about his plans for the council and for the crusade, and it is possible that he then decided upon Adhemar as legate for the expedition. Urban's reasons for the choice of Adhemar were probably the latter's record of ability and loyalty to the Cluniac papacy, his prestige in the area where the council was to be held, and his harmonious relationship with Raymond of Saint-Gilles, Count of Toulouse, the great prince who expected to be the military leader of the crusade. For Urban's preliminary relations with Adhemar and Raymond, see John Hugh Hill and Laurita L. Hill, *Raymond IV, Count of Toulouse* (Syracuse: Syracuse University Press, 1962), 29–34.

cided in the council and firmly agreed upon by all, the blessing of absolution was given and all departed. After they had returned to their homes they told those who were not informed of what had been done. When the edict of the council had been proclaimed everywhere through the provinces, they agreed under oath to maintain the peace which is called the Truce [of God].

3. Indeed finally many people of varied calling, when they discovered that there would be remission of sins, vowed to go with purified soul whither they had been ordered to go.

4. Oh how fitting, and how pleasing it was to us all to see those crosses made of silk, cloth-of-gold, or other beautiful material which these pilgrims whether knights, other laymen, or clerics sewed on the shoulders of their cloaks. They did this by command of Pope Urban once they had taken the oath to go. It was proper that the soldiers of God who were preparing to fight for His honor should be identified and protected by this emblem of victory. And since they thus decorated themselves with this emblem of their faith, in the end they acquired from the symbol the reality itself. They clad themselves with the outward sign in order that they might obtain the inner reality.

5. It is evident indeed that because a good intention brings about the accomplishment of a good work, a good work brings about the salvation of soul. If it is well to have good intentions it is still better after meditation to carry them out. Therefore it is best to lay up a store of good works so that through worthy deeds one acquires nourishment for the soul. Therefore let each one intend [to do] good so that he will finish by doing better and at length by deserving attain the best, which will not diminish in eternity.

6. In such a manner Urban, a wise man and reverenced
Meditated a labor whereby the world flowered.

For he restored peace and re-established the rights of the church in their former condition. He also made a vigorous effort to drive out the pagans from the lands of the Christians. And since he endeavored in every way to glorify everything which was of God,

nearly everyone freely submitted in obedience to his paternal
authority.

V

Concerning the Dissension Between Pope Urban and Guibert.

1. But the Devil, who always seeks man's destruction and goes
about like a lion, seeking whom he may devour [I Petr. 5:8],
stirred up, to the confusion of the people, a certain rival to Pope
Urban, Guibert by name.[1] This man, incited by pride and supported for a while by the impudence of the aforesaid emperor of
the Bavarians,[2] began to usurp the apostolic office while Urban's
predecessor Gregory, that is Hildebrand, rightfully held the see
and excluded Gregory himself from the limits of St. Peter's
Basilica.

2. And because Guibert acted thus perversely, the better people did not care to recognize him. Since Urban after the death of
Hildebrand was legally elected and consecrated by the cardinal
bishops,[3] the greater and more pious part of the people were in
favor of obedience to him.

3. Guibert, however, urged on by the support of the said emperor and by the passion of most of the Roman citizens, kept
Urban a stranger to the Monastery of the Blessed Peter[4] as long
as possible. But Urban during the time that he was excluded from
his church traveled about the country reconciling to God the
people who had gone somewhat astray.

---

1 Guibert had been the Archbishop of Ravenna. In the famous investiture controversy between the Emperor Henry IV and Pope Gregory VII [Hildebrand],
Guibert sided with Henry and as a result was chosen (anti-) pope in 1080, taking
the name of Clement III. He died in 1100.

2 Fulcher sarcastically refers to Henry IV not as Emperor of the Romans but of
the Bavarians. Henry had become Duke of Bavaria in 1055 and drew much of his
strength from that area.

3 Gregory died in 1085, and his successor, Victor III, reigned briefly from 1086
to 1087. Then the former Cluny monk, the Frenchman Odo de Lagny, Cardinal
Bishop of Ostia, was elected pope in 1088, taking the name of Urban II.

4 The term *monasterium* was sometimes used instead of *basilica* because the
clergy of many cathedral chapters lived according to the monastic rule (*HF* 147,
note 15, quoting Charles Du Fresne Du Cange, *Glossarium ad script. mediae et
infimae latinitatis* [6 vols. fol.; Basil, 1762]).

4. Guibert even as he was puffed up by his primacy in the church showed himself to be a pope indulgent to sinners. He exercised the papal office, albeit unjustly, amongst his adherents and ridiculed the acts of Urban as invalid.

5. But Urban, in the year in which the Franks first passed through Rome on their way to Jerusalem,[5] obtained the whole apostolic power with the aid of a certain most noble matron, Mathilda by name, who was then very powerful in her native region about Rome.[6]

6. Guibert was then in Germany. Thus there were two popes over Rome, but whom to obey many did not know, nor from whom to seek counsel or who should heal the sick. Some favored one, some the other.

7. But it was clear to the intelligence of men that Urban was the better; for he is rightly considered better who controls his passions just as if they were his enemies.

8. Guibert as the archbishop of the city of Ravenna was very rich. He was resplendent in pomp and wealth. It was remarkable that such riches did not satisfy him. Ought he to be considered by all an exemplar of right living who, a lover of ostentation, boldly presumes to usurp the scepter of God's authority? Certainly this office is not to be seized by force but accepted with fear and humility.

9. Nor is it a wonder that the whole world was disquieted and disturbed. For if the Church of Rome, the source of correction for all of Christianity, is troubled by any disorder, then immediately the members subject to it derive the malady through the chief nerves and are weakened by suffering along with it.

10. Yes, truly this church, which is indeed our mother, at whose bosom we were reared, by whose example we profited, and by

[5] Fulcher, in referring to the year (1096) when the Franks first passed through Rome, must have been writing after they had passed through again, that is, after the members of the Crusade of 1101 went through. By "Franks" Fulcher meant "crusaders" because most crusaders at that time (though by no means all) were Frenchmen.

[6] Mathilda, Countess of Tuscany, famous as the supporter of Gregory VII and Urban II against Henry IV and Guibert, sent troops to accompany Urban II to Rome early in 1096 after the Council of Clermont.

whose counsel we were strengthened, was rudely smitten by that proud Guibert. And when the head is thus struck the members are hurt immediately.

> If the head is afflicted the other members suffer.

11. Moreover when the head was sick in this way the members were enfeebled with pain because in all parts of Europe peace, virtue, and faith were brutally trampled upon by stronger men and lesser, inside the church and out. It was necessary to put an end to all these evils and, in accordance with the plan initiated by Pope Urban, to turn against the pagans the fighting which up to now customarily went on among the Christians.

12. Now therefore I must turn my pen to history in order to tell clearly the uninformed about the journey of those going to Jerusalem, what happened to them, and how the undertaking and the labor gradually came to a successful conclusion with the help of God. I, Fulcher of Chartres, who went with the other pilgrims, afterwards diligently and carefully collected all this in my memory for the sake of posterity, just as I saw it with my own eyes.[7]

VI

The Time of Departure of the Christians Together with the Names of the Leaders of the Pilgrims. 1. In the year 1096 of the Lord's Incarnation and in the month of March following the council, which, as has been said, Pope Urban held during November in Auvergne,[1] some who were more speedy in their preparation than others began to set out on the holy journey. Others followed in April or May, in June or in July, or even in August or September or October as they were able to secure the means to defray expenses.[2]

---

[7] Fulcher here identifies himself by name and as a member of the First Crusade. The phrase "successful conclusion" indicates that he wrote it at some time after, and not before, the conclusion of that crusade in 1099.

[1] November 18–28, 1095 (chap. i, note 7).

[2] Urban in his proclamation to the people of Flanders, December, 1095, set August 15, 1096, as the date of departure for the army under Bishop Adhemar (*Epistula Urbani II papae ad omnes fideles in Flandria,* in HEp 136–37). D. C. Munro suggests that this date was set in order to give the crusaders time to harvest

2. In that year peace and a very great abundance of grain and wine existed in all countries by the grace of God, so that there was no lack of bread on the trip for those who had chosen to follow Him with their crosses in accordance with His commands.

3. Since it is fitting to remember the names of the leaders of the pilgrims at that time I mention Hugh the Great, the brother of King Philip of France, the first of the heroes to cross the sea.[3] Hugh landed with his men near Durazzo, a city in Bulgaria,[4] but rashly advancing with a small force was captured there by the citizens and conducted to the emperor at Constantinople. Here he stayed for some time, being not entirely free.[5]

4. After him Bohemond of Apulia, a son of Robert Guiscard, of the nation of the Normans, passed with his army over the same route.[6]

5. Next Godfrey, Duke of Lorraine, traveled through Hungary with a large force.[7]

6. Raymond, Count of the Provençals,[8] with Goths and Gascons, and also Adhemar, Bishop of Le Puy, crossed through Dalmatia.

7. A certain Peter the Hermit, having gathered to himself a

---

their crops and to march through Anatolia in the cooler part of the year (*The Kingdom of the Crusaders* [New York, London: D. Appleton-Century Co., 1935], 39).

[3] Hugh, Count of Vermandois, younger brother of King Philip I, commonly called "Magnus," a Latin mistranslation of the French term "moins né," i.e., a younger brother (Bréhier [ed.], *Histoire anonyme de la première croisade*, 14, note 3).

[4] The reference to Durazzo, Albania, as a part of Bulgaria dates back to the great Bulgarian monarchy of Czar Samuel (d. 1014), destroyed by the Byzantine Emperor Basil II by 1018.

[5] The Emperor Alexius wanted Hugh to set a precedent for the other princes, to swear to return any former imperial lands that he might conquer, and to take an oath of allegiance for any others that he might conquer. Hugh, a vain man and powerless, did so willingly. See Frederic Duncalf, "The First Crusade: Clermont to Constantinople," in Setton (ed.), *Crusades*, I, 284.

[6] For Bohemond's life, see Ralph Bailey Yewdale, *Bohemond I, Prince of Antioch* (n.d. [probably Princeton, 1924]).

[7] In regard to Godfrey's life, see John C. Andressohn, *The Ancestry and Life of Godfrey of Bouillon* ("Indiana University Publications, Social Science Series," No. 5 [Bloomington, Ind., 1947]).

[8] For the career of Count Raymond, see Hill and Hill, *Raymond IV*.

crowd of people on foot but only a few knights, was the first to pass through Hungary.[9] Afterwards Walter the Penniless, who was certainly a very good soldier, was the commander of these people. Later he was killed with many of his companions between Nicomedia and Nicaea by the Turks.[10]

8. In the month of October, Robert, Count of the Normans, a son of William, King of the English, began the journey, having collected a great army of Normans, English, and Bretons.[11] With him went Stephen, the noble Count of Blois, his brother-in-law,[12] and Robert, Count of the Flemings,[13] with many other nobles.

9. Therefore since such a multitude came from all Western countries, little by little and day by day the army grew while on the march from a numberless host into a group of armies. You could see a countless number from many lands and of many languages. However, they were not gathered into a single army until we reached the city of Nicaea.

10. What then shall I say? The islands of the seas and all the kingdoms of the earth were so moved that one believed the prophecy of David fulfilled, who said in his Psalm, "All the nations whom Thou has made shall come and worship before Thee, O Lord" [Psalm. 85:9], and what those who arrived later deservedly

[9] In regard to Peter the Hermit, see Heinrich Hagenmeyer, *Peter der Eremite* (Leipzig: Otto Harrasowitz, 1879); and Frederic Duncalf, "The Peasants' Crusade," *AHR*, XXVI (1921), 440–53.

[10] Concerning Walter, see Theodore Wolff, *Die Bauernkreuzzüge des Jahren 1096* (Tübingen, 1891), 130–43, 185–87; and Duncalf, "The Peasants' Crusade," 443–44, 459–51.

[11] Robert (II) Curthose, Duke of Normandy, was the eldest son of William the Conqueror, King of England. See Charles Wendell David, *Robert Curthose, Duke of Normandy* ("Harvard Historical Studies," Vol. XXV [Cambridge: Harvard University Press, 1920]).

[12] Stephen was the Count of Blois and Chartres and the husband of Adela, daughter of William the Conqueror. He was also the father of King Stephen of England (1135–54). See James A. Brundage, "An Errant Crusader: Stephen of Blois," *Traditio*, XVI (1960), 380–95.

[13] Robert II, Count of Flanders, was the son of Robert (I) the Frisian and a cousin of Duke Robert of Normandy. See M. M. Knappen, "Robert II of Flanders in the First Crusade," in Louis J. Paetow (ed.), *The Crusades and Other Historical Essays Presented to Dana C. Munro by His Former Students* (New York: F. S. Crofts and Co., 1928), 79–100. This volume will hereinafter be cited as *Crusades-Munro*.

said, "We shall worship in the place where His feet have stood" [Psalm. 131:7].[14] Of this journey moreover we read much more in the prophets which it would be tedious to repeat.

11. Oh what grief there was! What sighs, what weeping, what lamentation among friends when husband left his wife so dear to him, his children, his possessions however great, his father and mother, brothers and other relatives!

12. But however many tears those remaining shed for departing friends and in their presence, none flinched from going because for love of God they were leaving all that they possessed, firmly convinced that they would receive a hundredfold what the Lord promised to those who loved Him [Matth. 19:29; Marc. 10:29–30; Luc. 18:29–30].

13. Then husband told wife the time he expected to return, assuring her that if by God's grace he survived he would come back home to her. He commended her to the Lord, kissed her lingeringly, and promised her as she wept that he would return. She, though, fearing that she would never see him again, could not stand but swooned to the ground, mourning her loved one whom she was losing in this life as if he were already dead. He, however, like one who had no pity—although he had—and as if he were not moved by the tears of his wife nor the grief of any of his friends—yet secretly moved in his heart—departed with firm resolution.

14. Sadness was the lot of those who remained, elation, of those who departed. What then can we say further? "This is the Lord's doing, and it is marvelous in our eyes" [Psalm. 117:23; Matth. 21:42].

VII

The Journey of the Count of the Normans and What Happened at Rome While They Were There. 1. Then we western Franks crossed Gaul and traveling through Italy came to Lucca, a most

---

[14] Hagenmeyer says that the phrase "arrived later . . . 'where His feet have stood' " indicates that Fulcher did not write this until after the conquest of Jerusalem in 1099 (*HF* 162, note 34). Fulcher used it again (I, xxxiii, 15).

famous city. Near there we met Pope Urban; and Robert the Norman, Count Stephen of Blois, and others of us who desired talked with him. After we had received his blessing we went on to Rome rejoicing.[1]

2. When we entered the Basilica of the Blessed Peter we found the men of Guibert, that stupid[2] pope, in front of the altar. With swords in hand they wickedly snatched the offerings placed there on the altar. Others ran along the rafters of the monastery itself and threw stones at us as we lay prostrate in prayer. For when they saw anyone faithful to Urban they straightway wished to kill him.

3. Moreover in one tower of the Basilica were the men of the Lord Urban. They were guarding it well and faithfully and as far as possible were resisting his adversaries. For that we grieved when we saw such an outrage committed there. But we heartily desired that nothing be done except as vengeance by the Lord. Many who had come thus far with us hesitated no longer but returned to their homes, weakened by cowardice.

4. We, however, traveled through the middle of Campania and reached Bari, a very wealthy city situated by the side of the sea. There in the Church of the Blessed Nicholas we prayed fervently to God, and then we went down to the harbor hoping to cross at once. But because the seamen objected, saying that fortune was perverse and the winter season was coming, which would expose us to dangers, Count Robert of Normandy was obliged to withdraw into Calabria and spent the entire winter there. But Robert, Count of Flanders, crossed with his whole force at once.[3]

5. At that time many of the common people who were left [to their own resources] and who feared privation in the future sold their weapons and again took up their pilgrims' staves, and re-

---

[1] Fulcher's frequent use of the first-person pronoun in chaps. vii, viii, ix, and x clearly indicates that he was traveling in the following of Duke Robert and Count Stephen, whose trip he describes, certainly as far as Nicea. Hagenmeyer dates the events at Lucca and Rome *ca.* October 25 and 28, 1096 (*HChr* 90, 92).

[2] The designation of Guibert as "stolidus" should not be interpreted literally, for Guibert was not stupid; rather, it should be seen as a term of contempt for a "pseudo" pope (*HF* 165, note 7). Fulcher's loyalty to Urban is quite apparent.

[3] At the beginning of December (*HF* 168, note 23).

turned home as cowards. For this reason they were regarded as despicable by God as well as by mankind, and it redounded to their shame.

VIII

The Drowning of the Pilgrims and the Miracle Divinely Revealed.

1. In the year of our Lord 1097, with the return of spring in March, the Norman count and Count Stephen of Blois with all of his followers, for Stephen likewise had been awaiting an opportune time for the crossing, again turned toward the sea. When the fleet was ready in the Nones of April, which then happened to be on the holy day of Easter,[1] they embarked at the port of Brindisi.

2. "How unsearchable are the judgments of God, how inscrutable His ways!" [Rom. 11:33]. For among all these ships we saw one near the shore which suddenly cracked through the middle for no apparent reason. Consequently, four hundred of both sexes perished by drowning, but concerning them joyous praise at once went up to God.

3. For when those standing round about had collected as many bodies of the dead as possible, they found crosses actually imprinted in the flesh of some of them, between the shoulders. For it was fitting that this same symbol of victory, which they had worn on their clothes while living, should remain by the will of God as a token of faith upon those thus occupied in His service. At the same time it was also proper that such a miracle should show those who witnessed it that the dead had now attained by the mercy of God the peace of eternal life. Thus it was most certainly manifest that the Scriptural prophecy had been fulfilled: "The just, though they shall be taken prematurely by death, shall be in peace" [Sapient. 4:7].

4. Of the others now struggling with death but few survived. Their horses and mules were swallowed up by the waves, and much money was lost. At the sight of this disaster we were much

---

[1] April 5, 1097.

afraid; so much so that many faint-hearted who had not yet embarked returned to their homes, giving up the pilgrimage and saying that never again would they entrust themselves to the treacherous sea.

5. We, however, relying implicitly on Almighty God, put out to sea in a very gentle breeze with sails hoisted and to the sound of many trumpets. For three days we were detained at sea by the lack of wind. On the fourth day[2] we reached land near the city of Durazzo, about ten miles distant I judge. Our fleet entered two harbors. Then joyfully indeed we set foot on dry land and crossed over in front of the aforementioned city.

6. And so we passed through the lands of the Bulgars in the midst of steep mountains and desolate places. Then we all came to a swift stream called the River of the Demon by the local inhabitants and justly so.[3] For we saw many people of the common sort perish in this river, people who hoped to wade across step by step but who were suddenly engulfed by the strong force of the current. Not one of the onlookers was able to save any of them. Wherefore we shed many tears from compassion. Many of the foot-soldiers would have lost their lives in the same manner had not the knights with their trained horses brought aid to them. Then we pitched camp near the shore and spent one night. On all sides were great mountains which were uninhabited.

7. At daybreak the trumpets sounded, and we began to climb the mountain which is called Bagulatus [Bagora]. After we had crossed the mountain and passed through the cities of Lucretia [Ochrida], Botella [Bitolj, Monastir], Bofinat [Edessa, Vodena], and Stella we reached a river called the Bardarius [Vardar].[4] Al-

---

[2] April 9, 1097.

[3] The route from Durazzo to Constantinople described by Fulcher followed the old Roman military road, the Via Egnatia. It ran up the valley of the Skumbi (anc. Genusus) River, here called "flumen Daemonis," but not to be confused with the Devol to the south (HF 172, note 18). See Adolf Stieler, Handatlas über alle Theile du Erde und über das Weltgebäude (Gotha: Justus Perthes, 1881), plate 56; William R. Shepherd, Historical Atlas (9th ed.; New York: Barnes and Noble, Inc., 1964), plates 10–11.

[4] These towns can be identified in the atlases cited above, and in Theophilus Luc. Fridericus Tafel, Via militaris Romanorum Egnatia (Partes occidentalis et orien-

though it was customary to cross this river only by boat we joyfully waded across with the aid of God. The following day we camped in front of the city of Thessalonica [Salonica], a city rich in goods of all kinds.

8. After a stop of four days[5] we traveled across Macedonia through the valley of Philippi [Angista] and through Crisopolis, Christopolis [Kavalla], Praetoria [Peritheorion, Jenidscheh], Messinopolis [Mosynopolis], Macra [Makri], Traianopolis [Orichova], Neapolis, Panadox [Panidos], Rodosto [Tekirdagh], Heraclea [Eregli], Salumbria [Silivri], and Natura [Athyra, Büyük Chekmeje] and thus reached Constantinople.[6] We pitched our tents before this city and rested fourteen days.[7]

9. But we did not try to enter the city because it was not agreeable to the emperor (for he feared that possibly we would plot some harm to him). Therefore it was necessary for us to buy our daily supplies outside the walls. These supplies the citizens brought to us by order of the emperor. We were not allowed to enter the city except at the rate of five or six each hour. Thus while we were leaving, others were entering to pray in the churches.[8]

---

talis; Tubingae: Typis Hopferi de l'Orme, 1841), 5–10, 39–43, 51–57; Joseph Arnim Knapp, "Reisen durch die Balkanhalbinsel während des Mittelalters nach der kroatischen Original-Abhandlung des Peter Matkovic," *Mittheilungen des kais. und kön. geographischen Gesellschaft in Wien*, XXIII, neuen Folge, XIII (1880), 42–43, 169–71; and HF 173, note 23. Knapp believes Stella to have been anc. Cella, modern Ostrova (p. 171); Hagenmeyer believes, from the order listed, that it was Pella (HF 173, note 23).

[5] April 22–26, 1097 (HF, 174 note 26).

[6] Most of these towns can be found in Stieler's *Handatlas* or Shepherd's *Historical Atlas* or in John Bartholomew (ed.), *The Times Atlas of the World* (5 vols.; London, Times Publishing Co., 1955–59), IV, plate 83. Neapolis is doubtful. Knapp says it cannot be identified ("Reisen durch die Balkanhalbinsel während des Mittelalters," 356), while Hagenmeyer suggests that it may have been Malgera or Ainadschik (HF 175, note 28). For discussion of this list of towns, see Tafel, *Via Egnatia*, 9–46, 55–58; Tafel, *De via militari Romanorum Egnatia, Dissertatio geographica* (Tubingae: Prostat apul H. Laupp., 1842), *Prolegomena*, pp. ix, xli–xlvi, lviii–lxxiii; Knapp, "Reisen durch die Balkanhalbinsel während des Mittelalters," 355–57; HF 175, note 28.

[7] May 14–28, 1097 (HF 175, note 29).

[8] The Emperor Alexius (I) Comnenus (1081–1118) was taking no chances with the men of Robert of Normandy and Stephen of Blois because he had had trouble with the hungry followers of Peter the Hermit, Godfrey of Bouillon, Bo-

IX

From Constantinople to Nicaea. 1. Oh what a noble and beautiful city is Constantinople! How many monasteries and palaces it contains, constructed with wonderful skill! How many remarkable things may be seen in the principal avenues and even in the lesser streets! It would be very tedious to enumerate the wealth that is there of every kind, of gold, of silver, or robes of many kinds, and of holy relics. Merchants constantly bring to the city by frequent voyages all the necessities of man.[1] About twenty thousand eunuchs, I judge, are always living there.[2]

2. After we were sufficiently rested[3] our leaders, after taking counsel, made under oath an agreement with the emperor at his insistence. Bohemond and Duke Godfrey who had preceded us had already agreed to it. But Count Raymond refused to subscribe. However, the Count of Flanders took the oath as did the others.[4]

---

hemond, and Raymond of Saint-Gilles. But Fulcher, writing in the mood of Pope Urban's desire to help the Byzantines as fellow Christians, did not object to Alexius' precautions and even worshipped in the Greek churches in disregard of the Schism of 1054.

[1] The anonymous *Gesta Francorum Iherusalem expugnantium* is eloquent at this point: "Oh how great a city, how noble, how delightful and how filled with churches and palaces built with wonderful skill, what spectacles and what marvels of engraving in brass and marble are contained within the city! On one side the sea and an impregnable wall bound the city; on the other a valley and a double ditch, and a wall of immense size and strength with towers in its circuit. Frequent voyages bring to the citizens at all times necessities in abundance. Cyprus, Rhodes and Mytilene, and Corinth and innumerable islands minister unto this city. Achaia, Bulgaria and all of Greece likewise serve the city and send to it all their choicest products. Moreover the cities of Romania in Asia and in Europe, and also the cities of Africa never cease sending donatives to Constantinople. Greeks, Bulgars, Alans, Cumans, Pigmatici (Petchenegs), Italians, Venetians, Romans, Dacians, English, Amalfitans and even Turks and many gentiles, Jews and proselytes, Cretans, Arabs and people of all nations come to this great city" (*RHC, Occ.,* III, 494).

[2] Fulcher, like other unsophisticated Westerners, believed that the Byzantine emperors kept harems and large numbers of eunuchs in their service. The statement is repeated by F. C. H. L. Pouqueville, October 1, 1833, quoted in Tafel, *Via Egnatia,* 10.

[3] The anonymous *Gesta Francorum Iherusalem expugnantium* states that they rested fifteen days (*RHC, Occ.,* III, 494).

[4] Hugh of Vermandois, Godfrey of Bouillon and his brother Baldwin, Bohemond, Robert of Flanders, Robert of Normandy, and Stephen of Blois agreed to restore to Alexius any former imperial lands that they might conquer and to owe allegiance to the emperor for any further lands that they might recover (Steven

3. For it was essential that all establish friendship with the emperor since without his aid and counsel we could not easily make the journey, nor could those who were to follow us by the same route. To them [the princes] indeed the emperor himself offered as many *numisma* and garments of silk as pleased them, and the horses and money which they needed for making such a journey.[5]

4. When this was done we crossed the sea which is called the Arm of St. George, and then hurried on to the city of Nicaea.[6] Lord Bohemond, Duke Godfrey, Count Raymond, and the Count of Flanders had already been besieging it since the middle of May. It was then in the possession of the Turks, a valiant race from the East skilled with the bow. They had crossed the Euphrates River from Persia fifty years before and had subjugated the whole Roman land as far as the city of Nicomedia.[7]

5. Oh how many severed heads and how many bones of the slain we found lying in the fields near the sea around Nicomedia! In that year [of the battle, 1096] the Turks had annihilated our people who were ignorant of the arrow and new to its use. Moved by pity at this sight we shed many tears.[8]

Runciman, "The First Crusade: Constantinople to Antioch," in Setton [ed.], *Crusades*, I, 284–88). Fulcher errs in part, for Count Raymond did take an oath, a special one in Provençal terms. He did not take an oath of vassalage, but he promised to respect the life and "honor," in this case the possessions, of the emperor and to restore to him any former imperial lands reconquered. See John Hugh Hill and Laurita L. Hill, "The Convention of Alexius Comnenus and Raymond of Saint-Gilles," *AHR*, LVIII (1953), 322–27; Hill and Hill, *Raymond IV*, 49–51; François-L. Ganshof, "Recherches sur le lien juridique qui unissait les chefs de la première croisade à l'empereur byzantin," in *Mélanges offerts à M. Paul-E. Martin* ("Mémoires et documents publiés par la Société d'Histoire et d'Archéologie de Genève," XL [Genève, 1961]), 49–63.

[5] The *Gesta Francorum Iherusalem expugnantium* explains that Alexius agreed to provide Robert and Stephen with horses, arms, silver (money) and other necessities, and transportation across the straits. In addition he gave them presents of money and *pallia* (cloaks) for themselves (*RHC, Occ.*, III, 494).

[6] They arrived on June 3, 1097 (HF 179, note 15).

[7] Seljuk Turkish nomads were west of the Euphrates as early as 1057 and 1067–68 and overran nearly all of Anatolia after defeating the Byzantines at Manzikert in 1071 (Claude Cahen, "The Turkish Invasions: The Selchükids," in Setton [ed.], *Crusades*, I, 147–49).

[8] This refers to the slaughter of the followers of Peter the Hermit in October, 1096.

X

The Siege of Nicaea and Its Capture.   1. When they who were besieging Nicaea heard, as has been said,[1] of the arrival of our leaders, the Count of Normandy and Stephen of Blois, they joyfully came out to meet us and escorted us to a place south of the city where we pitched our tents.

2. Once before the Turks had gathered in force[2] hoping to drive the besiegers away from the city if possible or else to defend it with their own soldiers more effectively. But they were fiercely thrown back by our men, nearly two hundred of them being killed. Moreover when they saw that the Franks were so inspired and so strong in military valor they retreated in haste into the interior of Romania until such time as they should feel the occasion opportune for attacking again.[3]

3. It was the first week in June when we, the last to arrive, reached the siege.[4]

4. At that time a single army was formed from the many that were there. Those skilled at reckoning estimated it to number 600,000 men accustomed to war. Of these, 100,000 were protected by coats of mail and helmets. In addition there were those not bearing arms, viz., the clerics, monks, women, and children.[5]

5. What further then? If all who departed from their homes to undertake the holy journey had been present there doubtless would have been 6,000,000 fighting men. But from Rome, from Apulia, from Hungary, or from Dalmatia, some, unwilling to undergo the hardships, had returned to their homes. In many places thousands had been killed, and some of the sick who went on with us finally died. You could see many graves along the

---

[1] Chap. ix, 4.   [2] May 16, 1097 (*HF* 182, note 5).
[3] The interior of Romania refers to Anatolia. The next attack was on July 1, 1097.
[4] The arrival was on June 3, 1097.
[5] Fulcher attempts to distinguish between the commonality and the better-armed, excluding the noncombatants. His figures are grossly large. See *HF* 183, note 11.

roads and in the fields where our pilgrims had been publicly buried.[6]

6. It should be explained that for as long as we besieged the city of Nicaea food was brought in by ocean ships with the consent of the emperor.[7] Then our leaders ordered machines of war to be made, battering-rams, *scrofae*, wooden towers, and *petrariae*. Arrows were shot from bows and stones hurled from *tormenta*.[8] Our enemies and our own men fought back and forth with all their might. We often assailed the city with our machines, but because there was a strong wall facing us the assault would be brought to naught. Turks struck by arrows or stones often perished and Franks likewise.

7. Truly you would have grieved and sobbed in pity when the Turks killed any of our men in any way near the wall, for they lowered iron hooks by means of ropes and snatched up the body to plunder it. None of our men dared or were able to wrest such a corpse from them. After stripping the bodies the Turks would throw them outside [the walls].

8. Then with the aid of oxen and ropes we dragged some small boats from Civetot over the land to Nicaea and launched them in the lake to guard the approach to the city lest the place be supplied with provisions.[9]

9. But after we had worn down the city by five weeks of siege and had often terrified the Turks with our attacks, they meantime held a council and, through intermediaries to the emperor,

[6] The desertions in Rome and Apulia have been mentioned (chap. vii, 3, 5). Those in Hungary must have been among the followers of Peter the Hermit, Walter the Penniless, and Godfrey and in Dalmatia, among the men of Raymond of Saint-Gilles (chap. vi, 7, 5, 6). In referring to the dead, Fulcher was doubtless influenced by his memory of the sight of the remains of the slain followers of Peter the Hermit around Nicomedia (chap. ix, 5).

[7] These supplies were unloaded at Civetot and then transported south up the valley of the Dracon (Yalak). For map, see Runciman, *Crusades*, I, 129.

[8] A *scrofa* ("sow") seems to have been a portable shed for protecting sappers, a *petraria* was apparently a mangonel or machine for hurling stones, and a *tormentum* was probably a stone-throwing lever powered by twisted ropes. Consult HF 186, notes 22–26; and McGinty (trans.), *Fulcher of Chartres*, 32, note 3.

[9] The crusaders had the city surrounded on three sides but could not completely blockade it until they cut off food coming in across Lake Ascanius (Isnik), west of the city. They launched the boats on the night of June 17–18 (HF 188, note 33).

secretly surrendered the city to him, a city already hard pressed
by our power and skill.[10]

10. Then the Turks admitted into it Turcopoles[11] sent thither
by the emperor. These latter took possession of the city with all
the money in it in the name of the emperor just as he had commanded. Wherefore after all this money was seized the emperor
ordered gifts to be presented to our leaders, gifts of gold and
silver and raiment; and to the foot-soldiers he distributed copper
coins which they call tartarons.[12]

11. On that day when Nicaea was seized or surrendered in this
manner the month of June had reached the solstice.[13]

XI

The Deadly Battle of the Christians with the Turks. 1. When
our barons received permission from the emperor to depart, we
left Nicaea on the third day before the Kalends of July to go into
the interior parts of Romania. But when we had been on our way
for two days, it was reported to us that the Turks had laid a trap
for us in the plains through which they thought we would have
to pass and that there they expected to do battle.[1]

2. When we heard this we did not lose courage.[2] But that eve-

[10] Anna Comnena, Emperor Alexius' daughter, tells in detail how the surrender
of the Turks was procured secretly by the imperial general Manuel Butumites
(*Alexiade: Règne de l'empereur Alexis I Comnène* [1081–1118], ed. and trans.
Bernard Leib ["Collection Byzantine pub. sous le patronage de l'Association Guillaume Budé"; 3 vols.; Paris: Société d'édition *Les belles lettres*, 1937–45], III,
10–16). However, Fulcher, trying to write in a vein still loyal to Pope Urban's
friendly feelings toward the Byzantines, reveals a touch of the bitterness of the
crusader rank and file, who felt that Alexius had snatched from them the fruits of
victory. Since their first contacts with the Byzantines, the Franks had begun to
regard the Greeks as enemies to be suspected rather than as fellow Christians to be
helped.

[11] These Turcopoles were light-armed cavalry of Turkish origin serving as mercenaries in Alexius' army.

[12] Cf. Alexius' similar treatment of the Franks as shown in chap. ix, 3.

[13] Fulcher's date is June 20; actually it was June 19, 1097 (HChr 160; HF 189,
note 39).

[1] The battle of Dorylaeum (Eskishehir), July 1, 1097. Runciman gives the best
summary (*Crusades*, I, 183–87). The date given is July 29, 1097.

[2] Fulcher was with Bohemond, Robert of Normandy, and Stephen of Blois in
the advance force. The crusaders divided forces at Lefke (Leucae), a day's distance

ning when our scouts saw many of the Turks a long distance away, they at once notified us of it. Therefore that night we had our tents protected on all sides by watchmen. Early in the morning, which was on the Kalends of July,[3] we took up our arms and at the sound of the trumpet divided into battle wings with the tribunes and centurions skillfully leading the cohorts and centuries.[4] With banners flying we began to advance in good order.

3. Then at the second hour of the day,[5] lo, their scouts approached our sentries! When we heard this we pitched our tents near a marsh and took off our pack saddles in order that we would be better able to fight.

4. After this was done, behold! there were the Turks, those pagan Persians whose amir and prince was that Soliman who had held the city of Nicaea and the country of Romania in his power.[6] They had at Soliman's command collected about him, having come to his aid for a distance of more than thirty days. There were present with him many amirs or princes, viz., Amircaradigum, Miriathos, and many others.[7] Altogether they numbered 360,000 fighters,[8] that is to say, bowmen, for it was their custom to be armed in that manner. All were mounted. On the other hand we had both footmen and bowmen.

---

from Nicaea, and Godfrey, Raymond, and Adhemar commanded the rear. Consult the anonymous *Gesta* (HG ix, 2); and Runciman, *Crusades*, I, 184–86, and map, p. 176. Runciman, from personal observation of the terrain, believes the battle was fought on the plain of Sari-su (Bathys), about eight miles northwest of Eskishehir (186, note 1).

[3] July 1, 1097. By early in the morning Fulcher meant the first hour, 6–7 A.M. (HF 197, note 7).

[4] Fulcher often used Roman terminology in describing military formations, there being none for feudal formations.

[5] Between 7–8 A.M.

[6] Kilij Arslan (I) ibn-Sulaimān, sultan of Rūm (Anatolia) from 1092 to 1107.

[7] These names are garbled and obscure. Hagenmeyer suggests that "Amircaradigum" may have meant "Amir Karaja" and that "Miriathos" may have meant "Amir Atsiz" (HF 193, note 16). One Karaja became governor of Homs in 1104, and an Atsiz held Palestine from 1071 to 1079 (Cahen, "The Turkish Invasions: The Selchükids," in Setton [ed.], *Crusades*, I, 173, 148, 151), but it is difficult to be certain whom Fulcher meant. He listed five other Turkish chieftains in his first redaction (HF 193, note d) but omitted them in his second, possibly as doubtful.

[8] This figure, 360,000, appears in the anonymous *Gesta* (HG ix, 9), where Fulcher probably obtained it.

5. At that time Duke Godfrey, Count Raymond, and Hugh the Great had been absent from us for two days. They had for some reason, I know not what, separated from us with a large number of men at a place where the road divided.[9] For that reason we suffered [in the ensuing battle] an irreparable loss because as many of our men were slain as there were Turks who escaped death or capture. Because those who were separated from us received our messengers late, they were tardy in coming to our aid.

6. Meanwhile the Turks were howling like wolves and furiously shooting a cloud of arrows. We were stunned by this. Since we faced death and since many of us were wounded we soon took to flight. Nor is this remarkable because to all of us such warfare was unknown.

7. And now from the other side of the marsh a dense mass of the enemy fiercely forced its way as far as our tents. The Turks entered some of these tents and were snatching our belongings and killing some of our people when by the will of God the advance guard of Hugh the Great, Count Raymond, and Duke Godfrey came upon this disaster from the rear. Because our men had retreated to our tents those of the enemy who had entered fled at once thinking that we had suddenly returned to attack them. What they took for boldness and courage was, if they could have known, really great fear.

8. What shall I say next? We were all indeed huddled together like sheep in a fold, trembling and frightened, surrounded on all sides by enemies so that we could not turn in any direction. It was clear to us that this happened because of our sins. For luxury had defiled some of us, and avarice and other vice had corrupted others. A great clamor rose to the sky, not only from our men and our women and children but also from the pagans rushing upon us. By now we had no hope of surviving.

9. We then confessed that we were defendants at the bar of justice and sinners, and we humbly begged mercy from God. The Bishop of Le Puy, our patron, and four other bishops were there, and a great many priests also, vested in white. They humbly be-

9 At Lefke. See note 2.

sought God that He would destroy the power of our enemy and shed upon us the gifts of His mercy. Weeping they sang and singing they wept. Then many people fearing that death was nigh ran to the priests and confessed their sins.[10]

10. Our leaders, Count Robert of Normandy and Stephen, Count of Blois, and Robert, Count of Flanders, and Bohemond also, resisted the Turks as far as they were able and often tried to attack them. They were also strongly assailed by the Turks.

XII

The Flight of the Turks and the Victory of the Christians. 1. The Lord does not give victory to splendor of nobility nor brilliance in arms but lovingly helps in their need the pure in heart and those who are fortified with divine strength. Therefore He, perhaps appeased by our supplications, gradually restored our strength and more and more weakened the Turks. For when we saw our comrades hastening to our aid from the rear[1] we praised God and regained our courage and formed into troops and cohorts and strove to resist the enemy.

2. Oh how many of our men straggling behind us on the road did the Turks kill that day![2] From the very first hour of the day until the sixth, as I have said, difficulties hampered us.[3] However, little by little our spirits revived as our comrades reinforced us and as divine grace was miraculously present, and then as if by sudden impulse the Turks all turned their backs in flight.

3. Shouting fiercely we followed them over the mountains and

[10] This story—that Adhemar heard confessions during the battle—is disproved by Anselm of Ribemont and the anonymous *Gesta*, which show that the bishop was one of the leaders in the fighting, one of those bringing up the rear guard (*Epistula I Anselmi de Ribodimonte ad Manassem archiepiscopum Remorum*, in HE*p* 145; and *HG* ix, 2, 6, 8).

[1] The army of Godfrey, Raymond, and Hugh.

[2] This would seem to mean stragglers from the advanced and beleaguered force of Bohemond and not from the relieving force of Godfrey.

[3] From 6–7 A.M. to 11–12 A.M. The author means that the advanced force was in danger from the time of muster in the early morning to the arrival of Godfrey *et al.* just before noon when the tide turned. The anonymous *Gesta* (*HG* ix, 9) places the time of the fight between the third to the ninth hours (8–9 A.M. to 2–3 P.M.), a statement not inconsistent with that of Fulcher.

through the valleys. We did not cease pursuing them until our swiftest men had reached their tents. Then some of our men loaded many of the camels and horses of the Turks with their possessions and even with the tents abandoned there in panic. Others followed the fleeing Turks until nightfall. Because our horses were famished and exhausted we kept a few of theirs.[4]

4. It was a great miracle of God that during the next and the third days the Turks did not cease to flee although no one, unless God, followed them further.[5]

5. Gladdened by such a victory we all gave thanks to God. He had willed that our journey should not be brought entirely to naught but that it should be prospered more gloriously than usual for the sake of that Christianity which was His own. Wherefore from East to West the tidings shall resound forever.

6. Then indeed we continued our journey carefully. One day we suffered such extreme thirst that some men and women died from its torments.[6] The Turks, fleeing before us in confusion, sought hiding places for themselves throughout Romania.

XIII

The Destitution of the Christians. 1. Then we came to Antioch, which they call the Lesser, in the province of Pisidia, and then to Iconium. In these regions we very often were in need of bread and other food. For we found Romania, a land which is excellent and very fertile in products of all kinds, terribly wasted and depopulated by the Turks.[1]

2. Often, however, you could see many people much revived

---

[4] Cf. the anonymous *Gesta* (*HG* ix, 9), used by Fulcher.

[5] The *Gesta Francorum Iherusalem expugnantium* includes an account in which it was related that two knights in white vestments, the Martyrs George and Demetrius (Byzantine saints much admired by the crusaders), pursued the Turks for three days (*RHC, Occ.,* III, 496).

[6] The hardships of the march south from Dorylaeum are best described in René Grousset, *Histoire des croisades* (3 vols.; Paris: Librairie Plon, 1934–46), I, 36.

[1] The crusaders arrived at Antioch in Pisidia (near modern Yalvach) about the end of July, 1097, and at Iconium (Konya) about the middle of August (*HF* 201, notes 3, 4). Fulcher's source, the anonymous *Gesta,* states that the Franks reached better country as they approached Konya (*HG* x, 4).

from the products of the scattered farms which we found from time to time throughout the country. This was with the help of that God who with five loaves and two fishes fed five thousand people [Matth. 14:17–20; Marc. 6:38–44; Luc. 9:13–16; and Joan. 6:9–10]. Wherefore we were well content, and rejoicing we acknowledged that these were gifts of the mercy of God.

3. Then indeed you would have laughed, or perhaps wept from pity, because many of our people who lacked beasts of burden since many of their own had died, loaded wethers, she-goats, sows, and dogs with their possessions, viz., clothing, food, or whatever baggage was necessary for pilgrims. We saw the backs of these small beasts chafed by the weight of this baggage. And sometimes even armed knights used oxen as mounts.[2]

4. And whoever heard of such a mixture of languages in one army? There were present Franks, Flemings, Frisians, Gauls, *Allobroges*, Lotharingians, *Alemanni*, Bavarians, Normans, English, Scots, Aquitanians, Italians, Dacians, Apulians, Iberians, Bretons, Greeks, and Armenians. If any Briton or Teuton wished to question me I could neither reply nor understand.[3]

5. But though we were of different tongues we seemed, however, to be brothers in the love of God and to be of nearly one mind. For if anyone lost any of his property he who found it would keep it very carefully for many days until by inquiry he found the loser and returned what was found. This was indeed proper for those who were piously making the pilgrimage.

XIV

The Deeds and Bravery of Count Baldwin, Brother of Godfrey, and the Acquisition of the City of Edessa Which is Called Roha.

1. When we reached the city of Heraclea, we beheld a certain

---

[2] Cf. HG x, 3.

[3] This list of names is in part rhetorical and exhibits Fulcher's knowledge of geography, partly classical. By *Franci* he meant men from northern France (his own area); by *Galli*, men from central France; by *Allobroges*, men from Dauphine and Savoy; by *Alemanni*, south Germans and Swiss; by *Daci*, men from Romania and eastern Hungary (HF 202, note 11).

sign in the sky which appeared in brilliant whiteness in the shape of a sword with the point toward the East.[1] What it portended for the future we did not know, but we left the present and the future to God.

2. We then came to a certain flourishing city which is called Marash. We rested quietly there for three days.[2] But when we had marched a day's journey from there and were now not farther than three days from Antioch of Syria, I, Fulcher, withdrew from the [main] army and with the lord Count Baldwin, brother of Duke Godfrey, turned into the country to the left.[3]

3. Baldwin was indeed a most capable knight. Previously he had left the army with those men whom he had brought with him and had taken with great boldness the city which is called Tarsus of Cilicia. He took it away from Tancred, who had introduced his own men with the consent of the Turks. Leaving guards in it Baldwin had returned to the [main] army.[4]

4. And so trusting in the Lord and in his own strength, Baldwin collected a few knights and set out toward the Euphrates. There he took many towns by force as well as by strategy. Among them was the most desirable, called Turbezel.[5] The Armenians who dwelt there gave it up peacefully to him, and many other towns were also subjected to him.

5. When the report of this had circulated far and wide, the

---

[1] This comet was seen in Europe from September 30 to October 14, 1097. Other information indicates that the Franks were at Heraclea from September 10 to 14, and Hagenmeyer calculates that the comet was seen by them not at Heraclea but around Caesarea (Kayseri). See HF 204, notes 2, 3.

[2] October 13–16 (HF 205, note 6).

[3] From this time, October 17, 1097 (HF 206, note 7), Fulcher followed the fortunes of Baldwin on the latter's Edessan venture. He was not a direct witness of the central story of the crusaders until Baldwin came to Jerusalem to become king late in 1100. The "country to the left" was an Armenian district from Tell Bashir to Edessa.

[4] The Tarsus episode between Baldwin and Tancred, here barely mentioned by Fulcher, lasted from about mid-September to mid-October, 1097. Consult Robert Lawrence Nicholson, *Tancred: Crusading Leader and Lord of Galilee and Antioch* (Chicago: University of Chicago Libraries, 1940), 38–56.

[5] Tell Bashir, a powerful fortress about thirty miles west of the crossing of the Euphrates at Bira (Birejik) that commanded the route from Edessa to Antioch.

prince of the city of Edessa sent a delegation to Baldwin.[6] This city is very famous and is in a most fertile area. It is in Syrian Mesopotamia about twenty miles beyond the above-mentioned Euphrates and about a hundred miles or more from Antioch.[7]

6. Baldwin was asked by the duke to go there so that they could become mutual friends, like father and son, as long as they both should live. And if by chance the duke of Edessa should die Baldwin was to possess the city and all the duke's territory immediately as a permanent inheritance just as if he were the latter's own son. Since the duke had neither son nor daughter and since he was unable to defend himself against the Turks, this Greek wished that he and his territory should be defended by Baldwin. He had heard that Baldwin and his knights were very formidable fighting men.

7. As soon as Baldwin heard this offer and had been persuaded of its truth under oath by the deputies from Edessa, he with his little army of eighty knights[8] proceeded to cross the Euphrates. After we had crossed this river we went on very hastily all night and, very much afraid, passed between the Saracen towns which were scattered about.

8. When the Turks who were in the fortified town of Samosata heard this, they set ambushes for us on the way through which they thought we would go. But on the following night a certain Armenian carefully sheltered us in his castle. He warned us to guard against these snares of the enemy, and for this reason we hid there for two days.[9]

---

[6] The ruler of Edessa was Thoros, an Armenian. He claimed authority as a Byzantine governor and at the same time had a vassal relationship with the neighboring Turks. He was detested by his subjects for both of these reasons and also because he was a member of the Greek Orthodox rather than the Armenian Jacobite Church and because of his high taxes and feeble military power. Consult J. Laurent, "Des Grecs aux croisés: Étude sur l'histoire d'Édesse," *Byzantion*, I (1924), 404–34; and Grousset, *Croisades*, I, 43–56. The time of the invitation was late in January or early in February, 1098 (*HF* 210, note 21).

[7] Edessa (Urfa) is about 45 miles east of the Euphrates and about 160 miles northeast of Antioch.

[8] Albert of Aix states that Baldwin left with two hundred knights (*RHC, Occ.*, IV, 352); Matthew of Edessa says that he arrived with sixty (*RHC, Arm.*, I, 36).

[9] The amir of Samosata was named Balduk (Matthew of Edessa, *RHC, Arm.*, I, 36; Albert, *RHC, Occ.*, IV, 353). The name of the friendly Armenian is not

9. But on the third day the Turks, irked by such delay, rushed down upon us from their place of hiding and with flags flying galloped in front of the castle in which we were located and before our eyes drove off as plunder the livestock which they found in the pastures.

10. We went out against them, but because we were few we were unable to contend with them. They shot arrows but wounded none of us. However, they left one of their men, killed by a lance, on the field. His horse was kept by the man who unseated him. Then the enemy left, but we remained there.

11. On the following day we resumed our journey. When we were passing by the towns of the Armenians, you would have been amazed to see them coming humbly to meet us, carrying crosses and banners, and kissing our feet and garments for the love of God because they had heard that we were going to protect them against the Turks under whose yoke they had been long oppressed.[10]

12. At length we reached Edessa where the aforesaid prince of the city and his wife, together with the citizens, joyfully received us and fulfilled their promises to Baldwin without delay.[11]

13. After we had been there for fifteen days the citizens wickedly plotted to slay their prince because they hated him and to elevate Baldwin to the palace to rule the land. This was suggested and it was done. Baldwin and his men were much grieved because they were not able to obtain mercy for him.[12]

---

known (*HF* 211, note 29), but the time seems to have been the two days before Balduk's attack *ca.* February 15 (*HChr* 238).

[10] The Turks had taken Edessa in 1087, and Thoros captured it in 1094 (Runciman, *Crusades*, I, 75).

[11] The wife of Thoros was the daughter of a neighboring prince, Gabriel of Melitene (Malatya). Her name is not known. Paul Gindler gives *ca.* February 4–6, 1098, as the date of arrival; Hagenmeyer, February 20; and Laurent, *ca.* February 6. See Gindler, *Graf Balduin I. von Edessa* (Halle A. S.: Hofbuchdruckerei von C. A. Kaemmerer & Co., 1901), 55; *HF* 213–14, note 36; and Laurent, "Des Grecs aux croisés," 431.

[12] Fulcher's brevity at this point is extremely disappointing. Probably he could not justify Baldwin's failure to defend Thoros nor explain Baldwin's willingness to be the beneficiary of Thoros' death; therefore he did not try. Consult Galust Ter-Grigorian Iskenderian, *Die Kreuzfahrer und ihre Beziehungen zu den Armenischen Nachbarfürsten bis zum Untergange der Grafschaft Edessa* (Weida i. Th.: Druck

14. As soon as Baldwin had accepted as a gift from the citizens the princely position of this man, who had been wickedly murdered, he began a war against the Turks who were in the country. Many times he defeated or killed them. However, it happened also that many of our men were killed by the Turks.

15. I, Fulcher of Chartres, was the chaplain of this same Baldwin. I wish now to resume the narrative, which I interrupted, of the army of God.

XV

The Arrival of the Franks at Antioch and the Vicissitudes of the Siege. 1. In the month of October the Franks came to Antioch in Syria, a city founded by Seleucus, son of Antiochus. Seleucus made it his capital. It was previously called Reblata. Moreover it lay on the other side of the river which they called the Fernus or Orontes.[1] Our tents were ordered pitched before the city between it and the first milestone. Here afterwards battles were very frequently fought which were most destructive to both sides. When the Turks rushed out from the city they killed many of our men, but when the tables were turned they grieved to find themselves beaten.

2. Antioch is certainly a very large city, well fortified and strongly situated. It could never be taken by enemies from without provided the inhabitants were supplied with food and were determined to defend it.[2] There is in Antioch a much-renowned church dedicated to the honor of Peter the Apostle where he,

---

von Thomas und Hubert, 1915), 42–47; and André A. Beaumont, "Albert of Aachen and the County of Edessa," in *Crusades-Munro*, 109–12. The murder was committed on March 9 (*HF* 214, note 38).

[1] The Franks arrived at Antioch on October 20–21, 1097 (*HF* 216, note 2). The city was founded by Seleucus (I) Nicator, a former general of Alexander the Great, in 300 B.C. Fulcher followed St. Jerome into the error that Reblata (Riblah) near Hamah [Num. 34:11; II Reg. 23:33; Jerem. 39:5] was Antioch. See Jerome, *Liber de situ et nominibus locorum Hebraicorum* (sometimes called the *Onomastikon*), *MPL*, XXIII (Paris, 1883), cols. 964 and 915; *HF* 216, note 5, and 710, note 29. Fulcher repeats this error later (III, xxx, 5).

[2] Fulcher could attest to the strength of the city, for he went through it in October, 1100 (II, i, 4).

raised to the episcopate, sat as bishop after he had received from the Lord Jesus the primacy of the church and the keys to the Kingdom of Heaven.[3]

3. There is another church too, circular in form, built in honor of the Blessed Mary, together with others fittingly constructed.[4] These had for a long time been under the control of the Turks, but God, foreseeing all, kept them intact for us so that one day He would be honored in them by ourselves.

4. The sea is, I think, about thirteen miles from Antioch. Because the Fernus River flows into the sea at that point, ships filled with goods from distant lands are brought up its channel as far as Antioch.[5] Thus supplied with goods by sea and land, the city abounds with wealth of all kinds.

5. Our princes when they saw how hard it would be to take the city swore mutually to cooperate in a siege until, God willing, they took it by force or stratagem.

6. They found a number of boats in the aforesaid river. These they took and fashioned into a pontoon bridge over which they crossed to carry out their plans.[6] Previously they had been unable to ford the river.

7. But the Turks, when they had looked about anxiously and saw that they were beset by such a multitude of Christians, feared that they could not possibly escape them. After they had consulted together, Aoxianus, the prince and Amir of Antioch, sent his son Sanxado to the Sultan, that is the Emperor of Persia, urging that he should aid them with all haste.[7] The reason was that they had

[3] The anonymous *Gesta* states that St. Peter founded the see of Antioch (*HG* xi, 7) and mentions the Church of St. Peter several times (*passim*). For discussion of the residence of Peter in Antioch, see Glanville Downey, *A History of Antioch in Syria* (Princeton, N.J.: Princeton University Press, 1961), 56 ff, 67 ff, and 581–82.

[4] The Church of St. Mary is twice mentioned by the *Gesta* (*HG* xxiv, 1; xxvi, 2). See Downey, *Antioch*, 525, 631.

[5] Silting and upward thrust caused by earthquakes have since ruined the channel (see Downey, *Antioch*, 18). The port of St. Simeon at the mouth of the Orontes was even then used instead (*HF* 218, note 19).

[6] For an excellent map, see Runciman, *Crusades*, I, 214.

[7] Fulcher used a letter of Stephen of Blois dated March 29, 1098, as the source of his information about "Aoxianus" and "Sanxado" (*Epistula II Stephani comitis*

no hope of other help except from Mohammed their advocate. Sanxado in great haste carried out the mission assigned to him.

8. Those who remained within the city guarded it, waiting for the assistance for which they had asked while they frequently concocted many kinds of dangerous schemes against the Franks. Nevertheless the latter foiled the stratagems of the enemy as well as they could.

9. On a certain day it happened that seven hundred Turks were killed by the Franks, and thus those who had prepared snares for the Franks were by snares overcome.[8] For the power of God was manifest there. All of our men returned safely except one who was wounded by them.

10. Oh how many Christians in the city, Greeks, Syrians, and Armenians, did the Turks kill in rage and how many heads did they hurl over the walls with *petrariae* and *fundibula*[9] in view of the Franks! This grieved our men very much. The Turks hated these Christians, for they feared that somehow the latter might assist the Franks against a Turkish attack.

11. After the Franks had besieged the city for some time and had scoured the country roundabout in search of food for themselves and were unable to find even bread to buy, they suffered great hunger.[10] For this reason all were very much discouraged, and many secretly planned to withdraw from the siege and to flee by land or by sea.

12. But they had no money on which to live. They were even obliged to seek their sustenance far away and in great fear by sep-

---

Carnotensis ad Adelam uxorem, HEp 150; HF 67 and 219, note 23). "Aoxianus" was Yaghi-Siyan, the Turkish governor of Antioch, and "Sanxado" was his son Shams-ad-Daulah. The latter's mission was actually to Dukak of Damascus and not to the Seljuk Sultan Berkyaruk (1094–1105), here called the "Emperor of Persia," in distant Khurasan. The anonymous *Gesta* has a somewhat different version (*HG* xxi, 1, 2). Consult Runciman, *Crusades*, I, 213–15.

[8] This refers to a demonstration against a neighboring Turkish fortress called Ḥārim (Harenc, Aregh) in mid-November, 1097 (*HF* 221, note 30). Fulcher's figure, seven hundred, is hearsay.

[9] *Fundibula*, like *petrariae*, were machines for hurling stones. The two types seem to have been much the same (*HF* 221, note 32).

[10] The Franks began to run out of food by the end of the year (*HG* xiii, 2; Raymond, *RHC, Occ.*, III, 243).

arating themselves forty or fifty miles from the siege, and there in the mountains they were often killed by the Turks in ambush.

13. We felt that misfortunes had befallen the Franks because of their sins and that for this reason they were not able to take the city for so long a time. Luxury and avarice and pride and plunder had indeed vitiated them.

14. Then the Franks, having again consulted together, expelled the women from the army, the married as well as the unmarried, lest perhaps defiled by the sordidness of riotous living they should displease the Lord. These women then sought shelter for themselves in neighboring towns.[11]

15. The rich as well as the poor were wretched because of starvation as well as of the slaughter, which daily occurred. Had not God, like a good pastor, held His sheep together, without doubt they would all have fled thence at once in spite of the fact that they had sworn to take the city. Many though, because of the scarcity of food, sought for many days in neighboring villages what was necessary for life; and they did not afterward return to the army but abandoned the siege entirely.

16. At that time we saw a remarkable reddish glow in the sky and besides felt a great quake in the earth, which rendered us all fearful. In addition many saw a certain sign in the shape of a cross, whitish in color, moving in a straight path toward the East.[12]

XVI

The Miserable Poverty of the Christians and the Flight of the Count of Blois. 1. In the year of our Lord 1098, after the area around Antioch had been stripped completely bare by the large number of our people, both the old and the young were increasingly distressed by excessive hunger.

---

[11] The *Gesta Francorum Iherusalem expugnantium* states that it was Bishop Adhemar who caused the expulsion of the women (*RHC, Occ.,* III, 499).

[12] The auroral display and earthquake were on December 30, 1097, according to Raymond of Aguilers (*RHC, Occ.,* III, 245). The "sign in the sky" may have been something imagined in the auroral display (*HF* 224, note 48).

2. Then the starving people devoured the stalks of beans still growing in the fields, many kinds of herbs unseasoned with salt, and even thistles which because of the lack of firewood were not well cooked and therefore irritated the tongues of those eating them. They also ate horses, asses, camels, dogs, and even rats. The poorer people ate even the hides of animals and the seeds of grain found in manure.[1]

3. The people for the love of God endured cold, heat, and torrents of rain. Their tents became old and torn and rotten from the continuous rains. For this reason many people had no cover but the sky.[2]

4. Just as gold is thrice tried in the fire and seven times purified [Psalm. 12:7], so I believe the elect were tried by the Lord and by such suffering were cleansed of their sins. For although the sword of the Assassin did not fail to do its deadly work, many of the people suffered long agony and gladly ran the full course of martyrdom. Perhaps they took consolation from the example of Holy Job who purging his soul by torments of the body always remembered God [Job 2:12]. When they struggled against the pagans they labored for God.

5. Although God, who creates all, orders all that He has created and sustains what he has ordered, governs with vigor and is able to destroy or repair whatever He wishes, I feel that at the cost of suffering to the Christians He wills that the pagans shall be destroyed, they who have so many times foully trod underfoot all which belongs to God although with His permission and as the people deserved. In truth He has permitted the Christians to be slain for the augmentation of their salvation, the Turks, however, for the damnation of their souls. But those of the Turks predestined to salvation it pleased God to have baptized by our priests.[3]

---

[1] Cf. HG xxvi, 5. The *Gesta Francorum Iherusalem expugnantium* states that some Franks ate the flesh of the Saracen slain (*RHC, Occ.*, III, 498).

[2] Hagenmeyer suggests that these references to the cold weather came from the *Epistula II Stephani comitis Carnotensis ad Adelam uxorem* (HEp 150; HF 67 and 226, note 9).

[3] Cf. HG xxix, 11, and letter of Bohemond and the princes to Urban II, September 11, 1098 (chap. xxiv, 11).

"For those whom He predestined, them He called and also glorified" [Rom. 8:30].

6. What then? Some of our men as you have heard about withdrew from a siege which was so difficult, some from want, some from cowardice, some from fear of death, first the poor, then the rich.

7. Then Stephen, Count of Blois, left the siege and went home to France by sea. We all grieved on this account because he was a very noble man and was mighty in arms. On the day following his departure the city of Antioch was surrendered to the Franks. If he had persevered he would have greatly rejoiced with the rest, for what he did was a disgrace to him. For a good beginning does not profit one if one does not end well.[4] In things regarding God I shall be brief lest I might go astray, for in these matters I must be careful not to wander from the truth.

8. From this month of October, as was said, the siege of the city continued throughout the following winter and spring until the month of June.[5] The Turks and Franks alternately staged many attacks and counterattacks. They conquered and were conquered. We, however, won more often than they. Once it happened that many Turks in fleeing fell into the Fernus River and miserably drowned.[6] On this side of the river and on the other side both peoples fought many times.

9. Our princes constructed forts in front of the city.[7] By frequent sallies from them our men sturdily held back the Turks. As a result they often denied pasturage to the animals of the enemy.

[4] This passage was written before Fulcher knew of Stephen's death at Ramla, May 19, 1102 (II, xix, 4). Fulcher omits the embarrassing statement from the anonymous *Gesta* that Stephen met the Emperor Alexius at Philomelium (Akshehir) and advised him to turn back (*HG* xxvii, 2). Brundage suggests that Stephen had been for two months resolved to leave as soon as he felt that the Frankish capture of Antioch was certain ("An Errant Crusader," 388). Stephen fled on June 2, 1098, and Antioch fell the next day (*HF* 228, note 22).

[5] October 20, 1097, to June 3, 1098.

[6] This may refer to skirmishes of November 18, 1097, or March 6, 1098 (*HF* 229, note 28).

[7] These forts were the Tower of Malregard east of Antioch, the Tower of La Mahomerie to the north, and the tower of Tancred to the west (*HF* 229, note 29; Runciman, *Crusades*, I, map, p. 214).

Nothing was brought in from the Armenians of the outlying areas; yet they often acted to our detriment.[8]

XVII

The Surrender of the City of Antioch. 1. When, however, God, appeased no doubt by their prayers, was pleased to end the labor of His people who had daily poured forth beseeching supplications to Him, in His love He granted that through the treachery of these same Turks the city should be secretly delivered up and restored to the Christians. Hear therefore of a treachery, and yet not a treachery.

2. Our Lord appeared to a certain Turk[1] predestined by His grace and said to him, "Arise, you who sleep! I command you to return the city to the Christians." Although wondering about it the man kept the vision a secret.

3. Again the Lord appeared to him. "Return the city to the Christians," He said, "for I who command this am Christ indeed." Wondering therefore what he should do the man went to his master, the prince of Antioch,[2] and made known the vision to him. The latter replied, "Do you wish, stupid man, to obey a ghost?" The man returned, and remained silent.

4. Again the Lord appeared unto him, saying, "Why have you not done what I have commanded? It is not for you to hesitate, for I who command this am the Lord of all." The Turk no longer doubting discreetly made a plot with our men by which they should obtain the city.[3]

---

[8] Cf. HG xix, 3.

[1] This man, mentioned again by Fulcher (chap. xxiv, 4), seems to have been an Armenian who had turned Muslim, who bore some such name as *Firuz* ("The Victorious One"), and who was of a family of armor makers (see Ralph of Caen, *RHC, Occ.,* III, 651-52; William of Tyre, V, xi; Ibn-al-Qalānisī, *The Damascus Chronicle,* 44; Ibn-al-Athīr, *Extrait de la chronique intitulée Kamel-Altevarykh,* in *Recueil des historiens des croisades, Historiens orientaux,* I [Paris: Imprimerie Nationale, 1872], 192; hereinafter referred to as *RHC, Or.;* and Kamāl-ad-Dīn, *Extraits de la chronique d'Alep, RHC, Or.,* III [Paris: Imprimerie Nationale, 1884], 580; cf. HG, xx, 1).

[2] Yaghi-Siyan (chap. xv, note 7).   [3] This tale is original with Fulcher.

5. When this agreement was made, the Turk gave his son as a hostage to the Lord Bohemond to whom this plan had first been proposed and whom he had first influenced. On the appointed night the Turk admitted over the wall twenty of our men by means of rope ladders. At once, without delay, the gate was opened. The Franks, who were ready, entered the city. Forty more of our soldiers who had already entered by means of the ropes slew sixty Turks whom they found guarding the towers. Then all the Franks shouted together in a loud voice, "God wills it! God wills it!" For this was our signal cry when we were about to accomplish any good enterprise.[4]

6. Hearing this the Turks were all extremely terrified. The Franks immediately began to attack the city, the dawn then growing lighter.[5] When the Turks first noticed Bohemond's red banner, now waving aloft, the great tumult already raging round about, the trumpets of the Franks sounding from the top of the wall, and the Franks running about through the streets with drawn swords and savagely killing people, they were bewildered and began to flee here and there. As many Turks as could fled to the citadel situated on a lofty cliff.[6]

7. Our common people indiscriminately seized whatever they found in the streets and houses, but the knights, who were experienced in the business of warfare, continued to seek out and kill the Turks.

8. The Amir of Antioch, Aoxianus by name, was beheaded while fleeing by an Armenian peasant, who at once brought the severed head to the Franks.

XVIII

The Discovery of the Lance. 1. It happened moreover that after the city was taken a certain man found a lance[1] in a hole in the

---

[4] Cf. *HG* xx, 4, 6, 7.

[5] The time was after 3 A.M., June 3, 1098 (*HG* 301, note 37).

[6] Cf. *HG* xx, 8–10. The citadel was on Mount Silpius, southeast of the city (Downey, *Antioch*, map on Plate 11, photographs on Plates 1, 12; and Runciman, *Crusades*, I, map on p. 214.

[1] Nearly all Christian sources, including the anonymous *Gesta* (*HG* xxv), and

ground under the Church of the blessed Apostle Peter.[2] When it was discovered the man asserted that it was the very lance with which Longinus had, according to the Scriptures, pierced Christ in the right side [Joan. 19:34].[3] He said that this had been revealed to him by St. Andrew the Apostle.

2. And when it had been discovered and the man himself told the Bishop of Le Puy and Count Raymond, the Bishop thought the story false, but the Count hoped that it was true.

3. All the people when they heard this exulted and glorified God. For almost a hundred days[4] the lance was held in great veneration and was carried gloriously by Count Raymond, who guarded it. Then it happened that many of the priests and laity hesitated, thinking that this was not the Lord's lance but another one dishonestly found by that doltish man.

4. Wherefore after three days of fasting and prayers had been decided upon and finished by all, they lighted a heap of wood in the middle of the field in front of the town of Archas in the eighth month after the capture of Antioch;[5] the bishops made the judicial benediction over the same fire; and the finder of the lance quickly ran clear through the midst of the burning pile to prove his honesty, as he had requested. When the man passed through the

---

one Muslim, Ibn-al-Athīr (RHC, Or., I, 195), mention the discovery of the lance; but the most complete account of the whole affair, including the ordeal, is in the chronicle of Raymond of Aguilers (RHC, Occ., III, 253–57, 262–70, and 279–88). Fulcher, who was at Edessa during all of this time, writes in a highly skeptical manner, but his factual details agree very well with those of Raymond. He seems to have sympathized with Bishop Adhemar and also with those who disliked the attempt of Count Raymond of Saint-Gilles to exploit custody of the lance. For discussion of the lance, see L. F. Sheffy, "The Use of the Holy Lance in the First Crusade" (Master's thesis, the University of Texas, 1915); Steven Runciman, "The Holy Lance at Antioch," Analecta Bollandia, LXVIII (1950), 197–205; Runciman, Crusades, I, 241–46, 247, 253–54, 273–74, and 284; and Hill and Hill, Raymond IV, 100–101, 106, and 123–25.

2 The lance was found by a peasant (Peter Bartholomew) on June 14, 1098, eleven days after the fall of Antioch (HF 258, note 21; 236, note 3).

3 Regarding Longinus, see HEp 346, note 40.

4 I.e., until late in September, 1098.

5 The date of the ordeal was Good Friday, April 8, 1099, in the tenth month after the capture of Antioch (HF 239, note 10). The place was 'Arqah, about thirteen miles northeast of Tripoli.

flames and emerged, they saw that he was guilty, for his skin was burned and they knew that within he was mortally hurt. This was demonstrated by the outcome, for on the twefth day he died,[6] seared by the guilt of his conscience.

5. And since everyone had venerated the lance for the honor and love of God, when the ordeal was over those who formerly believed in it were now incredulous and very sad. Nevertheless Count Raymond preserved it for a long time afterward.[7]

XIX

The Siege of the Christians Within Antioch by the Turks. 1. On the day following the capture of Antioch, related above, an immense multitude of Turks set up a siege around the city. For as soon as the sultan, that is the king of the Persians, learned that the Franks were besieging Antioch he at once collected a great number of men and sent an army against the Franks. Corbagath was the leader and satrap of these people.[1]

2. He remained three weeks before the city of Edessa, which was then possessed by Lord Baldwin. But since he accomplished nothing he hastened to Antioch to rescue Prince Aoxianus.[2]

3. Seeing these things the Franks were again discouraged, and no less than usual, because their punishment was doubled on account of their sins. For when they had entered the city many of them had at once commingled with unlawful women.[3]

4. Then about 60,000 Turks entered the city through the citadel on the side of the high cliff above and hemmed in our men by frequent and vigorous attacks. But they did not stay long, for they

---

[6] April 20, 1099 (*HF* 240, note 13).

[7] As late as the Crusade of 1101 in Anatolia (*HF* 241, note 14).

[1] Kerbogha, the personally ambitious *Atabeg* of Mosul, in theory represented the Seljuk Sultan Berkyaruk, then in Khurasan. Consult Runciman, *Crusades*, I, 78, 203–204, 213, 215, and 229–30.

[2] Fulcher was then in Edessa and must have witnessed this siege but unfortunately says nothing more. See Matthew of Edessa, *RHC, Arm.*, I, 39; and Albert of Aix, *RHC, Occ.*, IV, 396–97. The siege lasted from May 4–25, 1098 (*HF* 243, note 8).

[3] Cf. *HG* xxiv, 2; and Raymond of Aguilers, *RHC, Occ.*, III, 252.

were struck with terror and left the city to besiege it from outside.[4] The Franks, walled in, remained there more worried than can be imagined.

XX

The Visions Appearing Within the City. 1. In the meantime the Lord, not unmindful, appeared to many of the people, which fact they often related, and comforting them He promised them that presently they would rejoice in victory. Then the Lord appeared to a certain cleric who was fleeing because of fear of death and said to him, "Where, brother, are you going?" "I am fleeing," he said, "lest unluckily I shall perish."

Thus many fled, lest they perish by a terrible death.

To the cleric the Lord answered, "Flee not, but hasten back and tell the others that I shall be with them in battle. For appeased by the prayers of my Mother, I shall be merciful to the Franks. But because they have sinned they have almost perished. Let their hope in Me be constant, and I shall make them triumph over the Turks. Let them repent and they shall be saved. For I who speak to you am the Lord." The cleric turned back at once and reported what he had heard.[1]

2. Meanwhile many Franks wished to descend at night from the wall by ropes and escape, fearing to die of want or by the sword. Before one of those who was descending, his brother, already dead, appeared and said, "Where, brother, are you fleeing? Stay; fear not for God will be with you in your struggle; and your companions in this journey who have already preceded you in death will fight with you against the Turks." The other, astonished at the words of one who was dead, ceased to flee and told the rest what he had heard.[2]

[4] This was the citadel on Mount Silpius. The figure sixty thousand is mere rhetoric. The Turks were in a part of the city (*HG* xxvi, 4) from June 8–14 (*HF* 244, notes 12, 13).

[1] Cf. Raymond of Aguilers, RHC, Occ., III, 255–56; and *HG* xxiv, 3. The cleric seems to have been Stephan Valanti (Raymond, RHC, Occ., III, 255, 256, 257, 279, 282, and 286).

[2] See the account of the flight of William de Grant-Mesnil and others (Ray-

3. For they could no longer bear such anguish. They had nothing more to eat for which reason they as well as their horses were very weak. When it pleased the Lord to end the labors of His servants, they agreed upon a three-day fast with prayers and almsgiving in order that by these penances and prayers they might propitiate God.[3]

XXI

The Attack upon the Turks Ordered by the Franks. 1. Meantime after taking counsel the Franks notified the Turks through a certain Peter the Hermit that unless they quietly evacuated the land which had belonged to the Christians in former times they, the Franks, would most certainly attack them the next day. If the Turks preferred, the combat might be between five or ten or twenty or even a hundred knights chosen from each side, lest in the case of all fighting at once a great number should die. The side whose men overcame the others might freely receive the city and the rulership without further controversy.[1]

2. This was the demand, but it was not conceded by the Turks. They trusted in their great numbers and strength and thought that they could conquer and destroy us.

3. They were estimated to number three hundred thousand, both horsemen and footmen.[2] They knew that our knights had been reduced to weak and helpless footmen.

4. Then Peter, our legate, returned and gave their answer. When the Franks heard they unhesitatingly prepared themselves for battle, placing their hopes completely in God.

5. The princes of the Turks were many and were called *amirs.*

---

mond, RHC, Occ., III, 256; and HG xxiii, 2) on the night of June 10–11, 1098 (HF 246, note 7).

[3] The famine is mentioned by nearly all sources; the three-day fast is reported in the *Gesta* (HG xxix, 1) and in the *Epistula cleri et populi Luccensis ad omnes fideles* of October, 1098 (HEp 167).

[1] Cf. Raymond of Aguilers, RHC, Occ., III, 259; HG xxviii, 2–5; *Epistula II Anselmi de Ribodimonte ad Manassem archiepiscopum Remorum,* HEp 159–60. The date of Peter's mission was June 27, 1098 (HF 248, note 2).

[2] Fulcher's estimate of the strength of the Turkish army was still more extravagant in his first redaction, viz., 600,000 men (HF 249, note e).

They were Corbagath, Maleducat, Amisoliman, and many others too numerous to mention.[3]

XXII

The Preparation for Battle. 1. The princes of the Franks were Hugh the Great, Robert, Count of Normandy, Robert, Count of Flanders, Duke Godfrey, Count Raymond, Bohemond, besides many lesser nobles.[1] May God grant His blessing to the soul of Adhemar, Bishop of Le Puy, who, truly an apostolic man himself, always kindly comforted the people and strengthened them in the Lord.

2. Oh pious precaution! On the night before, Adhemar himself commanded by herald that each knight in the army of God should give his steed as much as possible of his dole of grain, however precious, lest the horse should collapse the next day in the hour of battle, weak with hunger. It was so ordered, and it was done.

3. And so thus prepared for battle they all went forth from the city at daybreak, which was on the fourth day before the Kalends of July.[2] The footmen and horsemen were organized into companies and squadrons preceded by their banners. Amongst them were the priests vested in white. These latter, weeping for the whole people, sang to the Lord and poured out many prayers from the depths of their devout souls.

4. Then a certain Turk named Amirdalis, a most excellent knight, when he saw our men advancing against them with banners flying, was greatly surprised. And when he had seen the flags of our leaders, which he recognized, advancing one by one in orderly fashion he knew that there would soon be a battle.

[3] Kerbogha, *Atabeg* of Mosul, Shams-al-Mulūk Dukak (1095–1104) of Damascus, and Amir Sulaimān, possibly a son of Il-Ghāzī (*HF* 250, note 12). Fulcher left out the names of about thirty other Turkish leaders mentioned in garbled form in his first redaction (*HF* 250, note d).

[1] Much of the material in this chapter Fulcher seems to have taken from the chronicle of Raymond of Aguilers (*RHC, Occ.,* III, 259–60) with some omissions and embellishments. Cf. *HG* xxix, 1; *Epistula II Anselmi de Ribodimonte ad Manassem archiepiscopum Remorum* (*HEp* 160); and *Epistula cleri et populi Luccensis ad omnes fideles* (*HEp* 167).

[2] July 28, 1098.

5. He was familiar with Antioch and had learned to know the Franks. He immediately hastened to Corbagath, told him what he had seen and said to him, "Why are you playing chess? Behold, the Franks are coming!" The latter replied, "Are they coming to fight?" Amirdalis answered, "Up to the moment I do not know, but wait a little."

6. And when Amirdalis discerned the flags of our princes being carried forward on the other side in a military manner and their serried lines of battle smartly following them he soon returned and said to Corbagath, "Look at the Franks!" "What do you think?" the latter replied. "I think there will be a battle," he said, "but wait a little. I do not recognize the banners which I see."

7. Then looking more closely he recognized the standard of the Bishop of Le Puy advancing with the third squadron.

> Waiting no longer he said to Corbagath,
> "Behold the Franks are coming; flee now or fight bravely
> For I see the banner of the mighty Pope advancing.

Tremble today lest you be overcome by those whom you thought you were going to utterly destroy."

8. Corbagath said: "I shall send word to the Franks that what they demanded of me yesterday I shall grant today." Amirdalis said, "You speak too late." Nevertheless Corbagath made the request, but what he sought he did not obtain. Amirdalis soon

> Withdrawing from his master, spurred on his horse.
> He considered whether to flee, but still urged all his comrades
> To fight bravely and to speed their arrows.[3]

XXIII

The Battle, the Victory of the Christians, and the Flight of the Turks. 1. Lo! Hugh the Great, Count Robert the Norman, and Robert, Count of Flanders, were the leaders in the first line of attack. Duke Godfrey followed in the second with the Germans and the Lotharingians. After them came the Bishop of Le Puy with the men of Count Raymond, the Gascons, and Provençals. The

---

[3] Fulcher made small attempts at versification throughout his chronicle.

Count himself remained in the city to guard it. Bohemond skillfully herded along the crowd in the rear.[1]

2. When the Turks saw that their ranks were being penetrated
by the fierce onslaught of the entire Frankish army, they began to
dart forward as individuals to shoot arrows as was their custom.[2]
But struck by a heaven-sent fear they all fled precipitately as if the
whole world had fallen down upon them. The Franks pursued the
fugitives as fast as they could.

3. But because the Franks had few horses and these were weak
from hunger, they did not capture as many of the pagans as they
should have taken. However, the tents of the Turks all remained in
their camps. In them the Franks found objects of many kinds,
namely gold, silver, robes, [other] clothing, utensils, and many
other things which the Turks in their panic and disorderly flight
through their camps had either left or thrown away. For example,
there were horses, mules, camels, asses, magnificent turbans, bows,
and arrows with quivers.[3]

4. Corbagath fled, swift as a deer, he who had so often slain the
Franks with ferocious words and threats. But why did he flee, he
who had such a large army so well provided with horsemen? Because he dared to contend against God, the Lord perceiving Corbagath's pomp from afar utterly destroyed his power.

5. Those Turks who had good and swift horses escaped, but the
stragglers were abandoned to the Franks. Many of these, especially
the Saracen footmen, were taken.[4] On the other hand few of our
men were injured. In regard to the women found in the tents of
the foe the Franks did them no evil but drove lances into their
bellies.

6. Then all in exultant voice blessed and glorified God.[5] In

---

[1] Cf. Raymond of Aguilers, *RHC*, *Occ.*, III, 259. Because Fulcher was skeptical
of the validity of the Holy Lance, he omits mention of its use as an object of inspiration. See Raymond, *ibid.*, 261; and *HG* xxix, 4. The date of this sortie was
June 28, 1098.

[2] Cf. Raymond, *RHC*, *Occ.*, III, 260, 261; and *HG* xxix, 4.

[3] Fulcher embellishes the *Gesta's* account of the booty. See *HG* xxix, 8.

[4] Cf. Raymond, *RHC*, *Occ.*, III, 261.

[5] Cf. *HG* xxix, 9.

righteous compassion He had freed them from the cruelest of enemies, those who, placed in great need and tribulation, had [nevertheless] trusted in Him. In His might He had scattered in conquered state the Turks who up to then had almost conquered the Christians. Our people, enriched by the booty of the foe, returned rejoicing to the city.

7.   When the ancient city of Antioch was captured
         Eleven hundred, if two be subtracted therefrom,
         Were the years of our Lord born of the Virgin,
         In the Sign of Gemini,
              when Phoebus had risen twice times nine.[6]

8. Then, on the Kalends of August, died the Bishop Adhemar, may his soul rest in eternal peace.[7] Amen! And then Hugh the Great departed for Constantinople with the consent of the princes, and from thence to France.[8]

XXIV

Concerning These Matters the Illustrious Band of Leaders of the Whole Army Addressed the Following Letter to the Roman Pontiff. 1. To the venerable Lord Pope Urban;[1] from Bohe-

[6] We would expect the date of the fall of Antioch to have been given when it occurred, but Fulcher puts it here at the end of his account of events at Antioch. Usually accurate with dates, he errs in dating the fall of the city June 4 instead of June 3 (*HF* 258, note 21); however, he uses the correct date later (chap. xxiv, 4).

[7] August 1, 1098.

[8] Hugh was sent early in July to offer Antioch to the Emperor Alexius if the latter brought aid as agreed (*HG* xxx, 2), but Alexius failed to do so.

[1] At this point Fulcher inserted into his work, in the first recension only, a curious letter purporting to be a report to Pope Urban II from the crusading princes at Antioch, written September 11, 1098 (*HF* 259, note 1). It denounced the Greeks and other Oriental Christians as heretics and urged Urban to make Antioch his seat from which to lead the crusaders on to the Holy Sepulcher. Compliance with this astonishing invitation would have wrecked the friendly relations with the Christians of the East that Urban had sought to promote at Clermont.

The letter seems to have been inspired by Bohemond, who was named first among the princes and again later in the first person. It may have been written by the *Gesta* author, who admired Bohemond, or more likely by someone familiar with the *Gesta* (*HEp* 96–97; and *HF* 259, note 1). In it Bohemond's plan to turn the crusade to his own advantage by breaking with the Byzantines and seizing Antioch for himself began to be evident. What Urban thought of this strange letter is unknown; he died before he could take any action. Consult Yewdale,

mond, Count Raymond of Saint-Gilles, Duke Godfrey of Lorraine, Count Robert of Normandy, Count Robert of Flanders, and Count Eustace of Boulogne,[2] greetings! and as from sons to a spiritual father: faithful service and true subjection in Christ.

2. We wish and desire that notice be made to you that through the great mercy of God as well as through His most manifest assistance Antioch has been taken by us; that the Turks, who had brought much shame to our Lord Jesus Christ, have been captured and slain; that we, pilgrims of Jesus Christ going to Jerusalem, have avenged the injury to God Almighty; that we who first besieged the Turks were afterwards besieged by other Turks coming from Khurasan, Jerusalem, Damascus, and many other places;[3] and how we were delivered by the mercy of Jesus Christ.

3. After the capture of Nicaea,[4] we overcame as you have heard the great multitude of Turks which met us on the Kalends of July[5] in the Valley of Dorylaeum and routed the mighty Soliman and stripped him of all his lands and possessions. Having acquired and subdued all of Romania, we advanced to the siege of Antioch.[6] In its siege we endured many hardships, especially from attacks of the neighboring Turks and pagans rushing in upon us so frequently and in such numbers that we might truly be said to have been besieged by those whom we were besieging in Antioch.

4. Finally all the battles were won and the Christian faith was

---

Bohemond, 49–84; Krey, "Urban's Crusade—Success or Failure," 239–41; and Anthony F. Czajkowski, "The Siege of Antioch in the First Crusade," *Historical Bulletin*, XXVI (1948), 82–84.

Fulcher seems not to have used this letter as a source of information for his preceding chapters but, rather, to have used the anonymous *Gesta* and Raymond of Aguilers. Why, then, did he incorporate it in his text? Probably in 1105–1106 he thought that including it would lend support to Bohemond's drive for a new crusade. Years later, in writing his second recension, Fulcher no doubt felt that the communication was superfluous and therefore omitted it.

Paul Riant has analyzed the letter ("Inventaire critique des lettres historiques des croisades," AOL, I, 181–83), and Hagenmeyer has edited it twice (*HEp* 88–93, 161–65, 341–58; and *HF* 258–64).

[2] Eustace III, Count of Boulogne and older brother of Duke Godfrey and Baldwin I. He returned home after the crusade.

[3] Cf. HG xxi, 1.

[4] June 19, 1097.

[5] July 1, 1097.

[6] October 20–21, 1097.

exalted by their successful issue in this way: I, Bohemond, made an agreement with a certain Turk who delivered the city to me. A little before dawn on the third day before the Nones of June[7] I placed ladders upon the wall, and thus we took the city which had been resisting Christ. We slew Cassianus, the tyrant of the city,[8] and many of his soldiers, and kept their wives, children, and families, together with their gold and silver and all their possessions.

5. However, we were not able to capture the citadel of Antioch, which had been previously fortified by the Turks.[9] But when we were ready to assail it the next day, we saw an infinite multitude of Turks moving about throughout the entire countryside. For many days we had been expecting that they would arrive to fight us while we were [still] outside the city. On the third day [after we had captured the city] they laid siege to us; and more than one hundred thousand of them[10] entered the aforesaid citadel, hoping to rush through its gate into the section of the city below it, which was held partly by us and partly by them.

6. But we, stationed on another height opposite the citadel,[11] guarded the path which was between both armies and which descended to the city so that the Turks in their great numbers could not break through. We fought inside and outside the walls night and day and finally compelled our enemies to return to their camp, through the citadel gate which led down into the city.

7. When they saw that they could not harm us on that side they surrounded us on all sides so that none could leave or enter the city. On that account we were all so discouraged and desolate that many of us, dying of famine and other afflictions, slaughtered and devoured our horses and asses,[12] which were also starving.

---

[7] June 3, 1099. [8] Yaghi-Siyan.

[9] The commander of the citadel was Aḥmad ibn-Marwan (Kamāl-ad-Dīn, *RHC, Or.*, III, 583). Consult Steven Runciman, "The First Crusade: Antioch to Ascalon," in Setton (ed.), *Crusades*, I, 319–23.

[10] "C eorum milia" in *HF* 262, but "centum eorum milites" in *HEp* 162, and "LX fere milia" in Fulcher's chronicle (*HF* 243; see chap. xix, 4). The first and third figures are obviously rhetorical (see *HF* 262, note 15).

[11] An excellent photograph of this height, Mount Staurin, and a topographical map may be found in Downey, *Antioch*, Plates 1, 3.

[12] Cf. *HG* xxiii, 4; xxvi, 5.

8. Meanwhile with the kindest mercy of Almighty God watching over us and assisting us we found the Lord's Lance with which the side of our Savior was pierced by Longinus.[13] It was revealed three times to a certain servant of God by St. Andrew the Apostle who showed him the place where the Lance lay in the Church of the Blessed Peter, Prince of the Apostles. Comforted by this discovery and by many other divine revelations, we were so strengthened that we who had previously been dejected and timid now most bravely and promptly urged each other to battle.

9. Thereafter having been besieged three weeks and four days, we, having confessed all our sins and entrusted ourselves to God, issued forth from the gates of the city in battle array on the eve of the Feast of the Apostles Peter and Paul.[14] We were so few that the enemy thought that we would not fight him, but would flee.

10. However, when we were all prepared and our foot and horse were drawn up in regular order, we boldly advanced with the Lord's Lance[15] toward the center of the greatest strength and power of the Turks and forced them to flee from their advanced position. They, however, as was their wont began to scatter in all directions. By occupying hills and roads wherever possible they thought to hem us in. Thus they hoped to slay us all. But we had been trained against their wiles and trickery in many a battle. The grace and mercy of God assisted us so that we who were so few in comparison with them forced them into a mass. With the right hand of God fighting on our side we compelled the Turks, thus herded together, to flee and to abandon their camps with all that they contained.

11. After we had overcome the Turks and pursued them for a whole day and killed many thousands of them, we returned to the city joyous and happy. Then a certain amir surrendered the citadel, previously mentioned, to Bohemond together with a thousand men in it. Through Bohemond he gladly yielded them with one accord to the Christian faith. Thus our Lord Jesus Christ delivered all of Antioch to the Roman religion and faith.

---

[13] See *HEp* 346, note 40.   [14] June 28, 1098.
[15] Fulcher omits mentioning that the Holy Lance was carried into battle.

12. And since something sad always happens in the midst of joys, the Bishop of Le Puy, whom you had sent us as your vicar, died on the Kalends of August.[16] This was after the battle, in which he had taken a noble part, and after the city had been pacified.

13. Now therefore we thy children, bereft of the father assigned to us, ask this of you, our spiritual father. Since you initiated this pilgrimage and by your sermons have caused us all to leave our lands and whatever was in them, since you have admonished us to follow Christ by carrying the Cross, and since you have urged us to exalt the name of Christ by fulfilling what you have preached, we beg you to come to us and to urge whomsoever you can to come with you. For it was here that the name of Christian originated [Act. 11:26]. After the Blessed Peter was enthroned in the church which we see daily,[17] they who were formerly called Galileans [Act. 1:11; 2:7] were here first and principally called Christians. Therefore what in this world would seem more proper than that you, who are the father and head of the Christian religion, should come to the principal city and capital of the Christian name and finish the war, which is your project, in person?

14. We have subdued the Turks and the pagans; but the heretics, Greeks and Armenians, Syrians and Jacobites, we have not been able to overcome. Therefore we ask and ask again that you, our most dear father, come as father and head to the place of your predecessor; that you who are the Vicar of the Blessed Peter seat yourself on his throne and use us as your obedient sons in carrying out all things properly; and that you eradicate and destroy by your authority and our strength all heresies of whatever kind. And thus you will finish with us the pilgrimage of Jesus Christ undertaken by us and proclaimed by you; and you will open to us the gates of the one and the other Jerusalem and will liberate the Sepulcher of our Lord and exalt the Christian name above all. For if you come to us and finish with us the pilgrimage that was inaugurated by you the whole world will be obedient to you. May God

---

[16] August 1, 1098.   [17] Consult HG 238, note 56.

who liveth and reigneth forever and ever suffer you to do this. Amen.¹⁸

XXV

The Campaign Against the Other Cities, the Siege Undertaken at Archas, the Journey of the Franks to Jerusalem and Their Arrival at that Place. 1. After our men and horses, wearied by many days of arduous labor, had been refreshed by rest and food for four months in the vicinity of Antioch, they were restored to their original health.¹ One part of the army, after taking counsel, went into the interior of Syria desiring to delay the march to Jerusalem. In this Bohemond and Count Raymond were the leaders.² The other princes still remained in the neighborhood of Antioch.

2. Those two leaders with their men seized the two cities of Barra and Marra³ in an attack showing great bravery. They very quickly captured the former, killed the citizens to a man, and confiscated everything. Then they hastened to the other city and besieged it for twenty days. Here our men suffered from excessive hunger. I shudder to say that many of our men, terribly tormented by the madness of starvation, cut pieces of flesh from the buttocks of Saracens lying there dead. These pieces they cooked and ate, savagely devouring the flesh while it was insufficiently roasted.⁴ In

---

¹⁸ A postscript, probably written in France at Bohemond's instigation during his recruiting campaign there in 1106, again denounces the Eastern Christians as heretics and urges Urban's active leadership (HF 264, note m; consult Hill and Hill, *Raymond IV*, 100).

¹ In this chapter Fulcher summarizes the history of the main army of the crusaders from Antioch to Jerusalem (June 28, 1098–June 7, 1099). He indulged his literary tastes by using Josephus' *Antiquitates Judaicae* for some geographical details.

² Soon after the defeat of Kerbogha, June 28, 1098, the crusader princes had sent word to the Emperor Alexius that he could have Antioch if he joined them by November 1. Bohemond and Count Raymond wanted to delay the march to Jerusalem because Bohemond hoped to acquire Antioch for himself and Raymond championed the rights of Alexius (HG xxx, 3; xxxi, 2–5; Raymond, RHC, Occ., III, 262, 266–67).

³ Al-Bāhrah, forty-two miles southeast of Antioch, and Ma'arrat-an-Nu'mān, eight miles east of al-Bāhrah. The first was taken by Count Raymond (HG xxxi, 1; cf. Raymond, RHC, Occ., III 266) ca. September 25, 1098 (HChr 316), and the latter was captured by Raymond and Bohemond on December 11 (HG xxxiii, 6; HChr 329).

⁴ For similar stories of cannibalism, see HG xxxiii, 8; and Raymond, RHC, Occ., III, 271.

this way the besiegers were harmed more than the besieged.

3. Meanwhile the Franks, having made such machines as they could and moved them up to the wall, with the blessing of God crossed over the top in an assault of great boldness. On that day and the next they killed all the Saracens from the greatest to the least and plundered all their possessions.

4. When Marra was destroyed in this way Bohemond returned to Antioch. He then expelled from it the men whom Count Raymond had placed there as guards for his sector.[5] Bohemond afterwards possessed Antioch together with the whole area, for he said that the city had been acquired by his negotiations and stratagems.

5. As a result Count Raymond joined Tancred to himself and resumed the advance to Jerusalem. Similarly Count Robert the Norman joined the same force on the day after the departure from Marra.[6]

6. In the year 1099 of the Incarnation of Our Lord this force proceeded to the stronghold called Archas at the foot of Mount Lebanon. We read that it was founded by Aracaeus, son of Canaan and grandson of Noah. But because it was very difficult to take they besieged it for almost five weeks but accomplished nothing.[7]

7. Duke Godfrey and Robert, Count of Flanders, followed this army not far behind. When they were besieging the stronghold of Gibellum, they received a message asking them to help the men at Archas. Hence they left Gibellum immediately and hurried to help the army as requested. But after they surrounded the city [Archas] the expected battle did not materialize.

8. In this siege of Archas, Anselm of Ribemont, a valiant knight, was struck by a stone and killed.[8]

---

[5] Raymond, RHC, Occ., III, 286.

[6] For Tancred, see ibid., 272; and for Robert, HG xxxiv, 3. The Gesta dates the departure of Count Raymond on January 13, 1099 (HG xxxiv, 3; HChr 339).

[7] 'Arqah, about thirteen miles northwest of Tripoli, was reached ca. February 14, 1099 (HG xxxiv, 11; HChr 352). The siege lasted not five but twelve and a half weeks, February 14–May 13 (HF 269, note 18). For Aracaeus, see Joseph. Ant. i. 138; Gen. 10:15–17; and I Paralip. 1:13–15.

[8] Raymond, RHC, Occ., III, 277; and HG xxxv, 1, 3. Gibellum (Jabala, class. Gabala) is fourteen miles south of Laodicea. Anselm was killed on February 25, 1099 (HChr 355).

9. At this point the Franks consulted together and decided that if they should remain there for a while and fail to take the fortress of Archas irreparable harm would be done to them all. They said that it would be wise to abandon the siege and continue the march, for while they knew that their route was devoid of commercial traffic there was still time to reach Jerusalem during the harvest season. If they should proceed thus they would be able to live everywhere on the harvests, on subsistence provided by God, and would with His leadership arrive at their much desired goal. Thus it was proposed and thus it was decided.[9]

10. Therefore after they had folded their tents they set out and passed through the city of Tripoli. This done they arrived at the fortress of Gibellulum. It was in the month of April, and already they were living off the harvests. Going on farther and passing some time near the city of Beirut they came upon another city which we read in our language as Sidon. It is in the Phoenician land and was founded by Sidon the son of Canaan, from whom the Sidonians are descended. From Sidon our men went on to Sarepta. From there they proceeded to Tyre, a very fine city. From here came Apollonius, whom we read about. Of these two cities the Evangelist says, "into the regions of Tyre and Sidon" [Matth. 15:21; Marc. 7:24]. The inhabitants of the area now call the first "Sagitta" and the other "Sur." In Hebrew it is "Soor."[10]

11. Then they came to a fortress called Ziph, in the sixth mile from Ptolemais. Next they passed in front of Ptolemais, formerly called Accon, which some of our people erroneously call Acharon. But Acharon is a Philistine city near Ascalon, between Jamnia and Azotus. In fact Accon, that is Ptolemais, has Mount Carmel to the south. Crossing by it the troops passed by the town called

[9] Cf. HG xxxv, 4.

[10] For this paragraph Fulcher used the Gesta more than Raymond (HG xxxvi, 1–3; cf. Raymond, RHC, Occ., III, 291). For the chronology from 'Arqah to Tyre, May 13–23, see HChr 371–76. Fulcher misunderstood a passage in the Gesta and thought the time was April (HG xxxv, 4; HF 271, note 25). Gibellulum (Jubail, class. Byblos) is twenty miles north of Beirut; and Sarepta, not mentioned by the Gesta or Raymond, is ten miles south of Sidon. For the references to Sidon, see Joseph. Ant. i. 138; cf. Gen. 10:15–19; and for the reference to Apollonius, see Joseph. Ant. xii. 261, 264; cf. HF 273, note 30. Sagitta is Sidon; Sur is Tyre.

Haifa, to their right. After that they came close to Dora and then to Caesarea in Palestine. This latter has been called since ancient times by another name, the Tower of Straton. In it Herod Agrippa, grandson of that Herod in whose time Christ was born, died miserably, consumed by worms [Act. 12:23].[11]

12. Next, leaving the sea and the town of Arsuf to the right, the Franks passed through the city called Ramatha or Arimathia. Its Saracen inhabitants had fled the day before. The Franks found much grain there, which they loaded on their beasts and transported to Jerusalem.

13. After tarrying there for four days, and appointing a bishop for the Basilica of St. George and stationing men in the defenses of the town, the Franks then directed their way toward Jerusalem. That day they marched as far as Emmaus, near which is Modin, the city of the Maccabees [I Mach. 2:1–15].[12]

14. The following night one hundred of the better knights mounted their horses and passing at daybreak close to Jerusalem hurried to Bethlehem. Tancred was one of them and Baldwin another.[13] When the Christians who dwelt there, Greeks and Syrians, discovered that the Franks had arrived, they were completely overcome with joy. However, at first they did not know who these people were and thought they might be Turks or Arabs.

15. But as soon as they beheld them clearly at a closer distance and were sure that they were Franks they, full of joy, immediately took up crosses and banners and went out to meet them, weeping

[11] Ziph or az-Zib, Biblical Achzib (Jos. 19:29; Judic. 1:31), called Arce by Josephus (*Ant.* v. 85; ix. 285), was about nine miles north of Acre. Consult *HF* 274, note 33, and 706, note 6. Ptolemais, Accon, or Acco will be hereinafter rendered "Acre," its usual modern name. Acharon (Bibl. Ekron) was four miles east of Jamnia (Jabneel, Frankish Ibelin), itself about the same distance from the Mediterranean, and both were about ten miles northeast of Azotus (Bibl. Ashdod). Hence, Fulcher errs in placing Acharon between Jamnia and Azotus.
[12] For events at Ramatha (Ramla) Fulcher chiefly depended on the *Gesta* (*HG* xxxvi, 4) and Raymond of Aguilers (*RHC, Occ.,* III, 272). He is the authority for the length of the stay, June 2–6, 1099 (*HChr* 382–83). The bishop chosen was Robert of Rouen (William of Tyre, VII, xxii). Emmaus ('Amwās) is seven miles south of Modin and fifteen miles west of Jerusalem.
[13] Baldwin of Le Bourg, a kinsman of Baldwin I, who became count of Edessa in 1100 and king at Jerusalem in 1118.

and devoutly singing. They wept because they feared that so few people might very easily and at any time be slain by the great multitude of pagans who they knew were in the country. They sang because they welcomed those whose arrival they had long desired and who they felt would restore the Christian faith, long abused by the heathen, to its original and rightful dignity.

16. Our men, after they had made devout supplication to God in the Basilica of the Blessed Mary, and after they had visited the place where Christ was born and had given the kiss of peace to the Syrians, went back in haste toward the Holy City, Jerusalem.

17. Behold! there appeared the rest of the army approaching the city. It had passed Gibeon to the left, fifty stades from Jerusalem, Gibeon, where Joshua gave orders to the sun and the moon [Jos. 10:12–13].[14] When the standard-bearers of the advanced guard displayed their banners aloft to the citizens, the latter immediately sallied forth against them. But they who speedily came out were even more speedily driven back into the city.

> June was already a-glow with the heat of its seventh sun[15]
> When the Franks surrounded Jerusalem in siege.

XXVI

The Site of Jerusalem. 1. The city of Jerusalem is located in a mountainous region which is devoid of trees, streams, and springs excepting only the Pool of Siloam, which is a bowshot from the city. Sometimes it has enough water, and sometimes a deficiency due to a slight drainage. This little spring is in the valley at the foot of Mount Zion in the course of the Brook Kedron which, in winter time, is accustomed to flow through the center of the Valley of Jehoshaphat.[1]

[14] Fulcher is the authority for the events at Bethlehem.

[15] Fulcher corrects the *Gesta*, which gives June 6 (*HG* xxxvii, 1; *HChr* 385).

[1] In this chapter the author provides a valuable eyewitness description of Jerusalem as it appeared early in the twelfth century. Raymond of Aguilers and the anonymous *Gesta* do not do so. Fulcher's account should be compared with those of Saewulf in 1102–1103 (*Relatio de peregrinatione ad Hierosolymam et Terram S. annis 1102 et 1103*, in *Recueil de voyages et de mém. pub. par la Société de Géographie*, IV [Paris, 1839], 818 ff, quoted in *HF* 282, note 1); the Russian Abbot

2. The many cisterns inside the city, reserved for winter rains, have a sufficiency of water. More, at which men and beasts are refreshed, are also found outside the city.

3. It is generally conceded that the city is laid out in such proper proportion that it seems neither too small nor too large. Its width from wall to wall is that of four bowshots. To the west is the Tower of David with the city wall on each flank; to the south is Mount Zion a little closer than a bowshot; and to the east, the Mount of Olives a thousand paces outside the city.

4. The aforesaid Tower of David is of solid masonry half-way up, of large squared blocks sealed with molten lead. Fifteen or twenty men, if well supplied with food, could defend it from all assaults of an enemy.

5. In the same city is the Temple of the Lord, round in shape, built where Solomon in ancient times erected the earlier magnificent Temple. Although it can in no way be compared in appearance to the former building, still this one is of marvelous workmanship and most splendid appearance.[2]

6. The Church of the Lord's Sepulcher is likewise circular in form. It was never closed in at the top but always admits the light through a permanent aperture ingeniously fashioned under the direction of a skillful architect.[3]

7. I cannot, I dare not, I know not how to enumerate the many objects which it now contains or contained in the past lest in some

---

Daniel in 1107 (*Vie et pèlerinage*, trans. B. de Khitrowo in *Itineraires Russes en Orient*, I [Genève: Fick, 1889], 1–83); the anonymous *Gesta Francorum Iherusalem expugnantium* (*RHC, Occ.*, III, 509–12); and the anonymous *Descriptio sanctorum locorum Hierusalem* (ed. Rosalind Hill, in *Gesta Francorum et aliorum Hierosolymitanorum*, 98–101). For an excellent map of twelfth-century Jerusalem and modern photographs, see Michel Join-Lambert, *Jerusalem*, trans. Charlotte Haldane (London: Elek Books; New York: G. P. Putnam's Sons, 1958), 193 *et passim*.

[2] The beautiful octagonal mosque Qubbat aṣ-Ṣakhrah ("Dome of the Rock," the *Templum Domini* of the crusaders), built by the Caliph 'Abd al-Malik in 691 over the sacred rock from which it is believed Mohammed ascended to Heaven in a nocturnal journey (*Koran*, Sura XVII).

[3] For an illustration of this aperture and a modern photograph, see Join-Lambert, *Jerusalem*, 183, 191.

way I deceive those reading or hearing about the matter. In the middle of the Temple, when we first entered it and for fifteen years thereafter,[4] was a certain native rock. It was said that the Ark of the Lord's Covenant along with the urn and tables of Moses was sealed inside of it, that Josiah, King of Judah, ordered it to be placed there saying, "You shall never carry it from this place" [II Paralip. 35:3]. For he foresaw the future Captivity.

8. But this contradicts what we read in the descriptions of Jeremiah, in the second book of the Maccabees, that he himself hid it in Arabia, saying that it would not be found until many peoples should be gathered together. Jeremiah was a contemporary of King Josiah; however, the king died before Jeremiah [II Mach. 2:4–9].

9. They said that the angel of the Lord had stood upon the aforesaid rock [II Paralip. 3:1; II Sam. 24:18–25] and destroyed the people because of the enumeration of the people foolishly made by David and displeasing to the Lord [II Sam. 24:1–2, 15–17; I Paralip. 21:15].[5] Moreover this rock because it disfigured the Temple of the Lord was afterwards covered over and paved with marble. Now an altar is placed above it, and there the clergy have fitted up a choir. All the Saracens held the Temple of the Lord in great veneration. Here rather than elsewhere they preferred to say the prayers of their faith although such prayers were wasted because offered to an idol set up in the name of Mohammed. They allowed no Christian to enter the Temple.

10. Another temple, called the Temple of Solomon, is large and wonderful, but it is not the one that Solomon built. This one, because of our poverty, could not be maintained in the condition in which we found it. Wherefore it is already in large part destroyed.[6]

---

[4] This statement may indicate that Fulcher was the chaplain of King Baldwin I for fifteen years and had entrée to the *Templum Domini* during that time. See HF 16; 282, note 1; 287, note 18.

[5] Cf. William of Tyre, VIII, iii.

[6] The al-Aqṣa Mosque ("the Farther Mosque"), the third most holy shrine of Islam. The reason for its dilapidated appearance was that King Baldwin had stripped its roof of lead and sold it (Fulcher, first redaction, HF 291). It was later the headquarters of the Knights Templars and was also the royal palace, according to William of Tyre (VIII, iii).

11. There were gutters in the streets of the city through which in time of rain all filth was washed away.

12. The Emperor Aeilus Hadrian[7] decorated this city magnificently and fittingly adorned the streets and squares with pavements. In his honor Jerusalem was called Aelia. For these and many other reasons Jerusalem is a most renowned and glorious city.

XXVII

The Siege of the City of Jerusalem. 1. When the Franks beheld the city and realized that it would be difficult to take,[1] our leaders ordered wooden ladders to be made. By carrying these to the wall and erecting them, and climbing with fierce energy to the top of the wall, they hoped with the help of God to enter the city.

2. These ladders were made, and on the seventh day after the arrival our leaders gave the command for the attack. At the sound of the trumpets at daybreak[2] our men attacked the city on all sides with remarkable energy. But when they had continued the attack up to the sixth hour of the day and were not able to enter by means of the ladders which they had prepared because the ladders were too few, they reluctantly gave up the assault.

3. Then after consultation our leaders ordered the engineers to make machines of war.[3] They hoped when these were moved up to the walls to attain the desired result with the help of God. Therefore this was done.

4. Meanwhile, however, our men did not suffer from lack of bread or meat. Yet because the area was dry, unwatered, and without streams our men as well as their beasts suffered for lack of water to drink. Wherefore, because necessity demanded it, they

---

[7] The Roman Emperor Hadrian (117–38).

[1] Fulcher follows the anonymous *Gesta* and Raymond of Aguilers in their accounts of the capture of Jerusalem, adding a few details but omitting much for the sake of brevity (*HG* xxxvii–xxxviii; and Raymond, *RHC, Occ.*, III, 293–300).

[2] June 13, 1099 (*HChr* 389). For the attack, cf. *HG* xxxvii, 3.

[3] The conference was on June 15 (*HChr* 391). Regarding the construction of the siege towers, see *HG* xxxviii, 1–2; and Raymond, *RHC, Occ.*, III, 297–98.

brought water daily to the siege from four or five miles away, laboriously carrying it in the skins of animals.[4]

5. When the machines were ready, namely battering rams and *scrofae,* our men again prepared to attack the city. Among those contrivances they put together a tower made of short pieces of timber because there was no large stuff in that area. When the command was given they transported the tower, in sections, by night to a corner of the city. In the morning they quickly erected it, all assembled, not far from the wall, together with *petrariae* and other auxiliary weapons which they had prepared. After they had set it up and well protected it on the outside with hides, they pushed it little by little nearer the wall.[5]

6. Then some soldiers, few it is true but brave, climbed upon the tower at a signal from the trumpet. The Saracens nevertheless set up a defense against them. With *fundibula* they hurled small burning brands soaked in oil and grease against the tower and the soldiers in it. Therefore many on both sides met sudden death in this fighting.[6]

7. From the side where they were located, namely Mount Zion, Count Raymond and his men launched a heavy attack with their machines. From the other side where Duke Godfrey, Count Robert of Normandy, and Robert of Flanders were stationed there was still greater assault upon the wall. These were the events of that day.

8. The next day at the sound of the trumpets they undertook the same task with still more vigor. As a result they made a breach in the wall by battering it in one place with rams. The Saracens had suspended two timbers in front of the battlements and tied them there with ropes as a protection against the stones hurled at them by their assailants. But what they did for their advantage

---

[4] The *Gesta* and Raymond state that there was a shortage of food but agree that there was a lack of water (*HG* xxxvii, 4, 8; cf. Raymond, *RHC, Occ.,* III, 293–94).

[5] Cf. *Gesta.* It dates the transfer of the tower (Godfrey's) on the night of July 9 (*HG* xxxviii, 2).

[6] The *Gesta* indicates that there were two days of fighting before the final assault (*HG* xxxviii, 3). Raymond has much to say about the use of flaming missiles (*RHC, Occ.,* III, 299).

later turned to their detriment, by Divine Providence. For when the Franks had moved the aforesaid tower up to the wall they used falchions to cut the ropes by means of which the two beams were suspended. With these timbers they contrived a bridge and skillfully extended it from the tower to the top of the wall.

9. Already one stone tower on the wall, at which those working our machines had thrown flaming brands, was afire. This fire, gradually fed by the wooden material in the tower, caused so much smoke and flame that none of the city guards could remain there any longer.[7]

10. Soon therefore the Franks gloriously entered the city at noon on the day known as Dies Veneris, the day in which Christ redeemed the whole world on the Cross.[8] Amid the sound of trumpets and with everything in an uproar they attacked boldly, shouting "God help us!" At once they raised a banner on the top of the wall. The pagans were completely terrified, for they all exchanged their former boldness for headlong flight through the narrow streets of the city. The more swiftly they fled the more swiftly they were pursued.

11. Count Raymond and his men, who were strongly pressing the offensive in another part of the city, did not notice this until they saw the Saracens jumping off from the top of the wall. When they noticed it they ran with the greatest exultation as fast as they could into the city and joined their companions in pursuing and slaying their wicked enemies without cessation.

12. Some of the latter, Arabs as well as Ethiopians,[9] fled into the Tower of David, and others shut themselves up in the Temples of the Lord and of Solomon. In the courts of these buildings a fierce attack was pressed upon the Saracens. There was no place where they could escape our swordsmen.

13. Many of the Saracens who had climbed to the top of the

---

[7] The details of pars. 8–9 are largely Fulcher's.

[8] Friday, July 15, 1099 (*HChr* 405).

[9] Fulcher refers elsewhere to Ethiopians in the Egyptian service, once as dark men and once as infantry. He distinguished between them and men of Arabic ancestry (chap. xxx, 3; II, xxxi, 1).

Temple of Solomon in their flight were shot to death with arrows and fell headlong from the roof. Nearly ten thousand were beheaded in this Temple. If you had been there your feet would have been stained to the ankles in the blood of the slain. What shall I say? None of them were left alive. Neither women nor children were spared.[10]

XXVIII

The Spoils Taken by the Christians. 1. How astonishing it would have seemed to you to see our squires and footmen, after they had discovered the trickery of the Saracens, split open the bellies of those they had just slain in order to extract from the intestines the bezants which the Saracens had gulped down their loathsome throats while alive! For the same reason a few days later our men made a great heap of corpses and burned them to ashes in order to find more easily the above-mentioned gold.[1]

2. And also Tancred rushed into the Temple of the Lord and seized much gold and silver and many precious stones. But he restored these things, putting them or their equivalent back into the holy place. This was in spite of the fact that no divine services were conducted there at that time. The Saracens had practiced their rule of idolatry there with superstitious rite and moreover had not allowed any Christian to enter.[2]

3.   With drawn swords our men ran through the city
    Not sparing anyone, even those begging for mercy.
    The crowd fell just as rotten apples fall
    From shaken branches and acorns from swaying oaks.[3]

[10] Fulcher's account in pars. 10–13, although based in part upon the *Gesta* and Raymond, shows some originality. They all have slightly different but graphic details about the hideous massacre around the Mosque al-Aqsa (*HG* xxxviii, 4–7; Raymond, *RHC, Occ.,* III, 300).

[1] Fulcher is the authority for these gruesome details. The men are said to have been Provençals arriving late for the sack of the city (*Gesta Francorum Iherusalem expugnantium, RHC, Occ.,* III, 516).

[2] Cf. Raymond of Aguilers, *RHC, Occ.,* III, 300; *HG* xxxviii, 7. Fulcher's story of the restitution of plunder by Tancred is doubted by Nicholson (*Tancred*, 97, note 1).

[3] Ovid. *Metam.* vii. 585, 586.

XXIX

The Stay of the Christians in the City. 1. After this great
slaughter they entered the houses of the citizens, seizing whatever
they found in them. This was done in such a way that whoever
first entered a house, whether he was rich or poor, was not challenged by any other Frank. He was to occupy and own the house
or palace and whatever he found in it as if it were entirely his own.
Thus they mutually agreed upon this right of possession. In this
way many poor people became wealthy.[1]

2. Then the clergy and laity, going to the Lord's Sepulcher and
His most glorious Temple, singing a new canticle to the Lord in
a resounding voice of exultation, and making offerings and most
humble supplications, joyously visited the holy places as they had
long desired to do.[2]

3. Oh day so ardently desired! Oh time of times the most memorable! Oh deed before all other deeds! Desired indeed because in
the inner longing of the heart it had always been hoped by all believers in the Catholic faith that the place in which the Creator of
all creatures, God made man, in His manifold pity for mankind,
had by His birth, death, and resurrection, conferred the gift of
redemption would be restored to its pristine dignity by those believing and trusting in Him. They desired that this place, so long
contaminated by the superstition of the pagan inhabitants, should
be cleansed from their contagion.

4. It was a time truly memorable and justly so because in this
place everything that the Lord God our Jesus Christ did or taught
on earth, as man living amongst men, was recalled and renewed
in the memory of true believers. And this same work which the
Lord chose to accomplish through His people, His dearly beloved
children and family, chosen, I believe, for this task, shall resound
and continue memorable in the tongues of all nations until the
end of time.

[1] Cf. Raymond, *RHC, Occ.*, III, 292; *HF* 304, note 2.
[2] Cf. Raymond, *RHC, Occ.*, III, 300; *HG*, xxxviii, 7.

XXX

The Creation of a King and Patriarch in the City, and the Discovery of the Cross of the Lord.

1. In the year eleven hundred minus one
   From the Virgin Birth of the Illustrious Lord
   When Phoebus had illumined July fifteen times,
   The Franks in their might captured Jerusalem
   And soon made Godfrey prince of the fatherland.

All the people of the Lord's army in the Holy City chose Godfrey prince of the realm[1] because of the nobility of his character, military skill, patient conduct, no less than for his elegance of manners, to protect and govern it.

2. Then too, they placed canons in the Church of the Lord's Sepulcher and in His Temple to serve Him.[2] Moreover they decided at that time that a patriarch should not be created as yet until they had inquired from the Roman pope whom he wished to place in authority.[3]

3. Meanwhile some Turks and Arabs and about five hundred black Ethiopians who had taken refuge in the Tower of David begged of Count Raymond, who was quartered near that citadel, that on condition they leave their money there, they be allowed to depart with their lives. He conceded this, and they withdrew to Ascalon.[4]

[1] Fulcher's reference to Godfrey as *regni principem* means that Godfrey was chosen not king but protector of the land. This was because of the objections of Count Raymond and some of the clergy. See Raymond of Aguilers, RHC, Occ., III, 301.
[2] Albert of Aix states that twenty canons were established (VI, xl). Consult HF 308, note 6.
[3] Raymond and the *Gesta* explicitly state that Arnulf of Chocques was chosen patriarch (Raymond, RHC, Occ., III, 301; and HG xxxix, 3). Fulcher supports the thesis that this was the prerogative of Pope Urban. The chapter title, mentioning the creation of a king and patriarch, was obviously written by someone other than Fulcher. Regarding the legal status of Godfrey and Arnulf in 1099, see Ch. Moeller, "Godefroid de Bouillon et l'avouerie du Saint-Sépulchre," *Mélanges Godefroid Kurth*, I (Liège, Paris, 1908), 75–79; Joseph Hansen, *Das Problem eines Kirchenstaates in Jerusalem* (Luxemburg: Luxemburger Kunstdruckerei A. G. vorm. Dr. M. Huss, 1928), 11–28.
[4] Cf. HG xxxviii, 6; xxxix, 2; Raymond, RHC, Occ., III, 300.

4. At that time it pleased God that a small piece of the Lord's Cross should be found in a secret place.[5] It had been hidden in ancient times by holy men. And now by the will of God it was discovered by a certain Syrian who with the knowledge of his father had carefully concealed and preserved it. This piece, fashioned in the form of a cross, partly covered by gold and silver work, they all carried aloft to the Lord's Sepulcher and thence to the Temple, singing triumphantly and giving thanks to God, who through all this time had preserved for Himself and us this, His treasure and ours.

XXXI

The Arrival and Attack of the Pagans, and the Victory of the Christians. 1. Moreover the king of Babylon and the commander of his forces, Lavedalius[1] by name, when they heard that the Franks had already entered their territories for the purpose of subjecting the Babylonian kingdom to themselves, gathered by edict a multitude of Turks, Arabs, and Ethiopians and hastened to go to fight against them.[2] And when they had heard through another set of messengers that Jerusalem had been captured with such fury the aforesaid commander waxed wroth and hurried to do battle with the invaders or besiege them confined within the city.

2. When the Franks learned this they adopted a plan of great boldness. They marched their forces toward Ascalon against those tyrants, taking with them the wood of the life-bearing Cross mentioned above.[3]

3. One day[4] when the Franks were scouring around Ascalon

[5] Raymond states that this relic was found by the initiative of Arnulf (*RHC, Occ.,* III, 302).

[1] To the Franks "Babylon" was Cairo, its "king" was the ninth Fāṭimid Caliph al-Mustaʿlī (1094–1101), and Lavedalius was the Vizier al-Afdal Shāhānshāh (1094–1121), the very astute power behind the throne (*HF* 311, note 2). Regarding the latter, consult H. A. R. Gibb, "The Caliphate and the Arab States," in Setton (ed.), *Crusades,* I, 94–98.

[2] Fulcher's account of the battle of Ascalon, August 12, 1099, and its antecedents depends mostly upon the anonymous *Gesta* and Raymond of Aguilers (*HG* xxxix, 5–21; Raymond, *RHC, Occ.,* III, 302–305).

[3] Raymond refers instead to the Holy Lance (*RHC, Occ.,* III, 303).

[4] August 11, 1099 (*HChr* 420).

and awaiting battle they discovered considerable booty in oxen, camels, sheep, and goats. When our men had gathered these beasts near their tents at the end of day, our leaders decreed by strict proclamation that the men should not drive their quarry with them on the morrow, when battle was expected, so that they should be unencumbered and the more free to fight.

4. The next morning the Franks learned from the scouts that had been sent out that the pagans were advancing. When this was known the tribunes and centurions at once formed their men into wings and phalanxes, arranged them in the best way for battle, and proceeded boldly against the enemy with banners aloft.

5. You might have seen the animals mentioned above advancing of their own will to the right and left of our formation as if by command; yet they were driven by no one. In this way many of the pagans, at a distance seeing the animals proceeding with our soldiers, concluded that the whole array was the army of the Franks.[5]

6. However, the pagans, an innumerable multitude, approached our formations like a stag thrusting forward the branches of his horns. They divided their advance formation, uncovering a flying wing of Arabs and managing to encircle our rear. As a result Duke Godfrey went back with a heavy body of mailed knights and rescued the rear line. The other princes advanced, some in the first line, others in the second.

7. When foe had approached foe at a distance of a stone's throw or less, our footmen began to shoot arrows into their opponents, whose lines were extended. Soon the lance took the place of the arrow as our knights, as if mutually agreed under oath, made a violent onslaught. In the slaughter the slower of the horses of the enemy were thrown over on their riders. In the short space of an hour many bodies became pale and lifeless.[6]

8. Many of the enemy in their flight climbed to the tops of trees. Yet here they were shot with arrows and, mortally wounded,

[5] Cf. Raymond, *RHC, Occ.,* III, 304.
[6] These details are original with Fulcher. Cf. *HG* xxxix, 12–13.

fell miserably to earth.[7] In the sweeping attack the Saracens perished on all sides. Those who escaped fled through their camp to the walls of Ascalon. This city is 720 stades from Jerusalem.[8]

9. Lavedalius, their leader, who had hitherto despised the Franks, now in the very first encounter turned his back in precipitate flight. He thus involuntarily abandoned his tent, which was pitched among the rest and was stored with much money. Thither the Franks returned, joyous in victory, and, reunited, gave thanks to God.

10. Then they entered the tents of the enemy and found vast princely wealth: gold, silver, long cloaks, other clothing, and precious stones. These latter were of twelve kinds, jasper, sapphire, chalcedony, emerald, sardonyx, sardius, chrysolite, beryl, topaz, chrysoprasus, jacinth, and amethyst [Apoc. 21:19–20]. They also found many vessels and many kinds of things such as helmets decorated with gold, the finest rings, wonderful swords, grain, flour, and much else.

11. Our men spent the night there and, by being very watchful, guarded themselves well. For they thought that on the following day the fighting would be renewed by the Saracens, but these latter, exceedingly terrified, all fled that same night.[9] When in the morning this fact was ascertained by scouts, the Franks, in voices overflowing with praise, blessed and glorified God, who had permitted so many thousands of infidels to be scattered by a tiny army of Christians. "Blessed therefore be God who hath not given us as a prey to their teeth!" "Blessed is the nation whose God is the Lord!" [Psalm. 123:6; 32:12].

12. Had not these very Babylonians threatened, saying, "Let us go and capture Jerusalem with the Franks enclosed therein. After slaying them all let us tear down that Sepulcher so dear to them, and cast the stones of the building out of the city, and let no further mention of the Sepulcher ever be made again!"[10] But with

[7] Ibid., 15.
[8] A distance of a day and a half, according to Raymond (RHC, Occ., III, 303), perhaps the same in Fulcher (HF 316, note 23).
[9] These details are original with Fulcher.   [10] Raymond, RHC, Occ., III, 303.

God's mercy this was brought to nought. Instead the Franks loaded the very horses and camels with the money of the Saracens. Not being able to carry to the Holy City the tents and all the spears, bows, and arrows thrown on the ground, they committed them all to the flames and then returned rejoicing to Jerusalem.[11]

XXXII

The Return of the Princes to Their Native Lands. 1. After these things were accomplished, some of the people wished to return to their native lands. As soon as they had bathed in the waters of the Jordan and had collected palm branches near Jericho, in what was said to be the Garden of Abraham,[1] Robert, Count of the Normans, and Robert, Count of Flanders, set out by ship for Constantinople and from there returned to France to their possessions. Raymond, however, returned to Laodicea in Syria, left his wife[2] there, and went on to Constantinople, expecting to return.[3] Duke Godfrey, keeping Tancred and several others with him, ruled the government at Jerusalem which, with the consent of all, he had undertaken to maintain.

XXXIII

Bohemond and Baldwin and Their Pilgrimage. 1. Lord Bohemond, a man wise and strong, was at that time ruling in Antioch while Lord Baldwin, a brother of the aforesaid Godfrey, ruled Edessa and the neighboring country on the other side of the River Euphrates.[1] When they heard that Jerusalem had been taken by

[11] Cf. HG xxxix, 20.
[1] Regarding the Garden of Abraham, see HF 320, note 2.
[2] Elvira of León and Castile (Hill and Hill, *Raymond IV*, 19–20).
[3] Fulcher passes over a very unpleasant incident, one in which Robert of Normandy, Robert of Flanders, and Raymond of Saint-Gilles found Bohemond and Archbishop Daimbert of Pisa, both crusaders, engaged in a scandalous siege of the Byzantines, who were fellow Christians, at Laodicea and forced them to desist. See Krey, "Urban's Crusade—Success or Failure," 244–45; and Hill and Hill, *Raymond IV*, 144–45.
[1] With this chapter Fulcher, absent with Baldwin I of Edessa since late in 1098 (chap. xiv), again becomes an eyewitness of the events he records.

their colleagues who had preceded them, they rejoiced and returned praise and prayers to God.

2. But if those who were first in speed of journey to Jerusalem had done well and advantageously, still it was not to be doubted that these latter two with their companions would be as brave although following later.

3. For it was necessary that the land and the cities taken from the Turks with such difficulty should be carefully guarded. These if rashly left unprotected might be conquered in a sudden attack by the Turks, now driven back as far as Persia. In this case great harm would befall all the Franks, both going to Jerusalem and returning. Perhaps it was Divine Providence which delayed Bohemond and Baldwin, judging that they would be more useful in what remained to be done than in what had been done.

4. Oh how many times, meanwhile, was this same Baldwin wearied in the battles against the Turks in the lands of Mesopotamia! How many Turkish heads were cut off there it would be impossible to say. Often it happened that Baldwin with his few men fought a great multitude of the enemy and with the help of God rejoiced in triumph.[2]

5. Now when Bohemond through messengers suggested to Baldwin that they both with their men should finish the journey to Jerusalem, which they had not yet completed, Baldwin in good time arranged his affairs and prepared to go.

6. But then when Baldwin heard that the Turks had invaded one section of his country he delayed starting on the trip. Since he had not yet gathered his little army for this journey to Jerusalem, he went against the Turks with only a few men. One day the Turks, thinking that Baldwin had already begun his journey, were feeling secure in their tents when they saw the white banner which Baldwin carried. They were terrified and fled as quickly as possible. After he had pursued them a little way with his few men he re-

[2] Here Fulcher, perhaps moved by criticism of Bohemond and Baldwin, justifies their reasons for staying behind while the main force of the crusaders went on to capture Jerusalem.

turned to the project which he had previously undertaken.[3]

7. Beginning the journey and passing Antioch to the right, he came to Laodicea where he bought provisions for the journey and reloaded the pack animals. Then we set out. It was in the month of November. After we had passed by Gibellum we came up to Bohemond encamped in his tents before a certain town called Valania.[4]

8. With him was a certain Pisan archbishop named Daimbert, who had come by sea to the port of Laodicea with some Tuscans and Italians and there had waited to go with us. A certain bishop from Apulia was there too. A third was with Lord Baldwin.[5] Of those thus assembled in friendship we estimated the number to be twenty-five thousand of both sexes, mounted and on foot.[6]

9. When we entered the interior lands of the Saracens, we were unable to obtain from the hostile inhabitants bread or anything else to eat. No one would give or sell, and as more and more of our provisions were being consumed it happened that many suffered grievously from hunger. The horses and beasts of burden suffered doubly from lack of food. They walked but had nothing to eat.

10. But in those cultivated fields through which we passed during our march there were certain ripe plants which the common folk called "honey-cane" and which were very much like reeds.[7] The name is compounded from "cane" and "honey," whence the expression "wood honey" I think, because the latter is skillfully made from these canes. In our hunger we chewed them all day

---

[3] This engagement cannot be identified, although it obviously occurred shortly before Baldwin set out in November.

[4] Bāniyās, on the coast south of Laodicea. Bohemond and Daimbert were lingering in the vicinity after their frustrated attack on the Byzantines in Laodicea.

[5] Archbishop Daimbert of Pisa, a powerful figure in his city and in papal circles, had arrived on the coast of Syria in mid-August with a Pisan fleet said to number 120 vessels. Because the Pisans and the Byzantines were trade rivals, he had inflicted depredations on Byzantine possessions while sailing east and had readily joined Bohemond in an assault upon the Greeks of Laodicea. Now with a powerful fleet behind him, Daimbert was ready for further adventures. For a discussion of his career, see Hansen, *Das Problem eines Kirchenstaates*, 29–113. According to Hagenmeyer, the bishop from Apulia may have been from Ariano, and Baldwin's bishop may have been Benedict of Edessa (HF 327, notes 24, 25).

[6] This estimate is perhaps excessive.   [7] Probably sugar cane.

because of the taste of honey. However, this helped but little.

11. Verily for the love of God we endured these and many other hardships such as hunger, cold, and heavy rains. Many men, starving, ate horses, asses, and camels. Moreover we were very often tormented by excessive cold and frequent rainstorms, for the heat of the sun was not sufficient to enable us to have our sodden clothes dried when another rain would harass us for four or five days.

12. I saw many people who had no tents die from chills from the rains. I, Fulcher of Chartres, who was with them, saw many persons of both sexes and a great many beasts die one day because of these freezing rains. It would be too long to tell and too tedious to hear since no anxiety, no misery missed the people of God.

13. Often many Franks were killed by Saracens lurking around the narrow paths along the way or were captured when they went in search of food. You might have seen knights of noble birth who had become foot-soldiers, having lost their horses in one way or another. You might have seen also, because of the lack of beasts of burden, goats and wethers taken from the Saracens greatly fatigued by the baggage loaded upon them and with their backs made sore by the chafing of their packs.

14. Twice on the way, and no oftener, we had bread and grain, purchased at a very high price, to wit, at Tripoli and at Caesarea.[8] From this it is evident that one cannot acquire anything great without corresponding effort. It was indeed a momentous event when we arrived at Jerusalem.

15. With this visit to Jerusalem our protracted task was finished. When we gazed upon the much longed-for Holy of Holies we were filled with immense joy. Oh how often we recalled to mind the prophecy of David which said, "We shall worship in the place where His feet have stood" [Psalm. 131:7]. Truly we saw that prophecy fulfilled in us at that moment, however much it

[8] Tripoli and Caesarea were held by Arab governors nominally subject to the Fāṭimid Caliph of Cairo. They had no wish to side with the Turks, who were supporters of the Abbasid Caliph of Bagdad, and only hoped that the Franks would leave them alone as they had done earlier in the year (chap. xxv, 10, 11). Consult Gibb, "The Caliphate and the Arab States," in Setton (ed.), *Crusades*, I, 89–98.

likewise pertained to others. "Thither" indeed we went up, "the tribes, the tribes of the Lord to confess His name" [Psalm. 121:4] in His holy place.

16. On the day of our entrance into Jerusalem the receding sun, having completed its winter descent, resumed its ascending course.[9]

17. When we had visited the Lord's Sepulcher and His most glorious Temple and the other holy places, we went on the fourth day to Bethlehem to celebrate the Nativity of the Lord. We wanted to assist personally that night in the prayers at the manger where the revered Mother Mary gave birth to Jesus.

18. After we had finished the appropriate devotions that night and had celebrated the third mass, we returned to Jerusalem in the third hour of the day.[10]

19. Oh what a stench there was around the walls of the city, both within and without, from the rotting bodies of the Saracens slain by our comrades at the time of the capture of the city, lying wherever they had been hunted down!

20. After we and our beasts had been refreshed for a while with a much-needed rest, and after the Duke and the other chief men had chosen the above-mentioned Lord Daimbert to be Patriarch in the Church of the Holy Sepulcher,[11] we replenished supplies, loaded our beasts, and went down to the River Jordan.

21. Some of the army, the last to arrive, chose to remain in Jerusalem; others that had come first preferred to go with us. Duke Godfrey continued to rule the territory of Jerusalem with a firm hand as before.

[9] The winter solstice, December 21, 1099.
[10] 9 A.M., December 25.
[11] Arnulf of Chocques had been chosen patriarch on August 1, 1099, although Fulcher did not record the fact. Daimbert was elected because of his prestige, his Pisan fleet, and the support of Bohemond. The latter wanted a legal title to Antioch by enfeoffment from a Latin patriarch of Jerusalem against the claims of the Emperor Alexius. Daimbert seems to have been neither papal legate nor patriarch-designate but an ambitious prelate who saw his opportunity and took it. Arnulf, whose position was weak, had to step aside. Consult Yewdale, *Bohemond*, 91; Hansen, *Das Problem eines Kirchenstaates*, 34–41; Krey, "Urban's Crusade—Success or Failure," 241, 245; and Fink, "Foundation of the Latin States," in Setton (ed.), *Crusades*, I, 377–78.

22. On the third of the Ides of August, dismal day,
The venerable Urban, Pontiff of Rome, passed away.[12]

XXXIV

The Return of Duke Bohemond and Count Baldwin to Their Own Lands. 1. In the year 1100 of the Incarnation of our Lord, on the first day of the year,[1] we all assumed the palm, having cut the branches in Jericho as is customary. On the second day we began the return journey.

2. It pleased our princes to go through the city of Tiberias, which is situated beside a sea. This sea, formed from fresh water, is eighteen miles long and five miles wide.[2] From there we passed through Caesarea Philippi which is called Paneas in the Syrian tongue. It is situated at the foot of Mount Lebanon at a place where two springs emerge and give rise to the River Jordan. It flows through the Sea of Galilee on into the Dead Sea.

3. Moreover this lake, called Gennesaret, is forty stades in width and a hundred in length, according to Josephus. The river flows on through its channel and pours into the sea called the Dead Sea because it yields no living thing. This latter lake, also called Asphaltites,[3] is believed to be bottomless because such cities as Sodom and Gomorrah were submerged into its depths [Gen. 19:24–29].

4. I made conjectures quite carefully concerning those springs mentioned by St. Jerome, whose book on the Prophet Amos I have read.[4] I concluded that Dan was within the limits of the land of Judea where Paneas is now located. Because the tribe of Dan built a city there, the people called it Dan after their forefather [Jos.

---

[12] This date, August 11, 1099, is incorrect, for Urban died on July 29, 1099 (*HF* 334, note 56).

[1] Usually Fulcher began his years with December 25, but in this case he seems to have begun with January 1. Apparently after Christmas, 1099, the Franks rested, elected Daimbert patriarch, and proceeded to the Jordan, all of which took several days. See *HChr* 441.

[2] Lake Tiberias is 7 by 13 miles by modern measurements.

[3] The lake sometimes floats asphalt or bitumen to its surface (Joseph. *Bell. Jud.* iii. 506, 515; iv. 479).

[4] *Comment. 3 in Amos* 8:14.

19:47; Judic. 18:7, 26–29]. For this reason I think one spring was called Dan and the other Jor, adjacent to it.[5]

5. Then we came to a very strong city called Baalbek, founded by Solomon, surrounded by him with high walls, and by him named Tadmor. This city is distant two days' march from upper Syria, six days from Babylon the Great, and one day from the Euphrates. The Greeks called it Palmyra.[6] Springs and many wells abound there, but water was never found in the desert.

6. Here about four hundred Turkish warriors from Damascus met us. Because they had learned that we were weak and very tired from our labors, they thought that they might injure us in some way. If by chance Lord Baldwin had not been the one to guard our rear that day, which he did carefully and closely, many of our men would have been killed. Their bows and arrows failed them due to rain, for in those lands glue was used in making those weapons. Bohemond commanded the front line. And thus with God's help the enemy gained no advantage of us.[7]

7. Then we camped before the aforementioned town. On the very next day we approached nearer the sea and passed in front of the cities of Tortosa and Laodicea. At Laodicea we found Raymond, whom we had left there. Because food was scarce we could buy no supplies on which we could live. Therefore we hurried on without stopping until we arrived at Edessa.

XXXV

The Capture of Duke Bohemond. 1. Bohemond[1] arrived first at Antioch where he was joyfully received by his friends[2] and where for six months he ruled as before.

---

[5] This idea is from Jerome *Comment. 3 in Matth.* 16:13. Paneas is modern Banyas, twenty-eight miles north of Lake Tiberias.

[6] Fulcher is in error, for he certainly did not go through Tadmor (Palmyra), the famous oasis about 140 miles northeast of Damascus. He probably misinterpreted I Reg. 9:18 and II Paralip. 8:4, 6, which state that Solomon founded Tadmor and a place called Baalath, which was not Baalbek.

[7] These Turks were warriors of Shams-al Mulūk Dukak of Damascus.

[1] Fulcher is an original although meager authority for these events. The best discussion is by Runciman (*Crusades*, I, 319–22).

[2] *Ca.* the end of January, 1100 (*HChr* 446).

2. But in the following month of July when he with a few men approached the city called Melitene[3] (which was to be turned over to him by its patron, Gabriel[4] by name, as the result of the exchange of pledges of mutual friendship), a certain amir named Danisman[5] advanced against him with a large body of Turks. His purpose was to intercept Bohemond, who was marching unaware of him.

3. And not far from the aforesaid city those wicked people sprang upon Bohemond from ambush on all sides. Our men, not daring to fight because they were few, immediately dispersed and fled. The Turks killed many of them and took all their money. They even seized Bohemond and led him into captivity.[6]

4. When this calamity was reported by those who escaped, a great despair arose among our people. However, Duke Baldwin of Edessa collected as many Franks as he could from Edessa and Antioch and promptly sought the aforesaid enemy in the place where he heard that they were.

5. Bohemond on his part cut a lock of hair from his head and by this token, prearranged between them, besought Baldwin for the love of God to bring aid at once. Danisman, when he learned of this, feared their vengeance and dared not linger longer before Melitene, which he had surrounded in siege. Instead he gradually retired ahead of us and managed to return to his own lands. For this reason we were much disappointed, for we had pursued the Turks for three days[7] beyond Melitene in the urgent desire to give them battle.

6. When we came back Gabriel, mentioned above, turned over the city of Melitene to Baldwin. The latter, having established

---

[3] Modern Malatya, about ninety miles north of Urfa (Edessa).

[4] Gabriel (Khōril) was an Armenian prince who ruled Melitene until 1103. During his life he was the father-in-law of both Thoros of Edessa and Baldwin II of the same place.

[5] Malik-Ghāzī Gümüshtīgīn ibn-Dānishmend, a Turk who ruled much of the interior of Anatolia from Sivas (class. Sebastia) during 1097–1105.

[6] Ca. August 15, 1100 (HChr 495).

[7] August 27–30, 1100, according to an estimate of Hagenmeyer (HF 348, note 16).

bonds of friendship and introduced his guards into Melitene, returned to the city of Edessa. The men of Antioch, bereft of their lord, returned to their homes.[8]

XXXVI

The Death of King Godfrey.[1] 1. Just as Baldwin was enjoying his prosperity, behold a messenger from Jerusalem announced[2] to him that Duke Godfrey, his own brother, had died there on the fifteenth day before the Kalends of August.[3]

> 2. At the beginning of the year after the city was captured,
> Upon you, Duke Godfrey, as a crown of merit, the Lord
> Bestowed this rule. But not for long
> Did you exercise it when by Nature's decree you perished.
> When the rising sun entered the Sign of the glowing Leo
> You rejoicing ascended to Heaven borne by Michael the
>   Archangel.

HERE ENDS BOOK ONE

[8] These events probably occurred in early September, before Baldwin heard of the death of his brother Godfrey *ca.* September 12 (*HChr* 499).

[1] This chapter heading was not written by Fulcher because Godfrey never had the title of king.

[2] *Ca.* September 12, 1100 (xxxv, note 8).

[3] July 18, 1100 (*HF* 351, note 7).

BOOK II

†

HERE BEGINNETH THE SECOND BOOK OF THE DEEDS
OF KING BALDWIN THE FIRST

I

How Baldwin Came to Rule Jerusalem. 1. When it was announced to the Lord Baldwin that all of the people of Jerusalem[1] expected him to succeed as hereditary prince in the kingdom,[2] he grieved somewhat at the death of his brother but rejoiced more over his inheritance. After taking counsel he granted the land which he possessed to a certain Count Baldwin, his cousin.[3] Then after he had gathered together his little army, numbering nearly two hundred knights and seven hundred footmen, he began the journey to Jerusalem on the sixth day before the Nones of October.[4]

2. Some marveled that he dared march through so much hostile territory with so few men. And many were for this reason fearful and timorous and withdrew furtively from our company without our knowledge.

3. Moreover when the Turks and Saracens discovered that we were making this journey, they collected as many of their men as possible and came out in arms against us where they thought they could harm us the most.

[1] Not all welcomed Baldwin, for Fulcher himself reveals that Tancred and Patriarch Daimbert were opposed (chap. iii, 10, 14).
[2] Fulcher's term *regni* might be translated "kingdom" because by this time, late 1100, he certainly thought of it in that way.
[3] Baldwin of Le Bourg, probably a second cousin, who was the king's successor not only as count of Edessa (1100–18) but also as king in Jerusalem (1118–31).
[4] October 2, 1100.

4. At that time we went through Antioch;[5] then we went past Laodicea, Gibellum, Maraclea, Tortosa, and Archas, and reached Tripoli.[6]

5. At this time the king of Tripoli sent to Lord Baldwin's tent bread, wine, wild honey, i.e., sugar, and wethers for eating. He informed Baldwin that Ducath, King of the Damascans, and Ginahadoles, King of Aleppo, were waiting with many Turks, Saracens, and Arabs massed along the route through which they knew we would come. Although we did not believe this to be entirely true, we realized later that it was.[7]

II

The Ambush Prepared by the Turks and the Remarkable Military Talents of Count Baldwin. 1. Not far from the city of Beirut, about five miles, is an extremely narrow place in the public road next to the sea.[1] It could not possibly be avoided by us or anyone else wishing to go through if an enemy were provided with food and wanted to block the way. A hundred thousand soldiers could not cross through if a hundred or even sixty armed men resolutely held it against them. Therefore our enemies planned to cut us off

[5] *Ca.* October 8–12 (*HChr* 504). Albert of Aix states that the people of Antioch later offered Baldwin I the regency of this city in the absence of Bohemond but that Baldwin declined (VII, xxxi).

[6] *Ca.* October 21, 1100 (*HChr* 507).

[7] The "king" of Tripoli was the *qadi* (judge) Djalāl al-Mulk ibn-'Ammār (*HF* 356, note 13; M. Sobernheim, "Ibn 'Ammār," *Encyclopaedia of Islam*, II [1927], 360–61). "Ducath" was Shams-al-Mulūk Dukak, the ruler of Damascus, and "Ginahadoles" was Janāh-ad-Daulah, *Atabeg* of Homs but formerly of Aleppo. See Cahen, "The Turkish Invasion: The Selchükids," in Setton (ed.), *Crusades*, I, 164, 172.

[1] This narrow place is a famous seaside pass 9 1/2 miles north of Beirut. For more than three thousand years conquerors have passed through it, in many cases leaving inscriptions upon the rocks. It was necessary for Baldwin to force his way through a section of an old Roman road 1 1/2 meters wide and 500 paces long, cut in the face of a steep cliff. Fulcher's account of the Battle of Nahr al-Kalb (Dog River; class. Lycus) is the only one of an eyewitness; however, the narratives of Albert of Aix (VII, xxxiii–xxxiv) and William of Tyre (X, v–vi), both partly dependent upon Fulcher, are also of value. Consult Munro, *Kingdom of the Crusaders*, 3–4; and Robert Boulanger, *Lebanon*, trans. J. S. Hardman ("Hachette World Guides" under the direction of Francis Ambière; Paris: Hachette, 1965), 93–95.

there on all sides and slay us. At this juncture we came right up to that place.

2. When our advance guard came near the aforesaid narrow place, our men saw some of the Turks,[2] who had separated from the others, advancing and scouting against us. When our scouts perceived them, they judged that a much larger number were concealed in ambush behind them. As soon as they saw this they immediately notified Lord Baldwin through a messenger.

3. When he heard this he ordered his troops to be suitably drawn up in order of battle. With banners aloft we moved toward the enemy step by step. When we thought that the battle was about to begin we, with contrite and pure hearts, devoutly prayed that as we encountered the foe aid would come from Heaven. The enemy was met one by one by our front line, and a number were killed at once. Only four of our men lost their lives.

4. And when both sides ceased the struggle we took counsel. It was ordered that our camp be moved and pitched in the place where we had approached closer to the enemy. We did not want to seem afraid as we would if we left the place as if in flight. We pretended one thing, but we thought another. We feigned boldness, but we feared death. It was difficult to retreat but more difficult to advance. On all sides we were besieged by our enemies. On one side those in boats on the sea, on the other those from the cliffs relentlessly pressed upon us. That day nothing went well;[3] we had no rest, nor were our thirsty beasts even watered. Indeed I wished very much that I were in Chartres or Orléans, and so did others. All that night we languished outside our tents keeping very watchful.

5. At the dawn of day when Aurora had begun to dispel the darkness from the land we, after discussing whether we should try to hold out or just die, decided to collect our tents and retreat through the way by which we had come. Our beasts loaded with

[2] These Turks were sent by Dukak of Damascus, according to William of Tyre (X, v), and also by Janāḥ-ad-Daulah of Homs, according to Albert of Aix (VII, xxxiii).

[3] Apparently October 24, 1100 (HF 360, note 14).

our possessions were to precede us, driven by the men of our baggage-train. The knights following were to defend them from the Saracens rushing in.

6. In the full light of morning when those cursed people, the Turks, saw that we had turned back, they immediately came down from the heights to pursue us as fugitives. Some with boats in the sea, others behind us in the road by which we had come, others from the mountains and the hills, horsemen as well as footmen, drove us through the narrow passage like sheep to the fold. They wanted to cut us off from a certain level place[4] which is at the very narrow exit between the sea and the cliff so that they could easily stop and kill us. But it did not turn out as they had hoped.

7. For our men stood firm saying to each other, "If we can intercept in that open place those who are following us, perhaps with the help of God we can turn against them and by fighting properly tear away from them."

III

A Most Desperate Battle Against the Turks. 1. By this time the Turks were jumping out of the boats, beheading the unwary who were wandering near the water, and coming after us into the level place mentioned above, shooting many arrows. On all sides they taunted us, yelling at us and howling like dogs or wolves as they brandished their swords. But what shall I say further? There was nowhere to flee nor any hope of safety in staying there.

Neither was Solomon wise nor Sampson able to conquer.

2. But the God of great mercy and power, gazing down upon the Earth from Heaven, saw our humility and also the great peril into which we had fallen for love of Him and in His service. He was moved by that ever-present compassion with which, as is just, He always assists His own. He gave our men bravery of such quality that when they turned suddenly they put their enemies

---

[4] This level place was probably at the north end of the pass (*HF* 361, note 21; consult Boulanger, *Lebanon*, 94–95).

to flight down a three-branched road[1] with the result that the latter never had a thought of defending themselves. Some betook themselves to a precipice in the high rocky crags, some fled hastily elsewhere to a place of safety while still others were overtaken and put to the sword. You might have seen some frantically put out to sea in boats as if we could have snatched them with our hands. Others quickly fled on foot through the mountains and hills.

3. And so rejoicing and glorying in so great a victory, we went back to the men of our baggage-train who meanwhile had been guarding our loaded animals in the road. Therefore then we gave the greatest thanks to God, who had become our bountiful helper in a great and incalculable emergency.

4. Oh how admirable are the works of God! Oh how very miraculous and how worthy of remembrance! We had been conquered but from being conquered we became conquerors. But we ourselves did not conquer. How, therefore, did we not conquer? He conquered who alone is the omnipotent Creator of all, in compassion for His creatures aiding Him. "If God be for us, who can be against us?" [Rom. 8:31]. Truly for us, and with us, and in us was fulfilled what He said through the prophet to the Israelites, "If you shall have obeyed my laws I shall enrich you with this gift, that five of you shall succeed against one hundred of the enemy, and one hundred of you against ten thousand" [Levit. 26:8]. And because we endured much suffering day and night in His service, and trusted no one else, He wondrously broke the pride of the enemy. And because we served the Lord with devout hearts in tribulation, He hath had regard for our humility.

5. Then our tents were ordered unfolded and pitched. Many rich Turks taken alive were brought before Lord Baldwin together with the arms of the slain. We had horses with saddles and golden bits.

6. When the following night was over, in the morning,[2] just as if it had been carefully planned, we went back four miles along

1 I have been unable to identify this three-branched road. Consult Boulanger, *Lebanon*, 94–95.
2 October 26, 1100 (HF 365, note 20).

the road. When our prince had divided the aforesaid plunder there, we rested that night under olive trees in the thickets of an abandoned castle.[3]

7. The next morning, when the light was bright, Baldwin, with his accustomed bravery, took some of his knights and rode up to the before-mentioned narrow pass to find out whether the Saracens who had previously blocked our way were still there. When he found none, for all had fled when they heard of the dispersion that had taken place, he praised God and immediately caused a fire to be lit on the top of the mountain. This was a signal for those of us who had remained in our camp, in order that we might more promptly follow those who had gone on ahead. When we saw it we praised God and quickly followed. We found our way clear and finished the journey as desired.

8. That day we camped near the city of Beirut. When the amir of this city[4] found out that we were there, he sent boats of food daily to Lord Baldwin, a gesture born more from fear than from love.

9. Those of other cities before which we passed did likewise, such as Tyre and Sidon and also Acre, i.e., Ptolemais. They feigned friendship but had none at heart.

10. Tancred already held the city called Haifa, which the men going to Jerusalem had seized earlier this very year. But we did not enter it because Tancred was unfriendly toward Baldwin. Tancred himself was not there, but his citizens sold us bread and wine outside the city, for they considered us brothers and wished to see us.[5]

11. We passed through Caesarea in Palestine and the strong-

[3] This place was Junia (Juniye), according to William of Tyre (X, vi). It is three miles north of Nahr al-Kalb. See Boulanger, Lebanon, 93 and 95.
[4] I have been unable to identify this amir.
[5] Baldwin arrived at the gates of Haifa, held by the men of Tancred, ca. October 30, 1100 (HChr 510). Tancred, who held a large fief around Tiberias, had disliked Baldwin since the latter ejected him from Tarsus in 1097. He and Patriarch Daimbert feared that the succession of Baldwin in Jerusalem would destroy the position of each of them, which actually happened, and they were therefore plotting against Baldwin. See Nicholson, Tancred, 42–48, 112–21; and Hansen, Das Problem eines Kirchenstaates, 57–87.

hold of Arsuth, which we then in ignorance thought was Azotus.[6] But it is not, because Azotus was one of the five cities of the Philistines [I Sam. 6:17] and is between Joppa and Ascalon. It is now reduced to a hamlet.

12. After passing Antipatrida we came at length to the maritime city of Joppa, which is in the territory of Dan. Here at this time our Franks gladly received Lord Baldwin as their king. We did not delay there but hurried on to Jerusalem.

13. When we approached the city[7] everyone came out to meet Baldwin, clergy as well as laity, Greeks also and Syrians, with crosses and candles. They conducted him to the Church of the Holy Sepulcher with great joy and honor, and praising God in ringing voices.

14. Patriarch Daimbert was not present at this gathering because he was under accusation by certain men around Baldwin and because as a consequence bad feeling had arisen between them. The greater part of the clergy even then held Daimbert in hatred. For this reason he resided on Mount Zion, deprived of his seat, and he was there until the sin of envy was expiated.[8]

15. When we had relaxed from our labors in needed rest at Jerusalem for six days and when the king had disposed of some of his affairs, we prepared to go on a new expedition. It is necessary that all who have enemies (I speak after the fashion of men) should press them on all sides incessantly and strenuously until they conquer them by tiring them in battle, or by force, or compel them to make peace.

IV

The Expedition of Baldwin into Arabia. 1. Therefore Lord Baldwin, having collected his men,[1] set out for Ascalon, traveling

---

[6] Arsuf, here miscalled Arsuth, is ten miles north of Joppa, and Azotus (class. Ashdod) is twenty-one miles south of Joppa, toward Ascalon. See HF 367, note 33.

[7] Ca. November 9, 1100 (HChr 514).

[8] Fulcher, chaplain of Baldwin, has the point of view of his master. Archbishop William of Tyre defends Patriarch Daimbert (X, vii).

[1] According to Albert of Aix, Baldwin started with 150 knights and 500 footmen (VII, xxxviii).

through Azotus, which is between Joppa and Ascalon and which was one of the five cities of the Philistines.[2] We had Acharon on our right near Jamnia, which is on the sea.[3] Moreover when we had come before Ascalon those who came out against us were vehemently driven back to the walls. Because it was useless for us to proceed farther, we returned to our tents, already pitched, to lodge there.

2. The following day[4] we went farther out into the country where we found food for ourselves and our beasts in prosperous areas and where also we devastated the land of our enemies. Then proceeding farther, we found villas where the Saracen inhabitants had hidden themselves and their beasts and other possessions from us in caverns. When we were unable to draw out any of them, we set fires near the entrances to the caverns. Soon on account of the intolerable smoke and heat they came out to us one after the other.

3. There were among them robbers who were accustomed to lurk between Ramla and Jerusalem and to kill our Christians. When we were told by some Syrian Christians who were kept in concealment among them that these malefactors were of this type, they were beheaded as soon as they came out of the cave. We spared these Syrians and their wives. Indeed we killed nearly a hundred Saracens.

4. And after we had eaten and consumed everything we found there, grain as well as livestock, and could find nothing more of use to us, we conferred with certain natives of the country who had formerly been Saracens but had newly become Christians.

---

[2] This chapter and the next tell of Baldwin's trip to the outskirts of the Egyptian base at Ascalon and to the area west and south of the Dead Sea, *ca.* November 15–December 21, 1100 (*HChr* 516). His purpose was to probe the defenses of Ascalon, explore the area through which the Cairo-Damascus caravans passed to avoid the Franks, and give Daimbert time to recognize the necessity of coming to terms with a new rival, Baldwin. The whole story illustrates Baldwin's prompt energy after coming to Jerusalem.

[3] Fulcher indicates that Baldwin swung south of Acharon. Jamnia (Jabneel) was later famous as the Frankish lordship of Ibelin.

[4] *Ca.* November 24, 1100 (*HF* 372, note 7).

We discussed what they knew of cultivated and desert areas far and wide and decided to go into Arabia.

5. And crossing the mountainous region near the sepulchers of the Patriarchs Abraham, Isaac, and Jacob, as well as of Sarah and Rebecca, where their bodies were gloriously buried, we came to a valley about fourteen miles from the city of Jerusalem.[5] Here the wicked cities of Sodom and Gomorrah were overthrown by the judgment of God [Gen. 19:24–25].

V

The Dead Sea. 1. There is there a great lake which is called the Dead Sea because no living thing is born in it.[1] It extends five hundred eighty stades in length and one hundred fifty in width.[2] It is so salty that no beast or bird of any kind whatsoever can drink from it. This I, Fulcher, learned by experience when I dismounted from my mule into the water and took a drink with my hand, testing it by the taste and finding it to be more bitter than hellebore.

2. From the north this lake receives the waters of the River Jordan, but in the south it has no outlet. No river has its source in it. Near this lake is a great and high salt mountain which is like natural salt rock, not, however, throughout but only in certain spots where it is very much like ice.[3] Moreover, no one can easily

[5] Baldwin's force crossed the Judean hills at Hebron where there is a walled enclosure that was called by the Franks the Castle of St. Abraham. Within it is a mosque over the Cave of Machpelah, inside of which Abraham, Isaac, Jacob, and their wives are believed to be entombed. From Hebron, Baldwin's troop made a dramatic descent of about 4,300 feet in seventeen miles to the shore of the Dead Sea. This was at Engeddi, according to William of Tyre (X, viii), which is twenty-three miles southeast of Jerusalem. However, the north end of the Dead Sea is about fourteen miles from Jerusalem.

[1] Fulcher's description of the area south of the Dead Sea is very interesting for three reasons. He is an eyewitness, he is quite accurate although he uses Joseph. *Bell. Jud.* iv. 476 ff. in places, and, finally, he gives an insight into Baldwin's energy in promptly exploring the southern limits of the petty state, an area not visited by Godfrey.

[2] Joseph. *Bell. Jud.* iv. 482.

[3] This probably refers to the Jabal Usdum, a lacustrine upthrust of saline deposits southwest of the Dead Sea. Consult *HF* 377, note 6; and Karl Baedeker,

submerge himself into the waters of this lake, even if one tries.[4]

3. I conjecture that this lake is thus so very salty for two reasons: first because it receives the salt of the mountain which is incessantly washed by the waves of the shore, and second it receives the rains descending from this mountain. Or perhaps the depth of the lake is so great that the Great Sea,[5] which is saline, flows below ground unseen into this lake.

4. Going around the lake on the south side, we found a village[6] most favorably situated and abounding in the fruits of the palm which they call "dates" and which we ate all day for their pleasant taste. We found little else there.

5. The Saracen inhabitants of the place had all fled when they heard rumors of us, all except some who were blacker than soot. These we left there, despising them as if they were no more than sea-weed.

6. I saw there among the trees some bearing a fruit. I gathered some of it wishing to know what it was. When I broke its shell I found a black powder inside, and from it a thin smoke came forth.[7]

7. Then we entered the mountains of Arabia and spent the following night in caverns there. The next morning[8] when we had ascended the mountains we found villages right away. But they were void of anything useful because the inhabitants, having heard of our approach, had hid themselves together with their possessions in a cavern of the earth. For this reason we profited little there.

8. So we promptly extended our journey into other areas with our guides always ahead of us. Then we found a valley very rich

---

Palestine and Syria (5th ed.; Leipzig: Karl Baedeker; London: T. Fisher Unwin; New York: Charles Scribner's Sons, 1912), 174.

[4] Cf. Joseph. *Bell. Jud.* iv. 476.

[5] The Mediterranean. See Prologue, 4; II, lvii, 2; III, xxxiv, 15.

[6] Fulcher identified this village as Segor (Zoar) in his first redaction (*HF* 378, note 2), perhaps from Joseph. *Bell. Jud.* iv. 482.

[7] Apples of Sodom or Dead Sea apples, mentioned in Joseph. *Bell. Jud.* iv. 484. See Baedeker, *Palestine and Syria*, 171 and cf. 129.

[8] *Ca.* November 25, 1100 (*HF* 380, note 17).

in the fruits of the earth, indeed the very one in which the devout Moses, instructed by God, twice struck the rock from which a fountain of living water flowed [Num. 20:11].[9] This fountain flows no less vigorously today than then, to such a degree that the millers of the region use the current of the stream for grinding. I watered my horses in this brook.

9. Furthermore we found at the top of the mountain the Monastery of St. Aaron where Moses and Aaron were wont to speak with God [Num. 20:7–8, 12, 23–26].[10] We rejoiced very much to behold a place so holy and to us unknown. But because the land outside that valley was desert and uncultivated, we did not care to go farther.

10. For three days we had luxurious ease in that valley which was so rich in everything. We also refreshed our animals with food. After our beasts were loaded with the necessary provisions, the king's trumpet sounded about the second hour of the fourth day, commanding us to begin the return journey.[11]

11. We returned therefore near Lake Asphaltites, as we had come, and past the graves of the patriarchs mentioned above, then through Bethlehem and through the place where Rachel is buried.[12]

12. We arrived safe at Jerusalem on the day of the winter solstice.[13] When the regalia were prepared which are suitable for the coronation of a king, and Daimbert had made his peace with the Lord Baldwin and with several of the canons of the Holy Sepulcher, because sensible men had labored to this end, their contention ceased.[14]

[9] Hagenmeyer identifies this valley as the Wādī Mūsâ (west of Petra and about fifty miles south of the Dead Sea) and the spring as the 'Ain Mūsâ (HF 380, note 20). Consult Baedeker, *Palestine and Syria*, 175, 178, 179, and cf. 'Ain Mūsâ, 165.

[10] Fulcher refers to the Jabal Harun (Mount Hor), containing a tomb dedicated to Aaron (Baedeker, *Palestine and Syria*, 186).

[11] This date cannot be determined, but it must have been in the first part of December, 1100. See HF 383, note 25.

[12] Lake Asphaltites was the Dead Sea (I, xxxiv, 3). The tomb of Rachel is a mile north of the Church of the Nativity in Bethlehem.

[13] December 21, 1100.

[14] We see that Patriarch Daimbert, who was hostile to Baldwin (chap. iii, 14),

VI

The Accession of King Baldwin and the Smallness of His King-dom. 1. In the year 1101 after the Incarnation of our Lord, and on the anniversary of His Nativity, Baldwin was ceremoniously appointed and crowned king by the above-mentioned patriarch in the presence of the other bishops, the priests, and the people in the Basilica of the Blessed Mary at Bethlehem.[1] This had not been done for his brother and predecessor because Godfrey had not wished it,[2] and there were others who did not approve of it.[3] Still, upon wiser consideration they decided that it should be done.

2. "Why should it be objected," they said, "since Christ our Lord was dishonored by abuse as a criminal and crowned with thorns in Jerusalem, and since He willingly gave Himself unto death for us? Besides, this crown was not, in the minds of the Jews, an emblem of honor and kingly dignity, but rather of igno-miny and disgrace. But what those murderers did as an insult to Him was by the grace of God turned to our salvation and glory.

3. "Moreover a king is not made king against the mandate of God, for when he is chosen rightly and according to God's will he is sanctified and consecrated with a lawful blessing. Anyone who receives that kingly power together with a golden crown takes upon himself at the same time the honorable duty of rendering

---

had had time to agree to a compromise. Hansen conjectures that Fulcher may have been one of the "sensible men" who intervened (*Das Problem eines Kirchen-staates,* 82, note 2).

[1] The coronation was held not at Jerusalem but at Bethlehem because Patriarch Daimbert regarded himself as lord of Jerusalem, an ecclesiastical state. He was therefore unwilling to crown Baldwin king in the capital city. In the spring of 1100 Daimbert had forced Godfrey to cede to him title to Jerusalem and Joppa and had expected Godfrey to conquer Cairo or some other possession for himself. Therefore, we may be sure that he expected Baldwin to be king elsewhere, but not in Jerusalem, a hope Baldwin was to ignore. See William of Tyre, IX, xvi; and letter of Daimbert to Bohemond, end of August, 1100, as quoted, *ibid.,* X, iv. For discussion, see Hansen, *Das Problem eines Kirchenstaates,* 83–85; and Jean Richard, *Le royaume latin de Jérusalem* (Paris: Presses Universitaires de France, 1953), 32.

[2] Godfrey was chosen "prince of the realm" (I, xxx, 1).

[3] Tancred, holding the area of Tiberias and Haifa, was also unwilling to recog-nize Baldwin as king and suzerain (Albert of Aix, VII, xliv).

justice. To him certainly as to the bishop in regard to the episcopate can this be fitly applied: 'He desires to do good work who
desires to rule, but if he does not rule justly, he is not a true king.' "

4. In the beginning of his reign Baldwin as yet possessed few
cities and people.[4] Through that same winter he stoutly protected
his kingdom from enemies on all sides. And because they found
out that he was a very skillful fighter, although he had few men,
they did not dare to attack him. If he had had a greater force
he would have met the enemy gladly.

5. Up to that time the land route was completely blocked to
our pilgrims. Meanwhile they, French as well as English, or
Italians and Venetians, came by sea as far as Joppa. At first we
had no other port. These pilgrims came very timidly in single
ships, or in squadrons of three or four, through the midst of hostile
pirates and past the ports of the Saracens, with the Lord showing
the way.

6. When we saw that they had come from our own countries
in the West, we promptly and joyfully met them as if they were
saints. From them each of us anxiously inquired concerning his
homeland and his loved ones. The new arrivals told us all that
they knew. When we heard good news we rejoiced; when they
told of misfortune we were saddened. They came on to Jerusalem;
they visited the Holy of Holies, for which purpose they had come.

7. Following that, some remained in the Holy Land, and
others went back to their native countries. For this reason the
land of Jerusalem remained depopulated. There were not enough
people to defend it from the Saracens if only the latter dared
attack us.

8. But why did they not dare? Why did so many people and
so many kingdoms fear to attack our little kingdom and our humble people? Why did they not gather from Egypt, from Persia,
from Mesopotamia, and from Syria at least a hundred times a
hundred thousand fighters to advance courageously against us,
their enemies? Why did they not, as innumerable locusts in a little

---

[4] Baldwin was in possession of Jerusalem, Bethlehem, and Joppa. The rest of
this chapter is an eloquent statement of Baldwin's feeble position.

field, so completely devour and destroy us that no further mention could be made of us in a land that had been ours from time immemorial?

9. For we did not at that time have more than three hundred knights and as many footmen to defend Jerusalem, Joppa, Ramla, and also the stronghold of Haifa. We scarcely dared to assemble our knights when we wished to plan some feat against our enemies. We feared that in the meantime they would do some damage against our deserted fortifications.

10. Truly it is manifest to all that it was a wonderful miracle that we lived among so many thousands of thousands and as their conquerors made some of them our tributaries and ruined others by plundering them and making them captives. But whence came this virtue? Whence this power? Truly from Him whose name is the Almighty, who, not unmindful of His people laboring in His name, in His mercy aids in their tribulations those who trust in Him alone. Moreover God promises to reward with everlasting glory in the life to come those whom He sometimes makes happy with very little temporal reward.

11. Oh time so worthy to be remembered! Often indeed we were sad when we could get no aid from our friends across the sea. We feared lest our enemies, learning how few we were, would sometime rush down upon us from all sides in a sudden attack when none but God could help us.

12. We were in need of nothing if only men and horses did not fail us. The men who came by sea to Jerusalem could not bring horses with them, and no one came to us by land. The people of Antioch were not able to help us, nor we them.[5]

VII

The Substitution of Tancred at Antioch. 1. Then it happened, in the month of March,[1] that Tancred turned over to King Bald-

[5] Trained horses, *destriers*, were needed for the knights. Antioch was more than three hundred miles away with hostile territory between it and Jerusalem. Bohemond, its prince, was a captive of Malik-Ghāzī Gümüshtīgīn ibn-Dānishmend of Sebastia (I, xxxv, 2).
[1] *Ca.* March 9, 1101 (*HChr* 542).

win Haifa, a city which he possessed, and Tiberias, and with his men marched to Antioch. The people of Antioch had sent representatives to him saying, "Do not delay, but come to us and rule us, and possess the city of Antioch and the land subject to it until the Lord Bohemond, our master and yours, shall come forth from captivity. For you are his kin, a prudent and excellent soldier, and more powerful than we are. You are better able to hold this our land than we. If sometime Lord Bohemond shall return then what is right shall be done." This was requested, and it was so done.[2]

VIII

The Siege of the Fortress of Arsuf and Its Capture. 1. During that same winter season a fleet of beaked Genoese and Italian ships had stayed at the port of Laodicea. In the spring when the men saw that the weather was calm and suitable for navigation they sailed as far as Joppa with a favoring wind. When they reached port they were gladly received by the king. Because it was near Easter and since it was customary for all who could to celebrate this solemn occasion, they beached their ships and went up to Jerusalem with the king.[1]

2. On Easter Sabbath everyone was much disturbed because the Holy Fire failed to appear at the Sepulcher of the Lord.[2] When the Easter solemnity was over, the king went back to

[2] Albert of Aix states that Tancred released his lands with the right of resumption within a year and three months if necessary and left with all of his knights and five hundred infantry (VII, xlv; see Nicholson, *Tancred*, 120–21, for discussion).

[1] Beaked or rostrated ships were war galleys (William of Tyre, X, xxviii). They usually had a superstructure on the bow, a ram, and oar propulsion. The nucleus of this fleet consisted of the twenty-six or twenty-eight galleys and the four to six (freight) ships that Caffaro the Genoese, an eyewitness, says left Genoa on August 1, 1100, for Laodicea where it wintered (*De liberatione civitatum orientis*, in *RHC, Occ.*, V [Paris: Imprimerie Nationale, 1895], 58, 60; Caffaro, *Annales Genuenses*, in L. A. Muratori [ed.], *Rerum italicarum scriptores*, VI [Mediolani: Ex typographia Societatis palatinae in regia curia, 1725], col. 248, also quoted in *RHC, Occ.*, V, 59, note f). The fleet left Laodicea *ca.* March 6, 1101, and arrived at Joppa on April 16; the men reached Jerusalem on April 18 (*HChr* 539, 552, and 555).

[2] The Holy Fire, which usually appeared in the Church of the Holy Sepulcher on the day before Easter, and which is still a feature of the Easter celebrations

Joppa[3] and made a convention with the consuls of the above-mentioned fleet. It was agreed that as long as the Genoese cared to stay in the Holy Land for the love of God, if with His consent and assistance they and the king could take any of the cities of the Saracens, they should have in common a third part of the money taken from the enemy with no injury done to the Genoese, and the king should have the first and second parts. Moreover they [the Genoese] should possess by perpetual and hereditary right a section in such a city captured in this way.[4]

3. When this had been agreed under oaths mutually exchanged they immediately besieged by land and sea the fortified place which is called Arsuf. But when the Saracen inhabitants realized that they could in no way defend themselves against the Christians, they shrewdly negotiated with the king and on the third day surrendered to him. Moreover they departed with all of their money. For those who set out in utmost dejection for Ascalon the king gave safe conduct.[5]

4. Then we joyfully gave thanks to God because we had been able to take this fortified place, so dangerous to us, without losing any lives.

5. This fortification, built by Solomon, was quite vexatious to us.[6] It had been besieged by Duke Godfrey the year before but had not been taken. Its inhabitants had frequently killed many of our people and rendered us miserable.

6. During the siege the Franks in hand-to-hand conflict had

---

there, did not appear on schedule in 1101, causing great consternation. Fulcher said little, perhaps feeling skeptical, but other writers said much. Consult HF 395, note 5.

[3] Ca. April 25, 1101 (HChr 559).

[4] In modern terms, the Genoese were to obtain a free port with extraterritorial rights for themselves. They offered naval aid, which Baldwin needed, for such privileges. This was to be a pattern for the future.

[5] The surrender was on April 29, 1101 (HChr 563). Baldwin circumvented his Genoese allies because he feared they would sack the town. He was statesman enough to want a prosperous and undamaged town and good commercial relations between it and the Arabs of Ascalon and those east of the Jordan.

[6] It is not known where Fulcher got the story that Solomon built the fortifications of Arsuf (HF 397, note 12).

seized the battlements of the wall. Then, as luck would have it, a wooden tower which they had attached to the wall from the outside had collapsed into pieces because of the large number of men climbing up within it. Nearly a hundred Franks who fell from it were desperately wounded.

7. The Saracens kept some of the captured Franks right there, crucifying them in the sight of all and shooting them with arrows. Some they killed in this way, and others they kept alive in loathsome confinement.[7]

IX

How the City of Caesarea Was Captured. 1. The king after garrisoning Arsuf with his own men, as was necessary, immediately marched against Caesarea in Palestine and surrounded it by siege. However, because the wall was very strong the city could not be taken quickly.

2. Therefore he ordered *petrariae* to be made and also a very high wooden tower to be constructed from the masts and oars of ships.[1] Our carpenters made the tower twenty cubits higher, I estimate, than the wall. The purpose was to enable our soldiers, when the tower should have been brought up to the wall, to bombard the enemy with stones and arrows. With the Saracens driven from the wall in this way our men might have free ingress into the city and take it.

3. But after the Franks had maintained the siege for fifteen days and had somewhat damaged the upper defenses of the wall with their *petrariae*, their righteous zeal would brook no further delay. So on a certain Friday they suddenly stormed the city with shield and spear, not using the wooden tower, as yet uncompleted, nor supplementary aids.[2]

4. The Saracens defended themselves as stoutly as they could,

[7] Fulcher refers to the unsuccessful siege of Arsuf conducted by Godfrey from October to December in 1099 (Albert of Aix, VII, i–vi; *HChr* 431).

[1] Very probably, most of the masts and oars of the Genoese ships.

[2] The siege lasted from May 2 to Friday, May 17, 1101 (*HChr* 564, 567).

encouraging each other. However, the Franks, whose Lord was God, quickly erected ladders, which they had prepared for this purpose, and ascended to the top of the wall. Then they slew with their swords everyone whom they encountered.

5. The Saracens, seeing that our men were so fierce and that the city was already taken by them, fled precipitately to wherever they thought they might preserve their lives a little longer. But they were unable to hide anywhere and instead were slain in a death that was well deserved.[3]

6. Very few of the male sex were left alive. But a great many of the women were spared because they could always be used to turn the hand mills. When the Franks captured the women they bought and sold them, the comely and the ugly, among themselves, and the men also.

7. The king spared the amir of the city and the bishop, which the Saracens called the *archadius*.[4] He did this for a ransom rather than for love. How much property of various kinds was found there it is impossible to say, but many of our men who had been poor became rich.[5]

8. I saw a great many of the Saracens who were killed there put in a pile and burned. The fetid odor of their bodies bothered us greatly. These wretches were burned for the sake of finding the bezants which some had swallowed and others had hidden in their mouths next to the gums, not wishing the Franks to get anything that belonged to them.

9. Hence it sometimes happened when one of our men struck the neck of some Saracen with his fist that from ten to sixteen bezants would be ejected from the mouth. The women also

---

[3] It is apparent that the rank and file among the Christians did not want Baldwin to deny them their plunder as he had after the fall of Arsuf.

[4] This refers to the *qadi*, a judge who sometimes exercised the functions of mayor. He dispensed Islamic law.

[5] Caffaro gives an insight into the wealth of this single Arab seaport. He says that after the Genoese paid off their leaders and ship captains, enough booty was left to give forty-eight *solidi* of Poitou and two pounds of pepper (spices) to each of eight thousand men (*De liberatione civitatum orientis*, RHC, Occ., V, 65). And the share of the Genoese was only one third of the total.

shamelessly hid bezants within themselves in a way that was wicked and which is more shameful for me to tell.[6]

10. It was the year eleven hundred plus one
When we took Caesarea with scaling ladders,
When we took the Tower of Straton, the city so named.[7]

X

How an Archbishop Was Chosen in Caesarea. 1. After we together with the Genoese had done as we pleased with Caesarea and with everything that we found in it, we installed there an archbishop whom we had chosen jointly.[1] Then we left a few men to guard the city and hastened to go to the city of Ramla, which is near Lydda. For twenty-four days we expected an attack to be made against us by the men of Ascalon and Babylon, who were assembled there for that purpose.[2]

2. Because we were few in number we did not dare to go against them. We feared that while we were attacking them at Ascalon they would lure us between their walls and ramparts by drawing back repeatedly and, having trapped us, would kill us. For this reason they did not take the offensive against us, thinking that things would happen in this way.

3. Perceiving their wiliness we shrewdly studied their tactic until at length we saw through their trickery.[3] Then, their spirits wilted from fear, they utterly gave up any thought of attacking

---

[6] Cf. I, xxviii, 1; and *HG* xxxiii, 8.

[7] Caesarea was also called the Tower of Straton (I, xxv, 11).

[1] The new archbishop was a cleric named Baldwin, said by Guibert of Nogent to have branded his forehead with the sign of the Cross and to have netted many gifts from the pious as a result (*RHC, Occ.,* IV, 182–83, 251). Perhaps Fulcher disdained to mention him for this reason (consult *HF* 405, note 4). The time was May 18–23, 1101 (*HChr* 568).

[2] May 24–June 17 (*HChr* 570 and 577).

[3] Around the verb *calleo* and its derivatives in the clause "Quorum calliditate comperta, tamdiu calliditatem eorum callidius callentes calluimus," Fulcher constructed a word play that must have given him much satisfaction. We may get its flavor, atrocious in English, if we use the verb "can" in its medieval sense of "to know" or "to understand." Thus, the translation might be, "Perceiving their canniness we, cannily canning, at length canned their canniness."

us. For this reason many of them became impatient of delay and, pressed by want, deserted their army.

4. When we learned of this we returned to Joppa, giving thanks to God that He had thus delivered us from their attack.[4]

XI

A Very Bloody Battle Between the Christians and the Turks, in Which the Christians Were the Victors. 1. But after we had waited quietly for seventy days with our ears ever intent upon our adversaries, the king was informed that they were moving upon us again with hostile intent and were now prepared to attack us.[1]

2. The king when he heard this promptly collected his men from Jerusalem, Tiberias, Caesarea, and Haifa.[2] Because it was urgent that we should have knights, the king ordered each one who could to make a knight of his squire. In this way our knights numbered about two hundred sixty and our footmen about nine hundred. At the same time eleven thousand knights and twenty-one thousand footmen opposed us.[3]

3. We knew this but because we had God with us we did not fear to go against them. We trusted in neither our arms nor numbers but placed our hope entirely in the Lord God. Our courage was great, but it was not audacity; rather it was faith and love.

---

[4] June 17, 1101 (*HChr* 577).

[1] The watching period occurred from *ca.* June 17–August 25, 1101 (*HF* 408, note 2). In this and the next two chapters Fulcher gives a graphic eyewitness account of King Baldwin's defeat of a formidable Egyptian invasion near Ramla on September 7–8, 1101. He shows much of Baldwin's character, his vigilance and energy, which gave the enemies no rest, his tactical skill, his eloquence, and even something of his sharp tongue. The reference in the chapter title to the Turks rather than to the Saracens or Arabs is an error by a later scribe. Ibn-al-Qalānisī states that the Egyptian army gathered at Ascalon in the beginning of Ramadan, A.H. 494 (June 30, 1101) (*The Damascus Chronicle*, 53).

[2] Ekkehard of Aura listed Baldwin's towns as Jerusalem, Caesarea, Nicopolis, Mount Tabor, Hebron, and Arsuf (*RHC, Occ.*, V, 33).

[3] Fulcher's estimate of Frankish strength is modest and probably accurate, but his view of Egyptian strength is as rhetorical as Ibn-al-Qalānisī's estimate of Frankish numbers—a thousand knights and ten thousand footmen (*The Damascus Chronicle*, 53).

We earnestly prepared to die for love of Him who mercifully deigned to die for us.

We went forth bravely prepared for battle or death.

4. The king had the wood of the True Cross carried forth, which gave us comfort. One day we set out from Joppa, and on the next we fought against our enemies.[4]

5. When we had advanced near to them, they had likewise come close to us, but we did not realize it. When we perceived their scouts from our lookout, we realized at once that the rest of them were following. When the king with some of his men went on ahead, he saw from a distance their vast camp shimmering in the plain. Having seen this, he at once put spurs to his horse and rode back to us in the rear, telling all that he had seen.

6. When we discovered that there would be a battle, we began to rejoice because we were eager for one. If our enemies would not advance against us, then certainly we would go against them. It would be better for us to fight in the open plain because when with God's help our foes should be defeated they would have farther to flee and would suffer more loss in flight than if we attacked them near their walls.

7. Then the king ordered us to take arms, and when all had done so he drew us up in proper battle array. In this way we committed ourselves trustingly into the hands of God and rode out against our enemies. A certain abbot, chosen by the king, carried the Lord's Cross in the sight of all.[5]

8. Then the king piously addressed his soldiers in these words: "Come then, soldiers of Christ, be of good cheer and fear nothing! Conduct yourselves manfully and ye shall be mighty in this battle. Fight, I beseech you, for the salvation of your souls; exalt everywhere the name of Christ whom these degenerate ones always vigorously revile and reproach, believing in neither His Nativity nor Resurrection. If you should be slain here, you will surely be

[4] September 6–7, 1101 (*HChr* 604, 605), but after September 27, according to Ibn-al-Qalānisī, who, however, was not present (*The Damascus Chronicle*, 53).

[5] Gerhard, perhaps from Schaffhausen. See Ekkehard, *RHC, Occ.*, V, 35, and note b; Albert of Aix, VII, lxvi; and *HF* 411, note 18.

among the blessed. Already the gate of the Kingdom of Heaven is open to you. If you survive as victors you will shine in glory among all Christians. If, however, you wish to flee remember that France is indeed a long distance away."

9. When he had spoken all agreed with him.

They hastened to the fray, a long delay was unendurable to all;
Each was now planning whom he would smite or cast down.

10. All at once those despicable people charged us viciously from the right and the left. Our men, although they were very few and divided into six lines[6] of battle, dashed into the surging cohorts of the enemy like fowlers into a mass of birds, shouting "God help us!" The number of the foe was so great and they swarmed over us so quickly that hardly anyone could see or recognize anyone else.

11. Already they had repelled and overwhelmed our two front lines, but the king seeing this brought aid from the rear with the greatest dispatch. When he saw that the strength of the enemy was greater, he rode up at full speed with his own squadron and vigorously opposed the attack of the infidels. Brandishing his lance, from which flew a white banner, in the face of their superior might, he ran through an Arab opposite him. The flag remained in the Arab's belly when he was knocked to the ground from his horse.[7] But Baldwin pulled out his lance as I, standing near, witnessed, and he at once carried it ready to slay others.

12. On our side and on the other the battle was bravely fought. Indeed in the short space of an hour you could see many riderless horses on both sides. We saw the ground thickly covered with shields and bucklers, daggers and quivers, bows and arrows, with Saracens and Ethiopians, either dead or mortally wounded, with Franks too, but not as many.

13. There was present with us the Cross of the Savior, mighty against the enemies of Christ. Against it by the grace of God the

---

[6] Five corps, according to Albert (VII, lxv).

[7] Baldwin's victim may have been the Egyptian commander himself, Sa'd ad-Daulah al-Qawāmisī, according to Ibn-al-Qalānisī (*The Damascus Chronicle*, 53–54; cf. Albert of Aix, VII, lxviii).

pomp of the pagans could not prevail. As if confounded by the presence of the Cross not only did they cease from attacking us but, struck with shame, all thought of precipitate flight. Those who had swift horses thus escaped death.

14. It would have been tiresome to collect all the shields, missiles, bows, and arrows which the fugitives threw to the ground. It would have been impossible for anyone, even if he wished, to count the lifeless bodies which lay there. It is said, however, that five thousand of their knights and footmen were killed there. Even the leader of the Babylonian army who led it to battle was killed with the others. We lost eighty of our knights, and more of the footmen.

15. On that day the king conducted himself most valiantly; he was the greatest source of comfort to us and was a dauntless fighter. His soldiers too, although they were few, were most brave. The battle was not long in doubt. Our enemies fled very quickly, and we pursued them at once.

XII

How Many Christians Perished There! 1. Oh war, hateful to the innocent and horrible to the spectators! War is not beautiful although it is thus called by antiphrasis.[1] I saw the battle, I wavered in my mind, I feared to be struck. All rushed to arms as if they did not fear death. There is dire calamity where love is lacking. The din arising from the mutual exchange of blows was excessive. One struck, his enemy fell. The one knew no pity, the other asked none. One lost a hand, the other an eye. Human understanding recoils when it sees such misery.[2]

2. Yet wonderful to relate, our army conquered in the van while it was defeated in the rear. There the Christians fell; in the front they vanquished the Saracens. We pursued them as far as Ascalon while some of them, having slain many of our men, rode

[1] The author plays upon the word *bellum*, using it first to mean "war," then to mean "beautiful."

[2] Fulcher, usually inclined to rejoice at the slaughter of Muslims, is here horrified by the carnage on each side.

off at once to Joppa. Thus on that day no one knew the outcome of the battle.

3. When the king and his men, by slaughter and pursuit, had cleared the field of the Saracens, he ordered us to spend the night in the tents which the fugitives had left. Thus it was ordered, and thus it was done.

4.   On the seventh day of the Ides of September[3]
       We fought this battle so worthy to remember,
       In which divine grace aided the Franks.

XIII

The Varying Fortunes of this Battle.   1. On the following day we gathered in the tent of the king and heard the mass of the Nativity of the Blessed Virgin Mary, to which event the day was sacred. Then we loaded up our beasts with the spoil of our enemies such as bread, grain, and flour as well as their tents. After this the signal to return to Joppa was given by the royal trumpet.

2. When we had turned around and had gone past Azotus, the fifth city of the Philistines, now deserted but commonly called Ibenium,[1] we beheld nearly five hundred Arabs coming toward us on their way back from Joppa. On the day of the battle they had rushed up to that place and seized what they could outside the city. For after they had made great slaughter of our footmen in the rear of our army and had utterly destroyed one line in the right wing, they thought our front ranks had been destroyed like the rear. They took up the shields, lances, and shining helmets of the slain and proudly adorned themselves. Then they hurried up to Joppa to show our arms to the men of the city and to say that the king and all of his men had been slain in the battle.

3. When those who had remained as guards in Joppa heard

---

[3] September 7, 1101.

[1] Fulcher errs here and again later (III, xviii, 3) in calling Azotus by the name of Ibenium (Ibelin), for the latter place, the Biblical Jabneel and the classical Jamnia, is about ten miles northeast of Azotus. Azotus was one of the five cities of the Philistines listed in the book of Samuel, but Jabneel was not one of them (I Sam. 6:17). Cf. chap. iv, 1, note 3.

this, they were bewildered and badly frightened and gave credence to the words of the Arabs, which seemed true. The Arabs had thought that the city would be surrendered at once by the terrified citizens, but their schemes came to naught. When they saw that they were accomplishing nothing, they began to retire to Ascalon.

4. When the Arabs saw us coming back to Joppa, they thought we were some of their people who, having killed us all in battle, wished to seek out the rest of the Christians living in Joppa. For this reason we were puzzled because they were approaching us in this way, not recognizing that we were Franks until they saw our knights attack them in a sudden charge.[2]

5. Then you should have seen our enemies abruptly flee hither and thither, none caring to wait for another. He who did not have a swift horse was soon beheaded. But because the Franks were excessively tired and many of them wounded in the battle they could not pursue the Arabs. Thus the latter got away while we went on to Joppa rejoicing.

XIV

The Message Sent from the People of Joppa to Tancred, Prince of Antioch. 1. Imagine the exultation and thanksgiving when they whom we had left in Joppa saw from the top of the wall that we were returning with banners flying! It will certainly not be easy to tell about it.

2. Two bearers of false news had hastened to Joppa, one after the other,[1] and had misled the people there by saying that the king and all his men were dead. The people of Joppa were unbelievably distressed by this news. Believing it they sent a short letter to Tancred, who was then ruling in Antioch. By order of

---

[2] The author of the *Gesta Francorum Iherusalem expugnantium* says that the Franks also used disguise, the equipment of Arabs, to lure the latter in closer (*RHC, Occ.*, III, 530).

[1] I have been unable to identify the bearers of false news, although Runciman says that one of them was Hugh of Saint-Omer (*Crusades*, II, 75). Hugh did come to Joppa during the crisis of 1102 (chap. xxi, 1).

Baldwin's wife[2] it was carried by a certain mariner who was just then embarking on his ship.

3. The letter contained these words of greeting: "Tancred, illustrious man and most valiant soldier, receive this brief message which those who inhabit Joppa, namely the queen and the few citizens of the city, have sent in haste to you by me, their legate. Read it through carefully because you will perhaps more easily believe what is written than what I might say.

4. "Oh great misfortune! The king of the men of Jerusalem, who went into battle against the Babylonians and the Ascalonites, in this encounter either has been defeated completely or perhaps has been killed in the fray with all his men. For those who barely escaped the sadness of this calamity fled to Joppa and reported this to us.

5. "For this reason I come as a legate to you, a prudent man, seeking help and begging that you set aside all else and hasten without delay to aid the suppliant people of God in their great distress and, as I believe, already near the end of their life."[3]

6. This it said. Tancred, when he heard this, was silent for a little. But when he believed that what he had heard was true, he as well as all those present began to weep in pity because of their great sadness and grief. Tancred gave an answer to the messenger and then ordered that preparations be made throughout his land for helping the men of Jerusalem.

7. And when they were all ready to undertake the journey, lo! another letter carrier suddenly arrived with a message different from the first one, and he gave it to Tancred. Whereas disaster had been reported in the first letter, good fortune was reported in

[2] This was Baldwin's first wife, an Armenian princess, the daughter of Taphnuz, married for her dowry (Albert of Aix, III, xxxi). She is sometimes called Arda but in no known original source, viz., Matthew of Edessa, William of Tyre, or Guibert of Nogent. Consult HF 421, note 7.

[3] Fulcher is the source of information concerning this appeal to Tancred, a man who had disliked Baldwin since their rivalry at Tarsus in 1098 (I, xiv, 3), and the incident here cannot be proven nor safely dismissed. However, Baldwin is said to have appealed to Tancred a year later during a similar time of crisis (Albert, IX, xiii). The queen's letter as it exists is obviously a rhetorical device. If Baldwin's wife wrote this appeal in 1101, we have the sense of it rather than the text, for Fulcher altered his "text" between redactions (HF 423, note 8).

the second. It read that the king had returned safe to Joppa and that without a doubt the Saracens had been wondrously conquered. Then those who had grieved at our distress rejoiced at our good fortune.

8. Oh wondrous mercy of God! We did not conquer our enemies because of numbers of men but because we trusted in divine power. And so saved from our enemies in this way we returned to Jerusalem rendering praise to God. Then during eight months we rested safe from war until the year in its course brought back the summer season.[4]

XV

The Army of Babylon Gathered Against the Christians. 1. In the next year, 1102, in the middle of May, the Babylonians gathered around Ascalon. Their king had sent them there to try to destroy entirely us Christians. There were present about twenty thousand horsemen and ten thousand footmen not counting the drivers of the pack animals, camels and asses laden with victuals.[1] These drivers carried staves and missiles in their hands for fighting.

2. The Babylonians came up to Ramla one day[2] and pitched their tents in front of it. Up ahead of them in a fortified tower of the city were fifteen knights whom Baldwin had left as guards. In front of the tower lived some rustic Syrians in a kind of suburb. The Saracens persistently molested and disturbed these Christians, trying to destroy them and to demolish the tower. They could not go around freely in the open country because of the men holding the tower.

3. They even attempted to seize the bishop of the city, who

---

[4] From September, 1101, to the middle of May, 1102.

[1] The "king of the Babylonians" was the Fāṭimid Caliph of Cairo, al-Āmir ibn-al-Mustaʻlī (1101–30), a child of five years set up by the powerful Vizier al-Afḍal (Philip K. Hitti, *History of the Arabs* [London: Macmillan and Co., 1937], 622–23). From a previous reference we know that Fulcher knew the difference between "king" (caliph) and al-Afḍal, the vizier (I, xxxi, 1). Ibn-al-Athīr states that the Egyptian commander was Sharaf-al-Maʻālī, the son of al-Afḍal (*RHC*, Or., I, 215). Fulcher's estimate of the size of the Egyptian army is extravagant.

[2] *Ca.* May 16, 1102 (*HF* 426, note 7).

dwelt in the Church of St. George with his dependents. One day they surrounded the monastery with wicked intent, but after seeing the strength of the place they returned to Ramla.[3]

4. Moreover that bishop when he saw the smoke and flames arising from the fires in the grain fields feared lest the Saracens would return and besiege him. As a precaution against future danger he immediately sent word to the king, who was in Joppa, to aid him at once because the Babylonians were encamped before Ramla and had already sent one cohort from there to surround and attack the monastery.[4]

5. The king when he heard this hastened to take arms and mount his horse. His knights at his command and at the sound of the trumpet followed him immediately.

6. There were then in Joppa a great many knights who had chosen to cross the sea and return to France and who were awaiting a favorable wind. They had no horses because in the preceding year when they had passed through Romania on their way to Jerusalem they had lost their horses and everything which they had. It is not out of place to insert mention of this here.[5]

XVI

The Second Pitiable Pilgrimage of the Franks and the Death of Hugh the Great. 1. When the great army[1] of the Franks marched to Jerusalem, as has been said, William, Count of Poitou,[2] and Stephen, Count of Blois, were present in the multitude.

---

[3] The bishop was Robert of Rouen, according to William of Tyre (VII, xxii; cf. Albert of Aix, VII viii; and consult *HG* 448, note 25). The church and monastery of St. George were in nearby Lydda, to the north (*HF* 427, note 12).

[4] May 17, 1102 (*HChr* 645).

[5] This refers to the members of the ill-fated Crusade of 1101 who had succeeded in reaching Palestine and were waiting to return home.

[1] The "great army," the crusaders of 1101, had dwindled to a few refugees by the time they reached Jerusalem early in 1102.

[2] Count William VII of Poitou is better known as Duke William IX (1086–1127) of Aquitaine. Fulcher, from Chartres, thought of William in connection with nearby Poitou. William was also a troubadour and the grandfather of Eleanor of Aquitaine, wife of Louis VII of France and later of Henry II of England. Consult *HF* 429, note 4; and James Lea Cate, "A Gay Crusader," *Byzantion*, XVI (1942–43), 503–26.

The latter had left our army at Antioch[3] but now sought to make up for what he had then abandoned. With him also was Hugh the Great, who after the capture of Antioch had returned to Gaul.[4] With him was Raymond, Count of Provence, who stayed at Constantinople after he had returned that far from Jerusalem.[5] Stephen, the noble Count of Burgundy,[6] was there also and an innumerable popular following of knights and footmen divided into two groups.

2. The Turk Soliman, from whom the Franks had long previously taken the city of Nicaea,[7] opposed these Franks in the country of Romania. Remembering his own defeat[8] Soliman with a great number of Turks unfortunately dispersed, confounded, and almost totally destroyed the army of the Franks.[9]

3. But because of the providence of God the Franks were marching in companies over many different roads; hence Soliman could not fight and kill them all. However, he learned that they were exhausted, distressed by hunger and thirst, and unfamiliar with the use of bowmen in warfare. Hence he killed more than a hundred thousand knights and foot-soldiers.

4. Indeed he slew some of the women and carried others away with him. Many Franks who fled in different directions through the mountains perished from thirst and want. The Turks got their horses and mules, their beasts of burden, and equipment of all kinds.

---

[3] I, xvi, 7. [4] I, xxiii, 8.

[5] Raymond of Saint-Gilles (I, xxxii, 1).

[6] Count Stephen's title inhered in that part of Burgundy east of the Saône, later known as Franche-Compté. He and two brothers, Count Reginald II and Archbishop Hugh of Besançon, all perished in the Crusade of 1101–1102. A fourth brother, Guy, became Pope Calixtus II (1119–24) and is mentioned later by Fulcher (III, iii, 1; xiii; and xxxviii, 4). Count Stephen should not be confused with Odo I, Duke of Burgundy west of the Saône. Consult James Lea Cate, "The Crusade of 1101," in Setton (ed.), *Crusades*, I, 349–50, 357, 363, 364, note 32.

[7] Nicea was surrendered on June 19, 1097 (I, x). "Soliman" was Kilij Arslan I, Selchuk Sultan of Rūm and son of the former Sultan Sulaīman.

[8] Kilij Arslan lost not only Nicea but also a great battle at Dorylaeum, July 1, 1097 (I, xi, note 1).

[9] These crusaders were defeated seriatim in several battles in the interior of Anatolia in 1101 (Cate, "Crusade of 1101," 355–62).

5. The Count of Poitou lost there whatever he had, his retinue and his money. Scarcely escaping death he reached Antioch on foot, despondent and bewildered in his misery. Tancred, sympathizing with him in his distress, received him kindly and supplied him from his own means.[10] Thus him the Lord "chastening hath chastized but has not delivered over to death" [Psalm. 117:18].

6. Indeed this, it seemed to us, had befallen him as well as the others because of their sins and their pride.

7. Those, however, who escaped did not delay going on to Jerusalem except Hugh the Great, who died and was buried in Tarsus of Cilicia.[11] When they reached Antioch, some by sea and some by land, they went on to Jerusalem. Those who were able to procure horses preferred to go by land.

XVII

The Capture of the City of Tortosa. 1. When the Franks arrived at Tortosa, which the Saracens then held, they did not hesitate but attacked it by sea and land. Why should I dwell on it? They took the city, killed the Saracens, confiscated their money, and then without a pause resumed their march.[1]

2. All were disappointed at seeing Count Raymond remain there, for they had hoped that he would go on to Jerusalem with them. But because he refused, and remained there and kept the city for himself, the others hurled curses upon him.[2]

3. These latter then advanced farther, passing by Archas and the cities of Tripoli and Gibellulum and then came to the very narrow defile near the city of Beirut.

4. There King Baldwin had been awaiting them for eighteen

---

[10] *Ibid.*, 362.   [11] *Ibid.*

[1] Naval aid was given by the Genoese (Caffaro, *De liberatione civitatum orientis,* RHC, Occ., V, 69). Hagenmeyer dates the event *ca.* February 18, 1102 (*HChr* 631).

[2] The contemporary *Gesta Francorum Iherusalem expugnantium* explains this resentment by saying that Raymond (since 1099) knew the way to Jerusalem (*RHC, Occ.*, III, 533).

days,[3] guarding the passage lest perchance the Saracens should seize it and deny transit to the pilgrims. He had received a deputation from the army asking for aid as it approached that place.

5. When the pilgrims found the king there to meet them, they earnestly thanked him and, having exchanged kisses, set out for Joppa where those who came by sea had already landed.

XVIII

A Disastrous Battle Between the Christians and the Turks, in Which the Christians Were Killed and the Turks[1] Were the Victors. 1. As Easter[2] was drawing nigh the men then went to Jerusalem, which they had longed to visit. After they had carried out the customary solemnities there they returned to Joppa.

2. Then the Count of Poitou because he was needy and destitute in every respect boarded ship with a few followers and set out for France.[3]

3. Stephen of Blois and a great many others then wished to cross the sea, but because the winds were unfavorable they could do nothing else but turn back. For this reason Stephen was at Joppa when, as related above,[4] the king mounted his horse to go against the enemy who had encamped before Ramla.

4. Geoffrey, Count of Vendôme,[5] Stephen, Count of Burgundy, and Hugh of Lusignan,[6] brother of Count Raymond, were

[3] For Archas and Gibellulum see I, xxv, 6, 10. The narrow defile was the seaside pass at Nahr al-Kalb (ii, 1). Hagenmeyer dates this interval as *ca.* February 18–March 8, 1102 (*HChr* 631, 634).

[1] The chapter heading is in error, for the enemies of the Franks were Arabs (par. 7), not Turks.

[2] April 6, 1102.

[3] William of Poitou (and Aquitaine) embarked at the end of April or the beginning of May (*HChr* 640).

[4] Chap. xvi, 1.

[5] Geoffrey III of Preuilly and I of Vendôme (Jean Besly, *Histoire des comtes de Poitou* [Paris, 1647], 115–17), perhaps the "Gosfridus brevis statura" of Albert of Aix (IX, iv).

[6] Hugh VI (the Devil), ancestor of the Lusignan kings of Jerusalem and Cyprus and half-brother of Raymond of Saint-Gilles by their mother, Almodis of La Marche ("Lusignan," *Grand Dictionnaire universel du XIXᵉ siècle*, ed. Pierre Larousse, X [1873], 795; Hill and Hill, *Raymond IV*, 4, 6, 7).

also there. They borrowed horses from their friends and acquaintances, mounted, and followed the king.

5. It was indeed very rash for the king to neglect to wait for his men and to proceed into battle in disorderly fashion because he should have known better. Without foot-soldiers and hardly waiting for his knights, he hurried to meet the enemy until at length he foolishly threw himself into a multitude of Arabs. And because he trusted more in his own excellence than he should have, he thought there were not more than a thousand or seven hundred of the enemy. Therefore he hurried to meet them before they might escape.[7]

6. But when he suddenly saw their army he roared, struck with fear. Then all at once assuming the strength of consolation he turned to his men and spoke to them piously: "Oh soldiers of Christ, my friends, refuse not this battle but armed with the strength of God fight valiantly for yourselves for 'whether we live or die we are the Lord's' [Rom. 14:8]. For if one is tempted to flee there is no hope of escape. If you fight you will conquer; if you flee you will perish."[8]

7. Then indeed since this was the place and the occasion to show valor, the Franks hastily plunged among the Arabs in a brave assault. And because our knights numbered no more than two hundred they were surrounded by twenty thousand. Our men were so seriously hemmed in by the pressure of the Gentiles that the greater part of them were slain in the space of an hour. The rest because they could not stand a strain of this kind turned to flight.

8. But although so much evil happened to our men, it was not before they were most handsomely revenged upon their enemies. For they killed many of them and drove them from their camp.

[7] The contemporary author of the *Gesta Francorum Iherusalem expugnantium* states that Baldwin thought he was meeting one small enemy party in search of plunder (*RHC, Occ.*, III, 533). The date was May 17, 1102 (*HF* 436, note 1).

[8] Baldwin is reported to have told Stephen of Blois scornfully that he, Baldwin, would attack even if Stephen and his friends were back in France (*Gesta Francorum Iherusalem expugnantium, RHC, Occ.*, III, 533) and to have said to Harpin of Bourges that if he, Harpin, were afraid let him flee to Bourges (Guibert of Nogent, *RHC, Occ.*, IV, 244).

Then by the will of God our men were vanquished by those whom they had vanquished.

9. The king escaped by the grace of God, and a few of his more notable knights. They got into Ramla by a quick flight but could not go farther.

XIX

The Flight of King Baldwin. 1. The king, since he did not wish to be trapped there, preferred to die somewhere else rather than be ignominiously taken in that place. He immediately took counsel and taking the chance of life or death attempted to escape. He took with him only five companions, but he did not have them with him very long since they were stopped by the enemy.[1] He himself sought flight to the mountains on a swift horse.[2] Thus the Lord snatched him from the hands of his enemies who were stronger than he. Baldwin would gladly have set out for Arsuf if it had been possible, but the enemy blocked him and he could not go there.

2. As to those who remained in the city of Ramla, they could not afterwards get outside the gate. They were besieged on all sides by those impious folk and then alas were captured by them.[3] Some were killed, and others taken away alive.

3. The bishop in the Church of St. George, hearing of this disaster, secretly got away to Joppa.

4. Alas, how many noble and brave knights we lost in this disaster, in the initial engagement as well as afterwards in the aforesaid tower. For Stephen of Blois, a prudent and noble man, and the other Stephen, the Count of Burgundy, were killed.

1 William of Malmesbury, hearing possibly through Edgar the Etheling, a crusader in 1102, says that Baldwin left with five companions: Robert the Englishman, hewing the way, Baldwin and a companion coming next, and three knights following, only Baldwin and his companion escaping (*De gestis regum Anglorum*, ed. William Stubbs [*Rolls Series*], II, 285, 384).

2 Baldwin's horse must have been famous, for she is called "Gazala" (Gazelle) in three chronicles (*Gesta Francorum Iherusalem expugnantium*, RHC, Occ., III, 534; Albert of Aix, IX, v; Ordericus Vitalis, MPL, CLXXXVIII, col. 772).

3 They were overwhelmed on the third day, reports Albert of Aix (IX, vi), which seems to have been May 19, 1102 (HF 443, notes 10, 12).

5. Three knights extricated themselves from there.[4] Sorely afflicted by cuts and blows they rode swiftly to Jerusalem on the following night. When they reached it they told the citizens of the disaster that had occurred. But as to whether the king was alive or dead they said they did not know. This immediately brought great grief to all.

XX

How the King, Fleeing, Entered Arsuf. 1. The king hid in the mountains the following night[1] for fear of the Arabs. On the third day[2] he emerged with only one knight and his squire,[3] wandering unknown as if he were just anyone and suffering from hunger and thirst in the byways of the desert. At length he entered his town of Arsuf.

2. The one circumstance which saved Baldwin was this. Five hundred enemy soldiers, who for some time had been riding around the walls of the town as scouts, had withdrawn a little before this. The king never could have evaded them if he had been seen by them.

3. On entering Arsuf the king was received by his men with great joy. He ate and drank and slept in safety. This was required by the human side of his nature.

XXI

How Hugh of Tiberias and the Patriarch of Jerusalem[1] Hastened to the Aid of the King, and How a Battle Was Fought with the Power and Help of the Holy Cross, the Christians Witnessing It.

[4] The *Gesta Francorum Iherusalem expugnantium* identifies them as Lithard (of Cambrai), the Viscount of Joppa, and Baldwin's squire (*RHC, Occ.*, III, 534). Fulcher, the source of the *Gesta*, omits the viscount in his second redaction (chap. xx, 1; *HF* 444, note b). Albert of Aix states that Baldwin escaped from Ramla with Hugo de Brulis and his squire (IX, v).

[1] Either May 17–18 or 18–19, 1102, according to Hagenmeyer (*HF* 444, note 2).

[2] May 19, 1102 (*HF* 445, note 4).

[3] Perhaps Hugo de Brulis and the squire.

[1] As Fulcher does not mention the patriarch in this chapter, the chapter title must have been written by another person.

1. Lo, on that day[2] Hugh of Tiberias, one of the great lords of the king,[3] came to Arsuf. He had heard of the king's discomfiture and wished to bring some solace to the survivors. The king, when he saw him, rejoiced greatly. This was because Hugh had with him eighty knights for whom there was pressing need. Then in response to a message from Jerusalem the king hastened to bring aid to the people of Joppa.

2. He did not dare to conduct his men by land because his enemies might be lying in wait for him in the guise of wayfarers. Instead he boarded a skiff and sailed to Joppa.[4] When he arrived at the port he was received with great joy since according to the Gospel, "He was dead and came to life again; he was lost and was found" [Luc. 15:24]. He whom they lamented as dead they now saw alive and safe.

3. The next day[5] the aforesaid Hugh left Arsuf and hastened in fear to Joppa. The king met him in order to help him if he should be attacked en route by their enemies.

4. When the king reached Joppa he did not deliberate very long, for he was admonished by necessity, before he summoned those who were at Jerusalem and St. Abraham,[6] to come to Joppa. He wanted to fight the Arabs who were camped near Joppa planning to seize the city.

5. While he was wondering whom he could send as a messenger, he saw a certain Syrian, a humble man and meanly clad, whom he earnestly besought to undertake the accomplishment of this mission because he could not find anyone who was able or dared

---

[2] May 19, 1102 (chap. xx, note 2).

[3] Hugh of Falkenberg near Saint-Omer succeeded Tancred as lord of Tiberias in 1101 (HF 447, note 3).

[4] Albert of Aix states that this vessel belonged to "Gudericus, an English pirate" (IX, ix). It is supposed that this was Godric of Finchale, the Lincolnshire peasant boy who became a traveler, merchant, and saint. See Thomas Andrew Archer, "Godric," Dictionary of National Biography, VIII (n.d.; reprinted London: Humphrey Milford, Oxford University Press, 1921–22), 47; and Henri Pirenne, Medieval Cities, trans. F. D. Halsey (Princeton: Princeton University Press, 1939), 116–19, 121, 125.

[5] May 21, the day after Baldwin reached Joppa (HF 448, note 7).

[6] Hebron.

to do it. No one dared to travel that way because of the snares of the enemy. But this man, having received courage from God, did not hesitate to make the trip. He went by a little-known and very difficult route, and in the darkness of night, lest he be seen by the enemy. On the third day[7] he reached Jerusalem, exhausted.

6. When he told the citizens the welcome news of the king and declared that he was alive, they all gave just praise to God for this. There was no longer any delay.

7. When they read the message which the Syrian carried, they immediately got ready as many knights as they could find in Jerusalem. There were ninety as I recall, knights as well as those who were able to obtain horses and set out without delay. Avoiding as far as possible the snares of the enemy and traveling by a devious route, they approached Arsuf by a side road.

8. When they were marching in great haste along the seashore their wicked enemies attacked them, hoping to cut them off and kill them there. Some of our men, because it seemed necessary, plunged into the waves in order to swim, so that one misfortune might be the remedy for another. By swimming, they were saved from the unbelievers, but they lost their animals. The knights, having swift horses, defended themselves and reached Joppa. Nevertheless they escaped with difficulty.

9. The king was much cheered and encouraged by their arrival and did not wish to delay any longer. On the following morning[8] he arranged his knights with his foot-soldiers and went forth to fight his enemies.

10. The latter in truth were not far from Joppa, about three miles. They were already preparing siege machines in order to besiege Joppa and take it right away. But when they saw our men advance against them to do battle, they immediately took arms and boldly met us. Because their number was great they encircled our men on all sides.[9]

11. When our men were surrounded in this way, nothing could

[7] Perhaps May 23 (*HChr* 653–54).   [8] May 27, 1102 (*HF* 451, note 18).
[9] Hagenmeyer conjectures that Baldwin might have had six or seven hundred men, or even eight or nine hundred (*HF* 451, note 20), but we cannot tell.

help them but divine aid. Trusting absolutely in the omnipotence of the Lord, they did not hesitate to strike with wondrous force where they saw the enemy formation was densest and strongest. When our men by vigorous fighting penetrated the hostile ranks in one place, it was immediately necessary to come back somewhere else. This was because our enemies, when they saw our footmen without the protection of knights, would rush at once to that place and slay those in the rear.

12. But our foot-soldiers were not cowards. They launched such a shower of arrows upon their assailants that you could see many arrows stuck in the shields or in the faces of their adversaries. And so since the Saracens were vigorously repulsed by the arrows of the infantry, because many of them were wounded by the lances of our knights, and since they had already lost their tents, God helping us, they turned their backs to the Franks and fled. However, they were not pursued very long, for the pursuers were few.

13. They abandoned their tents on the plain and all their provisions to the Franks. But they took away nearly all their horses except some that were wounded and some which died of thirst in flight. We[10] got many of their camels and asses. Many of the enemy perished as they fled, either of wounds or parched by thirst.

14. Truly it was right and just that they who were protected by the wood of the Lord's Cross should emerge as the victors over the enemies of that Cross. If indeed this benevolent Cross had been carried with the king in the previous battle, it cannot be doubted that the Lord would have favored His people.

15. But there are some people who trust more in their own strength than in the Lord, who trust too much in their own judgment, and who spurn the counsels of the wise.[11] They presume to accomplish their task hastily and heedlessly. Hence great harm

---

10 Fulcher's use of the plural pronoun in the first person may be rhetorical, for there is no other reason to think that he was present at this battle. He was probably in Jerusalem (HF 13, and 453, note 26).

11 It should be remarked as indicative of Baldwin's character that if he knew of this criticism by his chaplain he did not demand its excision.

often comes not only to them but to many others involved in the same task. For this reason such people are accustomed to blame the Lord rather than to recognize their own folly.

16. He who begins a thing foolishly does not consider the result. "The horse is prepared for the battle but the Lord bestows the victory" [Prov. 21:31]. If the prayer of the just is not always hearkened to by the Lord, how much less is that of the wicked? Or how can one blame God if one's desire is not fulfilled at once? Why should one be heard who merits no good? Does He not know what is to be done in all things?

17. Boëthius on this point says, "Although you see your hopes fall short of accomplishment, still there is a just order of things, and a perverse order is a matter of confusion in your mind. But the foolish man expects a turn of fortune, not what is deserved."[12] Many times indeed a man thinks something an evil to him which afterwards turns to his profit. On the contrary, it happens that what succeeded well with someone a little later thwarts him very much.

18. When the battle was over and the king was the victor, as has been said, he picked up his tents and went back to Joppa. After this the land was free of war during the following autumn and winter.[13]

XXII

The King Besieged the City of Acre. 1. In the year 1103, in the spring, after we had celebrated Easter[1] in Jerusalem as was customary, the king advancing with his little army besieged the city of Acre, which is also called Ptolemais. But because the city was very strong in its wall and outer defenses, the king was not able to take it at that time, especially since the Saracens within defended themselves with most wondrous bravery. After the king

---

[12] De consolatime philosophiae iv. pros. 6. 131–33; i. pros. 4. 156.
[13] Albert of Aix reveals that there was a futile eight-day siege of Ascalon by the Franks at the end of September, 1102 (IX, xv; HChr 673). Hagenmeyer suggests that Fulcher thought the event was unimportant (HF 455, note 37).
[1] March 29, 1103.

had destroyed their crops, orchards, and gardens he returned to Joppa.[2]

XXIII

The Liberation of Prince Bohemond from Captivity. 1. At that time there spread the most welcome rumor concerning the Lord Bohemond, that by the grace of God he had been freed from Turkish captivity.[1] He announced by messenger how he had been ransomed from captivity and how the citizens of Antioch had joyfully received him, their ruler of yore who now again possessed and exalted the land.

2. Moreover Bohemond took over the city of Laodicea, which Tancred had captured and wrested from the men of the emperor of Constantinople. Because of this he gave Tancred an adequate compensation from his lands and graciously placated him.[2]

XXIV

The Almost Fatal Wounding of the King. 1. At that time when King Baldwin was as usual struggling with the Saracens one day he happened to make an attack upon a few of them. Already sure of their destruction he was rejoicing at the prospect when behold! an Ethiopian lurking behind a rock stealthily waited for Baldwin in order to kill him. The Ethiopian threw a missile very hard which injured the king most severely, in the back near the heart. By this stroke he wounded the king nigh unto death. But because Baldwin afterwards sought to have himself carefully

---

[2] Albert of Aix has a detailed account of this siege (IX, xix, xx). He and Ibn al-Athīr (*RHC, Or.*, I, 213) agree that Baldwin, using siege machines, would have taken the city if it had not received relief by sea. For discussion, see Reinhold Röhricht, *Geschichte des Königreichs Jerusalem* (1100–1291) (Innsbruck: Verlag der Wagner'schen Universitäts-Buchhandlung, 1898), 43–44. Hagenmeyer dates the siege *ca.* April 6–May 16, 1103 (*HF* 456, note 4).

[1] Bohemond was captured by Malik-Ghāzī Gümüshtīgīn ibn-Dānishmend of Sivas in 1100 (I, xxxv, 3) and released in May, 1103 (*HChr* 691).

[2] Fulcher is very cryptic here. Patriarch Bernard of Antioch and King Baldwin had a hand in Bohemond's release. Tancred had to give up his recent conquests of Laodicea, Mamistra, Adana, and Tarsus in addition to the regency of Antioch and retained scarcely two small towns, according to Ralph of Caen (*RHC, Occ.*, III, 709). Consult Nicholson, *Tancred*, 136–37.

treated, after an incision he at length recovered from his trouble-some wound.[1]

XXV

The Capture of the City of Accon, Which Is Commonly Called Acre. 1. In the year 1104 after the winter was over and when spring was flowering, we celebrated Easter[1] in Jerusalem. Then King Baldwin gathered his men and proceeding to Acre besieged it again. The Genoese came there with a fleet of seventy beaked ships.[2] After the Christians had besieged the city with machines and frequent attacks for twenty days, the Saracens were greatly terrified and reluctantly surrendered it to the king.

2. This city was very necessary to us since it contained a port so commodious that a great many ships could be safely berthed within its secure walls.

> 3. Already Phoebus had risen nine times in the Sign of
>   the Gemini
> When Acre, which is called Ptolemais, was captured
> In the year eleven hundred and four.[3]
> This is not the city of Acharon which some called Acre,
> The former is a Philistine city [Jos. 13:3], the latter is called
>   Ptolemais.

4. After the city was captured in this way they killed many of the Saracens but permitted some to live. They took all of their possessions.[4]

---

[1] Baldwin was wounded in or before July, 1103 (*HChr* 701). The fullest account is given by Albert of Aix (IX, xxi–xxii). For the best discussion, see *HF* 460–61, notes 2, 3, and 4.

[1] April 17, 1104.

[2] Albert of Aix, whose account is the most complete, states that the fleet was a combined Genoese and Pisan squadron (IX, xxvi); Caffaro reports that forty of the ships of the original fleet were Genoese (*De liberatione civitatum orientis, RHC, Occ.*, V, 71); and Ibn-al-Qalānisī says that it was a fleet of more than ninety Genoese ships (*The Damascus Chronicle*, 61).

[3] May 26, 1104 (*HChr* 721).

[4] The city surrendered on terms granted by King Baldwin, but his greedy Genoese and Pisan allies killed and plundered many of the helpless citizens, according to Albert of Aix (IX, xxix). See also the *Gesta Francorum Iherusalem expugnantium* (*RHC, Occ.*, III, 537).

XXVI

Bohemond Arranged to Cross Over to Apulia.   1. After summer had passed Bohemond, greatly troubled by necessity, crossed over to Apulia with a few ships.[1] He committed all his territory to Tancred.[2] With him at that time went Daimbert, who had been Patriarch of Jerusalem, a man prudent and powerful in counsel.

2. Bohemond went in order that he could lead back with him men from the lands across the sea.[3] Daimbert went in order that he could make known to the Roman pope his complaint and the injury done to him by the king. He went and he gained what he sought, but he did not come back for he died on the way.[4]

XXVII

How the Men of Antioch Fighting Against the Parthians Were Captured and Some of Them Were Killed.   1. In that year the Parthians, Medes, Chaldeans, and all the inhabitants of Mesopotamia, our neighbors, were stirred to attack us Christians and to molest us in every way. When the report of this reached us, our leaders nevertheless all made preparations to engage our enemies in battle.[1]

2. Lord Bohemond and Tancred, Count Baldwin of Edessa,

---

[1] Bohemond's troubles included a disastrous defeat by the Turks at Harran on May 7, 1104 (chap. xxvii), subsequent aggressions from Ridvan of Aleppo and the Byzantines, and shortages in men and money. He left Antioch in the fall of 1104 and arrived at Bari in January, 1105. See Yewdale, *Bohemond,* 100–102.

[2] Tancred served as Bohemond's regent.

[3] The sequel was Bohemond's attack upon the Byzantines in Epirus in 1107–1108 (Yewdale, *Bohemond,* 115–34).

[4] Patriarch Daimbert, who wanted Jerusalem to be an ecclesiastical state headed by himself, had been forced out of Jerusalem by King Baldwin in 1101, had gone to Antioch and been temporarily restored by the influence of Tancred, and then had been immediately deposed in the fall of 1102. At the end of 1104 he started back to Italy with Bohemond, as Fulcher here states. He was declared restored by Pope Paschal II and died soon after at Messinia on the return journey. See *HF* 468, note 9; and Hansen, *Das Problem eines Kirchenstaates,* 95–113.

[1] Chapters xxvii–xxix, dealing with the affairs of Bohemond, are of Fulcher's second recension, which he began in 1124. He inserted them after chap. xxvi, where he stated that Bohemond went to the West in 1104 in order to raise troops.

Joscelin,[2] and likewise Daimbert of Jerusalem and the Archbishop of Edessa, Benedict by name,[3] were very soon ready together with a throng of knights and common people.

3. They marched on past the Euphrates River and up to the city called Harran near the Khabur River. Here they encountered the phalanxes of their enemies. They began battle at once near Raqqa, but because of the gravity of our sins the Christians were given over to dispersion and confusion. This engagement was far more disastrous than all previous battles, as the result showed.[4]

4. Lord Baldwin, Count of Edessa and future and second king of the men of Jerusalem, was captured there and with him Lord Joscelin, his kinsman. With them too was taken the archbishop mentioned above. Many men also were drowned and lost in the aforesaid river. Horses and mules and a great amount of wealth were lost.

5. However, Lord Bohemond and Lord Tancred fled here and there along unfrequented roads and bypaths, choosing neither the best route nor byway. They at length escaped, bewildered and confused.

6. Many men died transfixed by arrows and daggers. They who could have taken Harran without great difficulty, if they had besieged it at first, afterwards could not have taken it during either the outward or return journey. And because security sometimes works harm by deception, so fear and caution seem to be an advantage to the wary and the timid. For as it is written, often "delay is dangerous for those who are ready to act."[5]

7. For certainly two enemies, discord and envy, were hurtful to our people in this undertaking or rather misfortune. These

[2] Joscelin de Courtenay, successor of his cousin Baldwin II as Count of Edessa (1119–31). For his life, see Robert L. Nicholson, *Joscelyn I: Prince of Edessa* (Urbana: University of Illinois Press, 1954).

[3] In regard to Archbishop Benedict, see E. G. Rey (ed.), *Les Familles d'outremer de Du Cange* (Paris: Imprimerie Impériale, 1869), 769.

[4] For this campaign, see Nicholson, *Joscelyn*, 8. Ibn-al-Qalānisī is the only chronicler to give the date of the battle, May 7, 1104 (*The Damascus Chronicle*, 60). The Turkish leaders were Chökürmish of Mosul and Sokman ibn-Artuk of Mardin.

[5] Lucan. *Pharsalia*. i. 281.

enemies are accustomed to bring down men from the riches they have acquired to extreme poverty. We have often seen this. We have learned it by experience. I am not deceived, nor am I beguiled by deceptive circumlocution to meditate in terms of trivialities.

8. In this campaign so dangerous and fearful the Franks antagonized each other even before the disaster so that they almost wished to part company and break the alliance they had made.[6] Indeed he is foolish who does evil and expects good. For nothing is acceptable to God which is done in strife and without love. It is therefore cowardly and disgraceful to desert the society of Him whom I ought to serve unto death.

9. Moreover God aided the archbishop of Edessa, who was then in chains. The Turks had loaded him down with tools and utensils as if he were a beast of burden. With the help of a very valiant knight who devotedly risked his life, and by the will of God, the archbishop was snatched from the hands of the Turks in a deed of wondrous daring. For the knight did not hold his life more precious than self.[7]

10. Thus many men in this our pilgrimage burned with zeal for God and chose to sacrifice this life, endeavoring to die a blessed death and thus enjoy rest with Christ.

11. For example, one man, as some of our people heard and saw while we were around Antioch, when he heard the name of God blasphemed with great irreverence by a certain pagan, was stirred by a fiery zeal to contradict him in word and deed. He immediately put spurs to his horse and eagerly asked those standing around, "If any of you wish to sup in Paradise, let him now come and eat with me, for I am about to go there."

12. He promptly waved his lance and plunged amidst the thousands of the enemy, overthrowing and killing the first one who opposed him. Thus in the act of slaying he was himself slain

6 William of Tyre relates that Baldwin and Joscelin, on the verge of forcing the surrender of Harran, quarreled over who should have the city and gave the Turkish relief force time to come up (X, xxx).

7 I.e., the knight did not hold mortal life more precious than his soul.

forthwith. And so supported by faith and hope and strengthened by love he died joyfully. Who has ever heard the like? Still lying on the ground he was already glorified in Heaven.

13. Wherefore Heaven and those in it rejoice. And it was truly a source of joy and thanksgiving to us because the angels rejoiced at the addition of such a companion. For He was near who heard him and rewarded him with the gift which He had prepared, an everlasting abode [Joan. 14:2].

XXVIII

The Liberation of Count Baldwin and the Battle Between Him and Tancred. 1. After the Lord Baldwin had been kept in chains for about five years, after select hostages had been given and faith pledged with solemn oath that Baldwin would redeem them, and when afterwards these hostages had craftily killed their guards, then Baldwin escaped from prison.[1] In this he had a most faithful helper, Joscelin.[2]

2. But later when Baldwin returned to his city of Edessa, he could not go in because Tancred and his men forbade entrance.[3]

3. Finally because it was to the advantage of Baldwin and Joscelin, and because of the agreement which Lord Bohemond had previously caused to be made, that if at any time and in any way Baldwin should escape from captivity his land should be restored to him without controversy, the two allies immediately fought a battle against Tancred, the third party.[4]

4. They were in no wise appeased by Tancred's pleas and appeals for peace. Joscelin, having collected seven thousand Turks, provoked Tancred, who was unprepared, to battle and with the

---

[1] The best discussion of Baldwin's release and his subsequent war with Tancred is by Nicholson (*Tancred*, 172–78).

[2] Baldwin was captured in 1104 (chap. xxvii, 4) and was released not in 1109 but in 1108, in mid-August (W. B. Stevenson, *The Crusaders in the East* [Cambridge: at the University Press, 1907], 84, note 4; cf. *HF* 478, note 2). He was set free by ransom arranged by Joscelin (Nicholson, *Tancred*, 172, note 2).

[3] Tancred then controlled Antioch and Edessa and was very reluctant to release the latter (Nicholson, *Tancred*, 169, 173).

[4] Although there was some preliminary fighting before the battle mentioned in par. 4 (*ibid.*, 174), it is doubtful if Fulcher had this in mind.

aid of these Turks killed five hundred of the followers of Tancred. And although Tancred was at first almost overcome yet with the help of God, whose countenance always looks upon justice, he remained the victor on the field, the victor with honor.[5]

5. But when the chief men of the land saw the damage being done, they took mutual counsel and brought the contestants to agreement.

XXIX

Bohemond Crossed into Gaul. 1. Then Bohemond, discouraged in many ways as has been said above,[1] proceeded into Gaul.[2] There among other things he married the daughter of King Philip,[3] Constance by name, and brought her to Apulia. By her he had two sons. Of these the first-born died; the second, named for his father, remained the heir.[4]

XXX

Tancred Fighting the Turks Gained the Victory. 1. In the year of our Lord 1105, on the second day of the Kalends of March, died Count Raymond, a distinguished knight, in his stronghold before the city of Tripoli. His nephew William Jordan succeeded him.[1]

2. At the time the usual impudence of the Saracens and Turks

[5] This battle, fought near Tell Bashir in September, 1108, is highly interesting because Tancred on the one hand and Baldwin and Joscelin on the other had Turkish allies who were rivals of each other. It was a true double civil war (*ibid.*, 178).

[1] Chap. xxvi.

[2] Bohemond left for Apulia in the fall of 1104 and then went to France early in 1106 (Yewdale, *Bohemond*, 102, 109).

[3] Philip I (1060–1108).

[4] The first son, John, died in infancy; the second, Bohemond II, born *ca.* 1109, came to Antioch in 1126 and was the ancestor of the later princes of Antioch. Bohemond I died in Apulia in 1111. See Yewdale, *Bohemond*, 110, 131, 133; and Fulcher, III, lxi, 2.

[1] Fulcher is the principal authority for this date, February 28, 1105 (*HF* 484, note 2). Raymond's stronghold was Mount Pilgrim, built in 1102–1103 (Hill and Hill, *Raymond IV*, 154–55). Its ruins are still extant (Robin Fedden and John Thompson, *Crusader Castles* [Beirut: Khayat's College Book Cooperative, 1957], 24). Concerning William Jordan, see Runciman, *Crusades*, II, 61, note 2.

was not lacking, for in the month of April the king of Aleppo, Ridvan by name,[2] assembled an army of no small size from the lands about him. With excessive pride he raised his head to do battle with Tancred, Prince of Antioch.

3. But Tancred, placing the anchor of his hope not in a multitude of men but in the Lord, drew up his line of battle in good form and rode against the enemy without delay. Why should I tarry longer? Tancred rushed boldly against the enemy before Artasia. With the help of God the Turks were at once struck by fear and turned their backs in flight. They fled and were pursued. Those who could not flee did not escape death.

4. Of their dead there was no number, but Tancred took many of their horses. He also took the standard of the fugitive king. The latter fled, crushed and with his pride humbled. Thus glorified was God, who always comes to the aid of the faithful.[3]

5. Having mentioned this little bit about the men of Antioch, we shall now treat of those of Jerusalem.

XXXI

The King of Babylon Again Sent All His Army Against King Baldwin, Against Whom He Prepared Himself. 1. It should be related how in that same year the king of Babylon gathered many men and sent them in the service of the governor of Ascalon to do battle against Christianity.[1] He thought and intended to drive us all from the Holy Land. He had learned that we were very few and without the accustomed assistance of pilgrims. At

---

[2] Ridvan, son of the Selchükid prince Tutush of Syria (1078–1095), claimed to be his father's heir but only succeeded in possessing Aleppo (1095–1113). See Robert W. Crawford, "Riḍwān the Maligned," in James Kritzek and R. B. Winder (eds.), *The World of Islam* (London: Macmillan and Co., 1960), 135–44.

[3] For a discussion of this battle at Artāḥ, twenty-two miles east of Antioch, see *HF* 487, note 13; and Nicholson, *Tancred*, 154–56. Ibn-al-Qalānisī corroborates Hagenmeyer in regard to the date, April 20, 1105 (*HF* 486, note 5), and adds that Ridvan lost 3,000 men (*The Damascus Chronicle*, 70).

[1] The year was 1105, and the event was the final attempt (August 27) of al-Afḍal, vizier of the boy Caliph al-Āmir of Cairo (1101–30), whom Fulcher calls "king," to overthrow the Franks of Jerusalem. The governor of Ascalon was Jamāl-al-Mulk (Ibn-al-Athīr, *RHC, Or.*, I, 229; cf. chap. xxxii, 9).

Ascalon therefore were gathered together Arab horsemen and Ethiopian footmen. With them were more than a thousand Turks of Damascus, who were excellent archers.[2]

2. When this had been made known to King Baldwin he gathered all his men and awaited the enemy around Joppa. And because necessity demanded it, all who lived in the cities and were able to bear arms went forth to do battle, excepting only those who guarded the walls at night.

3. Fear and trembling then came upon us. We were afraid that our foes either might take one of our cities while it was denuded of manpower or might slay the king and his people in battle. It was in the month of August. Both sides shrewdly deferred battle, for we did not attack them nor they us.

4. But finally at a time divinely set, as I believe, that wicked race advanced from Ascalon and began to approach us. When this was discovered the king left Joppa and rode up to the city of Ramla.

5. And because "it was good for us in all things to cling to the Lord and to place our firm hope in Him" [Psalm. 72:28], the king at the inspiration of the Lord God sent a fleet messenger to the patriarch,[3] clergy, and common people of Jerusalem imploring them to pray with all their might for the mercy of Almighty God that He might deign to give aid from on high to His Christians placed in such difficult straits.

6. This messenger therefore although strongly urged declined to accept any pay. He feared that he might not be able to fulfill the mission or, if he lived, to collect the reward. He trusted that he would receive from God in some way the reward for his pious labor. And so commending his soul and body into the hands of his Creator he hastened to Jerusalem. With the guidance of the

---

[2] There was a rift among the Turks ruling Damascus because Irtash, brother of the prince Dukak (d. 1104), had fled in fear of the *Atabeg* Tughtigin, henceforth ruler of the city (1104–28). Irtash went to Bosra and appealed to Baldwin of Jerusalem. As a consequence of this, Tughtigin, a Sunnite, sent aid to the Shī'ite Egyptian force at Ascalon (Ibn-al-Qalānisī, *The Damascus Chronicle*, 70–71), thirteen hundred men according to Ibn-al-Athīr (*RHC, Or.*, I, 229).

[3] Evremar (1102–1108). See *HF* 513, note 3.

Lord he reached there and upon entering the city made known his mission.

7. When the news was announced the patriarch ordered the great bell to be rung and all the people to be assembled before him. "Oh my brothers," he said, "my friends and the servants of God, behold here in very truth is the battle which you heard would occur, for the messenger is announcing that it is beyond a doubt ready to come upon us. And because without divine aid we cannot resist such a great multitude, implore ye the clemency of God, that He deign mercifully to aid our King Baldwin and all his men in this impending struggle.

8. "The king today[4] deferred the battle, as he has just informed us by this messenger, until tomorrow, which will be the Lord's Day, the day on which Christ rose from the dead, in order that he the king might fight with greater hope of success. He begs that you offer to God your prayers and alms in order that he may be strengthened to fight with greater confidence.

9. "Hence keep the vigils tonight according to the dictum of the apostle, be firm in faith and let all that you do be in charity. Tomorrow go through the holy places in this city, barefooted, mortifying and humbling yourselves, devoutly beseeching the Lord God to deliver us from the hands of His enemies.

10. "I myself am now going to the king. I am leaving at once, urging that if any of you remaining here is able to bear arms that you come with me forthwith. For the king is in need of men."

11. Why should I delay further? They mounted their horses and were in all one hundred fifty men, knights as well as footmen. And so at nightfall they set out quickly and at dawn arrived at the city of Ramla.

12. Those who remained in Jerusalem gave themselves up zealously to prayers, alms, and tears. Up to the noon hour they continuously visited the churches. Chanting they wept, and weeping they chanted for the priests in the procession were doing this. I too, barefooted, was praying with the rest.[5] The old men fasted

[4] August 26, 1105.
[5] Fulcher here attests that he was a witness of these events at Jerusalem.

until the ninth hour of the day nor did the infants suck the breasts of their mothers until they cried from hunger. Generous alms indeed were bestowed upon the poor. For these are the works by which God is pleased, by which He is inspired to save us and "influenced," by which "he will not fail to leave His blessing behind Him" [Joel 2:14].

XXXII

The Battle of the Men of Jerusalem with the Turks, a Victory Gained by the Power of the Most Holy Cross. 1. And when the patriarch came through to Ramla as has been related, and the ensuing dawn began to dispel the twinkling stars,[1] all were delighted by his arrival and inspired to hurry to the priests to confess their sins to God and to them. Similarly, the chief men hastened to the patriarch desirous of hearing some salubrious words[2] from him and of being freed from their sins.

2. After this had been done the patriarch put on his pontifical vestments and took in his hands the glorious Cross of the Lord, which was usually carried on such occasions. When the companies of knights and footmen were properly arranged, they advanced against the hostile army.[3]

3. Our knights numbered about five hundred, excepting those who were not counted as knights although they were mounted. Our footmen were estimated at not more than two thousand.[4] Moreover, the pagans were thought to be fifteen thousand, footmen and horsemen. That night they were camped not more than four miles from Ramla.

4. In the morning when they saw the king advancing against them they hastily prepared for battle. However, their scheme was then somewhat spoiled since they had planned to send a part of their army, although a lesser part, against Ramla, so that it

[1] Ovid. *Metam.* vii. 100. The date was August 27, 1105 (*HChr* 756).

[2] Ovid. *Fast.* vi. 753.

[3] Albert of Aix states that the Franks were arranged in five divisions with Baldwin commanding the fifth, consisting of 160 men (IX, xlix).

[4] Fulcher's estimates of Frankish strength are conservative and possibly nearly accurate.

could deceive our army. However, they had decided to send the greater part to Joppa to attack and seize it unknown to us. But when they saw the king riding against them in this way they at once regrouped their forces, their plan thwarted.

5. There was no longer any delay; each side attacked the other.

"Then bucklers resounded and there was the swish of sword blades."[5]

In the mutual onslaught all our men shouted at the foe, "Christ conquers, Christ reigns, Christ rules," just as they had been ordered.

6. Our enemies surrounded us, thinking to utterly confound and shatter us. Moreover the Turkish archers, wheeling as was their custom, loosed showers of arrows. When they had performed their function of archers, they drew their swords from their scabbards and attacked us in close combat. When the king saw this his courage mounted, and he snatched his white banner from the hand of one of his knights, rushed thither with a few men, and started to aid those under attack.

7. Immediately with the help of God he dispersed the Turks by his attack and the slaughter and then returned to the attack against the greater body of the Saracens, Arabs, and Ethiopians.

8. But I shall not dwell on the attacks and the onslaughts of both sides because I wish to compress the narrative into more limited compass. For God Almighty, who is never unmindful of His servants, did not wish those infidels to destroy His Christians who for love of Him and for the glory of His name had come to Jerusalem from distant lands. Those impious people suddenly fled, going back to Ascalon.

9. Oh if Semelmulc, the commander of their army, could have been captured, how much money might have been paid for his ransom to King Baldwin! But Gemelmulc, the Amir of Ascalon and a very rich man, did not escape. He was slain, which caused no little desolation among those people.[6]

---

[5] Ennius *Annal.* xi. 1.

[6] These leaders were Sena-al-Mulk, a son of al-Afḍal, and Jamāl-al-Mulk, according to Ibn-al-Athīr (*RHC, Or.,* I, 228–29). Ibn-al-Qalānisī states that the

10. Another amir, formerly of Acre, was captured alive.[7] Our king caused him to be ransomed for twenty thousand pieces of money besides horses and other things.

11. The Ethiopians since they could not flee were slaughtered in the fields. Four thousand of the enemy were reported killed, horsemen as well as footmen, but of ours only sixty.[8] Their tents remained behind in our hands, and many beasts of burden, camels, asses, and dromedaries.

12. Then we praised and glorified God in whom we found great strength and who brought our enemies to destruction [Psalm. 59:14]. Oh wonderful decree of divine judgment! Behold those who said: " 'We shall come to kill all those Christians and we shall possess their holy places' [Psalm. 82:13]. But it did not happen thus, oh infidels, not thus" [Psalm. 1:4] because "God made you like whirling dust, like chaff before the wind [Psalm. 82:14] so that He might terrify you in His fury" [Psalm. 2:5]. By their law they had sworn never to flee because of the Franks, but at length they found their safety in flight. They preferred to perjure themselves rather than to die a stultified death.

13. The king finally returned rejoicing to Joppa where he distributed to his knights and footmen the booty taken in battle. This he did according to careful calculation.

XXXIII

The Fleet of the Babylonians. 1. Up to then there had been a fleet of Babylonian ships before Joppa. The Babylonians had been waiting there for some time hoping to find out how and when they might completely destroy us all by land and sea, together with our maritime cities. But when King Baldwin had his sailors throw the head of the Amir Gemelmulc, severed in battle, on

---

first was Sharaf-al-Ma'alī, the son of al-Afḍal who led the invasion of 1102 (*The Damascus Chronicle*, 58, 70; cf. chap. xv, note 1), but Ibn-al-Athīr explains that Sharaf was relieved of command because of events in 1104 (*RHC, Or.*, I, 228–29).

[7] Ẓahīr-ad-Daulah Bannā' Juyūshi (Ibn-al-Athīr, *RHC, Or.*, I, 220; Ibn-al-Qalānisī, *The Damascus Chronicle*, 61).

[8] Both sides lost about 1,200 men, reports Ibn-al-Athīr (*RHC, Or.*, I, 229); about equal numbers, writes Ibn-al-Qalānisī (*The Damascus Chronicle*, 71).

board one of the enemy ships, they were greatly alarmed and terrified by this discovery and did not care to remain there any longer. And so having learned of the disaster suffered by their people they retired to the ports of Tyre and Sidon, blown gently by a south wind.[1]

2. When later this fleet was returning to Babylon we were favored by the grace of God, for the enemy ships were scattered in a storm and blown wretchedly into our ports. We captured twenty-five ships full of Saracens.[2] The rest sailed away and barely escaped. God showed Himself our kind Helper in tribulation and thus manifested His omnipotence.

3. In consequence I wish to make known to all the date of the battle.

Phoebus had already risen for the tenth time in the Constellation of Virgo

When the full moon looked upon the Earth.

On the sixth day of the Kalends of September as it is read[3]

The Omnipotent granted it to the Franks to rejoice in triumph

When the Arabs as well as the Turks and Ethiopians fled,

Some to the mountains, while the rest remained dead on the field.

XXXIV

The Earthquake. 1. Since these deeds would be given over to oblivion if not recorded, and have not been written down either because of the neglect or the unskillfulness of writers or perhaps because these writers are few or are burdened by their own problems, therefore I, Fulcher, although rude in skill and weak in ability, would prefer to be known for the fault of temerity rather

[1] Albert of Aix says that this Egyptian fleet first retired to Tripoli, spent the night there, and then returned home via Ascalon (IX, 1). The *Gesta Francorum Iherusalem expugnantium* states that some ships went directly to Tripoli, the others to Alexandria (*RHC, Occ.,* III, 541). Consult HF 502, note 6.

[2] William of Tyre says that two thousand sailors and rowers were captured (XI, iii).

[3] August 27, 1105. Ibn-al-Qalānisī gives the same date (*The Damascus Chronicle,* 71).

than permit these accomplishments not to be known, as far as I have seen them with my own eyes or have learned by diligently seeking out reliable informants.[1]

2. Moreover I beg one reading this to charitably forgive my lack of skill and to correct, if he will, my diction if it has not yet been corrected in places by an eloquent writer. However, let him not change the arrangement of my history for the sake of pompous eloquence lest he deceitfully confuse the truth of events.[2]

3. After the deeds which have been related above, all of us who were in Jerusalem felt, toward the end of the year, a great earthquake which terrified us greatly. This was during the Vigil of the Lord's Nativity.[3]

XXXV

The Signs Appearing in the Sky. 1. In the year 1106 a comet appearing in the sky frightened us because we were suspicious of it. It was in the direction in which the winter sun is wont to set. It produced a brilliant white streak like a warp of linen thread of wondrous length.

2. This portentous sign began to redden in the month of February on the day of the new moon. But not presuming to prophesy from it we committed to God the whole problem of what it signified.

3. For fifty or more days that comet was seen every evening over the entire world. It is remarkable that from the beginning of its appearance the comet itself as well as its beautiful white streak faded a little every day until in the last days it lost the strength of its light and then ceased entirely to appear.[1]

[1] Fulcher names himself as the author of this chronicle, admits a lack of literary skill, declares his purpose to record events that might otherwise be forgotten, and states that he writes what he has personally seen or learned from others by careful inquiry.

[2] Fulcher indicates that another person was then reading his chronicle and rewriting it to improve its eloquence. For use of Fulcher's text by his contemporaries, see the Introduction, pp. 46–48, esp. notes 10–12.

[3] December 24, 1105.

[1] This comet of February–March, 1106, is mentioned by Ibn-al-Qalānisī (*The Damascus Chronicle*, 72), Matthew of Edessa (*RHC, Arm.*, I, 81), Anna Comnena (*Alexiade* [ed. Leib], III, 64), and by certain Chinese (*HF* 505, note 1).

4. Soon after in that same month, on the twentieth day of the new moon[2] and from the third hour until noon, we beheld in the sky two other suns seemingly to the right and left of the real one. However, they did not shine like the actual sun but glowed dimly in form and luminosity. Furthermore, around these suns a circular whiteness appeared which was in extent like unto a city. Inside this circle shone a half circle resembling a rainbow. It had four distinct colors. In the upper part of its curve it embraced the sun and even touched the two other suns already mentioned.[3]

5. Then in the following month at the hour of midnight a shower of stars was seen falling from the sky.[4]

XXXVI

The War of the Christians Against the People of Damascus.

1. In the following summer[1] Hugh, who then held the city of Tiberias, waged war against the soldiers of Damascus. After he had already been twice defeated by them in battle he was with the help of God the victor in a third attack. He killed two hundred of them and kept as many of their horses. The rest of the enemy took to flight. How wonderful to relate! Six scores of men dispersed forty times a hundred.[2]

2. Then immediately afterwards Hugh was killed by an arrow while he was on an expedition with King Baldwin in the same region.[3]

XXXVII

How the Patriarch Crossed the Sea to Rome; and the Battle Between the Men of Joppa and Those of Ascalon. 1. In the

[2] February 23, 1106 (HF 508, note 9).
[3] Regarding this solar phenomenon, see HF 508, notes 9–10.
[4] March, 1106. At this point ends the *Gesta Francorum Iherusalem expugnantium* (*RHC, Occ.,* III, 543).
[1] 1106.
[2] Baldwin and Hugh were harassing Tyre, trying to cut off its trade with Damascus. See Ibn-al-Qalānisī, *The Damascus Chronicle,* 71–72; Ibn-al-Athīr, *RHC, Or.,* I, 229–30; Sibṭ Ibn-al-Jauzī, *Mir'at az-zamān, Extraits,* in *RHC, Or.,* III (Paris: Imprimerie Nationale, 1884), 529–30; Albert of Aix, X, v–vi; William of Tyre, XI, v; and discussion in Runciman, *Crusades,* II, 95.
[3] Hugh's death may have been in September, 1106 (HF 512, note 8).

year 1107 the patriarch, Evremar by name, crossed the sea to
Rome to inquire from the Apostolic See whether he would remain
patriarch.[1] For Daimbert, mentioned above, had recovered the
patriarchate but later died on the return journey.[2]

2. At length in the month of November of the same year the
men of Ascalon, boiling over in their usual savagery, placed ambushes in the foothills of our mountains between Ramla and Jerusalem. Their purpose was to fall upon and seize a party of our people who they learned were about to go from Joppa to Jerusalem.

3. But when this was made known to the men of Joppa they at
once mounted their horses. When they reached the place of ambush, having been conducted thither by the reporter of the news,
for they had doubted up to then whether he spoke the truth, they
were terrified and very fearful when they saw the foe. For the men
of Ascalon were nearly five hundred horsemen and almost a thousand footmen while there were not more than sixty-five of our
men.

4. There was no time for the latter to consider what they
should do. There was no safety for them if they fled, and death
was at hand if they fought. They willingly chose to die an honorable death if necessary rather than to be known afterwards for
the shame of flight. Therefore they soon made a sudden attack,
penetrating the enemy line in marvelous wise and knocking down
and slaying the foemen. When the Saracens saw that they were
being badly beaten in this battle they lost courage, for it was the
will of God, and ceased to fight.

5. When our soldiers observed this they pressed the Saracens
still harder. They forced to flee those who had thought to force
our men to flee. They killed many of them and captured many of
their horses. Of our men we lost no more than three. However, the

---

[1] This is the only time that Fulcher mentions Evremar by name, although
he refers to him twice elsewhere (chap. xxxi–xxxii; and III, iv, 2). Evremar was
not restored by Pope Paschal, but his case was remanded to Jerusalem for decision
(Letter of Paschal, December 4, 1107, in Eugène de Rozière [ed.], *Cartulaire de
l'Église du Saint-Sépulcre de Jérusalem* [Paris: Imprimerie Nationale, 1849], No.
10). He was removed as patriarch in 1108. Consult *HF* 512–15, notes 2–4.

[2] Probably in 1105. See chap. xxvi, note 4.

enemy camp-followers stole some of our beasts of burden, but our men exacted a double toll from them.

XXXVIII

Bohemond, Having Collected an Army, Devastated the Territory of the Emperor. 1. In that same year Bohemond, after he had returned from Gaul, collected as many men as possible and prepared a fleet in the port of Brindisi, which is in Apulia. After waiting for a favorable time for crossing, the men embarked on the seventh day before the Ides of October and sailed to Bulgaria, landing at the port of Avlona.[1]

2. Capturing Avlona very quickly, they proceeded to the city of Durazzo and laid siege to it on the third day before the Ides of October.[2] But because that city was well supplied with men and provisions, it wore down the besiegers for a long time.[3] Lord Bohemond had five thousand knights and sixty thousand footmen.[4] Then too he allowed no women to cross with him lest they be an impediment and a burden to the army.[5]

3. The Emperor of Constantinople, Alexius by name, was at that time strongly opposed to our people. By trickery or open violence he thwarted or tyrannized over the pilgrims going to Jerusalem by land or sea. It was for this reason that Bohemond invaded Alexius' territory, trying to take his cities and fortresses.[6]

---

[1] Bohemond returned to Apulia in January, 1105, won the approval of Pope Paschal for a "crusade" against the Byzantine Emperor Alexius (II) Comnenus, went on a recruiting tour of France in 1106, returned to Italy in August of that year, spent the next year preparing his army and fleet at Brindisi, and sailed, as Fulcher says, on October 9, 1107, for Avlona in Epirus. For discussion, see Yewdale, *Bohemond,* 102–15.

[2] October 13, 1107.

[3] The siege of Durazzo lasted from October 13, 1107, to some time in September, 1108 (Yewdale, *Bohemond,* 117–27).

[4] Hagenmeyer and Yewdale estimate Bohemond's strength to have been 34,000 (HF 521, note 9; Yewdale, *Bohemond,* 115–16).

[5] Barth sarcastically remarks, "Noto hominis Itali continentiam," "Animadversiones," in Ludewig, *Reliquiae manuscriptorum,* III, 341, quoted in HF 521, note 10.

[6] It will be noted that by this time Fulcher had accepted Bohemond's thesis that Alexius had betrayed the members of the First Crusade and the Crusade of 1101 and was supporting Bohemond's cause.

XXXIX

The Peace Between the Emperor and Bohemond, Which Was Solemnized by Oaths. 1. In the year 1108 after the Incarnation of Our Lord, after Bohemond had already besieged Durazzo for one year, he had accomplished nothing whatever. He had prepared stratagems against the emperor, and the emperor had done the same against him. Finally after a treaty had been discussed through intermediaries and after the emperor with his army had approached Bohemond, they became friends with each other after several conferences.

2. The emperor, swearing upon the most precious relics, promised Bohemond that the pilgrims, of whom mention often has been made, would from that day forward be safe and unharmed by land and sea as far as the emperor's power extended, and that no one of them should be seized or maltreated. Bohemond on his part swore to observe peace and loyalty to the emperor in all things.[1]

3. Afterwards Bohemond, when occasion offered, returned to Apulia leading back the smaller portion of his army.[2] The greater part proceeded by sea to Jerusalem where it had vowed to go.[3]

4. In that same year Philip, King of France, died.[4]

XL

The Siege of the City of Tripoli. 1. In the year 1109, eleven years after the capture of Jerusalem,[1] Bertrand, the son of Count Raymond,[2] came to Tripoli bringing with him the Genoese and

---

[1] Yewdale has reconstructed the terms of the treaty of Devol, most of it from the elaborate statement of Anna Comnena (Yewdale, *Bohemond*, 127–30; Anna, *Alexiade* [ed. Leib], III, 125–39).

[2] In October, 1108 (*HF* 525, note 12).

[3] Fulcher's statement is doubtful, for there is no other record of a large influx of Bohemond's men to Jerusalem, although some may have gone there. Most must have returned to Italy.

[4] Philip I died on July 29, 1108.

[1] Fulcher counts 1099 as the first year.

[2] Bertrand was the son of Count Raymond by the latter's first wife. Her identity is uncertain (Hill and Hill, *Raymond IV*, 9–10, 13–14).

their fleet of about seventy beaked ships.[3] There they all landed.[4] Bertrand intended to besiege this city and to possess it by right of inheritance from his father.

2. As soon as they had surrounded it by siege, a quarrel arose between Bertrand and William Jordan, his kinsman, who had all along beset the city since the death of Count Raymond and who lived in a fortress near Tripoli called Mount Pilgrim.[5]

3. Bertrand said, "The city ought to be mine by hereditary right because my father, who originally began to attack Tripoli, built this mighty stronghold, namely Mount Pilgrim, in order to besiege the city, and while he was still alive bequeathed Tripoli to me to hold after his death."

4. William on the other hand said, "But it ought to be mine and justly so because since the death of Count Raymond I have vigorously held in check the hostile inhabitants of the land with my own forces, and I have striven and labored to annex the land adjacent to the city."

5. And since in discord greatness is wont to suffer and in concord pettiness to thrive,[6] William from hatred withdrew from the siege. Bertrand, however, strongly besieged the city with his men. He did not want William to succeed, and the latter did not want Bertrand to live.

"They struggled for uncertainties and were uncertain of certainties."[7] They struggled for temporal advantages and not for eternal values. They run who perchance catch nothing; therefore the prize remains in doubt. "So it depends not upon man's will

---

[3] Albert of Aix states that Bertrand left France with four thousand men and forty galleys and sailed to Pisa, where the Genoese joined him with about eighty galleys (XI, iii). Caffaro writes that Bertrand went to Genoa, where the Genoese joined him with sixty galleys (*De liberatione civitatum orientis*, RHC, Occ., V, 72). Ibn-al-Qalānisī says that Bertrand arrived at Tripoli with sixty ships loaded with Franks and Genoese (*The Damascus Chronicle*, 88).

[4] Hagenmeyer dates the arrival early in March (*HF* 527, note 4). Ibn-al-Qalānisī says the blockade began on May 4 (*The Damascus Chronicle*, 89).

[5] Raymond died February 28, 1105 (chap. xxx, 1). For the quarrel of William Jordan and Bertrand, see Runciman, *Crusades*, II, 66–68.

[6] Sallust. *Bell. Jugurth*. x.

[7] This play on words is typical of Fulcher. See *HF* 50.

nor exertion but upon the mercy of God" [Rom. 9:16]. They had not yet captured the city but already were quarreling about what they hoped to capture. At the nod of God moments pass, and thoughts of men are turned to vanities [Psalm. 93:11].

XLI

How the City of Tripoli Was Captured. 1. Soon after, King Baldwin arrived at the siege. He begged the Genoese to help him capture Ascalon, Beirut, and also Sidon during that year.[1]

2. And it happened while Baldwin was beginning to make peace between the two aforementioned counts that by some mischance which I do not understand William Jordan was killed. He was shot from ambush by a small arrow while riding one night. All asked who had done it, but they were not able to find out. Some grieved; others rejoiced. Some lamented a friend; others were happy over the death of an enemy. Bertrand remained the faithful vassal of King Baldwin.[2]

3. Then the city was besieged on all sides. Those outside worked hard; those inside were pressed hard. But when the Saracens were strongly beleaguered and had no hope of escape, an agreement was made, sealed by oaths, and confirmed by the king. It provided that the Saracens should not be killed but might go wherever they wished without being forbidden. By this agreement the king and his men were allowed entrance into one section of the city.

4. But while this was happening a great tumult suddenly arose for some reason or other among the common folk of the Genoese. They scaled the wall with ropes and ladders and entered the city. Any Saracen found there was at once beheaded. However, those

---

[1] Fulcher fails to say that Baldwin needed sea power to conquer seaports and was prepared to offer commercial concessions to the Genoese. Consult Fink, "Foundation of the Latin States," in Setton (ed.), *Crusades,* I, 398.

[2] Fulcher also omits the delicate negotiations between King Baldwin, Count Baldwin of Edessa, and Bertrand on the one hand and Tancred and William Jordan on the other. King Baldwin and Tancred each desired the area of Tripoli in his own sphere of influence. See Fink, "Foundation of the Latin States," 398.

in the vicinity of the king were protected according to the agreement made by him.[3]

    5. Phoebus had shone upon the Tropic of Cancer for thirty
        days less three
      When our fighting men in their might took the city of
        Tripoli.[4]

XLII

How the City of Beirut Was Captured. 1. In the year 1110, while the month of February[1] shut in the country with winter rains, King Baldwin set out for the city of Beirut and besieged it. To his assistance came Bertrand, the Count of Tripoli.[2] Bertrand's army camped at the first milestone from the city.

    2. After they had pressed upon the city from all sides for seventy-five days, as I estimate, and after our ships[3] had blockaded within the harbor those vessels[4] which had flocked thither to aid the enemy, our Franks moved wooden towers up to the wall and with great bravery leapt from them to the wall with drawn swords. From there they descended into the city while many others of our

---

[3] Baldwin for economic reasons wanted a very valuable seaport and its mercantile population taken intact while the common people of the newly arrived Genoese fleet were greedy for plunder. The Arab contemporary, Ibn-al-Qalānisī of Damascus, probably learning from refugees, gives a gruesome account of the sack of an opulent and cultivated city. He says that the governor, however, and some of his troops were spared by convention (*The Damascus Chronicle,* 89–90).

[4] Hagenmeyer interprets Fulcher's date as June 26, 1109, but admits some ambiguities (*HF* 534, note 14). Ibn-al-Qalānisī is precise with July 12 (*The Damascus Chronicle,* 89).

[1] Albert of Aix places the start of the siege in December, implying the year 1110, probably an error for 1109 (XI, xv; Stevenson, *Crusaders in the East,* 58, note 5).

[2] Fulcher neglects to say that Bertrand had become Baldwin's vassal for Tripoli. See Albert of Aix, XI, xi; and William of Tyre, XI, x.

[3] "Our ships" probably refers to vessels from the Genoese squadron, which had assisted in the recent capture of Tripoli. Ibn-al-Qalānisī states that the Genoese furnished forty ships filled with fighting men (*The Damascus Chronicle,* 100).

[4] Ibn-al-Qalānisī writes that nineteen Egyptian supply ships forced their way into the harbor (*ibid.,* 99–100). William of Tyre says that an enemy fleet from Tyre and Sidon was inside the port (XI, xiii).

men were coming in through the gates. They energetically pursued the fleeing enemy and eventually subdued those who were cut off and took all their money.[5]

3. In the year one thousand and one hundred and twice five
Our valor captured the mighty city of Beirut.
Twice ten times Phoebus had risen in the Sign of Taurus
And three and four times more when this event occurred.[6]

XLIII

How King Baldwin and Prince Tancred Set Out Against the Turks Besieging Edessa. 1. When[1] these things were done the king returned to Jerusalem to render thanks due to God through whom he had triumphed.[2] Then he prepared to go against the Turks who were besieging Edessa, a city in Mesopotamia.[3]

[5] Albert reports that about twenty thousand people of Beirut were killed after surrendering on terms (XI, xvii); however, Fulcher and Ibn-al-Qalānisī mention no terms, and there may have been none. Albert may have confused the massacre at Beirut with that at Tripoli (*HF* 536, note 12).

[6] Ibn-al-Qalānisī (*The Damascus Chronicle*, 100) agrees with Fulcher in regard to the date, May 13, 1110 (see *HF* 563, note 13).

[1] Fulcher's chapter on the Frankish relief expedition to Edessa in 1110 is disappointing. He speaks vaguely of a Turkish offensive against Edessa but gives no inkling that it represented a formidable effort in a series of *jihāds* led by a spirited new *Atabeg* of Mosul, Sharaf-ad-Din Maudūd, in alliance with *Atabeg* Tughtigin of Damascus. In fact, he mentions neither of them here and says nothing of the recent quarrel between Count Baldwin of Edessa and Tancred for the possession of that city (chap. xxviii, 1, 2) or of King Baldwin's statesmanship in effecting a new reconciliation with Tancred in order to relieve Edessa. The accounts of Ibn-al-Qalānisī (*The Damascus Chronicle*, 101–104), Matthew of Edessa (*RHC*, Arm., I, 91–94), and Albert of Aix (XI, xvi–xxv) give a better insight into these events. For discussion, see Stevenson, *Crusaders in the East*, 88–89; and H. S. Fink, "Mawdūd of Mosul, Precursor of Saladin," *Muslim World*, XLIII (1953), 20–21.

[2] King Baldwin returned for Pentecost, May 29, 1110 (Albert of Aix, XI, xviii; *HF* 537, note 2).

[3] Albert of Aix and Matthew of Edessa both relate that Count Baldwin of Edessa called for help from King Baldwin while the latter was besieging Beirut; the king, however, would not move until he had captured the city, which was on May 13 (Albert of Aix, XI, xvi; Matthew, *RHC*, Arm., I, 91–92; see *HF* 563, note 13, for date). Ibn-al-Qalānisī states that Maudūd's initial attack upon Edessa was on May 3–12 (*The Damascus Chronicle*, 102).

2. At that time we saw for several nights a comet with its rays extending toward the south.[4]

3. Tancred then assembled as many of his men as he could at Antioch and waited for some days for the king. They assembled their forces together in front of the River Euphrates.[5]

4. After they crossed they immediately encountered the Turks whom they were seeking. The Turks were scouring the country in bands looking for the arrival of the king. But because they knew that our knights were superb fighters remarkable at slaying with the lance, the Turks did not dare to join battle. By clever flight they broke away, neither daring to fight nor caring to retire into their own lands.

5. The Turks, not wishing to fight, tried for a great many days to wear down our men by their tedious craftiness. Then the king, considering both what was necessary and the best thing to do, provisioned the city of Edessa with food, which the inhabitants much needed. This was because the Turks had devastated the surrounding country and had captured the villages and the peasantry who supplied the aforesaid city with food.

6. The Franks did not delay further but returned to the river that we have mentioned. After the Franks had crossed over a little by little by means of a few small rafts, the crafty and rapacious Turks came upon them there. They seized many of our people who were on foot and carried them off to Persia, particularly the helpless Armenians whom they had already wickedly plundered.[6]

7. Because the river was difficult to cross at that time, the

[4] Ibn-al-Qalānisī mentions this comet of May 29 to mid-July (*The Damascus Chronicle*, 101).

[5] Albert says it took King Baldwin a month to reach the Euphrates, starting early in June. The two Baldwins then summoned Tancred (XI, xix, xxii).

[6] Fulcher correctly assesses the Turkish tactic of feigned retreat and counterattack. The other sources agree that the Turks retired to Harran, scene of their famous victory in 1104 (chap. xxvii, 2, 5). They also agree that the Frankish rear, largely Armenian, was caught on the east bank of the Euphrates and massacred (Ibn-al-Qalānisī, *The Damascus Chronicle*, 103–104; Matthew of Edessa, *RHC, Arm.*, I, 93–94; Albert of Aix, XI, xx, xxiii, xxiv). Matthew is plainest in saying that the area around the city of Edessa was depopulated. The date of this defeat is not recorded.

Franks continued on their appointed way, grieving much, Tancred going to Antioch and the king returning to Jerusalem.

XLIV

How Sidon, Also Called Sagitta, Was Besieged and Captured by King Baldwin and the Norwegians. 1. Meanwhile there landed at Joppa certain Norwegian people whom God had inspired to make the pilgrimage from the Western Sea to Jerusalem. Their fleet had fifty-five ships.[1] Their leader was a very handsome youth, a kinsman of the king of that country.[2]

2. When King Baldwin returned to Jerusalem he was filled with joy by the advent of these people. He conversed with them in a friendly manner, urging and even begging them to remain, for the love of God, in the Holy Land for even a very little time in order to aid in extending and glorifying the Christian name. Then having accomplished something for Christ, they could afterwards return to their own land rendering generous thanks to God.

3. They received the request favorably, replying that they had

[1] Sixty ships (Ibn-al-Qalānisī, *The Damascus Chronicle*, 106; Ibn-al-Athīr, *RHC, Or.*, I, 275; Albert of Aix, XI, xxvi).

[2] This youth, then about nineteen years of age, was Sigurd Jorsalafarer (the Crusader), jointly king of Norway (1103–30) with his brothers Eystein (1103–22) and Olaf, who died young. When their father King Magnus Barefoot was killed in 1103 during a raid on the coast of Ulster, Ireland, the older sons, Kings Eystein and Sigurd, began preparations for a crusade. When all was ready in 1107, Sigurd was chosen leader. He and his men spent the first winter in England as guests of King Henry I, the second winter in Galicia, northern Spain, and in fighting the Moors in Portugal, and the third among the kindred Normans of Apulia before they reached Palestine, *ca.* August, 1110. After cooperating with King Baldwin in the capture of Sidon, King Sigurd sailed on to Constantinople. There he was royally entertained, gave his ships to the Emperor Alexius, and left some of his men in the latter's service. He and the rest traveled overland to Denmark and crossed to Norway in the summer of 1111, thus returning much faster than they had come. Sigurd's head is now interred in the wall of Akershus Castle, Oslo. For reference, see Snorri Sturluson, *Heimskringla*, in Finnur Jonsson (ed.), *Nóregs Konunga Sogur* (4 vols. in 3; København: S. L. Mollers Bogtrykkeri, 1893–1901), III, 267–84; Paul Riant, *Expéditions et pèlerinages des Scandinaves en Terre Sainte au temps des croisades* (Paris: Ad. Laine et J. Havard, 1865), 194–203; and Knut Gjerset, *History of the Norwegian People* (2 vols.; New York: Macmillan and Co., 1915), I, 311–19.

come to Jerusalem for no other purpose. They said that wherever the king wished to go with his army, there they would gladly go by sea at the same time, provided that he would supply the necessary sustenance for them. This was conceded on one side and ratified on the other.

4. At first they were disposed to march against Ascalon,[3] but at last they adopted a more glorious project, to advance upon and besiege Sidon. The king moved his army from Ptolemais, which is more often called Acre; the Norwegians proceeded by ship from Joppa.

5. At that time the fleet of the amir of Babylon[4] was lying hidden in the port of Tyre. From it the Saracens very often went in piratical fashion against our Christian pilgrims and thus protected and encouraged the maritime cities up to then belonging to the king of Babylon. But when the Saracens heard reports of the Norwegians they dared not come forth from the port of Tyre and do battle with them.

6. When Sidon was reached the king besieged it by land and the Norwegians by sea. When our siege engines were completed, the enemy within the walls were so terrified that the garrison of mercenaries begged of King Baldwin that he permit them to go forth safely, and if he pleased he might retain in the city the peasants because of their usefulness in cultivating the land.

7. This they sought; this they obtained. The hired soldiers thus departed without their pay; the rustics remained peacefully under the aforesaid terms.[5]

> Nineteen times had the sun seen the Archer
> When they took the city of Sidon in December.[6]

---

[3] According to Albert of Aix, Sigurd originally anchored off Ascalon but finding it in enemy hands went on to Joppa (XI, xxvi).

[4] Technically, this refers to the child Caliph al-Āmir, who was dominated by his powerful vizier, al-Afḍal.

[5] It should again be noted that King Baldwin, remembering Tripoli and Beirut (chaps. xli, xlii), preferred to capture a city intact rather than one that had been sacked.

[6] Albert of Aix says the siege began in September and lasted six weeks (XI, xxxii, xxxiv). Ibn-al-Qalānisī is precise in saying that it began on October 19 and

· BOOK II ·

XLV

The Very Wicked Disturbances of the Turks and the Expedition of King Baldwin and Tancred Against Them. 1. In the year 1111[1] an immense multitude of Turks boiled up out of Persia, passed through Mesopotamia, crossed the river Euphrates, and besieged the fortress called Turbezel, delaying there a month.[2]

2. And when they could not capture it immediately, because it was strongly situated, they were annoyed with the delay and abandoned the siege, withdrawing into the territory of the city of Aleppo. This was because they craftily planned to provoke Tancred to come forth to fight them. Then with their great numbers they could intercept and completely destroy him far from Antioch.[3]

3. But Tancred met cunning with cunning, for he had no notion of compromising his fame with foolish boldness. He sent messengers to King Baldwin to most humbly beg the latter to hasten to aid the Christian cause. When the king heard this he promised to give the aid which was requested. Committing his land to custodians he hastened to war, taking with him Bertrand, the Count of Tripoli.

4. When they reached the town which they called Rugea, near

ended on December 4, 1110, lasting forty-seven days (*The Damascus Chronicle*, 107), although Fulcher indicates that it ended on December 5 (*HF* 549, note 18).

[1] In this chapter Fulcher, an eyewitness (par. 9), tells of the third campaign of Maudūd of Mosul against the Franks. For discussion, see Fink, "Mawdūd," 21–22.

[2] Two months, according to Albert of Aix (XI, xxxviii), and forty-five days, according to Ibn-al-Athīr (*RHC, Or.*, I, 282). But Ibn-al-Qalānisī, who should be better informed, states that the siege of Tell Bashir began on July 18, 1111, and that operations around Aleppo ceased by the end of *Safar*, *i.e.*, ca. September 6 (*The Damascus Chronicle*, 114, 116). If Kamāl-ad-Dīn is correct in saying that the episode of Aleppo lasted for seventeen days (*RHC, Or.*, III, 600), then the siege of Tell Bashir must have lasted about two weeks.

[3] Tancred of Antioch had been threatening Shaizar on the Orontes, about seventy-five miles southwest of Aleppo. Maudūd's plan to join with Ridvan of Aleppo against Tancred was good, but Ridvan was suspicious of the other Turks and shut his city gates against them. Maudūd's Iraqi allies, unwilling to go farther than Aleppo, deserted him. However, Tughtigin of Damascus, who wanted help, came up to join Maudūd. See Ibn-al-Qalānisī, *The Damascus Chronicle*, 114–17; and discussion in Nicholson, *Tancred*, 210–14.

Russa, Tancred was there.[4] He had been awaiting the arrival of the king for five days and received him with great joy. They unloaded and pitched their tents beside the Fernus River, the men of Jerusalem sharing the camp with those of Antioch.[5]

5. They did not delay there but marched to the city of Apamea. It was governed under the authority of Tancred, who had previously captured it in a very valiant manner.[6]

6. Then they proceeded against the Turks who were encamped before the city which they call "Sisara." I do not know how to name the city in correct literary form, but the inhabitants of the country commonly call it "Chezar." It is six miles distant from Apamea.[7]

7. The Turks though, because they now heard that the Franks were proceeding against them, hid themselves in the shrubbery and fortifications of the aforesaid city. This was in order to defend themselves the more securely if perchance they were surrounded by an onslaught of the Franks. Nevertheless when they saw our soldiers approaching them, they issued from the fortifications already mentioned, showing themselves to our men. Yet being cautious they did not dare to fight, nor wish to flee.

8. Our soldiers, drawn up in companies, when they saw the enemy running here and there through the country and not preparing battle, refrained from attacking them, not wishing to take any risk. And so the Turks, influenced as much by fear as by the

[4] Rugea (ar-Rūj) and Russa, today a ruin, were strongholds controlled by Tancred. They were east of the Orontes about forty miles southwest of Aleppo.

[5] Fulcher is eager to show that Baldwin and Tancred, usually rivals, were allies in a common cause. The river Fernus was the Orontes.

[6] On September 14, 1106, according to Kamāl-ad-Dīn (RHC, Or., III, 595). For discussion of this date, see Stevenson, Crusaders in the East, 83, note 4.

[7] Shaizar (anc. Larissa, Caesarea) was then the stronghold of Sulṭān ibn-Munqidh, uncle of the famous Arab writer Usāmah ibn-Munqidh, an eyewitness of the fighting around Shaizar, as was Fulcher. Usāmah indicates that Maudūd arrived there on September 15, 1111, after Tancred, and that the Franks were retiring toward Apamea by September 19. See Usāmah ibn-Munqidh, in An Arab-Syrian Gentleman and Warrior in the Period of the Crusades: Memoirs of Usāmah ibn-Munqidh (Kitāb al-I'tibār), trans. Philip K. Hitti ("Records of Civilization: Sources and Studies," ed. Austin P. Evans [New York: Columbia University Press, 1929]), 97–98. Fulcher errs in his estimate of the distance from Shaizar to Apamea, for Shaizar is actually about fifteen miles to the southeast.

craftiness of both sides, remained there. Our men returned by the way they came.

9. Since food was lacking for man and beast, the Franks could not remain there any longer. The king returned to Jerusalem, and I was with him. Tancred went back to Antioch.[8]

XLVI

The King Besieged Tyre, Which Is Called "Sur," But Accomplished Nothing. 1. Immediately afterwards, the king hastened his preparations and advanced against Tyre, called "Soor" in Hebrew,[1] and besieged it. After he had vigorously harassed it for four months and more, he as well as his men was exhausted from weariness and labor, and he reluctantly withdrew from there.[2]

2. He had ordered two wooden towers to be built higher than the wall and had moved them up to the wall, thinking thus to capture the city. But the Saracens, feeling that this would be fatal to them, defeated skill with skill, opposed cunning with cunning, and cheated bravery with bravery.

3. When they saw that the height of our towers far exceeded that of their walls they hastily effected a remedy. They built two towers upon their walls at night. These towers were of such height that the Saracens could defend themselves very well from above by setting fire to and burning our shorter towers.[3] Our soldiers were defeated by this mischance and were overwhelmed with despair. When the last thread of hope was broken the king returned to Acre.

[8] Albert of Aix states that the two armies faced each other for sixteen days and that the campaign was over by September 29 (XI, xli, xlii). Nearly all sources agree that Turkish harassment caused the Franks to lack food and water.

[1] See I, xxv, 10.

[2] The siege began on November 29, 1111 (Ibn-al-Qalānisī, *The Damascus Chronicle,* 120; Ibn-al-Athīr, *RHC, Or.,* I, 283; Sibṭ Ibn-al-Jauzī, *ibid.,* III, 543; Albert of Aix, XII, iv), and ended on April 10, 1112, according to Ibn-al-Qalānisī (*The Damascus Chronicle,* 125), or previous to April 7, according to Albert of Aix (XII, vii). Hagenmeyer errs in interpreting Albert's phrase "vigilia S. Andreae" to be November 28 rather than November 29 (*HF* 559, note 4).

[3] Ibn-al-Qalānisī, whose account is quite detailed, states that the two Frankish towers were burned by combustibles dropped from a mast and swinging yard mounted on the city wall (*The Damascus Chronicle,* 124).

4. That homely proverb is most true, "Many a slip between cup and lip."[4] Already our people were distributing the booty they expected to get; already some suspected others for their dubious share; already they counted as certain the day of the capture of the city. "The steed is prepared for battle," saith Solomon, "but the Lord giveth the victory" [Prov. 21:31]. Meanwhile men trust in their own strength not considering what they owe to God. They often invoke Him with their lips but neglect good works. They boast of their virtue in their successes more than they glorify the gift of God's mercy.

XLVII

The Death of Prince Tancred. 1. In the year 1112 Tancred, who ruled the principality of Antioch, paid his debt to death.[1]

> Now twice thirteen times had the sun seen the Sign of the Archer
> When Tancred submitted to the inexorable and became what
> he was predestined to be.[2]

Roger, his kinsman, succeeded him.[3] In that year we were entirely free from war.[4]

XLVIII

The Signs That Appeared. 1. In the year 1113 of the Incarnation of Our Lord, in the month of March and on the twenty-eighth day of the moon,[1] we saw the sun from early morning to the first hour. More than that we saw it wane by fading in one

---

[4] This idea may go back to Antinoüs' attempt to drink the contents of a golden goblet (Homer *Odys.* xxii, 10–20).

[1] Tancred had served as regent of Antioch since 1104 for Bohemond I (chap. xxvi, 1), who died on March 7, 1111 (Yewdale, *Bohemond,* 133), and then for his minor son Bohemond II in Apulia.

[2] Tancred died on December 12, 1112 (Nicholson, *Tancred,* 224, note 3).

[3] Tancred's successor in the regency of Antioch was Roger of Salerno (1112–19), son of Richard of the Principate, regent of Edessa (1104–1108), and of his wife, a sister of Tancred (*HF* 563, note 4).

[4] Jerusalem was free of war after April, 1112, when the siege of Tyre ended (chap. xlvi, note 2), and until the invasion of Maudūd of Mosul and Tughtigin of Damascus in June, 1113 (chap. xlix).

[1] March 19, 1113 (*HF* 564, note 2).

part. The section which first began to fade, at the top, at length came down like a round shape to the bottom. However, the sun did not lose its brightness, which was not diminished I think except in a fourth part. This part was in the shape of a small crescent.

This was an eclipse, which thus caused the sun to fail us.[2]

XLIX

The Battle Fought Against the Turks, in Which the King and the Christians Were Defeated and from Which Much Evil Followed. 1. Then in the summer time the Turks massed their forces and crossed the Euphrates in order to advance upon the lands of Jerusalem and, as they thought, to destroy us Christians.[1] They left the territory of Antioch to their right, traversed Syria not far from Apamea, left Damascus to their left, and crossed between Tyre and Caesarea Philippi, which is called Paneas,[2] into the regions of Phoenicia. They intended to attack King Baldwin. But he heard of their advance and moved his army out of Ptolemais, i.e., Acre, against them.

2. After providing themselves with what they felt was useful to them and while we were ignorant of what they intended, they circled around the Sea of Galilee through the territories of Napthali and Zebulun to the south end of the aforesaid sea.[3] There they hedged themselves between two streams, the Jor and Dan.[4]

---

[2] For discussion of this solar eclipse, see *HF* 564, notes 1–5.

[1] The date was near the end of Dhu'l Qa'da, A.H. 506 (ended May 18, 1113), according to Ibn-al-Athīr (*RHC, Or.*, I, 288). In this chapter Fulcher gives the principal Latin account of the great Turkish invasion of 1113, led by Maudūd of Mosul and Tughtigin of Damascus, which nearly destroyed the Frankish kingdom. Fulcher himself seems to have been in or near Jerusalem, not with King Baldwin (note 13). The most complete account is by another contemporary, Ibn-al-Qalānisī (*The Damascus Chronicle*, 132–39). See Fink, "Mawdūd," 23–25, for discussion.

[2] Banyas, about twenty-eight miles north of Lake Tiberias.

[3] Fulcher indicates that the Turks approached on the west side of Lake Tiberias. See *HF* 566, note 9.

[4] Fulcher is confused because these are not the springs of Jor and Dan he mentioned earlier (I, xxxiv, 4) but streams that he imagined were south of Lake Tiberias (cf. *HF* 567, note 10). He added these names in his second redaction (*HF* 567, note b).

3. An island lay between two bridges at this point.[5] It was so secure that anyone located there could not be attacked because of the narrow entrances at the bridges. When the Turks had pitched their tents, they soon sent out two thousand men across one of the bridges to prepare an ambush for our men. They were confident that these latter would rush up to that point without delay.

4. When therefore the king came up to encamp near the bridge that has been mentioned, the one leading to Tiberias, he saw nearly five hundred Turks who burst forth from their hiding places to attack our men. Some of the latter rashly charged the Turks and in slaying them did not hesitate to follow the foe up to the place of ambush. Here two thousand of the enemy issued from their hiding places, repulsed our men in a vigorous attack, and scattered them killing three times as many as they themselves lost.[6]

5. Oh great sadness! On that day our great sins brought great shame. The king fled losing his flag and his fine tent with many furnishings and silver vessels. Likewise the patriarch who was present also fled. We lost nearly thirty of our best knights and about twelve hundred footmen.[7]

6. Phoebus had risen three times four in the Sign of Cancer
When this faithless race scattered the incautious Franks.[8]

7. But all of the king's forces were not yet there. In particular Roger, prince of Antioch and son of Richard, was not present. He had been summoned in the name of the love of God and

---

[5] From Ibn-al-Qalānisī we learn that the Franks camped west of the bridge of aṣ-Ṣinnabrah and hoped to attack the Turks at al-Uqhuwānah (*The Damascus Chronicle*, 134–35), which is east of the Jordan. His account is followed by Ibn-al-Athīr (*RHC, Or.*, I, 288). Fulcher's version of an island and two bridges is to be doubted, although Hagenmeyer, who did not have access to Ibn-al-Qalānisī, accepts it (*HF* 567, notes 10, 11).
[6] Ibn-al-Qalānisī states that a Turkish foraging party crossed the bridge and encountered the Franks west of the Jordan (*The Damascus Chronicle*, 135).
[7] Nearly two thousand Franks were killed, according to Ibn-al-Qalānisī (*ibid.*).
[8] June 28, 1113. Ibn-al-Qalānisī agrees (*ibid.*, 136).

king and was coming from Antioch with all haste. A part of the men of Tripoli had already joined the royal army. They were all greatly dismayed. They denounced the impudence of the king in that he had rushed against the enemy in a rash and disorderly manner without waiting for their advice and aid.[9]

8. And because our men could not at that time do any damage to the Turks they camped not far from them. Thus each side could watch the other all day.

9. The leader of the enemy army was called Maledoctus. He had attached Tuldequinus, King of Damascus,[10] to himself as an ally. The former led a huge force; the latter had gathered an innumerable host from the part of Syria subject to himself.

10. The Turks were in the lowland; the Franks settled down upon a height.[11] The Turks did not dare issue from their island; the Franks could not attack them. One side schemed, the other feared; one side was crafty, the other wary.

> The heat of summer oppressed them both
> Yet they were not able to end such suffering.

11. The Franks who were absent wondered why those who were there delayed so long. The Saracens subject to us deserted us and as enemies hemmed us in on every side. In addition the Turks went out from their army in bands to devastate our lands and to send back booty and supplies to their army by means of our Saracens. Sichem, which we call the city of Neapolis, they not only took but destroyed with the help of the Saracens whom we ruled in the mountains.[12]

---

[9] This refers to Baldwin's youthful colleagues, Roger, regent of Antioch (1112–19), and Pons, Count of Tripoli (1112–37).

[10] Maudūd, Atabeg of Mosul, and Tughtigin, Atabeg of Damascus.

[11] This hill was west of the city of Tiberias (Ibn-al-Qalānisī, The Damascus Chronicle, 136).

[12] This paragraph is particularly enlightening because it shows how near the Franks were to total destruction. The Saracens mentioned were the native peasantry on the estates of the Franks, for they were never evicted. Ibn-al-Qalānisī writes that the Turks raided as far as the environs of Jerusalem and Joppa (ibid., 137). Neapolis was Nablus. The Turks gave up and went home after August 16.

12. Indeed the men of Ascalon, who were Arabs and Saracens, although few in number, advanced upon Jerusalem. One day they reached the outer wall of the city and set fire to the harvests gathered there. They wounded with arrows some of our men on the ramparts of the wall; yet many of their men were mortally wounded. Our soldiers were not in the city, for they had gone against the enemy. On the following night the people of Ascalon retired to the great relief of our men, for they dreaded a siege by the former.[13]

L

The Great Fear Which Then Possessed Everyone. 1. At that time it was almost impossible, because of the snares of the enemy, for a messenger sent by any of us to venture forth to the king nor for one from him to come through to any of our cities. Hence it was not known by the towns what the king was doing, nor could they tell him what they were doing.

> In many fields the ripened harvest withered
> And no one went into the fields to gather it [Matth. 9:37].

For none dared to do so. In that year the harvest was abundant, but while the sea is rough men fear to fish. Everything was in doubt to everyone, and all waited to see to whom God would give the victory. Our Christians ceased their business and their labors except to repair damages to the cities and their walls.[1]

LI

The Earthquake; and the Marriage of the King to the Countess of Sicily. 1. Meanwhile we twice felt an earthquake, to wit, on the fifteenth day before of the Kalends of August and again on

---

[13] The date of this foray from Ascalon cannot be determined. This paragraph and the next chapter seem to indicate that Fulcher was in or around Jerusalem, certainly not with Baldwin near Tiberias.

[1] Damage to the walls would seem to refer to the effects of the earthquakes of that summer (chap. li, 1).

the fifth day before the Ides of the same month: the first time at midnight, the second time at the third hour.[1]

2. Meanwhile the crafty Turks waited for two months[2] for an opportune time for scattering or conquering us, but in vain because in that season the pilgrims from overseas were arriving as was customary, and our army grew from day to day. In addition the men of Antioch did not leave us. At length the Turks withdrew into the territories of Damascus.[3]

3. King Baldwin then retired with his men to Acre where he found the Countess of Sicily. She had been the wife of Count Roger, brother of Robert Guiscard, but now was to be the wife of King Baldwin.[4]

4. Very soon after this event Maledoctus was killed at Damascus by a certain Saracen. The latter had a dagger concealed under his cloak and with it stabbed his victim thrice in the stomach. Thus he there committed a double homicide, for he both killed and was killed instantly by those present.[5] It is an ill-omened victory in which he who conquers is conquered. And so it transpired according to the saying of the philosopher:

"Fortune is of glass; while it is shining it breaks."[6]

5. Maledoctus was very rich and powerful and very renowned among the Turks. He was extremely astute in his actions but could not resist the will of God.[7] The Lord permitted him to scourge us for a while but afterwards willed that he should die a vile death and by the hand of an insignificant man.

[1] July 18 and August 9, 1113.

[2] During July and August, the two months after the battle at aṣ-Ṣinnabrah (chap. xlix, note 8).

[3] According to Ibn-al-Qalānisī, the Turks reached Damascus on September 5 (The Damascus Chronicle, 139).

[4] The countess was Adelaide, widow of Roger I of Sicily (d. 1101). Baldwin married her for her money and because he wanted diplomatic and naval support from her son, Roger II. See Runciman, Crusades, II, 102–103. Guiscard (d. 1085) was the father of Bohemond I.

[5] Maudūd was murdered in the great mosque of Damascus on October 2, 1113 (Ibn-al-Qalānisī, The Damascus Chronicle, 139–40).

[6] Publius Syrus Mim. 242 (quoted in HF 578, note 10).

[7] Fulcher could not resist admiring this very able foe.

LII

The Earthquake That Was Felt in Many Places. 1. In the year 1114 an infinite multitude of locusts swarmed out of a part of Arabia and flew into the land of Jerusalem. In a few days, during the months of April and May, they severely damaged our crops.[1]

2. Later, on the Feast of St. Lawrence,[2] there was an earthquake. Still later, on the Ides of November, an earthquake at Mamistra destroyed a part of the city.[3]

3. Likewise a greater quake, the worst ever heard of, shook the area of Antioch and destroyed a great many towns in whole or in part, including houses as well as walls. Some of the common people perished of suffocation in the ruins.

4. They say that this quake destroyed the city of Marash, which I think is about sixty miles north of Antioch. The houses and walls were completely demolished and the people living there, alas! were all killed.[4]

5. Another town called *Trialeth*, near the Euphrates River, was also destroyed.[5]

LIII

The Gathering of the Turkish Army, and the Siege of the People of Joppa by the Ascalonites and the Babylonians. 1. In the year 1115 the Turks, resuming their accustomed fierceness and audac-

[1] This plague is also mentioned by Walter the Chancellor (*Bella Antiochena*, Prolog., 2). Fulcher mentions another plague of locusts occurring in May, 1117 (chap. lx, 2).

[2] August 10, 1114.

[3] November 13, 1114. Mamistra was damaged by another earthquake in 1115 (chap. liv, 7).

[4] The effects of this earthquake, of November 29, 1114 (*HF* 579, note 7), upon Antioch are graphically described by Walter the Chancellor (*Bella Antiochena*, I, i, 1). The quake is apparently mentioned by several Arab writers (Kamāl-ad-Dīn, *RHC, Or.*, III, 607; Ibn-al-Athīr, *ibid.*, I, 295; and Ibn-al-Qalānisī, *The Damascus Chronicle*, 149). Marash is about a hundred miles north of Antioch.

[5] Trialeth cannot be identified, but Hagenmeyer suggests that it may have been Balis on the Euphrates, about 100 miles east of Antioch, the scene of an earthquake in a.h. 508 (June 7, 1114–May 26, 1115) recorded by Sibṭ Ibn-al-Jauzī (*RHC, Or.*, III, 551–52; *HF* 580, note 12).

ity, stealthily crossed the River Euphrates in June, entered Syria, and camped between Antioch and Damascus, to wit, in front of the city of Shaizar.¹ They had similarly taken a position here four years before, as has been written above.²

2. Tuldequinus, the King of Damascus, discovered this and realized that he was no less odious to these Turks than to us Christians because he had deceitfully been privy to the murder of Mandulf in a previous year, as was stated above.³ This Mandulf had been the chief satrap of their army. Tuldequinus made peace with King Baldwin and with Roger, Prince of Antioch, so that a third army was added to their two, and a triple cord, as it were, was made which could not afterwards be easily broken by the Turks. For he feared that if he remained alone he together with his kingdom would be entirely destroyed.⁴

3. Urged indeed by necessity and advised by an embassy from Antioch, King Baldwin came to the battle which he thought would occur. But when the Turks heard that he had already come up close to them they regarded this as the advance of the men of Antioch and Damascus which they had been expecting for nearly three months.⁵ Fearing for their lives if they fought so

¹ In this chapter Fulcher tells of the invasion of Syria by Bursuk ibn-Bursuk of Hamadan, commander-in-chief for the Selchükid Sultan Muḥammad ibn-Malik-Shāh in the *jihād* of 1115. According to Ibn-al-Athir, who was, however, a later writer, the crossing of the Euphrates was prior to the end of A.H. 508, *i.e.*, before May 26, 1115 (*RHC, Or.*, I, 296; cf. Stevenson, *Crusaders in the East*, 98, note 2). For discussion of this campaign, see Stevenson, *Crusaders in the East*, 98–100; and Cahen, *La Syrie du Nord*, 271–73.

² Chap. xlv, 6.

³ The murder of Maudūd of Mosul, Sultan Muḥammad's commander, in 1113 (chap. li, 4).

⁴ Fulcher correctly diagnoses the plight of Tughtigin. Tughtigin, who was practically independent, preferred an alliance with his neighbors the Syrian Franks to the presence in Syria of a powerful representative of the Selchükid sultan of Bagdad. Fulcher does not mention the regent Lu' lu' of Aleppo and Il-Ghāzī of Mardin, who also allied with the Franks in 1115. See H. S. Fink, "The Role of Damascus in the History of the Crusades," *Muslim World*, XLIX (1959), 45–47.

⁵ Walter the Chancellor, an excellent contemporary authority from Antioch, states that Roger, while at Apamea in August, summoned King Baldwin (*Bella Antiochena*, I, iii, 2), which bears out the statement of Fulcher. Two Arab writers, both later, indicate that Baldwin was with the allies for two months,

many although they were much more numerous, the Turks quietly retired and entered some caverns which were not very far from us.[6] When they did this King Baldwin and his allies thought that the Turks had departed entirely from our territories. For this reason the king went back to Tripoli.

4. While these things were happening the men of Ascalon, knowing that the land of Jerusalem was devoid of soldiers, rushed up to our city of Joppa and besieged it by land and sea.[7] Present there was the Babylonian fleet of nearly seventy vessels, of which some were triremes, some were beaked ships, and some were freighted with supplies for the undertaking.

5. The men of Ascalon approached, some by sea and the rest by land, prepared to attack the city. And when they made a vigorous effort to scale the wall with ladders which they brought with them, they were strongly repulsed by the citizens although the latter were few and weakened by sickness.

6. However, when the Ascalonites saw that they could not accomplish anything as they had planned, except to set fire to the gates of the city, they feared that perchance the people of Jerusalem who had already heard the news might bring help to Joppa, and hence they retired. Those that had come by land went back to Ascalon, and those that had come by sea sailed to Tyre.

7. Ten days later[8] the men of Ascalon returned to Joppa thinking that if they were prepared they might by sudden attack destroy their enemy unprepared. But the Omnipotent God as He has done before similarly protected and saved us a second time. In defending themselves the Franks killed some of the enemy and captured their horses. The Ascalonites began to besiege the city with *fundibula* and tried to enter it as before with

---

i.e., from June (Ibn-al-Athīr, *RHC, Or.*, I, 297; Sibṭ Ibn-al-Jauzī, *ibid.*, III, 554). By "three months" Fulcher refers loosely to June, July, and August.

[6] *I.e.*, Bursuk broke contact with his enemies. See *HF* 584, note 16.

[7] Fulcher is the sole authority for this campaign against Jerusalem. It may have been prior to August 15, 1115, since Albert of Aix speaks of an Egyptian fleet at Tyre between August 15–September 11 of that year (XII, xvii; see *HF* 585, note 18; 586, note 21).

[8] *Ca.* August 22, 1115, according to Hagenmeyer (*HF* 586, note 22).

ladders brought in small boats. After they had exhausted themselves during the course of six hours they sadly retired carrying with them their dead.

LIV

The Battle Between the Turks and the Men of Antioch in Which the Latter Gained the Victory.[1]   1. However, the Turks mentioned above, when they discovered that our army had returned home, went back to their former position and scoured the regions of Syria. They captured whatever castles they could, plundered villages, devastated the countryside, and carried off men and women into captivity.[2]

2. But when this was announced to the men of Antioch, who had already retired, they quickly turned back against the Turks by the way they had left. And when they had approached the Turks and noticed that the camp of the latter was closer than they had first thought, they at once formed battle lines and came down into the area of the camp, galloping against the enemy with banners flying. This battle was near the town of Sarmīn.[3]

3. As soon as the Turks saw the Franks, the Turkish corps of archers forthwith resisted furiously.[4] But our Franks were stirred by a mighty spirit of courage and chose to conquer if God willed or be conquered if He permitted, rather than be thus molested by the Turks every year. They assailed the enemy in wondrous manner wherever they saw the mass was densest.

4. The Turks at first resisted for a little while, then suddenly

[1] In this chapter Fulcher gives his account of the great victory of Roger of Antioch over the Selchükid generalissimo Bursuk ibn-Bursuk in the valley of Sarmīn near Tell Dānīth on September 14, 1115. Although Fulcher was not present, he agrees very well with Walter the Chancellor, of Antioch, whose account is quite complete (*Bella Antiochena*, I, iv, 6; vii, 5). For discussion see Grousset, *Croisades*, I, 504–10.

[2] Bursuk, after the departure of his enemies in August (chap. liii, 3) captured Roger's stronghold of Kafarṭāb and then ravaged the area around Ma'arrat-an-Nu'mān (Walter the Chancellor, *Bella Antiochena*, I, iv, 6–7).

[3] The town of Sarmīn is about thirty-three miles southeast of Antioch and about the same distance southwest of Aleppo.

[4] Apparently this is the attack made upon Roger by the Turk Tamirek of Sinjar (Walter the Chancellor, *Bella Antiochena*, I, vi, 8).

fled from those who smote and slew them. It is estimated that three thousand Turks were killed, and many captured. Those who escaped death saved themselves by flight. They lost their tents in which were found much money and property. The value of the money was estimated at three hundred thousand bezants. The Turks abandoned there our people whom they had captured, Franks as well as Syrians, and their own wives and maid-servants and many camels. Thousands of mules and horses were counted.[5]

5. Truly is God marvelous in all of His miracles. For while the men of Jerusalem along with those of Antioch and Damascus were prepared for battle they accomplished nothing whatever. For when did the victory of fighters ever depend upon the number of men? Remember the Maccabees, Gideon [I–II Mach.; Judic. 6–8], and many others who confided not in their own strength but in that of God and in that way overcame many thousands.

6. And so by this description the event shall be known to future generations.
Three nights went by before the Constellation Virgo went away
As deceptive fortune cruelly betrayed the Turks.[6]
Whence it is quite clear that manifestly all must fear
That before the end of a matter nothing is ever to be regarded as certain.

7. In that year the city of Mamistra was demolished by an earthquake. Other places in the area of Antioch suffered no less.[7]

8. In that same year the Bishop of Orange arrived, sent to Jerusalem by the Apostolic See, and deposed Patriarch Arnulf

[5] Kamāl-ad-Dīn also tells of the great quantity of booty (RHC, Or., III, 610). Walter the Chancellor writes that it took three days to divide it (Bella Antiochena, I, vii, 5).

[6] September 14, 1115. Two other Latin sources agree with Fulcher (Walter the Chancellor, Bella Antiochena, I, v, 3; Albert of Aix, XII, xx), while Usāmah the Arab gives September 15, 1115, as the date (An Arab-Syrian Gentleman, 105). See Stevenson, Crusaders in the East, 100, note 1.

[7] No other writer mentions this earthquake, nor is the exact day known (HF 586, note 1; 590, note 22).

from his seat. Wherefore Arnulf afterwards went to Rome and recovered the patriarchate.[8]

LV

The Castle Built in Arabia.   1. In that year[1] King Baldwin went into Arabia and built a castle strongly situated on a small mountain. It is not far from the Red Sea, about three days' journey, and about four from Jerusalem. He placed a garrison in it to dominate the country in the interest of the Christians. He decided to name this castle Montréal in honor of himself because he built it in a short time with a few men and with great boldness.[2]

LVI

The Expedition of the King into Arabia and What He Saw There.

1. In the year 1116 when the king went from Jerusalem with nearly two hundred knights to revisit his castle in Arabia, he advanced as far as the Red Sea to see what he had not seen and perchance to find something on the way that he might want.[1]

2. At that time they found the city of Elim on the shore of this sea where we read that the people of Israel camped after crossing the sea.[2] Those who dwelt there, when they heard of the

[8] Arnulf's reinstatement is announced in a letter of Pope Paschal II dated July 19, 1116 (Rozière, *Cartulaire de l'Église du Saint-Sépulcre*, No. 11; *HF* 590, note 24). Fulcher's original text refers to Paschal "qui tunc Romae papae praeerat," an indication that Fulcher was writing after 1118, when Paschal died (*HF* 591, note c; Fulcher, II, lxiii, 4).

[1] 1115.

[2] This castle, Krak de Montréal, destined to be famous in the time of Saladin, was built upon a ridge at ash-Shaubak, about ninety miles south of Jerusalem and seventy-five north of al-ʻAqabah on the Red Sea gulf of that name. Consult *HF* 592, note 4; 593, note 5; and Fedden and Thompson, *Crusader Castles*, 26, 28, 60. Baldwin reconnoitered this area in 1100 (chaps. iv–v).

[1] According to Albert of Aix, Baldwin advanced with two hundred knights and four hundred footmen to the vicinity of Mount Horeb, where he built a fortification in eighteen days, and then proceeded with sixty knights to the Red Sea (XII, xxi). However, Albert confused this story with that of the construction of the castle in 1115 (*HF* 593, note 25).

[2] Fulcher confuses Elim, where the Hebrews are said to have crossed the bed of the Red Sea (Exod. 15:27; Num. 33:9), presumably in the Gulf of Suez, with Elath (Ailah, modern al-ʻAqabah) at the head of the Gulf of ʻAqabah (I Reg. 9:26; II Paralip. 8:17).

king's approach, withdrew and embarking upon their little vessels rushed out to sea in great fear.

3. However, when the king and his men looked over the place as long as they wished, they returned to their castle of Montréal and then to Jerusalem.

4. When they told us what they had seen we were delighted with their tales as well as by the sea shells and certain precious stones which they brought and showed to us. I myself very eagerly questioned them to find what the sea was like, for until then I had wondered whether it was saline or fresh, stagnant water or a lake, whether it had an inlet and outlet like the Sea of Galilee, and whether it was confined by its own dimensions like the Dead Sea, which received the Jordan but had no outlet.[3] For on the south the Dead Sea is bounded by Segor, the city of Lot [Gen. 13:10; 19:22–23].[4]

LVII

The Red Sea. 1. This sea is called the Red Sea because the sand and stones in its bed are red, and so to those looking into it it appears red; but, however, in a vessel its water is as limpid and clear as that from any other sea. They say that this sea is derived from the Ocean to the south.[1] It extends like a tongue northwards as far as Elim, already spoken of, where it ends not far from Mount Sinai. The latter is a day's journey by horse.[2]

2. From the Red Sea or from Elim mentioned above to the Great Sea,[3] which is the way one proceeds from Joppa, Ascalon, or Gaza toward Damietta, they estimate the journey to be four or five days by horseback. In the region between these two seas is enclosed the whole of Egypt and Numidia and also Ethiopia,

[3] Cf. Fulcher's similar curiosity about the Dead Sea in 1110 (chap. v, 1–3).
[4] See reference to Segor in chap. v, 4, note 6.
[1] The Indian Ocean.
[2] Fulcher continues to confuse Biblical Elim with Elath. He is also vague about Mount Sinai, for if he is thinking of the traditional site, the Jabal Mûsâ, it is about ninety miles south of Elath.
[3] The Mediterranean Sea.

which Gihon, the river of Paradise, which is the Nile, compasseth, as we read [Gen. 2:13].[4]

LVIII

The River Gihon. 1. I can admire but never explain how and in what way this River Gihon, which we read comes out of Paradise with three others,[1] seems to have found a second source since it has to the east the Red Sea and to the west our sea,[2] into which it flows. For it has between itself and the east the Red Sea, and yet we read that Paradise is in the east. Therefore I greatly wonder how it resumes its course on this side of the Red Sea and how it crosses that sea, or whether it does cross it.

LIX

The Euphrates. 1. We say the same thing about the Euphrates, which has a second origin, in Armenia. It then crosses Mesopotamia about twenty-four miles from Edessa I think.[1]

2. Let him who wishes inquire the reason for this; let him who is able learn the reason, for I have very often sought to learn it by inquiry from many persons but have not been able to find anyone who could explain it to me. I leave the explanation to Him who miraculously causes the water to be in the clouds, the streams to arise in the mountains, hills, and valleys and to run swiftly through the crevices of hidden channels and at last, wonderful to tell, to find the sea and be swallowed up in it.

3. When the end of that year[2] was approaching the king was attacked by a growing bodily illness and feared death. For this reason he dismissed his wife Adelaide, the Countess of Sicily men-

---

[4] "Ut in bibliotheca legimus" appears at this point in Fulcher's first redaction, an indication that he was using a library at Jerusalem at the time he was writing.

[1] Paradise here refers to Eden. The four rivers said to flow from it are the Pison, the Gihon, which Fulcher regards as the Nile, the Tigris, and the Euphrates (Gen. 2:10–14).

[2] The Mediterranean.

[1] "Twenty miles" in I, xiv, 5. Actually, the distance is about forty-five miles.

[2] 1116.

tioned above,[3] whom he had unlawfully wed, since she whom he had lawfully married in the city of Edessa was still alive.[4]

LX

The Great Plague of the Locusts. 1. In the year 1117 of the Incarnation of Our Lord this queen who has been mentioned[1] departed from the port of Acre on the day on which, in accordance with the rule of the church, the greater litany is chanted[2] and with seven ships in her company crossed over to Sicily.

2. Then in the month of May an infinite multitude of locusts swarmed into the land of Jerusalem devouring more completely than usual the vines, field crops, and trees of all kinds.[3] You could see them advance like an army of men in good order as if they had previously arranged it in council. When they had made their day's journey, some on foot and some flying, they mutually chose a resting place for themselves. And so when they had eaten up everything green, and had gnawed the bark of the trees, the wingless locusts as well as the others departed in companies.

3. Oh the wickedness of men who persist in their wicked perversity! How often and how much our Creator touches us with His reproaches and admonishes us, terrifies us by His portents, stirs us by His threats, instructs us by His lessons, and represses us by His punishment. But we always persist in our iniquities, despise

[3] Chap. li, 3.
[4] The dismissal of Adelaide and the reinstatement of Patriarch Arnulf (chap. liv, 8) were connected. Arnulf had arranged the marriage, which was, in fact, bigamous. He was reinstated by Pope Paschal II provided that he would persuade King Baldwin to dismiss Adelaide. This Baldwin was willing to do because he had spent Adelaide's dowry and also felt guilty forebodings of death. Albert of Aix, dependent upon Fulcher but using a system of chronology beginning the year with March, dates Baldwin's sickness in March, 1117 (XII, xxiii; *HF* 601, note 7). Consult letter of Paschal, dated "XIV *kalendas augusti*, . . . MCXVII," which was apparently July 19, 1116. See Rozière, *Cartulaire de l'Église du Saint-Sépulcre*, No. 11; *HF* 591, notes 24, 25; William of Tyre, XI, i, xxix; and Mayer, *Kreuzzüge*, 82. Baldwin's first wife is called Arda, granddaughter of Roupen I of Armenia, by Dulaurier, editor of the chronicle of Matthew of Edessa (*RHC, Arm.*, I, li, cxiii); but I have been unable to find her named in any original source.
[1] Adelaide. [2] April 25, 1117 (*HF* 602, note 3).
[3] Cf. locust plague in May, 1114 (chap. lii, 4).

His admonitions, and contemptuously violate His precepts.

4. What wonder that the Saracens or other wicked lords should take from us our lands since we ourselves reach out with thievish hands into the fields of our neighbors! Indeed we wrongfully cheat them with the furrow of the plow or otherwise secretly rob them with greedy acts of fraud and thus sinfully enrich ourselves from their possessions.

5. What wonder is it that, God permitting, the mice destroy our crops while they are sprouting from the roots in the ground or the locusts devour them ripened in the ear, or that they are damaged in the granaries by worms of every kind or by rotting, when we dishonestly sell the tithes owed to God or sacrilegiously retain them entirely?

LXI

The Portent of the Moon. 1. In the following month, which was June, the moon appeared to us who were looking at it in the sky after cockcrow, first entirely red; very soon, however, the redness changed to black so that the moon lost the strength of its light for nearly two hours. This happened on the thirteenth of the month. If it had happened on the fourteenth we would certainly have thought it an eclipse.[1]

2. Therefore we regarded it as a portent. From this redness some conjectured that blood would be shed in battle; from the blackness others prophesied that a famine was coming. But we committed the matter to the disposition and providence of God,

---

[1] Fulcher, here using the Golden Number system of chronology, a lunar system for calculating the dates of Easter, expected the new moon on June 4, which he, however, regarded as the first of the month. He expected the full moon to occur fifteen days later on June 18 (or June 15 by his reckoning). However, his calculations were incorrect in this instance: the new moon came on June 2, and the full moon followed in fifteen days, on June 16 (which he regarded as June 13). Hence his astonishment and superstititious awe. He adds that if the full moon had appeared on the fourteenth day (*i.e.*, at any other interval than fifteen days) he would have regarded it as an eclipse. For further discussion, see *HF* 604, note 3; and Henri Wallon, edition of Fulcher, *RHC, Occ.*, III, 434, note b. Regarding the Golden Number system, see A. Giry, *Manuel de diplomatique* (Paris: Librairie Hachette et Cie, 1894), 148.

who foretold to His disciples that there would be portents in the sun and the moon [Luc. 21:25].

3. He moreover as He wills causes the earth to tremble and then to be still. This subsequently happened in the same month in the silence of an unseasonable night, on the sixth day before the Kalends of June.[2]

LXII

The Castle Built near Tyre. 1. Then the king built a castle near the city of Tyre, within five miles. He named it *Scandalion*, which interpreted means "Field of the Lion."[1] He repaired the breaches in it and placed a garrison within to be a restraint upon the people of Tyre.

LXIII

The Marvelous Portent Appearing in the Sun. 1. In the same year, in the month of December, on the fifth night after the eclipse of the moon which happened on the thirteenth of the month,[1] in the beginning of the night we all saw the northern sky streaked with the bright color of fire or of blood. Thinking that this phenomenon was full of wondrous portents, we marveled greatly.

2. Through the midst of this redness, which first began to increase a little by little, we saw a great many white rays rise in a remarkable way from the bottom upwards, now in front, then in the rear, then in the center.[2] In the lower part the sky appeared light as if it were dawn when the sky is wont to brighten just before sunrise. In front of this phenomenon, to the east, we saw a white-

---

[2] June 26, 1117.

[1] Fulcher apparently errs in his interpretation of *Scandalion*, for William of Tyre explains that it was named after Alexander the Great, called "Scandar" in Arabic (XI, xxx).

[1] Fulcher, again using the Golden Number system, began his reckoning for the month of December on November 29, 1117, the date of the new moon. The thirteenth day, counting November 29, was December 11, and the fifth day after that was December 16. This time his calculations were correct. See *HF* 607, note 3; and Wallon, edition of Fulcher, *RHC, Occ.*, III, 435, note d.

[2] This was a display of the aurora borealis.

ness as if the moon were about to rise there. For this reason the land and all the places about us glistened clearly in apparition.

3. If this had happened in the morning we would all have said that the day was bright. Therefore we conjectured that either much blood would be shed in war or that something no less threatening was forecast. But what was uncertain to us we humbly committed to the Lord God for His disposition.

4. However, some people, prophesying, declared that this was a portent of death for those who were to die during the next year. And subsequently these did die: Pope Paschal in the month of January; Baldwin, king of the people of Jerusalem, in April; also his wife in Sicily, whom he had forsaken; Arnulf, the Patriarch of Jerusalem; Alexius, the Emperor of Constantinople; and many others of the great men of the world.[3]

LXIV

The Death of King Baldwin I. 1. In the year of the Virgin Birth, 1118, toward the end of the month of March, King Baldwin attacked and plundered the city of Faramia, as it is called.[1] Then one day he went walking along the river which the Greeks call the Nile and the Hebrews the Gihon, near the city, enjoying himself with some of his friends. Some of the knights very skillfully

---

[3] Pope Paschal died on January 21, 1118; King Baldwin, on April 2; ex-Queen Adelaide on April 16; Arnulf, possibly on April 28; and Alexius on August 15 (HF 608, notes 12–16).

[1] The city was al-Faramā' (class. Pelusium), about twelve miles east of the modern Suez Canal. The chronology must be worked out in connection with Albert of Aix. He states that Baldwin reached al-Faramā' on Thursday "before the middle of Lent," that the Franks entered the city on Friday "the next day," stayed there Friday, Saturday, and Sunday (XII, xxv), discussed retirement on Sunday "in the middle of Lent," decided to retreat on Monday when Baldwin grew ill (XII, xxvi), and that Baldwin died on a Tuesday (XII, xxvii). As Lent in 1118 began on Ash Wednesday, March 6, Monday, March 25, was the twentieth day or the middle of Lent and the day of Baldwin's illness; the preceding Thursday was March 21; the capture of the city occurred on Friday, March 22. Hagenmeyer errs in locating the third Sunday in Lent, Oculi Sunday, on March 17 and therefore dates the day of arrival March 14 rather than March 21. But he is correct in saying that Sunday in mid-Lent was March 24 (HF 609, note 3). Albert's chronology thus accords with Fulcher's statement that these events took place "toward the end of the month of March."

used their lances to spear the fish found there and carried them to their camp near the city and ate them. Then the king felt within himself the renewed pangs of an old wound and was most seriously weakened.[2]

2. The news was at once announced to his men. When they heard of it they were all devoutly sympathetic and were saddened and disturbed. They decided to return to Jerusalem, but since the king could not ride they prepared for him a litter made from tent poles and laid him in it. The order to return to Jerusalem was given by the sound of the herald's trumpet.[3]

3. When they reached the village called Laris[4] Baldwin finally died, his body nearly wasted away by illness. They took out his intestines, salted them and laid them in the coffin, and hurried on to Jerusalem.

4. On the day when it was customary to carry branches of palms,[5] by the will of God and by a most unexpected circumstance the funeral train carrying its mournful burden met the religious procession when it was descending from the Mount of Olives into the Valley of Jehoshaphat.

5. At the sight of this and as if Baldwin were a kinsman, all who were present gave themselves over to mourning rather than song, to grief rather than joy. The Franks wept, the Syrians, and even the Saracens who saw it grieved also. For who, who piously wept there, could not control himself? Therefore returning then to the city the clergy as well as the people did what was fitting and customary for the sorrowful occasion.

6. They buried Baldwin in Golgotha[6] next to Duke Godfrey, his brother.

7.   The Epitaph of King Baldwin
When the king died the pious race of the Franks wept,
For he was their shield, their strength, and their support.

---

[2] Possibly the wound received in 1103 (chap. xxiv, 1).
[3] Apparently on Monday, March 25. See note 1.
[4] Al-ʿArīsh (class. Rhinocolura), about fifty miles east of al-Faramāʾ.
[5] Palm Sunday, April 7, 1118 (*HF* 612, note 17).
[6] A chapel in the Church of the Holy Sepulcher (*HF* 613, note 22).

He was the right arm of his people, the terror and adversary
of his enemies,
The mighty leader of his country, as was Joshua.
Acre, Caesarea, Beirut, and Sidon also
He took from the impious native foe.
Afterwards he added to his rule and subjected to his authority
The lands of the Arabs or at least those which touched
the Red Sea.
He captured Tripoli and with no less might took Arsuth
and likewise performed many other honorable deeds.[7]
8. For eighteen years the king bore rule,
Then passed to his fate as he was fated to do.
Sixteen times had Phoebus seen the Constellation of Aries
When the great king Baldwin passed away.[8]

Here Ends the Second Book

[7] Acre fell on May 26, 1104 (chap. xxv, 3, note 3); Caesarea, on May 17, 1101 (chap. ix, 4–5); Beirut, on May 13, 1110 (chap. xlii, 3, note 6); Sidon, on December 4 or 5, 1110 (chap. xliv, 7, note 6); Tripoli, on June 26 or July 12, 1109 (chap. xli, 5, note 4); and Arsuf, on April 29, 1101 (chap. viii, 5, note 5).
[8] Tuesday, April 2, 1118 (HF 614, note 28).

BOOK III

†

HERE BEGINNETH THE THIRD BOOK,
THE DEEDS OF BALDWIN II

I

The Consecration of King Baldwin on Easter Day. 1. As a result of the death of King Baldwin the people of Jerusalem called a council at once lest lacking a king they be considered the weaker. They chose as their king Baldwin, Count of Edessa, a kinsman of the deceased king. It happened that he had crossed the Euphrates River and had come to Jerusalem to consult with his predecessor. On Easter Day he was chosen unanimously and was consecrated.[1]

II

The Gathering of the Babylonian Army. 1. That same year when the summer had come the Babylonians assembled a very large army estimated at fifteen thousand horsemen and twenty thousand footmen with the intention of destroying the Christians of Jerusalem in battle.[1] When they reached Ascalon, Tuldequinus,

---

[1] Count Baldwin II of Edessa (1100–18) was a son of Hugh I of Rethel, a first cousin of Godfrey and Baldwin I (*HF* 616, note 4). He was consecrated on Easter Sunday, April 14, 1118, but not formally crowned until December 25, 1119 (chap. vii, 4), by which time it was apparent that his elder brother, Count Eustace III of Boulogne, would not come to claim the inheritance. Consult Reinhold Röhricht, *Geschichte der Kreuzzüge im Umriss* (Innsbruck: Verlag der Wagner'schen Universitäts-Buchhandlung, 1898), 71.

[1] The main sources of information for this campaign are Fulcher, William of Tyre (XII, vi), dependent in part upon Fulcher, and Ibn-al-Athīr; the most complete discussion is by Hagenmeyer (*HF* 617–19, notes 1–16). Ibn-al-Athīr states that the Egyptians sent a force of seven thousand horsemen to Ascalon following

· 225 ·

the King of Damascus,[2] who had crossed the Jordan, advanced to aid them with his men. In addition a dangerous fleet of no small size had come by sea to Ascalon. However, this fleet, of war vessels as well as supply ships, went on to Tyre. But the men who had come by land remained at Ascalon expecting battle.

2. Then King Baldwin with the men of Antioch and Tripoli,[3] whom he had summoned by messengers to this struggle, hurried off prepared to do battle against the hostile army. When they passed by Azotus, an ancient city of the Philistines,[4] he ordered the tents to be unloaded from the pack animals and pitched not far from the Babylonians so that both armies could be seen every day by each other.

3. But because each side greatly feared to attack the other, and because they preferred to live rather than to die, for nearly three months[5] both sides managed to postpone fighting for reasons of this kind. Then the Saracens, worn out by the delay, abandoned the war. The men of Antioch returned home, but detailed three hundred soldiers to Baldwin. This was in order that they might if necessary strengthen the king in battle if the Egyptians should try to renew the war.

III

The Battle and the Slaughter of the People of Antioch Who Were Fighting with the Turks. 1. In the year 1119 of the Incarnation the Lord, Pope Gelasius, the successor of Paschal, died on the fourth day before the Kalends of February[1] and was buried at Cluny. Calixtus, who had been the archbishop of the city of Vienne, was chosen as his successor.[2]

---

the raid of Baldwin I on al-Faramā' (*RHC, Or.,* I, 315). Fulcher's figures are far too high.

[2] Tughtigin, *Atabeg* of Damascus.

[3] Antioch was governed by Roger of Salerno, and Tripoli by Count Pons.

[4] Biblical Ashdod (I Sam. 6:17; cf. II, xiii, 2, note 1).

[5] July, August, September, 1118 (*HF* 618, note 10; 619, note 14).

[1] Gelasius II, pope for only a year, died on January 29, 1119.

[2] Calixtus II (1119–24), brother of several members of the Crusade of 1101 (II, xvi, note 6).

2. We do not wish to encumber our history by enumerating all the unfortunate events which took place that year in the region of Antioch, how Roger, prince of that city, together with his leading men and his people, went out to fight against the Turks and was killed near the town of Artasia;[3] how seven thousand of the men of Antioch were killed but of the Turks only twenty.

3. Nor is it to be wondered at that God permitted Roger and his men to be confounded since reveling in riches of all kinds they in their sin did not respect God or man.[4]

4. The prince himself shamefully committed adultery with many others while living with his own wife.[5] He deprived of his inheritance his own lord, the son of Bohemond, then living in Apulia with his mother.[6] He and his leading men, living in pride and luxury, were guilty of many other sins. To them that verse of David may be appropriately applied: "Their iniquities came forth as it were from their fatness" [Psalm. 72:7]. For moderation was scarcely preserved in the midst of copious delights.

IV

King Baldwin, Having Assumed the Cross of the Lord, Hastened to the Aid of the People of Antioch. 1. The massacre of the men of Antioch was followed by a second great victory[1] which through the favor of God very marvelously fell to the people of Jerusalem.

2. For when the aforementioned Roger had notified the king at Jerusalem through messengers that the latter should hasten to his

---

[3] Artāḥ (II, xxx, 3, note 3). The battle is often identified with nearby Sarmadā.

[4] Unfortunately, Fulcher knew little or did not care to write much about Roger's defeat and death at Sarmadā, often called *Ager sanguinis* ("The Field of Blood"), on June 28, 1119. Instead, he used clerical license to scold Roger for his sins. The battle, a great victory for Il-Ghāzī ibn-Artuk (d. 1122) of Mardin and Aleppo, is widely mentioned in other sources and is treated at length by Walter the Chancellor (*Bella Antiochena*, II, i–vi) and William of Tyre (XII, ix–x). Consult Cahen, *La Syrie du Nord*, 283–87.

[5] Probably Cecilia, a sister of Baldwin II. See Cahen, *La Syrie du Nord*, 266.

[6] Fulcher refers to Bohemond II, ruler of Antioch from 1126 to 1130. See II, xlvii; III, lvii, lxi.

[1] The battle near Tell Dānīth and Hāb, August 14, 1119 (v, i).

aid, because the Turks were coming against him with a large
army, the king dropped his other affairs. He had gone to fight
the men of Damascus not far from the Jordan and had taken with
him the patriarch with the Lord's Cross.[2] After he had vigorously
driven the enemy out of the fields in his territories, he hurried on
without a pause to help the people of Antioch. He took with
him the Bishop of Caesarea,[3] who later carried most gallantly
the Cross of the Lord in battle against the enemy. The king also
brought with him the Count of Tripoli. They had together two
hundred and fifty knights.[4]

3. When they reached Antioch the king sent a delegation to
the people of Edessa,[5] ordering them to hasten by forced march
to the campaign being planned against the Turks. After they had
joined the king and the soldiers of Antioch who had either fled
from the first battle or had escaped death by some chance, the
battle was begun near the town called Sardanaium,[6] which is
twenty-four miles from Antioch. Our knights numbered seven
hundred, those of the Turks, twenty thousand. Their leader was
Gazi.[7]

4. I think I should not omit to say that a certain Turk, noticing
that one of our knights knew the Persian language, addressed him
saying, "I say to you, Frank, why make a fool of yourself since
you labor in vain? You can in no wise prevail against us, for you

[2] Albert of Aix relates that Baldwin was then defending the area of Tiberias
against Tughtigin of Damascus (XII, xxxii). See HF 625, note 5. The patriarch
was Gormond (1118–28).

[3] Evremar, former Patriarch of Jerusalem. See II, xxxvii, 1, note 1.

[4] Count Pons of Tripoli. Fulcher's modest estimate of the number of Frankish
knights is probably nearly correct.

[5] King Baldwin apparently had not relinquished his responsibility as Count of
Edessa. Nicholson thinks Baldwin enfeoffed Joscelin, then of Galilee, with
Edessa in late August or early September, 1119 (*Joscelin*, 56).

[6] Zardanā (Zaredna, Sardone), about forty miles southeast of Antioch, taken
by the Turks on August 13, 1119 (Kamāl-ad-Dīn, RHC, Or., III, 620; and
Walter the Chancellor, *Bella Antiochena*, II, xi).

[7] Fulcher's estimate of the Frankish strength is probably trustworthy, but his
estimate of the enemy's number is rhetorical. See HF 627, note 18. The Turkish
leaders were Il-Ghāzī ibn-Artuk of Mardin and Aleppo, and Tughtigin of Damascus, whom Fulcher does not name.

are few and we are many. Indeed your God has abandoned you seeing that you do not keep your law as you should, nor preserve faith and truth among yourselves. We know this, we have learned it and take note of it. Tomorrow without a doubt we shall conquer and overcome you." Oh! what a great shame to the Christians that the faithless reproach us about our faith! For this reason we ought to be exceedingly ashamed and by being tearful and penitent correct our errors.

<h2 style="text-align:center">V</h2>

The Battle and the Victory Gained by the Power of the Most Holy Cross, and the Reception of the Cross in Antioch. 1. Therefore a very severe struggle, as has been said, was begun on the following day.[1] Victory for either side was for long in doubt until the Almighty compelled the Turks to flee by wondrously inspiring the Christians against them. Nevertheless, the Turks in attacking the Christians in the beginning scattered them into small parties and pursued them as far as Antioch, the Christians being unable to regroup their colleagues. But on the other hand God did disperse the Turks, some getting inside the city of Aleppo for safety and others fleeing home to Persia.[2]

2. Moreover the Jerusalem king and the Tripolitan count and their men had shown themselves to be allies of the Most Glorious Cross. They carried it forth to battle as servants of the Lord, fighting around it constantly and gallantly and not deserting it, manfully standing their ground on the field of battle. Through the power of this Most Holy and Precious Cross, Almighty God snatched His servants from the grasp of the abominable race of Turks and saved His people for some future mission in His service.

3. After the king stood guard on the battlefield for two days and

---

[1] August 14, 1119. The battle is usually identified with Tell Dānīth, scene of Roger's great victory in 1115 (II, liv), although sometimes with the adjacent village of Hāb. For this campaign, see Walter the Chancellor, *Bella Antiochena,* II, x–xiii; and Cahen, *La Syrie du Nord,* 289–90.

[2] By "Persia" Fulcher means Iraq. He thought of the Turks in connection with Persia because they had originally reached Iraq through Persia.

no Turks returned to fight he took up the Lord's Cross and advanced to Antioch.[3]

4. And the patriarch of Antioch[4] went forth to meet the Most Holy Cross, the king, and the prelate who carried it. They all rendered thanks to God and poured out sweet praise to the Almighty, who through the power of the Most Holy Cross gave victory to the Christians and brought back the Cross unharmed to Christendom. They wept from piety and sang from joy; adoring they bowed with repeated genuflections before the Cross so worthy of veneration, and rising gave thanks again with uplifted countenances.

> 5. The Sun had appeared twice during the Constellation of
>   the Virgin
> When this battle was waged, in which the Parthians were
>   thus conquered.
> At that time the crescent of the Moon had been shining
>   clear for ten days.[5]

VI

The Reception of the Holy Cross in Jerusalem.   1. After the Franks had rested themselves for a short time in Antioch they decided to return to Jerusalem with the blessed Cross of the Lord, as was proper. The king, having provided as many soldiers as was necessary, sent the Cross back to Jerusalem. With it they entered the Holy City rejoicing, on the day when they celebrated the festival of its exaltation, as the Emperor Heraclius had done when he brought it back from Persia.[1] All who were in Jerusalem received the Cross with ineffable joy.

---

[3] Apparently Baldwin spent August 15–16 around the battlefield and reached Antioch a day or two later. See *HF* 630, note 9.

[4] Bernard of Valence (1100–35).

[5] Fulcher gives the date August 19, 1119, but it was actually August 14 (*HF* 631, note 13). It is strange that Fulcher, usually accurate with dates, errs here.

[1] September 14, 1119, the anniversary of the day in A.D. 629 when Heraclius, Roman Emperor in the East (610–41), returned to Jerusalem with the Holy Cross after defeating Chosroes II, the Persian who had removed it in 614.

VII

The King Obtained the Principality of Antioch. 1. However, the king remained in Antioch because necessity demanded it until he granted out the lands of the deceased nobles in legal form to the living, until he had united widows, of whom he found many, to husbands in pious affection, and until he had reorganized much else in need of restitution. For as much as up to this time he had been simply king of the people of Jerusalem, now by the death of Prince Roger of Antioch, Baldwin was made king of the people of Antioch in that other realm as well.[1]

2. I, therefore, admonish the king and beseech that he love God with his whole heart and all his understanding and all his strength and that as a faithful servant he dedicate himself completely and with thanksgiving to God and that he who has found the Lord to be his faithful friend confess himself His humble servant. For which of Baldwin's predecessors has the Lord elevated as much as he? The Lord has made others the possessor of one kingdom but Baldwin of two. Without fraud, without the shedding of blood, without the trouble of litigation, but peacefully by divine will he acquired them.

3. God gave to him the land far and wide from Egypt to Mesopotamia.[2] The Lord has shown a bountiful hand toward him; let him then take care not to have a grudging hand toward God, who gives abundantly and does not cavil. If Baldwin desires to be a king let him endeavor to rule justly.[3]

[1] Fulcher indulges in rhetoric, for Baldwin was never king in Antioch. However, the death of Roger, Baldwin's brother-in-law, on June 28, 1119, threw the responsibility for the defense of Antioch upon Baldwin. He provided the many widows of Roger's vassals with husbands in order that these men might perform the military obligations due from their fiefs. He exercised the regency of Antioch until the arrival of Bohemond II in 1126 (chap. lxi).

[2] This statement is also rhetorical; yet there is some truth in it. Baldwin was king of the people of Jerusalem, suzerain of Count Pons of Tripoli, regent of Antioch, and Count of Edessa. However, it seems that he soon granted Edessa as a fief to Joscelin of Galilee in late August or early September of that year (chap. iv, note 5).

[3] Fulcher's use of the present tense here and in par. 2 above indicates that this chapter was written not long after the events recounted.

4. The king, after he had accomplished many things, returned from Antioch to Jerusalem. He was, together with his wife, crowned with the royal diadem in Bethlehem on the Day of the Nativity.[4]

VIII

The Remission of the Tax. 1. In the year 1120 of the Incarnation of the Lord, King Baldwin II absolved from all tax all those who wished to bring grain, barley, or legumes into the city of Jerusalem. Christians as well as Saracens were to have freedom to come in or go out and to sell whensoever and to whomsoever they wished. Besides, he remitted the customary tax per measure.[1]

IX

The Gathering of the Turks and the Expedition of the King Against Them. 1. When we had passed six months of that year in Jerusalem, messengers came from Antioch announcing to the king and to all of us who were present[1] that the Turks had crossed the Euphrates[2] and had entered Syria to molest the Christians as they had already done in the past.

2. Then having taken counsel as necessity demanded, the king

[4] Baldwin's wife, never mentioned by Fulcher, was called Morphia by William of Tyre (X, xxiv; XII, iv). She was the daughter of Gabriel of Malatya. Baldwin I had set the precedent of having the coronation in Bethlehem, and on Christmas Day (II, vi, 1). The delay of the coronation is explained in chap. i, note 1.

[1] The text of this decree may be found in Rozière, *Cartulaire de l'Église du Saint-Sépulcre*, No. 45. It also removed tolls levied upon pilgrims, a matter Fulcher does not mention. One of Baldwin's purposes was to stimulate commerce with the Arabs (William of Tyre, XII, xv), as Godfrey had attempted long before by means of his treaties with the Arabs (Albert of Aix, VII, xiv). It may be significant that Il-Ghāzī abolished the tolls at Aleppo and made peace with Baldwin, probably about the same time (Ibn-al-Qalānisī, *The Damascus Chronicle*, 162; Sibṭ Ibn-al-Jauzī, *RHC, Or.,* III, 562; and Kamāl-ad-Dīn, *ibid.,* 625).

[1] This was in June, 1120, as Fulcher says in par. 4. It will be noted that he was then in Jerusalem.

[2] According to Kamāl-ad-Dīn, who has the most complete account of this campaign, Il-Ghāzī crossed the Euphrates on May 26, 1120, on a raid into Syria that ended south of Aleppo at Qinnasrīn. Here most of his army was disbanded, and meanwhile the Franks mobilized (*RHC, Or.,* III, 623–24). For discussion, see Röhricht, *Königreich,* 147–48; and Cahen, *La Syrie du Nord,* 291–92.

most humbly begged of the patriarch and the clergy that the Victorious Cross of the Lord be entrusted to him. He said that he and his men ought to be fortified by it for battle, since he believed that the Turks could not be expelled from the country, which they were already devastating, without a hard battle. Because he did not trust in his own power nor in the many men that he had, he preferred to possess that Cross together with the Lord's help and favor than many thousands of men. Otherwise, without the Cross neither he nor the others dared to set out for the war.

3. Because of this there arose a strong difference of opinion between those going to war and those to remain in Jerusalem, whether in such a crisis for Christianity the Cross ought to be carried off to Antioch and whether the Church of Jerusalem ought to be deprived of such a treasure. And we said, "Alas, what will we do if God permits us to lose the Cross in battle as the Israelites once lost the Ark of the Covenant?" [I Sam. 4:10–11].

4. But why record more? Necessity admonished us; reason taught us. We did what we did not wish, and what we did not wish we decided to do.[3] And after many tears had been shed in devotion for the Cross and canticles had been sung in praise of it and the king and patriarch and all the people besides, barefooted, had accompanied it out of the city, the king weeping departed with it while the populace returned to the Holy City. This was in the month of June.

5. Thereupon they went to Antioch, which the Turks were by this time harassing so closely that the inhabitants hardly dared to go a mile outside of it. When the Turks heard of the approach of the king they at once departed, retiring toward the city of Aleppo, where they thought they would be safer. There they were joined by three thousand soldiers of Damascus.

6. But after the king by a bold march approached them in order to do battle and after many on both sides were wounded or killed by arrows, the Turks nevertheless refused a general engagement. After three days of inconclusive strife of this kind our men re-

[3] Note the play on words, typical of Fulcher.

turned to Antioch and the greater part of the Turks went home to Persia.[4]

7. Finally the king sent back the Holy Cross in fitting honor to Jerusalem while he himself remained in the region of Antioch in order to protect the land. And so on the thirteenth day before the Kalends of November we joyously welcomed back the most glorious Cross of the Lord into Jerusalem.[5]

X

The Expedition of the King Against the Damascans and the Demolition of Their Castle. 1. In the year 1121 of the Incarnation of the Lord the king gathered his men all the way from Sidon to Joppa and on the third day before the Nones of July[1] crossed the Jordan. He marched against the king of the Damascans[2] who with his Arab allies and associates was devastating our lands adjacent to the Tiberiad, with no one resisting him.

2. When the latter perceived our king approaching him with an army, he immediately gathered up his tents and, avoiding battle, took refuge in his own territories.

3. After our king pursued him for two days and after the enemy had not dared to fight, our king retired. He went back to a certain stronghold which Tuldequinus, the King of Damascus, had caused to be constructed the preceding year for the purpose of harassing us. We judge that it was sixteen miles from the Jordan. The king laid siege to it, attacked it with machines, took it by force, and received its surrender. He permitted its garrison, to wit, forty

---

[4] Kamāl-ad-Dīn reports that by this time Tughtigin of Damascus had joined Il-Ghāzī. They hung on the flanks of the Franks as far as Ma'arrat-Miṣrīn and then retired, agreeing upon a truce very favorable to the Franks (*RHC, Or.,* III, 624–25). The chronology of these events is not known.

[5] October 20, 1120. Fulcher's presence in Jerusalem rather than on the campaign is apparent.

[1] July 5, 1121.

[2] Tughtigin. Fulcher is the principal source of information for this campaign except for a vague statement by Ibn-al-Athīr that Tughtigin fought and defeated some Franks in the month of I Jumādā A.H. 515 (July 18–August 17, 1121), the place not being specified (*RHC, Or.,* I, 344–45).

Turks, to depart on terms, and then he razed the castle to the ground.

4. The inhabitants of the area called this fortress Jarash. It was inside a city wondrously and gloriously built in ancient times on a strong site. The castle was built of large squared stones. But when the king considered that he had taken the place with difficulty and that it would be hard to provide it with the necessary men and provisions, he ordered the castle destroyed and all his men to return home.

5. This city, once famous in Arabia, was called Gerasa.³ It was adjacent to Mount Gilead, in the land of the tribe of Manasseh.

6. This year ended happily in all respects,
Peaceful, prosperous, and rich in fruits of all kinds.

XI

The Expedition of the King Against the Count of Tripoli; and Then Against the Turks. 1. In the year 1122 of the Nativity of the Lord an archbishop of Tyre, Odo by name, and the first of the Latin race, was appointed in Jerusalem.¹

2. Then the king set out for Acre where he gathered his men, both footmen and horsemen. Putting his army in motion and carrying the Lord's Cross with him, he set out for Tripoli. He intended to take revenge for the injury and contempt which the count of that region, Pons by name, had brought upon him by refusing to submit to him as Bertrand, the father of Pons, had done.² But by the will of God and the conciliatory words of the

³ This stronghold was Jarash (class. Gerasa), about twenty miles east of the Jordan and twenty-three miles north of Amman. The former beautiful structures to which Fulcher refers were built by the Romans between A.D. 130–80. Fulcher's language in par. 5 betrays its origin in Jerome's *Liber de situ et nominibus locorum Hebraicorum* (MPL, XXIII, col. 946).

¹ Little is known of Archbishop Odo except that Fulcher originally said he died in this same year (1122) and then dropped the statement from his second redaction (HF 647, note c); William of Tyre said that Odo died during the siege of Tyre (XIII, xiii; XIV, xi), *i.e.*, between February 15–July 7, 1124. See HF 647, note 2.

² Bertrand became the vassal of Baldwin I in 1109 (II, xli, 2). Krey suggests

nobles present on both sides the count listened to reason, and Baldwin and Pons were made friends with each other.

3. After they were reconciled an archbishop[3] appeared there, sent by the people of Antioch, urging the king to hasten to Antioch as soon as possible to give them assistance against the Turks. The latter were already devastating the land with no Christian leader resisting them.

4. When the king heard this he hurried off at once, taking with him three hundred picked knights and four hundred of the very best footmen brought in from elsewhere. The rest of his men either returned to Jerusalem or to their homes. But when the king reached the place where he had heard the Turks had gathered and were already besieging, a fortress called Sardanaium, the Turks betook themselves away not wishing to encounter the king. When the latter learned this he went back to Antioch.[4]

5. Then the Turks returned anew to their project. When the king heard of this by report he rode against them at once. But these people, since they are truly Parthian in battle tactics and equipment and characteristically never remain long in any one place (more quickly than can be imagined they turn now their faces and now their backs to those opposing them, suddenly fleeing in pretense of despair and then quickly returning to attack again), have not trained themselves to fight confined to any certain area, but entirely avoid an encounter and flee as if defeated.[5]

6. Therefore, blessed be the standard of the Most Holy Cross of the Lord, the help everywhere present for all the orthodox, under whose protection and consolation the faithful are fortified.

---

that Baldwin II may have been aggressive in his desire to control Pons (*A History of Deeds Done Beyond the Sea, by William, Archbishop of Tyre*, I, 539, note 55).

[3] Henri Wallon in his edition of Fulcher suggests that this may have been Archbishop Peter of Apamea (*RHC, Occ.*, III, 447, note f), but the matter is highly uncertain (*HF* 648, note 7).

[4] This refers to an invasion of Syria beginning on June 25, 1122, and an attack upon Zardanā by Il-Ghāzī of Aleppo and his nephew Nūr-ad-Daulah Belek, apparently in conjunction with Tughtigin of Damascus, between July 27–August 11, 1122 (Kamāl-ad-Dīn, *RHC, Or.*, III, 631–32). See Röhricht, *Königreich*, 152–54, for discussion.

[5] Kamāl-ad-Dīn states that the Turks soon after made a second provocative attack upon Zardanā (*RHC, Or.*, III, 633).

It permitted our Christians to return to their homes without any harm. The number of the enemy was estimated in truth to be ten thousand soldiers, ours to be twelve hundred, not counting the body of footmen.

7. And when the king had returned to Tripoli along with the Cross of the Lord an occasion arose which caused him to return with some men to Antioch. The Cross of the Lord was borne into Jerusalem with great joy and restored to its place with great honor on the twelfth day before the Kalends of October.[6]

> This was the time in which Libra weighs equal hours,
> Equal in number as well as alike in length.[7]

XII

The Capture of the Count of Edessa. 1. Meanwhile Joscelin, Count of Edessa, was captured and Galeran, his kinsman, with him. Not less than a hundred of Joscelin's men were killed. They were craftily ambushed by Belek, a certain amir.[1]

> 2. This year ended as abundant as the previous year
> In products of all kinds, whatever is reaped in the fields.
> A measure of wheat sold for a denarius
> Or forty for the gold piece.
> At that time neither Parthia nor Babylonia undertook any
>   wars.[2]

XIII

The Peace Between the Pope and the Emperor. 1. In the year 1123 after the birth of Our Lord, and in the first indiction, King

---

[6] September 20, 1122.   [7] Vergil. *Georg.* i. 208.

[1] Il-Ghāzī's able and active nephew, Nūr-ad-Daulah Belek, ambushed and captured Joscelin and the latter's first cousin, Galeran of Bira (Birejik), on September 13, 1122, near Sarūj. He demanded Edessa as the price of their release and, failing in this, imprisoned them in the castle of Kharput (chap. xxvi, 1). For discussion of this incident, see Nicholson, *Joscelyn,* 62–63; and for the life of Galeran, see John L. La Monte, "The Lords of Le Puiset on the Crusades," *Speculum,* XVII (1942), 106–108.

[2] By Parthia, Fulcher meant Iraq and Iran, held by the Selchükid Turks; and by Babylonia he meant Egypt, held by the Fāṭimid Caliphs of Cairo.

Henry of Germany was reconciled with Pope Calixtus. Thanks be to God, because throne and church were united again in love![1]

XIV

The Preparations of the Venetians to Hasten to Jerusalem. 1. In the same year[1] the Venetians were inspired to sail with a great fleet[2] to Syria in order with the help of God to extend Jerusalem and the area adjacent, all for the advantage and glory of Christendom. They had left their own land the year before[3] and had wintered on the island called Corfu,[4] awaiting a favorable season for sailing farther.

2. Their fleet was of one hundred and twenty ships, excepting small boats and skiffs. Some vessels were beaked, some were merchant ships, and some triremes.[5] They were built of these three types.

[1] Fulcher refers to the Concordat of Worms between the Emperor Henry V and Pope Calixtus II, settling the controversy over the investiture of prelates who were imperial vassals. The agreement was made on September 23, 1122, and ratified on March 18, 1123.

[1] The Venetians arrived at Acre and other Palestinean ports at some time before the middle of May, 1123 (chap. xvi, 3; xx, 1).

[2] This fleet, under the command of the Doge Domenico Michiel, started out in an ambitious attempt to obtain commercial concessions in the ports of the crusader states and conquests along the way among the islands held by the Byzantines, who were commercial rivals. It sailed after extensive preparations, ostensibly as an answer to the appeal of Patriarchs Bernard of Antioch and Gormond of Jerusalem and of King Baldwin II of Jerusalem for aid following the disastrous defeat of Roger of Antioch in 1119 (chap. iii, 2). For the organization and departure of the fleet, see, in addition to Fulcher, who must have learned from eyewitnesses, the *Historia ducum Veneticorum*, ed. H. Simonsfeld in *Monumenta Germaniae historica*, G. H. Pertz (ed.), *Scriptores*, XIV (Hannov., 1883), 73; Cerbanus Cerbani, *Translatio mirifici Martyris Isidori a Chio insula in civitatem Venetam*, ed. Paul Riant in *RHC, Occ.*, V (Paris: Imprimerie Nationale, 1895), 322–23; William of Tyre, XII, xxii; and Andrea Dandulo, *Chronicon*, in L. A. Muratori (ed.), *Rerum italicarum scriptores*, XII (Mediolani: Ex typographia Societatis palatinae in regia curia, 1778), col. 269, partly dependent upon William of Tyre.

[3] Probably on August 8, 1122 (*HF* 656, note 5).

[4] The Venetians attempted to conquer the Byzantine garrison of Corfu (*Historia ducum Veneticorum*, ed. Simonsfeld, *Monumenta Germaniae historica, Scriptores*, XIV, 73).

[5] Estimates of the size of the Venetian fleet vary from seventy-two (William of Tyre, XII, xxii) to two hundred vessels (*Historia ducum Veneticorum*, ed. Simonsfeld, *Monumenta Germaniae historica, Scriptores*, XIV, 73).

3. In them were loaded very long timbers which when skillfully made into siege machinery by the carpenters could be used for scaling and seizing the high walls of cities.

XV

The Time When They Set Out. 1. In the spring[1] when the sea routes were open to their ships the Venetians delayed no longer in fulfilling their long-standing vows to God. After they had made ample provision for the voyage and had set fire to the huts in which they had wintered and had invoked the help of God, they joyfully sounded their trumpets and hoisted their sails.

2. The ships, painted in various colors, delighted with their brightness those who beheld them from afar. In them were fifteen thousand armed men, Venetians as well as pilgrims[2] whom they had associated with themselves. In addition they took three hundred horses.

3. And so when the wind blew gently from the north they expertly cut away from their gangplanks and set course for Methone[3] and then to Rhodes.

4. It was needful for them to travel together and not scattered about. Due to fluctuations in wind they often had to exercise foresight and change course lest they suddenly become separated from each other. For these reasons they sailed short distances and by day rather than by night. They landed for daily supplies at the frequent ports which they found so that they and their horses would not suffer thirst from lack of fresh water.[4]

XVI

Baldwin Is Captured and a Certain Eustace Is Substituted for Him. 1. At that time it happened that Baldwin, king of the

---

[1] 1123, after wintering on Corfu.

[2] Hagenmeyer suggests that these pilgrims were Germans going to the Holy Land via Venice (*HF* 657, note 7).

[3] A port on the coast of Messinia.

[4] Fulcher's graphic description of this voyage indicates that he must have obtained his information from eyewitnesses. He gives valuable insight into the methods of coastal navigation prevalent at that time.

people of Jerusalem, was captured.[1] For Belek who some time before had taken Joscelin and Galeran as prisoners[2] now seized Baldwin also. The latter had not expected this and was not prepared. Nothing could have been more joyful to the pagans or more horrible to the Christians.

2. After this news reached us at Jerusalem all came to an assembly in the city of Acre to take counsel concerning what would have to be done. They chose, and established, as the guardian and leader of the land one Eustace, a stout man of honest character who at that time possessed Caesarea and Sidon.[3] The patriarch of Jerusalem[4] together with the great men of the land made this decision and decreed that it would last until they heard for a certainty of the fate of their captured king.

3. This was the situation in the middle of May when suddenly we heard that the Babylonians had arrived at Ascalon with a host in two parts, one coming by land and one by sea. Getting ready a very fast small ship we decided to send messengers to the Venetian fleet to exhort and pray the Venetians to sail swiftly to our aid in the crisis which had already begun.[5]

XVII

The People of Joppa Are Again Besieged by the Babylonians and Are Much Afflicted. 1. The Babylonians moreover by rushing down upon Joppa with their fleet and sallying forth from their ships with great pomp and with the noise of brass trumpets surrounded the city in siege.[1] They immediately set up machines for

---

[1] April 18, 1123 (*HF* 658, note 2).

[2] September 13, 1122 (chap. xii, note 1).

[3] Eustace Garnier (Grenier), a Fleming, lord of Caesarea and Sidon and long prominent in the kingdom (*HF* 660, note 7).

[4] Gormond.

[5] This swift ship (*liburna*) was probably sent from Joppa, which was threatened (chap. xvii, 1), to the doge, who had landed at Acre (chap. xx, 1) before this time, the middle of May.

[1] The Arab historian Ibn-Muyassar states that this campaign was initiated by proposals of cooperation made by Tughtigin of Damascus and Aksungur al-Bursukī, governor of Mosul and claimant of Aleppo, to the Fāṭimid Caliph al-Āmir of Cairo, although it never materialized (*Extraits d'Ibn-Moyesser* in *RHC*,

battering the walls and other apparatus, which they had brought in the larger ships,[2] and attacked the city on all sides. They kept it under duress by hurling stones of unprecedented size.

2. This was because they had very powerful *tormenta* with which they shot stones farther than the flight of an arrow. The Arab or Ethiopian infantry which they had brought with them together with a body of knights made a heavy assault upon the citizens of Joppa. On both sides some men hurled spears, some hurled stones, and others shot arrows. Moreover, those within the city, fighting manfully for themselves, slew those without by oft-repeated blows.

3. The Ethiopians held shields in their hands and thus covered and protected themselves. The women of Joppa were constantly ready with generous aid for the citizens who were struggling mightily. Some supplied stones, and others water to drink.

4. In the space of five days[3] the Saracens did some little damage to the wall and destroyed many of the battlements by bombarding them with stones. Then they heard of our approach when it was near and broke off the fight with the sound of the trumpet. They dismantled their siege engines and took them back into their ships.

5. If they had dared to stay there longer they would without a doubt have taken the city, for those defending it were few. They had already dug around the wall here and there in the hope of penetrating it the more quickly. In addition they had a fleet of eighty ships.[4]

XVIII

The Battle with the Turks and the Victory of the Christians Won with the Help of the Holy Cross. 1. When therefore our people learned by rumor bearers that danger was imminent, they

---

Or., III [Paris: Imprimerie Nationale, 1884], 468–69). See H. A. R. Gibb, "Zengi and the Fall of Edessa," in Setton (ed.), *Crusades*, I, 454–55.

[2] See chap. xx, 7.

[3] Six days, according to Ibn-Muyassar (*RHC, Or.*, III, 469); May 23–28, 1123, according to Hagenmeyer (*HF* 663, note 12).

[4] Seventy galleys, states William of Tyre (XII, xxi); forty, reports Ibn-Muyassar (*RHC, Or.*, III, 469).

gathered from all sides into an army in front of a certain castle which the local inhabitants call *Kakun*.[1] They came from the Tiberiad, from Acre, Caesarea, and Jerusalem. After the Lord's Cross had been brought to this place of assembly our people hurried forth ready to fight the enemy near the city of Ramla which is next to Diospolis.[2]

2. But we who remained at Jerusalem, Latins, Greeks, and Syrians alike, did not cease to pray for our brothers who were thus placed in tribulation, to bestow alms upon the needy, and at the same time to visit piously in barefooted procession all the churches of the Holy City.

3. Meanwhile our leaders, arising at the break of day, ordered our men, who were arranged properly in cohorts, to proceed from Ramla. After the patriarch gave his blessing and absolution the battle was begun near Azotus. This was once one of the five cities of the Philistines,[3] but is now called Ibenium and has been reduced to a small village.

4. However, this battle did not last long because when our foes saw our armed men advance in excellent order against them their horsemen immediately took to flight as if completely bewitched, going into a panic instead of using good sense. Their foot-soldiers were massacred.

5. All their tents together with possessions of many kinds remained in the field. Three very rich banners, which we call *standarz*, were wrested from them. Our men brought back many kinds of things, mattresses and cushions, many wagons with baggage, together with four hundred camels and five hundred asses.

6. Of the sixteen thousand of the enemy who came to battle six thousand were killed.[4] Few, however, of our men were slain. Our men were estimated at eight thousand, but they were brave, very skillful, and deeply inspired to fight, trusting in the love of God, and were perfectly fortified by confidence in Him.

---

[1] Kakun (Caco), ten miles southeast of Caesarea.
[2] Lydda.   [3] Earlier stated in II, iii, 11.
[4] Fulcher's first redaction gave twelve thousand as the number of enemy slain by land *and sea*, out of a total of thirty thousand (*HF* 667, note n).

7. Phoebus had risen twelve times in the Sign of Gemini[5]
When that cruel people were ruined by the power of God.
Their bodies lying upon the plains of the Philistines
Became the food of wolves and hyenas.

XIX

The Reception of the Holy Cross by the People of Jerusalem. 1.
After the battle, as has been narrated, was won in this way
through the power of God and to the glory of His name and to
the exaltation of Christendom, the patriarch returned to Jerusalem with the Lord's Cross. It was received outside the Gate of
David[1] by a glorious procession and conducted with the highest
honor into the Basilica of the Lord's Sepulcher. Chanting "Te
Deum laudamus," we rendered praises to the Almighty for His
blessings.[2]

XX

*The Arrival of the Venetians and Their Naval Battle with the
Saracens.* 1. On the very next day after this happy success was
won more news followed.[1] We were delighted to hear that a fleet
of Venetians had entered many of the ports of Palestine. Indeed
rumor had for a long time foretold its arrival.[2] As soon as the doge
of the Venetians,[3] who commanded this fleet, had landed at Acre,
he was informed at once of what had happened at Joppa by land
and sea, and how the Babylonians had done as much damage as
they could, and having accomplished their purpose, had departed.
But if the doge wished to pursue them energetically he could certainly overtake them, with God's help.

[5] May 29, 1123, according to Fulcher; May 30, according to Ibn-Muyassar
(*RHC, Or.*, III, 469). The best discussions of this battle may be found in Röhricht, *Königreich*, 164; and Stevenson, *Crusaders in the East*, 114.
[1] The Joppa Gate.
[2] Fulcher's presence at Jerusalem is implied.
[1] Fulcher's date is not clear. He may refer to the victory of May 29, 1123, at
Ibelin (chap. xviii, 7) or to the undated return of the relic of the Cross to Jerusalem soon after (chap. xix).
[2] See chaps. xiv, xv, xvi.
[3] Domenico Michiel (chap. xiv, note 2).

2. He immediately held a council with his mariners and divided his fleet. He himself assumed command of one squadron and sailed toward Joppa. He very craftily sent the other out upon the high sea in order that the Saracens might unwittingly think it was bringing pilgrims to Jerusalem from the direction of Cyprus.

3. When the Saracens saw eighteen ships of the Venetian fleet approaching them, they began to exult as if their booty were already in hand and prepared to sail against the Venetians and boldly engage them in battle.[4]

4. But our men, pretending to be afraid to fight and shrewdly awaiting the gradual arrival of the other and larger squadron of their ships in their rear, were disposed neither to flee nor to fight until the Saracens saw our rearward ships loom up with sails unfurled and oars straining.

5. For this reason the spirits of the Venetians rose. They rushed upon their enemies with indescribable fury and hemmed them in on all sides so that they could not find anywhere an avenue of escape. The Saracens were confined in such a remarkable manner that neither their ships nor seamen could escape in any direction while the Venetians boarded their ships and cut their men to pieces.

6. The fact is hard to believe because it is unheard of, but the feet of the assailants in the ships were tinged with blood. In this way ships laden with much wealth were captured. After the corpses were cast out of the ships you could have seen the sea redden for four miles outward.[5]

7. Then when our men rowed on past Ascalon[6] to investigate whatever they might find, they discovered ten other ships, laden with supplies of different kinds, coming toward them. In these vessels were straight timbers of great length suitable for constructing war machines. They took those ships together with much war

---

[4] William of Tyre states that the Venetians used large, one hundred-oared, rostrated (beaked) vessels called *chatz*, of which they originally had twenty-eight, plus four large merchantmen as their van to entice the Egyptian fleet (XII, xxii).

[5] Two miles, according to William of Tyre (XII, xxiii).

[6] They went as far as Al-'Arīsh (Laris, Rhinocolura), according to William of Tyre (*ibid.*).

equipment, gold and silver coinage, pepper, cumin, and many kinds of aromatics.

8. They burned on the beach some ships which had fled to shore, but they brought more of them intact to Acre. Thus the Lord gratified His servants many times over with rewards in abundance.

XXI

The People of Jerusalem Were Not Abandoned Although Their King Was Captured. 1. Oh how good and glorious for men always to have God as their helper! Oh how "blessed are the people whose Lord is God" [Psalm. 32:12].[1] For the pagans said, "Let us go and utterly destroy the Christian people and erase the memory of them from the earth. For they do not now have a king; the members are without a head." They spoke truly, for they did not believe that we had God for our king.

2. We had lost Baldwin,[2] but we had adopted God as King of all. We invoked Him in our necessity and through Him we miraculously triumphed.[3] Perhaps he was no king whom we had lost by accident, but He who recently won the victory is not only King in Jerusalem but over all the Earth. Truly we must confess that we have had in reality a King in battle, and have now and shall have, since in our undertakings we shall prefer Him to all others. For He is present always, present to all who call upon Him in truth [Psalm. 144:18].

3. For He saw us in our humility afflicted greatly, and mercifully considering our humility He freed us [Psalm. 114:6]. He fought for us and brought our enemies to naught. He is accustomed to conquer always, never to be conquered; He overcomes but is not overcome; He does not deceive nor is deceived. He is King indeed, for He rules with justice.

4. How indeed shall one be king who is always conquered by his vices? How does one deserve to be called king if he is always

---

[1] A quotation used twice before by Fulcher (Prologue, 4; I, xxxi, 11).
[2] Chap. xvi, 1.　　　　　　　　　　[3] Chaps. xviii, xx.

outside the law? Because he does not keep the law of God, he is not obeyed; and because he does not fear God, he shall fear the man who is his enemy. Whoever is an adulterer, a perjurer, or a sacrilegious man, such a one has lost the name of king. A deceiver and a cheat, who will trust in him? If he is favorable to the impious how will God listen to him? If he is a robber of churches, if he is an oppressor of the poor, then he does not reign but confounds.

5. Let us cleave to the King above and place our hope in Him, and we shall not be confounded in eternity.

XXII

The Death of Eustace and the Succession of William. 1. Likewise in that difficult time died Eustace, who had been chosen regent of our land, on the seventeenth day before the Kalends of July.[1] It was decided that William of Bures, who then held Tiberias, should succeed him.[2]

XXIII

How King Baldwin Escaped from Prison. 1. Then in the middle of the month of August[1] King Baldwin of Jerusalem, through the mercy of Divine Providence, escaped from the fetters and prison of Belek by whom he had been held captive in a certain castle.[2] This place was very strongly situated and, because of its great height, very difficult to take. With Baldwin were also imprisoned

[1] June 15, 1123.
[2] William of Bures, lord of Tiberias, constable, and long prominent in the kingdom (John L. La Monte, *Feudal Monarchy in the Latin Kingdom of Jerusalem* [Cambridge, Mass.: Mediaeval Academy of America, 1932], *passim*).
[1] Baldwin's release from his cell must have been previous to August 7, 1123, when the news is reported to have reached Nūr-ad-Daulah of Aleppo (Kamāl-ad-Dīn, *RHC, Or.,* III, 637). The news probably reached Fulcher at Jerusalem in mid-August, as Stevenson suggests (*Crusaders in the East,* 110, note 1). It should be noted that Baldwin and the other Franks were merely released from their cells and not from the castle, as the chapter title erroneously indicates.
[2] A castle called Kharput in Turkish and Ḥiṣn Ziyād in Arabic, about 110 miles north of Edessa and 35 east of the Euphrates. Consult J. H. Kramers, "Kharput," *Encyclopaedia of Islam,* II (1927), 914–16.

Joscelin, Count of Edessa, and several others.[3] The narrative of this affair is rather long but is blessed with divine intervention and adorned with miracles.[4]

2. After they had languished concealed in that castle for a long time with no assistance from their friends, they began to discuss among themselves all kinds of plans and schemes by which they might in some way escape from there. Wherefore through trustworthy messengers they constantly sought aid wherever they had friends. They endeavored in every way to conspire with the Armenians living about them with this end in view, that if ever they could get help from their friends outside the Armenians would continue to be loyal helpers.

3. When this was agreed, after some gifts and many promises and a mutual exchange of oaths, about fifty agents[5] were sent very craftily from the city of Edessa to the castle for this affair. In the guise of the humblest of men carrying and selling merchandise they, when the opportunity came, introduced themselves little by little as far as the doors of the inner castle.

4. And when the commander of the guards was carelessly playing chess near a door with one of the men loyal to us, our clients warily and most craftily approached as if to complain to him of some injury done to them. Then putting aside all caution and fear they unsheathed their daggers and instantly slew the commander. They seized the lances which they found there and without hesitation smote and slew manfully.

5. A great clamor arose there, and all inside and outside were confused. Those who quickly hurried to the scene of the tumult were soon more quickly cut down. In truth there were nearly a

[3] For the capture of Joscelin and Baldwin see chaps. xii, 1, and xiv, 1.

[4] Fulcher's account in this and the next chapter is rather detailed, is in part fanciful, and must have been learned from eyewitnesses. William of Tyre makes some use of it (XII, xviii). For discussion, see Iskenderian, *Die Kreuzfahrer*, 100; and Nicholson, *Joscelyn*, 65–66.

[5] Matthew of Edessa reports fifteen men (*RHC, Arm.*, I, 133); the *Anonymous Syriac Chronicle*, "some twenty" ("The First and Second Crusades from an Anonymous Syriac Chronicle," trans. A. S. Tritton, notes by H. A. R. Gibb, *Journal of the Royal Asiatic Society* [1933], 92). Stevenson considers a smaller figure more probable than Fulcher's (*Crusaders in the East*, 110, note 2).

hundred Turks. And immediately the king and the others were freed from prison.

6. Some were still in fetters when they ascended ladders to the top of the citadel. Thus the truth was made manifest. In this same citadel were the wife of Belek and others dear to him.[6]

7. The castle was immediately surrounded on all sides by the Turks. Ingress and egress were entirely prohibited to those inside and outside. The doors were closed and the bolts were shot into place.

XXIV

How the Count of Edessa Escaped from Prison. 1. I do not think I should be silent regarding a misfortune revealed to Belek in a vision. For he saw (and he afterwards reported it) his eyes torn out by Joscelin himself. He told this at once to his priests in order that he might learn from them the interpretation of his dream. "Truly," they said, "this will happen to you, or something equally bad, if you should fall into his hands." Upon hearing this, Belek promptly sent men to kill Joscelin, lest he be killed by the latter as had been prophesied.[1] But before the slayers reached Joscelin, the latter, thanks be to God, had already escaped from captivity in a manner now to be related.

2. King Baldwin and all his men took solemn counsel together in regard to any means whatsoever by which they might save themselves. When they thought the time most suitable the Lord Joscelin placed his life in peril of death, commended himself to the Creator of the universe, and stole away from the castle, followed by three servitors.[2] With as much fear as boldness Joscelin

---

[6] Ordericus Vitalis identifies, doubtless from legend, three wives of Belek (*Hist. eccl.*, MPL, CLXXXVIII, col. 824).

[1] Hagenmeyer suggests that this tale may have reached the Franks at Jerusalem through Joscelin's squire (*HF* 680, note 3; see chap. xxxi, 7).

[2] With no one, according to Kamāl-ad-Dīn (*RHC, Or.*, III, 637); with an Armenian, writes Gregory Abû'l Faraj (*The Chronography of Gregory Abû'l Faraj . . . commonly known as Bar Hebraeus*, trans. Ernest A. Wallis Budge, I [London: Humphrey Milford, Oxford University Press, 1932], 251); with a certain Geoffrey the Slender, says Ordericus Vitalis (*Hist. eccl.*, MPL, CLXXXVIII, col. 823); and with an escort of knights, according to Matthew of Edessa (*RHC, Arm.*, I, 134).

passed through the midst of the enemy in the moonlight.[3] At once
he sent back to the king one of his men with his ring to show that
he had wormed his way through the besiegers, as he and Baldwin
had previously agreed should be done.

3. Later, by fleeing and hiding and proceeding more by night
than by day he came through to the River Euphrates almost barefooted, his shoes worn out. And because there was no boat he did
not hesitate to do what fear commanded. And what was that? He
inflated with air two leather bags which he carried with him,
placed himself upon them, and thus launched himself into the
river.[4] Because he did not know how to swim his companions
struggled hard to sustain him and with the help of God brought
him safely to the shore.

4. He was excessively fatigued by his unusual journey, famished, racked by thirst, and gasping for breath, but there was none
to lend him a helping hand. Exhausted by his labors and overcome
by drowsiness, he allowed himself to drop off to sleep under a nut
tree which he found there. He covered himself with brambles and
brush in order not to be recognized if seen. Meanwhile he ordered
one of his servitors to seek out and beg some native to give or sell
him bread at any price, for he was greatly tormented by hunger.

5. The servant found an Armenian rustic carrying dried figs and
clusters of grapes in a field nearby and, after cautiously accosting
him, brought him to his master.[5] For the latter in his hunger
craved even such fare.

6. The peasant in approaching Lord Joscelin recognized him
and fell at his feet saying, "Hail, Joscelin!" The latter, alarmed at
hearing what he did not wish to hear, answered, "I am not he
whom you address, but may God help him wherever he may be."
The countryman replied, "Do not, I beseech you, deny your

[3] Hagenmeyer invites attention to Vergil's "radiantes imagine lunae" (*Aen.*
viii. 23; *HF* 681, note 8). He dates the escape August 8, 1123.
[4] In that area inflated skins of animals are still sometimes used for crossing
streams.
[5] According to Ordericus Vitalis, this peasant was a Saracen who in his youth
had been a servitor of Joscelin (*Hist. eccl.*, MPL, CLXXXVIII, col. 824).

identity, for certainly I know you well. But tell me what has befallen you in these parts and how. I beg you not to fear."

7. To him the count replied, "Have pity on me," he said, "whoever you are. I beg of you not to make known my misfortune to my enemies but lead me to a place of safety and thus deserve to receive this piece of money. For I am fleeing, with the help of God, having escaped from imprisonment by Belek, from the castle which is called Kharput, which is in Mesopotamia on this side of the Euphrates.

8. "For you will do a good work if you assist me in this my necessity, that I fall not again into the hands of Belek and perish miserably. But if it please you to come with me to my castle of Tell Bashir, it will be well with you all the days of your life. Therefore tell me what and how much property you own in these parts, that I may in true affection restore to you even more in my domain, if you wish."

9. The peasant answered, "I do not seek anything from you but to lead you to safety wherever you wish. For I remember that once you kindly made me eat bread with you. Hence I am ready to return your kindness. My lord, I have a wife, a little daughter, and also a small ass, two brothers, and two oxen. I entrust myself entirely to you because you are a man prudent and most wise. Even now I am going with you with all that I have. I also have a little pig. This I will cook at once and bring to you."

10. "No, brother," Joscelin replied, "you are not accustomed to eat a whole pig at one meal; do not cause your neighbors any suspicion."

11. The Armenian departed and returned with all that he had, as they agreed should be done. The count mounted the peasant's little ass, he who had been accustomed to ride the finest mule. He carried in front of him the little child, a girl[6] and not a boy. Thus he who had not been permitted to father her was permitted to carry her as if he were her father. This was in order that, although he did not have a daughter of his own, he could cause those who did not know to think that he really had hope of descendants.

[6] A girl of six years, according to Ordericus (*ibid.*).

12. However, when the infant began to worry Joscelin by constant crying and screaming he was not able to quiet her in any way. There was no nurse to suckle her or soothe her with lullabies. For these reasons he thought of abandoning in fear this company so dangerous to him in order to proceed more safely alone. But when he perceived that this would upset the peasant he did not wish to offend the man but rather he persevered in the task which he had undertaken.

13. And when he arrived at Tell Bashir[7] joyful was the reception of such guests. His wife[8] rejoiced, his household exulted. Nor can we doubt with what great joy all rejoiced, what tears flowed for very joy, and what sighs there were. As to the peasant, without delay he received a worthy remuneration for his kindness, and in place of one yoke of oxen he received two.

14. Because Count Joscelin could not remain longer among his friends, he went to Antioch[9] at once and thence to Jerusalem.[10] There he rendered to God the praise he owed for His mercy and made an offering of the two fetters he had carried with him, hanging them reverently upon Mount Calvary in memory of his captivity and the glory of his liberation. One was of iron, the other of silver.

15. After three days[11] he left Jerusalem, following the Lord's Cross which had already been taken to Tripoli. For the army of Jerusalem was to go with the Cross to Kharput, the castle of Belek, where the king and several others were held, not in chains, but in the security of the fortress.

16. Blessed be the universal God who so regulates His will and His power that when He wishes He casts down the mighty from on high and raises the lowly from the dust. So in the morning Baldwin ruled as king; in the evening, however, he served as a slave. No less happened to Joscelin. It is quite clear that nothing in this

---

[7] In the second half of August (*HF* 686, note 26; Nicholson, *Joscelyn*, 67).

[8] Maria, a second wife, sister of Roger of Antioch (Runciman, *Crusades*, II, 126, note 3, and 161, note 2; Nicholson, *Joscelyn*, 62, note 351).

[9] At the end of August (*HF* 686, note 29; Nicholson, *Joscelyn*, 67).

[10] Mid-September (*HF* 686, note 29; Nicholson, *Joscelyn*, 67).

[11] This date cannot be precisely determined.

world is certain, nothing stable and nothing agreeable for long. Consequently it is not good to sigh for terrestrial goods, but it is better to keep the heart always turned toward God. Let us not put our trust in worldly goods lest we lose eternal life.

17. I have now completed my sixty-fifth year as I reckon it,[12]
But never have I seen a king confined as is this one.
Whether it signifies anything I know not, only God knows.

XXV

The Expedition of the Men of Jerusalem and the Second Capture of King Baldwin. 1. While the men of Jerusalem were proceeding to the place agreed upon, the men of Tripoli and Antioch joined them at Antioch. But when they all reached Tell Bashir,[1] they learned that the king and the castle, called Kharput,[2] in which he had been blockaded were captured again.[3] When they heard this they changed their plan and at once ordered a return.

2. Desiring to gain something for themselves, they sounded a trumpet and turned toward the city of Aleppo.[4] They devastated and destroyed everything which they found outside the walls after having first fiercely driven within all who had come out against them. But after they had delayed there four days[5] and had accomplished nothing further, they decided to return home because they were already suffering from a shortage of food. Count Josce-

[12] Fulcher indicates that he was writing at this very time, the fall of 1123, and that he was then sixty-five years of age.

[1] The time when the Franks reached Tell Bashir is not definitely known, but it was probably early in October between the departure from Jerusalem in mid-September (chap. xxiv, note 10) and the devastation of the lands of Aleppo, *ca.* October 20 (note 5).

[2] The text of Fulcher refers in error to "Carra," the name usually given to Harran, but it is plain from the rest of the sentence and from chap. xxvi, 4, that Fulcher had the castle of Kharput in mind.

[3] September 16, 1123 (Kamāl-ad-Dīn, RHC, Or., III, 637).

[4] The Franks ravaged the lands of Aleppo because Belek had acquired possession of the city on June 26, 1123 (Ibn-al-Qalānisī, *The Damascus Chronicle*, 167; Kamāl-ad-Dīn, RHC, Or., III, 636).

[5] The devastation of the lands of Aleppo is described by Kamāl-ad-Dīn, who dates Joscelin's withdrawal on October 23, 1123 (RHC, Or., III, 638). If Joscelin was there for four days he must have arrived *ca.* October 20.

lin, however, remained in the territory of Antioch.[6]

3. When the men of Jerusalem had returned as far as Acre and before the neighboring Saracens noticed it they suddenly crossed the Jordan. But after they had hurried through that region which is bordered by Mount Gilead and Arabia and had seized numbers of Saracens of both sexes and a great many animals, they returned to that part of the Tiberiad nearest them with a huge train of camels and sheep and also of children and adults. After they had divided the booty among themselves according to custom they convened at Jerusalem from all sides and deposited in its place the Lord's Cross, which they had brought with them.[7]

4. But now I must return to that subject which I have for a little while abandoned.

XXVI

How Belek Besieged the King and Captured Him Again. 1. When Belek heard what had happened at Kharput and how Count Joscelin had escaped from captivity, he hastened to go there as soon as possible. Speaking in flattering terms to the king, he demanded that Baldwin return his castle to him on condition that he, Belek, having given select hostages, permit Baldwin to depart peacefully and have him conducted safely as far as Edessa or Antioch. Otherwise it would be the worse for one or both of them.

2. But when the king declined to agree to these terms Belek went wild with rage and threatened to seize the king and castle by force and most assuredly take vengeance upon his enemies. He immediately ordered the rock on which the castle was situated to be undermined and props to be placed along the tunnel to support the works above. Then he had wood carried in and fire introduced. When the props were burned the excavation suddenly fell in, and the tower which was nearest to the fire collapsed with a loud noise.[1]

---

[6] Joscelin did not remain around Antioch very long, for he was again ravaging the lands of Aleppo by November 10, 1123 (*ibid.*, 639–40).

[7] Fulcher is the chief authority for these events.

[1] The *Anonymous Syriac Chronicle* (93) states that two towers were under-

3. At first smoke rose together with the dust since the debris covered up the fire. But when the fire ate through the material underneath and the flames began to be clearly manifest a stupor caused by the unexpected event seized the king. His empty hopes chilled him, for he was dismayed by this demolition and greatly alarmed by the event. And so having lost their courage with their judgment, the king and his men surrendered[2] as suppliants for the mercy of Belek, expecting nothing more than punishment according to their deserts.

4. However, Belek spared Baldwin and granted him his life and likewise one of the king's nephews[3] and Galeran as well. But of the Armenians who had given aid to the king, some Belek hung, some he flayed, and some he cut in two with the sword. He had the king and three of his men removed from the castle and taken to the city of Harran.[4]

5. Because these things happened far from us we were with difficulty able to learn with any certainty of the affair. Nevertheless as exactly as I was able I have written down what others have told me.[5]

6. This year ended short of rain and drouth-bound
   Which caused the people of Jerusalem frequent lament.
   Thus far our history has run on for twenty-four years
   After the beginning of the famous expedition of pilgrims
   from every land.[6]

---

mined: one was over the water supply of the castle; Matthew of Edessa states that "the great tower," i.e., the citadel, fell (RHC, Arm., I, 135).

[2] On September 16, 1123 (Kamāl-ad-Dīn, RHC, Or., III, 637).

[3] The presence of a nephew of King Baldwin is also mentioned by Kamāl-ad-Dīn, who calls him the son of a sister (RHC, Or., III, 637), and by William of Tyre (XII, xix), who used Fulcher. Neither names him, and who he was is not known. Consult HF 692, note 16; La Monte, "The Lords of Le Puiset on the Crusades," 107 and genealogical chart facing p. 100; Runciman, Crusades, II, 165, note 1, genealogical chart, Appendix III.

[4] Two of these men may have been Galeran and the man called Baldwin's nephew. Kamāl-ad-Dīn speaks of the presence of a nephew of Tancred (RHC, Or., III, 637), but Tancred's known nephew, Roger of Antioch, had been killed in 1119 (chap. iii, 2).

[5] Fulcher thus indicates that he learned of these events from others. He was probably at Jerusalem during this time.

[6] Fulcher is not quite accurate because the year 1123 was twenty-four years

XXVII

The Preparations for the Siege of Tyre.   1. In the year 1124 after the birth of our Lord Jesus we celebrated the Nativity of the Savior in Bethlehem as well as in Jerusalem, as was proper.[1] The Doge of Venice[2] and his men were also present to celebrate devoutly this event. It was agreed by common and voluntary consent under oath to carry on a siege of either Tyre or Ascalon after Epiphany.[3]

2. But because a lack of money at that time hindered us all, a large sum was collected man by man to pay knights and hired footmen. Such a project as the proposed siege could not be completed without payments to the men. For this reason we had to pledge the most valuable ornaments of the Church of Jerusalem in order to obtain money from our creditors.[4]

3. Therefore all convened from all sides just as had been agreed and in the place named.[5]

When Aquarius had been thrice refreshed by the heat of the sun
The people departed together from Jerusalem to meet the enemy.
This was on Sunday, the first day of the new moon.[6]

XXVIII

How Tyre Was Besieged by the Patriarch and the Venetians.

1. When they arrived at Acre they arranged with the Venetians to go to Tyre and besiege it. Therefore the patriarch[1] with all those subject to him and the doge with his seamen and ships surrounded

---

after the end of the First Crusade in 1099, not after its beginning in 1095–96.

[1] Fulcher here begins his discussion of the Frankish capture of Tyre in 1124, a great event because Tyre was a highly important seaport, the outlet for Damascus, and the last port north of Ascalon still in Muslim hands. In contrast to the futile siege of 1111–12, which he briefly mentions (II, xlvi), Fulcher devotes eight chapters (xxvii–xxxiv) to the siege of 1124, although with long digressions.
[2] Domenico Michiel (chaps. xiv, note 2; and xx, 3).
[3] January 6, 1124.
[4] Perhaps the Venetians (*HF* 695, note 9).
[5] "The place named" probably refers to Acre. See chap. xxviii, 1.
[6] January 20, 1124 (*HF* 695, note 11).
[1] Gormond of Picquigny.

the city of Tyre, precisely on the fifteenth day before the Kalends of March,[2]

"When the sun was entering Pisces."[3]

2. When the men of Ascalon, who could never curb their usual perversity, heard this they did not hesitate to do us as much harm as possible. One day,[4] having divided their army into three parts, they led the greater part of their cohorts up to Jerusalem. At once they cruelly killed eight men who were trimming vines outside the city.

3. As soon as their approach was discovered, the trumpet sounded above on the Tower of David to make it known to us; and our Franks and Syrians went against them and opposed them valiantly. After each side had worn itself out for three hours[5] in the presence of the other, the men of Ascalon sadly withdrew carrying off a great many wounded.

4. Our men followed them a little way, but lacking knights and fearing ambush they did not dare to follow them very long. Nevertheless in the end seventeen severed heads of the enemy were brought back and as many horses. Three horsemen were taken alive, and others were killed.[6] If we had had knights few of the enemy would have escaped. But our knights were with the army. Then we rendered praise to God to whom praise is always due.

XXIX

Tyre and Its Renown. 1. Meanwhile the people of Tyre were hemmed in closely within their city neither seeking peace nor

---

[2] February 16, 1124, rather than February 15, for 1124 was a leap year (*HF* 696, note 4). Ibn-al-Qalānisī, who is less precise and probably less accurate, states that the siege began during the month of I Rabī', A.H. 518, *i.e.*, between April 18–May 17 (*The Damascus Chronicle*, 171).

[3] Ovid. *Fast.* ii. 471; iii. 400.   [4] This date cannot be determined.

[5] William of Tyre reports that these were three hours of watchful waiting (XIII, viii).

[6] Fulcher in his first redaction stated that forty-five men were killed (*HF* 698, note k); William of Tyre, forty-two (XIII, viii).

submitting to capture. For abounding in wealth and supported by assistance from the sea, they were always accustomed to be insolent.[1]

2. This city is of all those in the Promised Land the richest and most renowned except Hazor, which Jabin, King of Canaan, possessed in ancient times and which Joshua afterwards destroyed along with a great many other cities [Jos. 11:1–14; Judic. 4:2].[2] Indeed Hazor boasted, so we read, of being defended by nine hundred iron chariots [Judic. 4:3, 13]. On the other hand Josephus says that it had three thousand iron chariots, three hundred thousand men-at-arms, and ten thousand horsemen, of which army Sisera was the leader.[3]

3. Both of these cities, Tyre and Hazor, were built in the land of the Phoenicians. The former was renowned for both its retailers and its huge wholesale business [Isai. 23:8], the latter, for its very great population.[4] Tyre was situated on the coast and Hazor was located in the uplands.

4. When Gideon was judged in Israel [Judic. 6:11–40; 7–8], Tyre was built by the Phoenicians a little before the time of Hercules.[5] For this city was in the land of the Phoenicians. It is the city to which Isaiah referred, reproaching it for its pride [Isai. 23]. In it is dyed the finest purple, whence the expression "noble Tyri-

[1] The wealth and military strength of Tyre are eloquently described by William of Tyre, who was archbishop of that city from 1175 to ca. 1185 (XIII, iii, v). When it was attacked by the Franks in 1111–12 and again in 1124, it received much support by sea from Egypt and by land from Damascus. See II, xlvi, and especially the Damascan writer Ibn-al-Qalānisī, *The Damascus Chronicle*, 119–26, 128–30, 142, 165–66, and 170–72.

[2] At this point Fulcher digressed to show his Biblical and classical erudition, as he continued to do later.

[3] Joseph. *Ant.* v. 199.

[4] Fulcher's notion of Hazor's great size probably came from Josephus (*Ant.* v. 199; *HF* 701, note 12).

[5] I have been unable to find Fulcher's authority for this statement regarding the founding of Tyre. For the origin of the city, see Frederick C. Eiselen, *Sidon: A Study in Oriental History* ("Columbia University Oriental Studies," Vol. IV [New York: Columbia University Press, 1907]), 16–28; and Wallace B. Fleming, *The History of Tyre* ("Columbia University Oriental Studies," Vol. X [New York: Columbia University Press, 1915]), 6–15.

an purple."[6] The word "Tyre" is interpreted "strait," which is called "Soor" in Hebrew.[7]

5. Shalmaneser, King of the Assyrians, in fighting against Syria and Phoenicia conquered Tyre at the time Helusaeus ruled there. But since the people of Tyre hated to be subject to the king of the Assyrians they were besieged for five years. Menander writes about it and Josephus at more length.[8]

6. Then at this time the Tyrians crossed the sea under the leadership of Dido, daughter of Belus, and founded Carthage in Africa.[9] Its site is described by the historian Orosius as surrounded by a wall thirty miles in extent without entrances, and as nearly all surrounded by the sea. The harbor mouth was three miles wide. The wall of Carthage, made of squared rocks, was thirty feet wide and forty cubits in height.[10]

7. The citadel, which was called Byrsa, occupied a space of more than two miles.[11] Carthage, founded by Helisa seventy years before the city of Rome,[12] was destroyed in the seven hundredth year of its existence and the entire stone wall broken up. Publius Scipio, the consul for the preceding year, brought upon the city its ultimate fate, in which it burned wretchedly for seventeen whole days.[13]

[6] Regarding this dye, see Fleming, *History of Tyre*, 144–45; and Philip K. Hitti, *History of Syria* (New York: The Macmillan Co., 1951), 94–96.

[7] Fulcher errs, for "sur" in Semitic means "rock," and this gave Tyre its name (Philip K. Hitti, *Lebanon in History* [London: The Macmillan Co.; New York: St. Martin's Press, 1957]), 99, note 1.

[8] Joseph. *Ant.* ix. 283–87, quoting the *Annals* of Menander of Ephesus, a work now lost. The king of Assyria was Shalmaneser V (727–22 B.C.), and King Helusaeus (Elulaios, Luli, Elu-eli) ruled in Tyre from 725 to 690 B.C. See Hitti, *Lebanon*, 143–44.

[9] Vergil. *Aen.* i, 622, 730.

[10] Orosius *Hist. adv. paganos libri VII* iv. 22. Our modern text of Orosius states that the wall was twenty-two miles in length.

[11] *Ibid.*

[12] *Ibid.*, iv. 6. Our modern text states that Carthage was founded seventy-two years before Rome. Helisa was Dido.

[13] *Ibid.*, iv. 23. Our modern text states that Carthage was destroyed in its 606th year. Hagenmeyer suggests that Fulcher may have gotten his figure 700 from Livy or Eutropius. See Liv. *Ab urbe condita* li; Eutrop. *Brev. ab urbe condita* iv. 12; and *HF* 705, note 28. The consul was Publius Cornelius Scipio Aemilianus Africanus the Younger, who was elected in 147 B.C. Publius Scipio

XXX

The Former Captivity of Tyre and by Whom It Was Besieged in Olden Times. 1. Moreover Tyre, mentioned above, languished depopulated for seventy years according to Isaiah [Isai. 23:15, 17]. When the people of Cyprus revolted from Tyre, King Helusaeus conquered them.[1] Shalmaneser, King of the Assyrians, attacked Tyre again[2] and retired. At that time the cities of Sidon, and Arce, which is called Actipus, Old Tyre,[3] and many others gave themselves up to the king of the Assyrians.

2. Since Tyre was not subjugated, Shalmaneser advanced against her again with sixty ships and nine hundred oarsmen[4] furnished by the [other] Phoenicians. The Tyrians sailed against them with twelve ships, dispersed their vessels, and captured five hundred men. For this reason the honor of Tyre waxed greatly.

3. The king of the Assyrians returned and placed guards along the river[5] and aqueducts of the city in order to prevent the people of Tyre from drawing water. Although this was done for five years the Tyrians endured it, drinking water from wells which they dug. These facts about Shalmaneser, King of the Assyrians, are written in the archives of Tyre.

4. He it was who besieged Samaria and took it in the sixth year of King Hezekiah and carried off Israel into Assyria [IV Reg. 17:3–6; 18:9–11].[6] Previous to Shalmaneser had come Pul, King

---

besieged Carthage, captured, and destroyed it in 146 B.C. during the Third Punic War.

[1] From this point to the end of par. 3 Fulcher used Joseph. *Ant.* ix. 283–87. His Latin shows that he used Rufinus' translation of Josephus (*HF* 706, note 3).

[2] See chap. xxix, 5.

[3] Arce (Actipus) was Ziph (az-Zib), about nine miles north of Acre (I, xxv, note 11). Old Tyre was that part of the city on the mainland, not on the peninsula (Fleming, *History of Tyre,* 4).

[4] Eight hundred oarsmen, according to Rufinus' translation of Josephus' original text (*HF* 706, note 3; 707, note 9).

[5] Possibly the Nahr al-Kasimije (*HF* 707, note 11) or Litani (Baedeker, *Palestine and Syria,* 274), whose outlet is about five miles north of Tyre.

[6] There are two views, one, that Shalmaneser V took Samaria in 723 B.C. (A. Ten Eyck Olmstead, *History of Assyria* [Chicago: University of Chicago Press, 1951], 205), and the other, that he began the siege but that his successor,

· THE EXPEDITION TO JERUSALEM ·

of the Assyrians [II Reg. 15:19],[7] and after him Tiglath-Pileser, King of the Assyrians, who took Kedesh and Hazor in Napthali near Banyas, and Janoah and Gilead and all of Galilee and carried off the people among the Assyrians [II Reg. 15:29].[8] Then came Sargon, King of the Assyrians, who sent Tartan to war against Azotus and Tartan took it [Isai. 20:1].[9] And thus because of the sins of the people, the Promised Land was devastated and reduced to captivity first by the Assyrians and then by the Chaldeans.

5. Nebuchadrezzar, King of Chaldea as well as of Babylon, besieged and took Jerusalem. For this reason King Zedekiah fled but was captured near Jericho and brought to the king of Babylon in the region called Reblata, in the land of Emath. Jerome says Emath the Greater is in Antioch and Emath the Lesser in Epiphania. There Nebuchadrezzar caused the eyes of Zedekiah to be put out and his sons slain in his presence. Then came Nebuzaradan, captain of his army, and burned the house of the Lord and the king's house and destroyed the wall of Jerusalem throughout its entire circuit.[10]

6. Moreover after an interval of time came King Alexander, who besieged and took Tyre, subjugated Sidon and before that, Damascus. He also captured Gaza in the space of two months, but he had besieged Tyre for seven months. Then Alexander hastened to the city of Jerusalem. Since he was received with honors he conferred great honors upon the high priest, Jaddua by name. Alexander, approaching alone, did scrupulous reverence to Jaddua, who

---

Sargon II (722–705), took the city in 722 or 721 (Hitti, *History of Syria*, 196; Dimitri Baramki, *Phoenicia and the Phoenicians* [Beirut: Khayat's College Book Cooperative, 1961], 29).

[7] Pul, once thought to have been an Assyrian king who ruled from 775 to 770 B.C. (*HF* 708, note 15), was, according to Olmstead, the name assumed by Tiglath-Pileser III (747–27 B.C.) of Assyria when he took the crown of Babylon in 729 B.C. (*History of Assyria*, 181).

[8] See discussion by Hitti, *History of Syria*, 167, 196.

[9] The king was Sargon II (note 6). "Tartan" was not a proper name but the title of an Assyrian army commander.

[10] Fulcher's sources for the suppression of the kingdom of Judea by Nebuchadrezzar of Chaldea (604–562 B.C.) *ca.* 587 were IV Reg. 25:1–10; and Jerem. 39:1–9. Reblata was about forty-eight miles south of Hamah (Emath, class. Epiphania). For Fulcher's reference to Jerome in this connection, see I, xv, note 1.

· 260 ·

wore a *cidaris* upon his head, a robe of hyacinth and gold, and a golden plate on which the name of the Lord was written. After arranging the affairs of Jerusalem, Alexander led his army against other cities.[11]

7. After the space of many years, because the sins of the Jews called for it, Antiochus Epiphanes challenged their law and harshly constrained the Maccabees.[12] After him came Pompey, who overthrew the people of Jerusalem in most melancholy fashion.[13] Finally came Vespasian with his son Titus, and the latter destroyed Jerusalem completely.[14] And so through a varying succession of events even to our own days the Holy City and the territory subject to it have been sorely troubled.

8. Most of Palestine and part of Phoenicia, which took its name from Phoenix,[15] brother of Cadmus, is waste country; then there is Samaria and then the land of Galilee, which latter, however, is designated by two names, Upper and Lower Galilee. They are bordered on two sides by Phoenicia and Syria.

9. That part which is beyond the Jordan extends in length from Macherus to Pella and in width from Philadelphia to the Jordan. Its northern part is Pella; on the west is the Jordan; in the south it is bounded by the land of Moab and in the east by Arabia, Philadelphia, and Gerasa.

10. The land of Samaria is situated between Judea and Galilee. On the other hand the width of Judea extends from the Jordan to Joppa; in the center is the city of Jerusalem, which is the navel of the land.

[11] Joseph. *Ant.* xi. 317, 326, 331–32, 340. Damascus and Sidon surrendered to Alexander probably late in 333 B.C. and Tyre and Gaza in 332. The story of his visit to Jerusalem is believed to be a myth.

[12] Fulcher may have used Joseph. *Ant.* xii, 234–64; Joseph. *Bell. Jud.* i. 31–40; and I Mach. 11–16 as the sources of his reference to the Seleucid King Antiochus (IV) Epiphanes (175–64 B.C.).

[13] Joseph. *Ant.* xiv. 69–79. The Roman general Gnaeus Pompeius occupied Palestine in 63 B.C.

[14] Joseph. *Bell. Jud.* i. 21, 23; iii. 3–8; vii. 1–4.

[15] Hagenmeyer refers to Apollodor. *Bibl.* iii. 1.1 and Hygin. *Fabul.* 128 as possible sources for this tradition (*HF* 713, note 48). Krey indicates Solin. *Polyhistor* and Ovid. *Metam.* (in *A History of Deeds Done Beyond the Sea*, by William, Archbishop of Tyre, II, 1, note 2).

11. Then Lower Galilee, which extends from the Tiberiad to Zebulun, to Acre, Carmel, and the mountains of Tyre, contains Nazareth and Sepphoris, a very strong city, and Tabor, Cana, and many others besides. It is bounded by the Lebanon and the sources of the Jordan, which is now Banyas or Dan or Caesarea Philippi by another name. Around it is the Trachonitis country and Nabatanea [Nabataea]. On the south are Samaria and Scythopolis, which is Bethsan.

12. The city of Beersheba bounds Judea; within the latter are Timnah, Lydda, Joppa, Jamnia, Tekoa, Hebron, Eshtaol, Zorah, and many others.[16]

13. Now I return to the main path, for I have been running through different bypaths for a long time.

XXXI

The Victory of the Men of Antioch Against the Turks, and the Death of Belek. 1. While we were laboring outside Tyre,[1] carefully preparing siege engines, Belek lost no time in raising his army and allies against us.[2] Setting out from the city of Aleppo, commonly called *Halapia*,[3] he reached Hierapolis in the beginning of the month of May with five thousand horsemen and seven thousand footmen. The city is commonly called Manbij. When the

[16] Fulcher used Joseph. *Bell. Jud.* iii. 35–58, for most of the statements in pars. 8–12. Macherus (Mukawir) was five miles east of the Dead Sea; Pella (Tabaqat Fahl) was seven miles southeast of Baisan (Bethsan) and three east of the Jordan; Moab was southeast of the Dead Sea; Philadelphia is modern Amman; Gerasa (Jarash) was twenty miles east of the Jordan (chap. x, 4, 5). Zebulun is here not the land of the tribe of Zebulun west of Lake Tiberias but Chabolo or Chabulon, a vague district south of Biblical Zebulun (HF 716, note 60). The Trachonitis country was the area about forty or fifty miles east of Lake Tiberias; and "Nabatanea" refers not to the area of Petra south of the Dead Sea but to the Batanea lands about twenty to forty miles east of Lake Tiberias, between the lake and the Trachonitis district. The towns mentioned in par. 12 were in ancient Judea. Joppa, Jamnia, and Lydda have been mentioned (II, iii, 12; iv, 1; x, 1).
[1] The Frankish siege of Tyre in 1124 lasted from February 16 to July 7 or 8 (chap. xxviii, note 2; xxxiv, 3, note 3).
[2] Nūr-ad-Daulah Belek, who succeeded his uncle Il-Ghāzī ibn-Artuk as master of Aleppo early in 1123, was then holding King Baldwin as prisoner (chap. xvi, 1; xxv, 1; xxvi, 4).
[3] Arabic *Ḥalab*.

possessor of this city refused to surrender it, Belek summoned him to a meeting outside the city and treacherously beheaded him.[4]

2. The city was immediately besieged by Belek. Messengers at once informed Joscelin, then staying at Antioch, and the latter hastened to go to Hierapolis with the men of Antioch. Although the number of the Christians was very small Joscelin was not afraid to advance against the multitude of pagans. There was not much delay before a fierce battle ensued.

3. With the help of God the Turks were repulsed three times, and three times they boldly returned to the fight. Belek, mortally wounded in the melee, turned aside as much as he could, in a dying condition.[5] As soon as his men discovered this, those who could did not hesitate to flee. Indeed many who were able to flee were not, however, able to escape.

4. It is reported that three thousand of their knights were slain. The number of footmen, however, is not known. Thirty of our knights fell dead and also about sixty of our footmen who were driving pack animals.

5. Joscelin wished, however, to know to a certainty whether Belek was dead or had somehow escaped alive. After those who looked around among the dead had examined the bodies with great care, Belek was recognized from indications on his armor familiar to those who knew him. The man who cut off Belek's head carried it with congratulations to Joscelin and received forty *nomismata* as had been promised would be given him.

6. Joscelin immediately ordered the head to be carried to Antioch as a token of his success. The man who carried Belek's head in a sack to Tyre and Jerusalem, and who announced and described the story to us all, had actually been present with the combatants in this memorable battle.

[4] Manbij is fifty miles northeast of Aleppo. Belek treacherously caused the arrest, not death, of its governor Ḥassān ibn-Gümüshtigin. Ḥassān's brother ʿĪsā refused to surrender Manbij to Belek's officers and called upon Joscelin for aid; hence Joscelin's approach (Kamāl-ad-Dīn, RHC, Or., III, 641; cf. Ibn-al-Athīr, ibid., I, 355; consult Nicholson, *Joscelyn*, 70).

[5] Belek was killed by an arrow from the fortress of Manbij (Kamāl-ad-Dīn, RHC, Or., III, 642; Ibn-al-Athīr, ibid., I, 355; *Anonymous Syriac Chronicle*, 94). For further details consult Nicholson, *Joscelyn*, 70, note 385.

7. In truth the messenger was Joscelin's squire. Since he had brought this most welcome news to our army encamped before Tyre, he was provided with the arms of a knight and elevated from squire to knight.[6] Indeed it was the Count of Tripoli who raised him to this rank.

8. And we all praised and blessed God because Belek, the raging dragon who had oppressed and trampled upon Christianity, was suffocated at last.

> 9. Nineteen times had the sun shone in the light of Taurus
> When Belek fell or when Fortune failed him.[7]

10. Behold how the interpretation of the dream mentioned before was made manifest, the dream that Belek like a prophet of his own fate had reported, at the time when Joscelin escaped miraculously from captivity. For in a dream he saw his own eyes put out by Joscelin.[8] In truth Joscelin utterly destroyed Belek since he deprived him of head and members.

> Belek neither saw, nor heard, nor spoke, nor sat, nor walked;
> Nor was there a place for him in the sky, the earth, or waters.

XXXII

What Happened During the Siege of Tyre. 1. One day while those who were conducting the memorable siege of Tyre[1] were taking their ease the Tyrians, both Turks[2] and Saracens, seeing their chance, flung open the gates of the city and sallied forth. They all rushed with drawn swords upon the most formidable of our machines.

---

[6] Presumably Fulcher's information came from this squire.

[7] May 5, 1124 (*HF* 727, note 24). Nicholson has May 6 (*Joscelyn*, 70).

[8] See chap. xxiv, 1.

[1] This chapter contains most of the actual details that Fulcher, who was probably at Jerusalem, furnishes regarding the siege of Tyre. Archbishop William of Tyre has much to add to Fulcher (XIII, vi–vii, ix–xi, xiii).

[2] Tughtigin, the Turkish ruler of Damascus, because Tyre was his Mediterranean outlet, defended the city in 1112 and with Egyptian consent maintained a garrison there from 1112 to 1122 and again in 1124. See chap. xxix, note 1, with numerous references to Ibn-al-Qalānisī. William of Tyre states that there were seven hundred Damascan soldiers in the city in 1124 (XIII, vii).

2. Before our men who were guarding it could take arms, the enemy drove them away wounded and set fire to the machine.[3] It had been used to shatter the towers of the city walls by hurling rocks and riddling the defenses with holes.

3. In this foray we lost thirty men, but the enemy twice as many. The people of the city injured and wounded our men very much by the rapid fire of arrows, darts, and rocks from the pinnacles of the wall.

4. Meanwhile, some of our Venetians, not more than five, embarked in a skiff and, enjoying their usual good fortune, pillaged a little house near the wall of the city. They beheaded two men whom they found there and then at once returned rejoicing over their modest booty. This happened in the eleventh day before the Kalends of June.[4]

5. But this did not avail much because a little before, some Tyrians stole a boat one night and dragged it into the harbor of the city. In struggles of this kind such things often happen.[5]

One fails, one succeeds, one rejoices, and one weeps.[6]

XXXIII

The Melancholy Invasion of the Men of Ascalon. 1. The men of Ascalon, knowing the fewness of our numbers, were not slow in molesting us when they thought they could weaken us and do us the most damage. They devastated and burned a little village near Jerusalem called Bira[1] and carried off all the petty plunder they found there, along with their dead and many wounded.

2. The women and children got into a certain tower built there

---

[3] William has more details (XIII, x). The time is not known.

[4] William does not use this story. The date was May 22, 1124 (*HF* 730, note 12).

[5] William states that this boat was kept moored for emergencies and was abducted by some swimmers from Tyre (XIII, vi, xi). It may have been the one mentioned in par. 4.

[6] I have been unable to find the origin of this statement. Perhaps it was original with Fulcher.

[1] Bira (Bibl. Beeroth, med. Mahumeria maior) is about nine miles north of Jerusalem, between Ramallah and Bethel. See *HF* 731, note 4.

in our time and thus saved themselves. Thus the Ascalonites roving through the land stole, killed, captured, and did whatever damage they could, nor was there anyone to resist them.

3. For we were all intent upon the siege of Tyre, hoping for mercy from on high, that with God as our agent and helper we might finish our task.[2] It was more than we could bear to strive at night and toil by day.

XXXIV

The Surrender of the City of Tyre. 1. When the king of Damascus[1] saw that his Turks and the Saracens, shut up in the city, could in no way escape from our hands he preferred to redeem them alive with some humiliation rather than mourn after them dead. Therefore he inquired through sagacious intermediaries how he might get out his people with all of their property and then turn over the empty city to us.

2. After both sides had haggled over this matter for a long time, they mutually exchanged hostages, the Muslims came forth from the city, and the Christians entered peacefully. However, those of the Saracens who chose to remain within the city did so in peace according to the terms of the agreement.[2]

3. The Sun had risen twenty-one times in the Sign of Cancer
When Tyre was taken, surrendered, and overcome.
This happened on the Nones of July.[3]

4. Therefore we ought not to cease nor indeed to hesitate to seek out the Lord as our kind and beneficent Helper in our tribulations, and to entreat Him with prayers to lend a favorable ear to our entreaties. This indeed we did in Jerusalem by repeatedly vis-

[2] Fulcher's presence at Jerusalem is apparent.
[1] Tughtigin, *Atabeg* of Damascus.
[2] According to Ibn-al-Qalānisī, the Tyrians who chose to leave could take out only the property they could carry (*The Damascus Chronicle,* 172). William of Tyre states that the Christian soldiery were bitterly disappointed at not being able to plunder (XIII, xiii).
[3] Fulcher's date was July 7, 1124 (HF 735, note 7). Ibn-al-Qalānisī gives the time as 23 Jumādā I, A.H. 518, which was July 8 (*The Damascus Chronicle,* 172).

iting the churches, shedding tears, distributing alms, and mortifying the body with fasts. God, seeing this from on high, as I believe, did not leave without bestowing His benediction behind Him [Joel 2:14], and He will hear our prayer.

5. While we were waiting with ears open to learn any bit of news, behold! three messengers arrived in great haste bearing letters from our patriarch[4] announcing the capture of Tyre.

6. When this was heard a most joyful clamor arose. The "Te Deum laudamus" was forthwith sung with exultant voices. Bells were rung, a procession marched to the Temple of God, and flags were raised on the walls and towers. Through all the streets many-colored ornaments were displayed, thankful gestures made, the messengers suitably rewarded according to their deserts, the humble and the great mutually congratulated themselves, and the girls were delightful as they sang in chorus.

7. Justly Jerusalem like a mother rejoices over her daughter Tyre at whose right hand she sits crowned as befits her rank. And Babylon mourns the loss of her prestige, which sustained her until recently, and the loss of her hostile fleet, which she used to send out against us each year.

8. Indeed although Tyre is lessened in worldly pomp she is augmented in divine grace. For whereas among the heathen the city had a high priest or arch-priest in authority, according to the institutions of the fathers she shall have a primate or patriarch in Christian law. For where there were high priests Christian archbishops shall be instituted to rule over provinces.

9. Where there was a metropolis, which is interpreted "mother city," there were metropolitans who presided over three or four cities within the province of the mother or greater city.

10. For when smaller cities had priests or counts there bishops were instituted. Moreover the priests and the rest of the clergy in minor orders were known, not foolishly, as tribunes of the people.

11. Every secular power corresponds in dignity to its rank, that first there is the Augustus or emperor, then the Caesars, then

---

4 Gormond of Picquigny. Fulcher's presence at Jerusalem is again indicated.

kings, dukes, and counts. So said Popes Clement, Anaclete, Anicet, and many others.[5]

12. Praise be to God on high because He has returned Tyre to us, not by the might of men but by His own good pleasure and without the effusion of blood.[6] Tyre is a noble city, very strong and very difficult to take unless God lays upon it His own right hand.

13. The people of Antioch failed us in this affair, for they furnished us no aid nor wished to be present at the task. But blessed be Pons of Tripoli since he was our most faithful ally.[7]

14. May God reconcile the Church of Antioch with that of Jerusalem, divided as are the two over Tyre, the third in rank. The former says that Tyre was subordinate to her in the time of the Greeks; the latter says she was strengthened by grant of privileges from the Roman pontiff.[8]

15. For in the Council of Auvergne, so authoritative and justly renowned, it was decreed by unanimous consent that whatever city across the Great Sea could be wrested from the yoke of the pagans should be held forever without contradiction. Moreover this was reaffirmed and conceded by all at the Council of Antioch, over which the Bishop of Le Puy presided.[9]

[5] Fulcher's references to canon law in pars. 8–11 show that he was quoting the decrees ascribed to Popes Clement I (ca. 92–101), Anaclete (ca. 79–92), Stephen I (254–57), and Anicet (ca. 155–68) in Isidor Mercator's *Decretalium Collectio*, now regarded as a forgery of the ninth century. See texts in MPL, CXXX, cols. 30, 72–73, 178, and 115–18, or excerpts quoted by Hagenmeyer from Paul Hinschius (ed.), *Decretales pseudoisidorianae et capitula Angilrami* (Lips., 1863), in HF 737, note 23; 738, note 24. See also HF 739, note 27.

[6] Fulcher means that Tyre was finally taken by capitulation and not by storm.

[7] Tripoli had been a fief of Jerusalem since its capture in 1109 (II, xli, 2).

[8] Fulcher refers to the fact that in Byzantine times the patriarchs of Antioch had had jurisdiction over the archdiocese of Tyre, but recently the patriarchs of Jerusalem claimed jurisdiction as a result of the Frankish conquests (William of Tyre, XIII, xxiii; XIV, xii) and on the basis of a decree by Paschal II in 1111 (*ibid.*, XI, xxviii). For discussion, see HF 739–41, notes 30–36; 742, note 1; and Röhricht, *Königreich*, 98–99. In 1122, before the siege of Tyre began, Patriarch Gormond had consecrated Odo as archbishop (Fulcher, chap. xi, 1), but Odo died before the city was taken (William of Tyre, XIII, xiii; XIV, xi). No new archbishop of Tyre was consecrated until 1128. Fulcher wrote this passage during this interval and shows the tension that existed. William of Tyre gives much information about this controversy as it continued (XIII, xxiii; XIV, xi–xiv).

[9] See text of decree in Rozière, *Cartulaire de l'Église du Saint-Sépulcre*, No. 9.

16. Besides it was in Jerusalem that Duke Godfrey and Lord Bohemond received their land from Patriarch Daimbert for the love of God.[10]

17. From time to time Pope Paschal confirmed these privileges and transmitted them to the Church of Jerusalem, which privileges, by the authority of the Roman Church, she should enjoy in perpetual right. These privileges are contained in this document.

XXXV

The Privilegium *of Pope Paschal.* 1. Paschal,[1] servant to the servants of God, to his most reverend brother Gibelin, Patriarch of Jerusalem,[2] and to his canonical successors.

2. In accordance with the mutations of time, so change the kingdoms of the earth. For this reason it is fitting that the boundaries of ecclesiastical parishes in most provinces should be changed and transferred. The boundaries of Asian churches were in ancient times distributed in accordance with fixed limits. These distributions have been disturbed by the influx of diverse peoples of diverse faiths. However, thanks to God, in our times both the cities of Antioch and Jerusalem with the provinces suburban and adjacent to them have been returned to the power of Christian princes.

3. Whence it is necessary that we put our hand to this divine change and transference and dispose of what must be disposed in accordance with the times. Accordingly, we concede to the Church of Jerusalem those cities and provinces which have been acquired by the grace of God through the sagacity of King Baldwin and by the blood of the army following him.

4. Therefore to you, Gibelin, dearest brother and co-bishop, and to your successors and through you to the Holy Church of

---

[10] Fulcher implies that Patriarch Daimbert at the end of 1099 or at the beginning of 1100 had granted to Godfrey and Bohemond their fiefs at Jerusalem and Antioch with the rights appertaining thereto.

[1] The text of this *privilegium* may also be found in William of Tyre, XI, xxviii; G. D. Mansi (ed.), *Sacrorum concilium nova et amplissima collectio* (new ed.; 53 vols. in 60; Paris: H. Welter, 1900–27), XX, col. 1005; Robert de Torigni, *Chronique*, ed. Léopold Delisle (2 vols.; Rouen: A. Le Brument, 1872–73), I, 90; and MPL, CLXIII, cols. 289–90.

[2] Gibelin of Arles (1108–12).

Jerusalem we grant, by the text of the decree here present, the rule and disposition by patriarchal and metropolitan right of all cities and provinces which Divine Grace has restored to the rule of the aforesaid king or shall deign to restore in the future.

5. For it is fitting that the Church of the Lord's Sepulcher shall obtain due honor according to the desires of the soldiers of the Faith and that, freed from the yoke of the Turks and the Saracens, it shall be exalted more generously by the hand of the Christians.[3]

XXXVI

The Distribution of the Lands Around Tyre. 1. The affairs of Tyre were settled as was proper. A tripartite division was made in which two equal parts were turned over to the authority of the city. The third part, lying within the city as well as around the harbor, was as a result of reciprocal concessions made one by one turned over to the Venetians to hold by hereditary right.[1] Then all returned home.

2. The patriarch of Jerusalem returned to Jerusalem with the soldiers of the city, and the clergy and people received the Holy Cross of the Lord with due veneration.

XXXVII

The Sign That Appeared at That Time. 1. At that time the sun appeared to us in dazzling color for almost one hour. It was changed by a new and hyacinthine beauty and transformed into the shape of the moon as in a two-pronged eclipse. This happened

---

[3] Hagenmeyer believes that this *privilegium* was written on June 8 or 9, or possibly July 11, 1111 (*HF* 742, note 1). The date is June 8, 1111, in Röhricht (ed.), *Regesta*, No. 61; and Philipp Jaffé and Samuel Löwenfeld (eds.), *Regesta pontificum Romanorum* (2nd ed.; 2 vols.; Lipsiae: Veit et comp., 1885–88), I, 747, No. 6298 (4670).

[1] See William of Tyre (XII, xxv) for the text of the agreement, which he dates 1123, Indiction II, at Acre. The indiction is correct, but the year is wrong, for the treaty must have been signed at Acre between January 20, 1124, when the Franks left Jerusalem, and February 16, 1124, when they began the siege of Tyre (chaps. xxvii, 3, note 6; xxviii, 1, note 2; cf. *HF* 696, note 2). For discussion of the treaty, see Runciman, *Crusades*, II, 167–68.

on the third day before the Ides of August when the ninth hour of the day was waning.[1]

2. Therefore do not marvel when you see signs in the heavens because God works miracles there as he does on earth.[2] For just as in the heavens so also on earth He transforms and arranges all things as He wills. For if those things which He made are wonderful, more wonderful is He who made them. Consider, I pray, and reflect how in our time God has transformed the Occident into the Orient.

3. For we who were Occidentals have now become Orientals. He who was a Roman or a Frank has in this land been made into a Galilean or a Palestinean. He who was of Rheims or Chartres has now become a citizen of Tyre or Antioch.[3] We have already forgotten the places of our birth; already these are unknown to many of us or not mentioned any more.

4. Some already possess homes or households by inheritance. Some have taken wives not only of their own people but Syrians or Armenians or even Saracens who have obtained the grace of baptism. One has his father-in-law as well as his daughter-in-law living with him, or his own child if not his step-son or step-father. Out here there are grandchildren and great-grandchildren. Some tend vineyards, others till fields.[4]

5. People use the eloquence and idioms of diverse languages in conversing back and forth. Words of different languages have become common property known to each nationality, and mutual

[1] This eclipse of August 11, 1124, was noted by several European chroniclers (HF 747, notes 2, 3).
[2] Fulcher regarded the success of the crusaders as miracles of God (see Prologue, 3–4; II, iii, 4; liv, 5). He wrote this remarkable chapter to show prospective crusaders from Europe how attractive, as well as divinely protected, was life in the Latin Orient.
[3] By a Roman, Fulcher meant a man from Rome or at least Italy; by a Frank, one from Gaul; by a Galilean, probably one from the principality of Tiberias; and by a Palestinean, one from southern Palestine or the area of Jerusalem. Cf. HF 748, note 6.
[4] Guizot may have better represented the sense of Fulcher's meaning by his free translation, "tel autre a chez lui ou son gendre, ou son bru, ou son beau-père, ou son beau-fils" (Histoire des croisades, par Foulcher de Chartres, in Collection des mémoires relatifs à l'histoire de France, XXIV, 241).

faith unites those who are ignorant of their descent. Indeed it is written, "The lion and the ox shall eat straw together" [Isai. 62: 25]. He who was born a stranger is now as one born here; he who was born an alien has become as a native.

6. Our relatives and parents join us from time to time, sacrificing, even though reluctantly, all that they formerly possessed. Those who were poor in the Occident, God makes rich in this land. Those who had little money there have countless bezants here, and those who did not have a villa possess here by the gift of God a city.

7. Therefore why should one return to the Occident who has found the Orient like this? God does not wish those to suffer want who with their crosses dedicated themselves to follow Him, nay even to the end.

8. You see therefore that this is a great miracle and one which the whole world ought to admire. Who has heard anything like it? God wishes to enrich us all and to draw us to Himself as His dearest friends. And because He wishes it we also freely desire it, and what is pleasing to Him we do with a loving and submissive heart in order that we may reign with him throughout eternity.

XXXVIII

The King's Release from Captivity, and the Siege of the City of Aleppo. 1. By the favor of Almighty God, the king of the people of Jerusalem came forth from the captivity of the Turks on the fourth day before the Kalends of September, after he had been kept in prison a little more than sixteen months.[1] But because he was first required to provide selected hostages for his release he did not depart altogether free. He and the hostages were obliged to be anxious about a future that was uncertain and doubtful.[2]

[1] The date was August 29, 1124, according to Fulcher; August 30 (17 Rajab, A.H. 518), according to Kamāl-ad-Dīn (*RHC, Or.,* III, 644). Baldwin had been a prisoner since April 18, 1123 (chap. xvi, note 1).

[2] By agreement of June 25, 1124 (Kamāl-ad-Dīn, *RHC, Or.,* III, 643), Baldwin gave as hostages his own daughter (Joveta), aged five (chap. xliv, 2; William of Tyre, XIII, xvi; cf. Kamāl-ad-Dīn, *RHC, Or.,* III, 644; Matthew of Edessa, *RHC, Arm.,* I, 139), a son of Joscelin of Edessa, and about fifteen other people (Kamāl-

2. A little later after taking counsel, of necessity the king hastened to besiege the city of Aleppo.[3] He intended by blockading
it either to extort the release of his hostages through the citizens
themselves or perchance to be able to seize the place while it was
hard hit by famine. For he had learned that it was already suffering greatly from lack of food.

3. This city is about forty miles from Greater Antioch.[4] It was
here that Abraham, while journeying from Harran to the land of
Canaan, had his herdsmen pasture his cattle, both those that had
borne or were about to bear calves, in this very fertile area. While
here he had the milk milked into pails, curdled, and the curds
squeezed in bags and finished as cheese. For he was wealthy in
possessions of all kinds.[5]

4. Pope Calixtus died on the thirteenth day before the Kalends
of January.[6]

XXXIX

*The Gathering of the Turkish Army for the Purpose of Breaking
Up the Siege.* 1. In the year 1125 of the Savior of the World,
in the third indiction, the Jerusalem king and his men[1] besieged

---

ad-Dīn, RHC, Or., III, 644; Matthew of Edessa, RHC, Arm., I, 139). A large
ransom was also promised. See Röhricht, *Königreich*, 171–72; and Runciman,
Crusades, II, 171–72.

[3] Complicated politics were involved here. Baldwin had engaged to assist
Timurtash ibn-Il-Ghāzī of Aleppo, who had released him, against Dubais ibn-
Sadaqah of Hilla, but instead Baldwin allied with Dubais against Timurtash
(Kamāl-ad-Dīn, RHC, Or., III, 643–45; Ibn-al-Athīr, RHC, Or., I, 360). Con-
sult Nicholson, *Joscelyn*, 71–72.

[4] Aleppo is about fifty-five miles east of Antioch. Fulcher refers to Antioch as
"Antiochia magna" in contrast to "Antiochia parva" in Pisidia (I, xiii, 1).

[5] The story that Abraham pastured and milked his flocks around Aleppo is
found in Arab tradition. See H. A. R. Gibb (trans.), *The Travels of Ibn Baṭ-
tūta, A.D. 1325–1354* (2 vols.; Ser. 2, Nos. 110, 117; Cambridge: Pub. for the
Hakluyt Society at the University Press, 1958, 1962), I, 97, note 113. The Book
of Genesis says that Abraham stopped at Harran and was rich in herds but does
not mention Aleppo (Gen. 11:31; 12:1–5, 16; 13:2, 7).

[6] The accuracy of Fulcher's date, December 20, 1124, is a matter of doubt.
Ulysse Robert without much evidence suggests December 19 (*Histoire de pape
Calixte II* [Paris: Alphonse Picard; Besançon: Paul Jacquin, 1891], 202). There
is also evidence for December 12, 13, and 14 (HF 752, note 13).

[1] Baldwin headed a Frankish-Muslim coalition during this siege. It was com-

the city of Aleppo for five months[2] and accomplished nothing. The Turks, alert as usual, crossed the great river of Paradise, the Euphrates [Gen. 2:8, 10, 14], and hastened by a very rapid march to the aforesaid city for the purpose of breaking up the siege. They feared that unless they relieved Aleppo very quickly it would soon be captured. Our people had already besieged it for a long time.

2. There were seven thousand enemy horsemen and nearly four thousand camels loaded with grain and other provisions.[3] But since our men were unable to prevail against the enemy they had to abandon the siege. The next day they withdrew to the stronghold nearest them, Cereph,[4] for it belonged to us.

3. After one part of the Turks pursued us for a little while it lost two of its bravest men, who were thrown from their horses and killed. We lost one of our camp-followers and six tents.

4. The enemy attack was on the fourth day before the Kalends of February.[5] Because the Turks came suddenly by night they easily found us unprepared and confounded us.

5. This is indeed most vile to say, most dishonorable to know, tedious to report, and shameful to hear! But I who tell it do not depart from the truth. What then? Who can resist the will of God? Moreover, the proverb is true in which a certain wise man said, "Events which are still in the future do not contend nor do they allow themselves to be overcome."[6] In truth this enemy at-

---

posed of himself as regent of Antioch, Joscelin of Edessa, Pons of Tripoli, Dubais of Hilla, Sulṭān-Shāh ibn-Ridvan of Aleppo, 'Isā of Manbij, and Yaghi-Siyan of Bālis. The principal Muslim authority is Kamāl-ad-Dīn (RHC, Or., III, 646). Consult Nicholson, Joscelyn, 72–73.

[2] Aleppo was besieged from October 8, 1124 (26 Sha'bān, A.H. 518), according to Kamāl-ad-Dīn (RHC, Or., III, 645), to January 29, 1125, according to Fulcher (par. 4, note 5).

[3] The Turkish leader was not Timurtash, who had lost interest in Aleppo when the inheritance of Maiyafariqin suddenly opened up to him, but Aksungur al-Bursukī, now Atabeg of Mosul. Aksungur was joined by Tughtigin of Damascus and Kir-Khan ibn-Karaja of Homs (Kamāl-ad-Dīn, RHC, Or., III, 647–49). See Grousset, Croisades, I, 625–31, for a thorough discussion.

[4] Al-Athārib, about twenty miles west of Aleppo. The date was January 30, 1125, the day after the relief of Aleppo (par. 4).

[5] January 29, 1125. Kamāl-ad-Dīn agrees, "eight days before the end of Dhu'l-Hijja, A.H. 518" (RHC, Or., III, 649).

[6] The author of this proverb is not known (HF 755, note 14).

tack was bound to occur, but no one knew it beforehand. If it had been foreseen it never could have happened because a thought in mind comes to naught unless there is a will to act. For one who foresaw the attack would have brought it to naught, and what had been negated would not have happened.

6. At length King Baldwin retired to Antioch, and Joscelin went with him. The hostages which the king had given when he was released from captivity were neither returned nor redeemed. And so the people of Jerusalem as well as those of Tripoli all returned to their homes.

7. Divine Dispensation, however, checks him whom human worth makes prosperous lest he become puffed up. It deservedly vexes the wicked also so that they do not enjoy the luxuries of extended prosperity.

8. For who gives every good and repels all evil but God, the Director and Solace of the spirit, who from His highest vantage point in Heaven sees and comprehends all things? A little while before, He in His bounty gave to us, the Christians, the powerful and glorious city of Tyre and took it away from its possessors. Now it pleases Him to withdraw His hand.

9. Perhaps He has reserved His vineyard for the more faithful husbandmen to cultivate who would desire and be able to return from it rich fruit in due season. Indeed certain people when they have more do less. They do not return the thanks which they owe the Giver of all good things. Moreover they are deceitfully guilty of lying repeatedly to God about those things which they have promised in prayer, and in deceiving they deceive themselves.

XL

The King Is Received in Jerusalem with Great Joy. 1. After the king had been most cruelly confined in chains by the pagans for about two years he returned to revisit his own realm at Jerusalem. On the third day before the Nones of April we all received him in solemn procession.[1] After he had been with us for a little while

---

[1] King Baldwin had been a prisoner from April 18, 1123, to August 29 or 30,

he returned in haste to Antioch in response to a summons. The Turks had already devastated that land. The most powerful of their leaders was Borsequinus,[2] who led six thousand horsemen.

XLI

The Venetians, While Returning to Their Homes, Devastated the Islands of the Emperor. 1. At that time it was made known to us that the Venetians on their homeward journey after the capture of Tyre had laid violent hands upon the islands of the emperor among which they had passed, namely Rhodes, Methone, Samos, and Chios. They threw down the walls, carried off the boys and girls into miserable captivity, and took away with them money of all kinds. But since we could not change the fact on hearing of it we grieved in pity to the depths of our hearts.[1]

2. For the Venetians raged most fiercely against the emperor, he against them, and then both against each other. Truly they were mutual enemies. But "woe to the world because of scandals! And woe also to them through whom scandals come!" [Matth. 18:7]. If the fault is the emperor's then indeed he has governed wickedly; if the Venetians' they have acquired damnation for themselves.

3. Indeed from pride all sins proceed. Is not man proud when he does what God forbids? The Venetians had the purpose of avenging themselves; the emperor, of defending himself, which was, he says, more just. However, the innocent, placed in the mid-

---

1124, about sixteen months (chap. xxxviii, note 1). Fulcher indicates that he was present in Jerusalem when Baldwin returned.

2 Aksungur al-Bursukī of Mosul.

1 It is not known when or how Fulcher learned of the attacks of the Venetian fleet upon the possessions of the Emperor John II Comnenus (1118–43) during its return in the winter of 1124–25. Rhodes was attacked first, then Chios, Samos, and Methone on the coast of Messinia. The Venetian Cerbanus Cerbani tells about this in some detail (*Translatio mirifici Martyris Isidori*, in RHC, Occ., V, 321–34). See Riant's annotation of Cerbani's work in RHC, Occ., V, 321–34; HF 758–59, notes 1–8; and Ferdinand Chalandon, *Jean II Comnène (1118–43) et Manuel I Comnène (1143–80)* (2 vols.; Paris: Picard, 1912; New York: reprint by Burt Franklin, 1960), I, 158.

dle, suffer punishment for injustices for which they are not to blame, and perish unjustly.

4. But what is to be said of those who by piracy never cease to do all the harm they can to the pilgrims of God who go by sea to Jerusalem with so much labor and suffering, for love of the Creator?[2] If the meek, as God says, shall deserve to be blessed [Matth. 5:7], on the contrary what mercy shall the remorseless receive for their impiety? They are accursed, excommunicated, and shall die impenitent of their perfidy. Further, such people shall go down to Hell while still alive [Psalm. 54:16]. They have not obeyed the apostle, they have scorned the patriarch,[3] and they have held in contempt the words of the holy fathers.

5. I know, I know what to say of them, and I am not afraid to say it. The time will come when they shall hear from the Lord, a very stern judge: "I know not whence ye are [Luc. 13:25, 27], ye who clamor that the door be opened to you. Ye have come too late and bring no good with you. For the door is already shut [Matth. 25:10]. Formerly ye did not wish to hear me, and now I do not think it fitting to listen to you further. I who once called 'Come' now in truth say 'Depart' [Matth. 11:28; 25:41]. I say, I say 'Amen,' say I. I change in no way the sentence I have given." What remains to them is horrible and unendurable; then shall be perpetual misery to them who merit it.

6. But now for the sake of continuing the relation of events in their proper order and of not letting the narrative be broken I shall take care to mention briefly each event.

XLII

The Evils Perpetrated by Borsequinus and the Battle Waged Against Him. 1. Therefore Borsequinus, whose bravery and unscrupulousness we have already undertaken to report,[1] after he had day by day gradually increased his army, surrounded a certain

---

[2] It is not certain what pirates Fulcher had in mind, but he plainly felt that the actions of the Venetians were a disturbing influence.

[3] These are probably references to the papacy. See *HF* 761, note 19.

[1] Chaps. xxxix, xl.

town called Cafarda and took it by siege.[2] It was surrendered to him by the men who had entered it as defenders, since they could not hold the place any longer and had no hope of aid from any source. Neither our king had gotten through to them[3] nor the count of Tripoli,[4] whom he was taking with him.

2. Moreover the king had with him only a few of the men of Jerusalem, for in the present and preceding year they had been much exhausted.

3. For how could they constantly endure such labors, they who were able to rest in their homes for scarcely a month? Certainly one has a hard heart who is not moved by compassion for those who live around Jerusalem, who day and night endure much suffering in the service of the Lord, and who also, when they go from their homes, wonder in their fear whether they will ever be able to come back. If they go far they of necessity go loaded with provisions and utensils.

4. If they are poor men, either peasants or woodsmen, they are captured or killed by the Ethiopians in ambush in ravines and forests. On this side the Babylonians suddenly attack them by land and sea; on the north the Turks take them by surprise. Here in fact ears are attentive to the sound of the trumpeter if perchance the tumult of war shall have been noised abroad. Therefore if we had not at times fallen away into sin we would in sooth be completely the friends of God.[5]

5. Borsequinus in trampling upon Lower Syria[6] and in carefully

[2] Kafartāb, about fifty-five miles southwest of Aleppo. Kamāl-ad-Dīn furnishes the date, May 9, 1125 (*RHC, Or.*, III, 651).

[3] Baldwin had his hands full as ruler of Jerusalem and regent of Antioch. He was at Acre on May 2, 1125 (*HF* 745, note 1), ratifying the agreement made between Patriarch Gormond and the Doge of Venice early in 1124 (chap. xxviii, 1), and was probably not yet aware of Aksungur's approach.

[4] Count Pons.

[5] Fulcher is thinking of the perils of the Frankish peasantry living around Jerusalem. By Ethiopians he probably refers to black infantry in the Egyptian service (I, xxvii, 12, note 9; *HF* 763, note 14); by Babylonians he probably means Egyptians (I, xxxi, 1); and by Turks he doubtless refers to Tughtigin's men from Damascus.

[6] By Lower Syria, Fulcher meant the lower or northern basin of the Orontes (*Joseph. Ant.* xii. 119) in contradistinction to the higher southern area around Baalbek (I, xxxiv, 5).

seeking out what would be best for him laid siege to the castle of Sardanaium.[7] But accomplishing nothing there he directed his army to the town called Hasar,[8] which he immediately besieged, harassing it grievously with siege machines and *tormenta*.[9]

6. To him hastened the king of Damascus[10] in response to a call for assistance. By this time Borsequinus, worried by the news of the approach of our king, had collected his tents and sent them away with his baggage.

7. But after Hasar had been vexed to the point of capture and the time was at hand for assaulting our garrison, behold! our king arrives with thirteen companies of men arranged in perfect order. The men of Antioch were stationed on the right wing, the two counts, of Tripoli and Edessa,[11] on the left, while the king was in the rear with the denser formation.

8. Since the Turks were divided into twenty-one phalanxes, their number was indeed very great. They promptly shifted their bows, already strung, from their hands to rest in their arms and drawing their swords attacked our men in hand-to-hand combat.

9. Our king seeing this hesitated no longer but, armed with the protection of prayer and the sign of the Cross, shouted "God help us!" With a loud blast of the trumpets he attacked the Turks and ordered his men to do the same, for they did not dare to begin the battle until the king had ordered it.

10. The Turks in truth at first resisted bravely. Then by the will of the Creator of the Universe they wilted in despair and became confused by the great carnage, and those who could turned and scattered in flight.[12]

---

[7] Zardanā, about twenty-five miles southwest of Aleppo.

[8] 'Azāz, about twenty-five miles north of Aleppo.

[9] Aksungur had twelve *ballistae*, according to Matthew of Edessa (*RHC, Arm.*, I, 143).

[10] Tughtigin, *Atabeg* of Damascus. According to Kamāl-ad-Dīn, he joined Aksungur at Hamah *before* the siege of Kafarṭāb (*RHC, Or.*, III, 651).

[11] Pons of Tripoli and Joscelin of Edessa.

[12] Fulcher is the chief Latin source for this campaign. Other reports are given by Matthew of Edessa (*RHC, Arm.*, I, 143–45), Ibn-al-Athīr (*RHC, Or.*, I, 362–63), and Kamāl-ad-Dīn of Aleppo (*ibid.*, III, 651). The best discussion is by Nicholson (*Joscelyn*, 75–76).

11. The Gemini had risen five times five
When the Lord gave us this victory.
This battle, to be remembered in honor of the Lord,
Was fought on the third day before the Ides of torrid June.[13]

XLIII

The Number Slain in this Battle. 1. The truth regarding the number of dead or wounded in this or any other battle cannot be determined since large numbers can only be estimated.[1] Often when different sorts of writers speak falsely the cause of such falsity is really adulation. They try to heap up praise of the victorious men of their country and to extol the power of their land for the benefit of present and future generations. Hence it is very plain that such is the shamelessness of lying that they will exaggerate the number of the enemy slain and minimize or omit entirely the losses of their friends.

2. However, those who were present in this battle reported to us that two thousand Turks perished, and the Turks who escaped testified to the same thing.[2] On both sides a very large number of horses perished from the agony of exhaustion or thirst.

3. The day was hot, and strenuous exertion made it hotter;[3]
A grievous battle was waged; one man went mad and
another died;
One pursued, another fled, and none recovered from a fall;
The fields and roads were red with the blood of the slain.[4]
Breastplates glistened, helmets and javelins glittered,
Shining equipment was everywhere thrown to the ground;
One man threw down his shield and another his quiver or bow.

4. Borsequinus did not care to spare the lash, and Tuldequinus

---

[13] June 11, 1125 (HF 767, note 31).
[1] This chapter is of interest because Fulcher makes some very shrewd observations about the reliability of medieval numerical estimates. However, in par. 4 he seems to exhibit the weaknesses he describes. In par. 3 he gives an extremely realistic description of the horrors of a hard-fought battle.
[2] Fulcher states that he learned of this battle through eyewitnesses.
[3] Ovid. *Metam.* v. 586.   [4] Cf. Vergil. *Aen.* viii. 695.

preferred to dwell barefoot in Damascus and carefully preserve his rule. The Turks lost fifteen satraps in that battle. We lost no more than twenty men of whom five were knights. We had eleven hundred knights when the battle began. The Turks had fifteen thousand soldiers. We had two thousand footmen.[5]

XLIV

The Redemption of the Daughter of the King. 1. Borsequinus after tarrying among us for only a few days crossed the Euphrates River into his own country. He brought back to his friends in Parthia not glory but grief and lamentation.[1] He who had come hither trumpeting and threatening returned by the grace of God weakened and bereft of sympathy.

2. Then our king, after he had paid a cash ransom for his five-year-old daughter who had been held as a hostage,[2] and also for several of his servitors likewise held in captivity as had been agreed by both sides, hurried on to Jerusalem.[3] He went to give thanks to God and to render Him the highest praise for the magnificent victory over Borsequinus.

3. And rightfully was the king going to praise God and render thanks. After he had by now been trampled upon for a long time and brought to the lowest point by the wheel of fortune, and had almost come to the point of giving up shamefully and miserably, now by the will of God the king was made strong again and restored to his pristine glory.

4. Six times ten, and two times three years have gone by

[5] All other sources agree that Aksungur and Tughtigin suffered a disastrous defeat at 'Azāz (Matthew of Edessa, *RHC, Arm.*, I, 145; Kamāl-al-Dīn, *RHC, Or.*, III, 651; and Ibn-al-Athīr, *ibid.*, I, 363).

[1] The date of Aksungur's return to Mosul is not known, but it must have been soon after his defeat at 'Azāz on June 11, 1125 (chap. xlii, 11, note 13). However, it was not before he took time to arrange a settlement with Baldwin (Kamāl-ad-Dīn, *RHC, Or.*, III, 651) that included the ransom of Baldwin's daughter and other hostages (Matthew of Edessa, *RHC, Arm.*, I, 145).

[2] This daughter, Joveta, was later for many years the Abbess of the Convent of St. Lazarus at Bethany (William of Tyre, XVIII, xxvii; XXI, ii).

[3] The date is not known. Hagenmeyer suggests that it was in July, 1125 (*HF* 770, note 11).

From the time when I was born until we reach the present
year.[4]
May God similarly direct and rule what remains of my life.

XLV

The Castle Built by the King. 1. In this year, in the month of
October, the king built a castle in the mountains of Beirut in a
region which was very fertile. They call it *Mons Glavianus* from
"digladio" because those who are condemned to death in Beirut
are beheaded there. It is six miles distant from the city. Previously
the Saracen peasantry had been unwilling to pay taxes for their
lands, but afterwards they were forced to do so.[1]

XLVI

The Expedition of the King and the Battle with the Turks.
1. Next after this the king prepared an expedition into Syria
against Damascus since the peace between him and Tuldequinus
had been broken.[1] He seized, ruined, and destroyed three of the
richest villages and returned to his own territory with as much
booty as he could carry off.[2]

2. After he had divided and distributed the spoils among the
knights and other participants according to equitable and estab-

[4] Fulcher here reveals his age, sixty-six years in 1125, and that he was writing
contemporaneously.

[1] Fulcher is the original source of information for the construction of this
castle. E. G. Rey identifies the site with Deir al-Kalaah (*Les colonies franques
de Syrie au XIIe et XIIIe siècles* [Paris: Alphonse Picard, Éditeur, 1883], 524).
This place is six miles from Beirut (as Fulcher says) and to the east, is 2,200 feet
above sea level, dominates the confluence of the Wādī Salima and Wādī Ham-
mana, which form the Nahr Beirut, and is the site of an ancient temple dedicated
to Baal Marcod and of a modern Maronite monastery (Baedeker, *Palestine and
Syria*, 287 and map facing p. 285). René Dussaud, without giving reasons, doubts
Rey (*Topographie historique de la Syrie antique et médiévale* [Paris: Librairie
orientaliste Paul Geuthner, 1927], 73). The French word *glaive* (sword) is
from the Latin *gladius*, as Fulcher indicates. Hagenmeyer takes no stand (*HF*
771, note 4).

[1] The settlement between Baldwin and Aksungur, and probably Tughtigin as
well, as Fulcher indicates, which was made in the summer of 1125 (chap. xliv,
2, note 1).

[2] The names of these villages are not known.

lished rules, he directed his expedition the next day toward the land of the Philistines.[3]

3. At that time new troops had recently gathered at Ascalon, sent there from Babylon.[4] Our force of knights, wishing to show its bravery in our land, now thought it would be victorious. The citizens of the aforesaid city, Ascalon, when they saw our men approach with banners raised, went out against them boldly and with loud cries.[5]

4. However, the king had not yet come to the front line of his men because he was shrewdly delaying in the rear so that he could be of help if necessary, should some of his men furtively try to flee. Our horsemen who were in advance, not wanting in courage, attacked the enemy with incredible ferocity, shouting "God help us!" They trampled on and pressed against the enemy with such vigor and spirit that they pushed within the gates of the city, smiting, knocking down, and killing the foe. As far as one can tell, if we had had a few more men ready at that place they could without any doubt have penetrated into Ascalon along with those who were involved in the pursuit.

5. The Ascalonites who survived bewailed and lamented the death of more than forty of their best men and were tremendously surprised at this unexpected misfortune.

6. The king, after the trumpets had sounded, rested his men that night in their tents outside and near the city. While by the grace of God they had repose, the enemy spent the night sleepless and sad. For as Josephus says, "He who is over-confident will be careless, but fear teaches prudence."[6]

7. It should be recorded that on that day our horsemen who were in advance found no prey around the city. The men of Ascalon, forewarned of the approach of the king, had wisely concealed their flocks.

[3] The area around Ascalon.
[4] William of Tyre states that the Egyptians were accustomed to send four fresh expeditions to Ascalon each year to keep the garrison continually renewed (XIII, xvii).
[5] William's version is that Baldwin lured the Egyptians into an ambush (*ibid.*).
[6] Joseph. *Bell. Jud.* i. 374.

XLVII

The Saracens Send Letters by Pigeons. 1. It is a custom of the Saracens who live in Palestine to transport from one city to another pigeons trained to carry letters back to the city which was recently home to them. These letters, written on paper tied to the feet of the pigeons, instruct the finder and reader about what is to be done after that. It is very plain that this is what happened in this case.[1]

XLVIII

The Diversity of Customs. 1. Manners and customs differ everywhere according to divisions of lands.[1] France has certain customs; England, Egypt, and India have still others.

2. Countries differ as to birds, fish, and trees. In Palestine I have seen neither a whale[2] nor a lamprey, nor among the birds a magpie or warbler. It has wild asses, porcupines, not to mention hyenas which dig out the graves of the dead.[3] Among the trees, I have seen neither the poplar, the hazel, the elder, the butcher's-broom, nor any maple.

XLIX

The Different Kinds of Beasts and Serpents in the Land of the Saracens. 1. Recently we have all seen around Neapolis[1] a certain beast the name of which no man has ever known or heard. It has a face like a he-goat, a hairy neck like a little ass, cloven hoofs, a tail like a calf, and it is larger than a ram.[2]

---

[1] By "in this case" Fulcher means that the men of Ascalon were forewarned of Baldwin's approach, enough to save their cattle.

[1] In this and in three later chapters (xlix, lix, lx) Fulcher digresses aimlessly into the field of natural history as if to find something about which to write. As a source of information he twice says he is using Solinus (chaps. xlix, 17; lix, 5), a writer of the first half of the third century A.D. Fulcher takes details from Solinus' *Collectanea rerum memorabilium* just as Solinus drew from Pliny's *Historia Naturalis* in the description of fabulous creatures.

[2] Solin. *Col.* 52, 42.   [3] *Ibid.*, 27, 27; 30, 28; 27, 24.

[1] Nablus (Bibl. Shechem).

[2] Solinus gives no clue to the identity of this mythical beast. However, Fulcher's description fits that of a capricorn. See HF 778, note 3.

2. In Babylonia[3] there is another beast which they call a chimera, which is tall in front but not in the rear.[4] Upon it on festival days they lay the richest mantle together with other magnificent things when they wish to serve their prince.

3. And there is the crocodile, an evil quadruped which is equally at home on land or in the river. It does not have a tongue, it moves the upper jaw, and its bites clamp with horrible tenacity. It grows to more than twenty ells in length. Like geese it lays eggs but hatches the young only where the Nile cannot reach them at high water. It is armed by claws of immense size. It lives in the water at night and lies on the ground through the day. It is encased in a very tough hide.[5]

4. In one stream of Caesarea in Palestine there are also quadrupeds of this type. It is said that they were brought there recently from the Nile itself by malicious deceit. Hence now they often devour other animals and do much other damage in that area.[6]

5. The hippopotamus lives only in the Nile River and also especially in India. It is similar to a horse in back and mane, in its neighing, its turned-up snout, cloven hoofs, close-fitting teeth, and twisted tail. At night it pastures in the grain fields. It approaches them facing away in sly deceit so that no one, because of its deceptive trail, may prepare a trap for it upon its return.[7] The body of this beast is larger than that of an elephant.[8] In regard to these and other animals, great and small, God creates all. And what it pleases Him to create should please us, and therefore we should render praise to Him.

6. The mouths of real dragons are small and not used for

[3] Egypt.
[4] Fulcher's description of the chimera, usually regarded as a leonine and goatlike creature, fits that of a giraffe. See HF 778, note 5.
[5] Solin. Col. 32, 22–24.
[6] This statement originates in Plin. Hist. Nat. v. 17, although it apparently is not in any present text of Solinus. The Nahr az-Zerka, two miles north of Caesarea, is still called the Crocodile River (HF 779, note 11; Baedeker, Palestine and Syria, 237, and map facing p. 225).
[7] Solin. Col. 32, 30.
[8] Cf. Epistula Alexandri in Rypins (ed.), Three Old English Prose Texts, 84, sec. 25.

biting. They are a kind of passage through which these animals breathe and stick out their tongues. Hence they have venom not in their teeth but in their tails. They injure not by biting but by threshing about. There is a stone which is cut from its brain.[9] The dragon is the largest of all serpents if not of all living things on earth.[10] It is often enticed from its cave into the open, and then there is a violent commotion in the air. Moreover this animal is crested. Whatever it seizes, dies; indeed the elephant in spite of its great size is not safe from it.

7. It is born in India and in Ethiopia in the heat of perpetual summer. It lurks around the paths which elephants are accustomed to use; it ties the legs of its victim into knots and thus slays it by suffocation.[11] It does not have feet.

8. In Asiatic Scythia are the griffins, extremely savage birds, mad beyond all insanity.[12] Then there are the Hyrcanians, a wild forest race whose land teems with huge wild beasts, among them tigers. This kind of beast is remarkable for its markings of brilliant yellow. I do not know which contributes most to its speed, its natural fleetness of foot or its determination. Nothing is so far away which it does not quickly reach, nothing so far ahead which it does not overtake on the spot.[13]

9. In Hyrcania there are panthers covered with small spots. It is said that herds of [other] animals are remarkably affected by the smell and sight of them. When these animals become aware of panthers they immediately herd together and are not frightened except only by the fearful aspect of the panther's jaws. Panthers are killed more often by poison than by weapons because of their rugged tenacity of life.[14]

10. The elk is to be compared to the mules in that it has an overhanging upper lip. For this reason it cannot pasture unless it moves backward.[15]

11. The chameleon, a four-footed animal, is born mostly in

[9] Solin. Col. 30, 15–16.
[10] Cf. ibid., 52, 33.
[11] Ibid., 25, 10.
[12] Ibid., 15, 22.
[13] Ibid., 17, 4–5.
[14] Ibid., 17, 8–10.
[15] Ibid., 20, 6.

India. It looks like a lizard except that its legs are straight and longer and are attached to the belly. It has a long twisted tail, subtly curved talons, a sluggish pace, a rough body, and a hide such as we see in crocodiles. Its mouth is always open and has no other use.[16]

12. It is loathed by the raven. Whichever raven kills it, it kills its slayer. For if the raven devours even a small morsel of the chameleon the bird dies on the spot. However, the raven has a remedy, for if it eats laurel leaves it regains its health. The body of the chameleon is without flesh, its vitals are without spleen, and it takes on the color of whatever it comes next to.[17]

13. It is called a salamander in Greek, *stellio* in Latin.
     The flame-potent *stellio*, the salamander, the rough
         chameleon
     Has three names but in body it is one and the same.

14. There is a bird called the pegasus which has no horselike qualities except the ears.[18] There are people so tall that they can mount elephants as easily as horses.[19] They are a race that is white in youth but grows black in old age.

15. The *leucocrotta* is a beast which surpasses all other wild animals in speed. It is the size of a wild ass with the haunches of a stag, the breast and legs of a lion, the head of a badger, cloven hoofs, a mouth stretching from ear to ear, and continuous bone instead of teeth. Such is its form; on the other hand in voice it mimics the sound of a man.[20]

16. Among them is born a beast called the *mantichora*. It has three rows of teeth coming together and used alternately, a face like a man's, sparkling eyes, blood-red color, a body like a lion's, a spiked tail with a sting like a scorpion's, and a voice so sibilant that it sounds like the music of a flute. It voraciously seeks after human flesh. It is so swift of foot and can leap so far that neither the broadest space nor the most extensive obstacle can contain it.[21]

[16] *Ibid.*, 40, 21–23.
[17] *Ibid.*, 40, 23–24.
[18] *Ibid.*, 30, 29.
[19] *Ibid.*, 52, 20.
[20] *Ibid.*, 52, 34.
[21] *Ibid.*, 52, 37.

17. But who can know or inquire into so many or such mighty works of God in this vast and spacious sea [of life] in which live so many animals and reptiles whose number cannot be counted? The very little that I have said I have excerpted as far as possible from that most sagacious investigator and skillful writer Solinus. What Alexander the Great likewise found in India and saw there I shall relate later on,[22] if not all at least in part.

18. Now this year is drawing to a close; may God continue
to govern
According to the manner of the time; just now the year
is passing into the next.

L

The Expedition of the King of the People of Jerusalem Against the King of the Damascans. 1. In the year 1126 after the birth of our Lord during the third indiction, after the celebration of the festal days of His Nativity in Jerusalem,[1] the king gathered his army in order to attack the Damascan king.[2] After the mobilization was announced by heralds the entire manpower of the realm of Jerusalem, horse and foot, was put into motion. The men of Joppa and Ramla and those who were in Lydda, passing through Neapolis, took the road through Scythopolis, that is Bethsan. The men of Acre and Tyre took the northern route.

2. Under the leadership of the king they left the city of Sepphoris and Mount Tabor to their right and arrived at Tiberias. The men of Jerusalem joined them here. Then they all crossed the Jordan and rested peacefully under their tents.[3]

---

[22] Chap. lx, 9.   [1] December 25, 1125, not 1126.

[2] The *Atabeg* Tughtigin. Fulcher is the chief Latin source of information for Baldwin's thrust against Damascus in January, 1126. He probably wrote in that year or the next, and he wrote vividly and factually, probably from eyewitness information. He was used by William of Tyre (XIII, xviii). The best Arabic account is by Ibn-al-Qalānisī (*The Damascus Chronicle*, 175-77), followed by Ibn-al-Athīr (*RHC, Or.*, I, 372-73), and Sibṭ Ibn-al-Jauzī (*ibid.*, III, 565-66), who used Ibn-al-Qalānisī. For discussion, see Röhricht, *Königreich*, 177-79; and especially Grousset, *Croisades*, I, 637-41.

[3] Fulcher indicates that Baldwin's southern troops marched to Tiberias via

The night was clear, serene, and cloudless
And the horns of the sixteenth moon were shining.[4]

3. Toward dawn the trumpet gave the signal [for the men] to set out from their camp. They struck their tents and all prepared for the march. They loaded the mules, camels, and other beasts of burden with baggage, which caused much tumult. The asses brayed, the camels grumbled, and the horses whinnied. When the scouts had begun to locate the trail for the marchers, the trumpets sounded at the same time, and the men carefully picked out the path they knew would be best for them.

4. After they penetrated more deeply into hostile territory they were wisely willing to march with flags down and to wear their armor as a protection lest they be surprised by unforeseen danger. They then went through the defile of Roob and entering the territory of Damascus stopped for two nights beyond Medan. Here arises a stream which flows toward Scythopolis from the Sea of Galilee and joins the Jordan.

5. Next they destroyed a tower which they came upon ahead of them. And so they came to the stronghold called *Salome*. The Syrian Christians living in it came out in procession to meet the king.

6. After that they came to the valley which is called *Marcisophar*, that is "Sophar in the Meadows."[5] This is the place where

Nablus (Neapolis) and Baisan (Bethsan) and that the northern force came via Saffūrīyah (Sepphoris), later famous as King Guy's point of departure for his disastrous defeat at Hattin in 1187. They must have crossed the river near the outlet of Lake Tiberias and near the scene of the defeat of King Baldwin I at al-Uqhuwānah in 1113 (II, xlix, note 5).

4 January 15, 1126 (*HF* 786, note 9).

5 Baldwin's route was apparently up the valley of the Yarmuk, the stream mentioned as flowing toward Scythopolis. He probably went to the area of Arbil (Arbela), where he crossed the Wādī ar-Rāhūb (Roob) and Wādī al-Meddān (Medan) to the vicinity of al-Muzeirib. He then followed the ancient pilgrim route to aṣ-Sanamein (Salome, according to *HF* 788, note 19, and Grousset, *Croisades*, I, 638) and went on to the Marj (prairie) aṣ-Ṣuffar, which is between Tell ash-Sharkhūb on the south and Kiswe on the north. The latter is on the Nahr al-'Awaj (class. Pharpar), north of which is the plain of Ghūtah and the city of Damascus. See Grousset, *Croisades*, I, 638; Baedeker, *Palestine and Syria*, 161, 169, and map facing p. 155; and Dussaud, *Topographie historique de la Syrie*, cartes I, II.

the Apostle Paul was struck by the Lord, losing his sight for three days [Act. 9:3–9]. They paused there for two days. From there they saw the tents of the Damascans, who were awaiting our army in that locality.[6]

7. The son of King Tuldequinus, after he had been away energetically collecting a force of three thousand horsemen from every possible quarter, returned to his father ready for battle.[7] He rejoined his people on the day before the fray.

8. Soon after, our horse and foot were organized in twelve formations in such a way that each could support the other if necessary. After all had heard mass and partaken of the consecrated bread, they formed ranks all along the line and began battle crying, "God help us!"

9. The Turks shouted also and fought most bitterly. They marveled at the wondrous bravery of those whom they had scorned as if already conquered. Their courage failed them and, struck by fear and trepidation, they resolved to flee. Tuldequinus fled and also his son.[8] And although our men were pressed beyond endurance their courage increased more and more, and they remained firm and resolute in spirit.

10. Nevertheless such a shower of Turkish arrows poured in upon the Christians that no part of their bodies was safe from bruise or wound. Indeed for our men no battle was ever more violent or terrible. The running about of excited men and the roar and shock of battle were very great. The trumpets and horns blared loudly.

11. By this time our men were surrounded by the Turks and a

---

[6] If indeed the battle was fought on January 25, 1126 (note 10), then Baldwin camped in the Marj aṣ-Ṣuffar on January 23–24. Ibn-al-Qalānisī also relates that Tughtigin was gathering his troops on this plain (*The Damascus Chronicle*, 175).

[7] Tughtigin's son and heir was Taj-al-Mulūk Böri, *Atabeg* of Damascus from 1128 to 1132.

[8] This part of Fulcher's account is confused. Ibn-al-Qalānisī states (*The Damascus Chronicle*, 176) that the Turks attacked first and put the Franks to rout (see Fulcher, par. 11); then the Franks rallied, turned, and put the Turks to rout, as Fulcher also says. Fulcher's account is therefore misleading in stating that the Turks fled first, but it is very graphic in telling about events in the battle. Ibn-al-Athīr states that Tughtigin fell from his horse, causing panic among his men (*RHC, Or.*, I, 372).

great many were being wounded. They took to flight, but after experiencing this for four miles they wheeled against the Turks as needs they must and began to fight, filled with martial courage.[9]

> This holy day of battle was on the anniversary of
> the Conversion of Paul,
> Paul who was chosen by God.[10]

The strife of battle began during the third hour of the day. Evening brought it to an end with a victory bestowed by God.

12. Battle is dangerous, flight is shameful; but it is preferable to live as a weakling, than to be dead and to mourn forever. And so the Turks chose flight in order to retain life. Indeed a little more than two thousand Turks were left slain on the battlefield. There is no count of the footmen. We lost fourteen knights and eighty footmen.[11]

13. Our king conducted himself magnificently on that day, together with all of his knights and camp-followers, since God Almighty was with them in person. The king of Syria fled with all who could follow him.[12] Our king returned in joyful triumph to Jerusalem.

14. After the return was ordered our men surrounded and captured a tower along with ninety-six men whom they killed. The king took another tower and the twenty Turks who had taken refuge in it.[13] When these latter realized that our men were digging around the tower and prying huge stones out of it they sur-

[9] Ibn-al-Qalānisī presents much the same picture—an initial Turkish attack and then a Frankish rally (*The Damascus Chronicle*, 176).

[10] The Feast of the Conversion of St. Paul is on January 25. Ibn-al-Qalānisī (*ibid.*, 175) and Sibṭ (*RHC, Or.*, III, 566) date the battle 27 Dhu'l-Hijja, A.H. 519, which in that year was January 24, not January 25.

[11] We cannot rely upon Fulcher's figures. Ibn-al-Qalānisī states that the Turkish infantry was cut to pieces (*The Damascus Chronicle*, 177); he (p. 176) and Ibn-al-Athīr (*RHC, Or.*, I, 372) write that the Frankish footmen suffered heavily in the beginning.

[12] Fulcher's statement in par. 9 that Tughtigin fled belongs here. The Muslim authorities state that he fled into Damascus and prepared to resist but that the Franks got no farther than the pass of Shuhura, ten miles south of the city, and retired the next morning (Ibn-al-Qalānisī, *The Damascus Chronicle*, 177; and Sibṭ, *RHC, Or.*, III, 566).

[13] These towers cannot be identified. Grousset describes them as being in the Jawlān (*Croisades*, I, 640), the general area northeast of Lake Tiberias.

rendered both themselves and the stronghold to the king in their fright. By agreement the king let them depart, but he had the tower torn down. It was very necessary that it be seen destroyed, for its fortifications would have incited many to revolt. For it could have stood out as a secure refuge for its possessors and a source of doubt and worry for its assailants.

15. Perhaps it will bore the hearers of my story if all things are reported which happened in the war or for the sake of it, either by force or by strategy. For the Damascans brought along young men chosen for their agility. They were armed and mounted behind the Turkish horsemen. When they met the enemy they jumped off and at once fought as footmen while the horsemen who had brought them were attacking on the other side.[14]

LI

The Siege of the City of Raphania; and the River Sabbaticus.

1. It is written, "Nothing is blessed in every way."[1] We cannot be blessed in respect of this battle since we lost fourteen of the bravest knights in addition to some stout footmen. But this is trifling compared to the slaughter done to the enemy.

2. The word "Damascus" is interpreted "the kiss of blood" or "drinking blood."[2] We read that it was in Damascus where the blood of Abel was shed.[3] Indeed the people of Damascus could bathe in the blood of the slain or could even drink their own blood by flinging themselves prostrate face down.

3. At length the king returned with his army to Jerusalem where we all spent the day as a holiday and in thanksgiving.[4]

4. A short while later the king, moved by a prayer of the count

[14] Arabic accounts state that Böri had sent out irregular troops (Ibn-al-Qalānisī, *The Damascus Chronicle*, 175; Sibṭ, *RHC, Or.*, III, 566).

[1] Horat. *Od.* ii. 16, 27.

[2] Fulcher may have confused a reference "sanguinis succi et sanguinis osculi" in Hieron. *Comment. in Ezech.* 27:18 (HF 794, note 4).

[3] The murder of Cain by Abel is related in Gen. 4:8, but that Damascus was the scene is from Arab tradition. See Jakut, *Reisen*, ed. Ferdinand Wüstenfeld in *Zeitschrift der deutsch. morgenländ. Gesellschaft*, XVIII, 456; and *Abulfedae tabulae Syriae*, ed. Köhler (Lips., 1766), 100, quoted in HF 794, note 5.

[4] The return to Jerusalem was probably in early February.

of Tripoli,[5] set out to help the latter besiege a town which we call Raphania, situated at the foot of Mount Lebanon.[6] In this region, as Josephus relates, "Between Archas and Raphania there flows a river which has something peculiarly remarkable about it. For when much water flows the current is brisk; yet after six days its springs fail, and the place seems to be dry. Then although no change seems to have occurred, on the seventh day the river rises again, and it has been found to keep this routine perpetually and exactly. Whence this river is called 'the Sabbaticus' after the seventh day sacred to the Jews.

5. "Indeed Titus the prince spent some time around Beirut. Then he left, praising this most magnificent spectacle in all the Syrian cities which he visited. He greatly admired this river, seeing in it something most worthy of spontaneous recognition."[7]

LII

Concerning Another River. 1. The same historian reports another marvel, saying that near the city of Acre "there was a very small stream a quarter of a mile away, called the Belus, near the sepulcher of Memnon. It is indeed most worthy of admiration.

2. "It has the shape of a circular valley, and it yields glassy sand. After many ships have come there and carried away this sand the place fills up again. The winds naturally bring more sand down from the hills surrounding the valley. The place immediately turns the material which it receives into vitreous sand.

3. "What seems more remarkable to me is that whenever a part of this sand which has become glassy is thrown out to the edge of the place it is again converted into common sand."[1]

---

[5] The date was prior to March 14, 1126 (chap. liii, note 3). Fulcher is referring to Pons.

[6] Raphanīya is about twenty-seven miles southwest of Hamah.

[7] Joseph. *Bell. Jud.* vii. 96–99. The stream has been identified as the Fuwar ad-Der (*HF* 796, note 16). Titus captured Jerusalem in A.D. 70 and was Roman Emperor in A.D. 79–81.

[1] Joseph. *Bell. Jud.* ii. 189–91. The stream is the Nahr Naʿman (*HF* 797, note 2). See Baedeker, *Palestine and Syria*, map facing p. 225.

LIII

The Capture of the City of Raphania. 1. The fall of Raphania, a city I have already begun to discuss briefly,[1] was in this wise. After the king and count[2] had vigorously besieged the Saracens within for eighteen days by hurling stones with their *tormenta*, the inhabitants surrendered the city and went out unharmed. This happened on the last day of March.[3] And so in this way the aforesaid count received the city as its possessor for the future. He fortified it, and the king returned to Jerusalem.

LIV

The Death of the Roman Emperor. 1. While we were celebrating Easter Day[1] in Jerusalem, tales from pilgrims reached us saying that the Roman Emperor had died.[2] They added that the Saxon duke, Lothair by name, had been elevated to the royal and imperial throne.[3]

When Henry died the Constellation of the Gemini was shining;[4]
After this Lothair the son of a duke ruled as king.[5]

LV

The Departure of the King Against the Babylonians. 1. Not long afterwards[1] the king set out from Tyre and descended into Lower Syria,[2] leaving part of his horsemen behind and taking part

---

[1] Chap. li, 4.   [2] Baldwin and Pons.
[3] March 31, 1126, according to Fulcher; the end of Safar, A.H. 520 (March 26), according to Kamāl-ad-Dīn (*RHC, Or.,* III, 652). Fulcher says the siege began March 14.
[1] April 11, 1126. Fulcher here indicates that he was in Jerusalem at this time.
[2] Emperor Henry V died in Germany on May 23, 1125 (*HF* 799, note 4).
[3] Lothair became Duke of Saxony in 1106, king in Germany in 1125, and emperor in 1133. He died in 1137.
[4] Began *ca.* May 21.
[5] Lothair was the son of Count Gebhard of Supplinburg, who died in 1075, not attaining the title of Duke of Saxony.
[1] After Easter, 1126.
[2] Northern Syria. See chap. xlii, 5, note 6.

with him. This was in spite of the fact that he had heard rumors
that the Babylonians were prepared for war and were about to
come against us.

2. For he proposed to hurry first to the place where he had
heard the enemy would attack. Like a wild boar surrounded by
dogs and beset by their repeated bites, he had to defend himself
right and left by furiously lashing out with his teeth. As we are
accustomed to say metaphorically, "The hand goes where there
is pain."[3]

3. But before the king arrived there, the Turks had already
besieged and taken a pseudo castle. Because this place was a nui-
sance to the Turks it was necessary for us to have it. Our soldiers
had escaped by a very clever egress during the night, leaving their
wives and children, preferring to save part than lose nearly all.[4]

4. Then that summer in the middle of the month of July a
comet began to appear between the east and the north.[5] It rose
before dawn and gave out its rays until about the ninth hour,
manifesting itself with a pale light. We strove to discern it for
eighteen days but left its meaning to the Creator of us all.

5. By this time the Turks, of whom Borsequinus was the most
important, had besieged the town called Cereph. However, hearing of the approach of the king, who was already following them,
they withdrew to safer defenses, frustrated in their design. For
there were not more than six thousand soldiers. Therefore the
king returned to Antioch.[6]

[3] "Ubi dolor, ubi manus." I have been unable to find the source of this
quotation.
[4] This place was apparently Ḥiṣn-ad-Dair, a fortress contrived from an old
convent near Sarmadā, according to Kamāl-ad-Dīn. He adds that it was taken by
Aksungur's officer, Babek ibn-Thalmās (RHC, Or., III, 653). See Röhricht,
Königreich, 180.
[5] This comet lasted from ca. July 15 to the beginning of August, 1126, and
may have been seen in China (HF 802, notes 12–14).
[6] The fortress was al-Athārib, twenty miles west of Aleppo (chap xxxix, 2,
note 4). Kamāl-ad-Dīn states that Aksungur al-Bursukī destroyed two outworks
before Baldwin's approach and that the Franks retired to Maʿarrat-Miṣrīn in
August and then returned home (RHC, Or., III, 653–54). Fulcher implies that
the Turks felt that their force of six thousand men was not sufficient. For discussion, see Röhricht, Königreich, 180; and Nicholson, Joscelyn, 77–78.

LVI

The Babylonian Fleet. 1. In this year the Babylonians, having repaired and assembled their fleet, sailed along with a south wind and entered the land of the Philistines.[1] They passed by Pharamia and Laris,[2] Gaza and Ascalon, and also Joppa, Caesarea, Acre, Tyre, and Sidon. They explored and stealthily examined the coast as far as the city of Beirut, hunting and searching from port to port to see if they could find any advantage for themselves which would be a disadvantage for the Christians.

2. But since they were then suffering greatly from lack of fresh water they were obliged to make a landing in order to fill their buckets from the streams and springs and thus assuage their thirst.

3. However, the citizens of the aforementioned city took this ill and boldly came out against them at once. Joining to themselves travelers who by chance had gathered there they made an attack. One hundred and thirty of those pirates were struck down, both killed and mortally wounded. In truth there were five thousand who disembarked to fight, not counting those who took care of the ships in the meantime. Twenty-two of these ships were triremes or *catos*,[3] and there were fifty-three other ships.

4. Thus were our enemies harsh and pitiless toward all whom they could get into their power, gloating in their cruelty toward our people.

5. But thanks to God they gained no advantage in this case. Our knights with their lances and our bowmen with their arrows drove them into the sea and in this way unexpectedly routed them. They promptly hoisted sail and directed their course toward Tripoli, then Cyprus.[4]

---

[1] Palestine.

[2] Al-Faramā', at one of the mouths of the Nile, reached by Baldwin I in 1118, and al-'Arīsh, about seventy-five miles east of there, where he died (II, lxiv, 1, 3).

[3] A *catus* was a ship that carried siege machines and took its name from them (Edward Heyck, *Genua und seine Marine in Zeitalter der Kreuzzüge* [Innsbruck, 1886], 85, quoted in *HF* 804, note 14).

[4] Fulcher must be in error, for the defeated Egyptians would not make for ports in Christian hands. See *HF* 805, note 19.

LVII

The Voyage of Bohemond the Younger. 1. How many times in this year[1] did not messengers or pilgrims announce to us, and relate to us, the coming of Bohemond the Younger?[2] But they deceived us by their manifold rumors. For Bohemond was afraid of the Babylonian or piratical fleet which he had heard was scattered abroad upon the sea. Besides he was much concerned about his own land. Unless he had it securely placed among his vassals he could lose it by being fraudulently circumvented by malicious schemes.[3] Indeed it is written in the proverbs of the peasants that "Whoever has a bad neighbor has a bad morning."[4]

2. Finally after he had several times prepared for his journey he collected at Otranto, a city of Apulia, as many ships as he could, viz., twenty-two, of which ten were long ships provided with oars, and began to speed preparations for his voyage.[5] This was after he had committed his land to the duke of Apulia, whom he chose and designated as his heir if he should be the first to depart this life. The duke freely granted and confirmed the same privilege too in case he himself should die first.[6] This was done in the presence of the leading men on both sides, who acted as witnesses.

[1] 1126.

[2] Bohemond II, Prince of Antioch, son of Bohemond I and Constance of France (II, xxix; III, iii, 4). King Baldwin II had been his regent for Antioch since 1119 (III, vii, 1). Consult Grousset, *Croisades*, I, 645–46.

[3] For the character of these vassals, see Ferdinand Chalandon, *Histoire de la domination Normande en Italie et en Sicile* (2 vols.; Paris, 1907; reprinted in New York: Burt Franklin, 1960), I, 382; and Edmund Curtis, *Roger of Sicily and the Normans in Lower Italy, 1016–1154* (New York and London: G. P. Putnam's Sons, The Knickerbocker Press, 1912), 109, 119.

[4] I have not been able to find the source of the quotation, "Qui habet malum vicinum, habet malum matutinum."

[5] Nineteen triremes and six ships of burden, according to Romuald of Salerno (*Chronicon*, in L. A. Muratori [ed.], *Rerum italicarum scriptores*, VII [Mediolani: Ex typographia Societatis palatinae in regia curia, 1725], col. 185).

[6] This duke of Apulia was William (1111–27), a first cousin of Bohemond II, both being grandsons of Robert Guiscard. However, when Duke William died in 1127, Roger II of Sicily claimed to be his heir and seized his lands, including those left by Bohemond (Alexander of Telese, *De rebus gestis Rogerii II Siciliae*, in L. A. Muratori [ed.], *ibid.*, V [Mediolani: Ex typographia Societatis palatinae in regia curia, 1724], 616–17; and Romuald of Salerno, *Chronicon*, cols. 183–85).

3. And so Bohemond put out to sea in the middle of September.[7] He passed through the Cyclades, which are scattered over the surface of the sea, came to Methone and to Rhodes, Pamphylia and Lycia, and arrived in the rough waters of Adalia, which are full of terrors for those sailing upon them. Then he passed by Antioch the Lesser, came to Antioch the Greater, and passed by Isauria and the city of Seleucia. He had Cyprus on the right and Tarsus and the famous city of Mallos, long since in ruins, on the left.[8]

4. At that time many two-faced and gluttonous people recently arrived from over the sea spread among us at Jerusalem[9] the tale that Bohemond had actually landed at Antioch, but they spoke falsely. Nevertheless, they thought they spoke the truth because they had come with some of his soldiers as far as Patara, together with the hawks and falcons, fowlers and dogs which he had sent on ahead.

LVIII

Perils Encountered at Sea. 1. Many are the troubles which, God willing or permitting, meet those sailing at sea. Sometimes the anchor breaks loose, sometimes a sail-yard or the carved ornamental stern[1] is broken, or the cables part.

2. When the winds veer the wind vane is watched in order to ascertain whether the ship is proceeding properly. There is danger that the course may be lost at night. When the stars are hidden by the clouds, or if the ship is run upon the rocks, there is imminent danger of shipwreck and death [Act. 27:20, 29–30]. As on land so also there are perils at sea.

3. Why do we wonder about ourselves if we remember the shipwreck of the Apostle Paul? His pilots let down a plummet to

[7] Romuald of Salerno, *Chronicon*, cols. 184–85; and *HF* 807, note 14.

[8] Fulcher is inaccurate with his geographical order. It should be Methone (chap. xv, 3), the Cyclades, Rhodes, Lycia, Adalia, Pamphylia, Cyprus, Seleucia (Silifke), Isauria, Tarsus, Mallos, and Antioch in Syria. The location of Antioch the Lesser (not in Pisidia) is obscure (*HF* 807, note 19).

[9] Fulcher indicates his presence in Jerusalem at this time.

[1] *Aplustre.*

sound the depth of the sea [Act. 27:28]. If he had not seen the vision of an angel in his extremity he would have despaired of his life [Act. 27:23–25].

LIX

The Great Sea. 1. Many ships are accustomed to run into danger in the Gulf of Adalia. The winds are wont to blow in violently from all sides, down the mountains into the valleys, to be deflected through lowland defiles, and to converge into a whirlwind in the Gulf. If sometimes the mariners meet a pirate ship they are robbed and pitilessly ruined.[1] But those who suffer this for the love of God, will they ever be disappointed in His rewards?

2. Let us say a few words about our sea. "We must not omit saying whence the Mediterranean comes. Some think it originates in the Straits of Cadiz and has no other origin than the inflow of the surging ocean. Those who think the contrary say that all the flowage comes from the Straits of Pontus. They support this by the solid argument that the tides from the Pontus never turn back."[2]

3. Therefore praise and honor be to the Creator of all who "fixed the limits of the sea and set the bounds and entrances. For He said unto it, 'Thus far shall you come and here your waves shall be thrown back upon you.' "[3] For when the sea dashes in its fury upon the coast it is turned into foam and cast back by the simple barrier of the shore.[4]

4. "Further, unless the power of a heavenly law inhibits, what prevents the Red Sea from joining the Egyptian Sea through the plain of Egypt, which lies considerably lower than the other flat valleys with which it is connected? Finally it is taught that two kings wished to connect these two seas and pour one into the other, first Sesostris the Egyptian and then Darius the Mede.[5] The

[1] For these dangers consult *HF* 811, note 2.
[2] Solin. *Col.* 18, 1–2.
[3] Job 38:10–11, quoted in Ambros. *Hexaemeron* iii. 2. 10.
[4] Vergil. *Aen.* i. 105.
[5] Sesostris is a legendary name in Egyptian history. Consult James H. Breasted, *A History of Egypt from the Earliest Times to the Persian Conquest* (2nd ed.;

latter in view of his greater power wished to accomplish what had been attempted by the indigenous prince.

5. "This is proof that the Indian Ocean, in which lies the Red Sea, is higher than the Egyptian Sea, which lies lower rather than on the same level. And perhaps it was to prevent the sea from flowing from a higher level to a lower and thus flooding the land that the two kings each gave up the undertaking." Thus it is stated in the *Exameron* of Ambrose.[6] It is otherwise in Solinus.[7]

6. Therefore the works of God are marvelous, but much more wonderful is He who created and arranged them. If any seem ugly in our sight nevertheless they are to be praised because the Creator of all made them. On the other hand these works are no less useful.

7. God has provided a medicine in the bug *cimex*.[8] He has given slyness to the polyp as well as to the sea urchin. To the serpents He has given wisdom [Matth. 10:16]. Sometimes these animals provide a remedy; sometimes they cause disease or even death. Sometimes they bring comfort, at other times harm. It is said that when an antidote for snake bite is prepared from the body of a serpent, although the poison and flesh of the snake is harmful when taken alone, such an antidote when mixed with other substance is safe and healthful.[9]

LX

Kinds of Serpents.   1. The basilisk is half a foot long, white as a mitre, and has a striped head.[1] It is given not only to the destruc-

---

New York: Charles Scribner's Sons, 1937), 189; and Percival G. Elgood, *Later Dynasties of Egypt* (Oxford: Basil Blackwell, 1951), 89. Darius is today known as Darius I, King of Persia (522–486 B.C.), the son of Hystaspes.

[6] Ambros. *Hexaemeron* iii. 2. 11. Ambrose may have used Plin. *Hist. Nat.* vi. 33. 165–66.

[7] Fulcher apparently refers to his previous remarks about the Mediterranean in par. 2, based upon Solinus (note 2).

[8] Perhaps the chinch bug (bedbug).

[9] I have been unable to find the source of Fulcher's remarks in par. 7. If he used Solinus, the passage would appear to be lost today. Solinus may have used Plin. *Hist. Nat.* xxix. 17. 61–62, which in this way may have been the source for Fulcher's remarks about the *cimex* and even about remedies for snake bites.

[1] In this chapter Fulcher, as if looking for something to occupy his time, re-

tion of men and beasts but of the earth itself, which it poisons and scorches. Wherever it has been it leaves a lurking place which is deadly, for at length the grasses and trees die. It pollutes the very atmosphere so that a bird cannot fly safely through the air infected by its pestilential breath.

2. When the basilisk moves half of its body crawls, and the other half is high and erect. Even the serpents tremble at its hiss. When they take flight they all rush off wherever they can. Whatever the basilisk kills with its bite no wild animal will eat, no birds will touch. Yet it is overcome by weasels, which men put into the dens in which it hides.

3. Indeed the people of Pergamum provided at the cost of a full *sestercium* the remains of a basilisk in order that the spiders might not cover with webs nor the birds invade a temple that was made remarkable by the hand of Apelles.[2]

4. The *amphisbaena* has two heads, the second being in the place of the tail. *Cerastes* have four small horns. They carefully cover their bodies with sand and then show their horns to look like food in order to decoy and kill birds.[3]

5. The *haemorrhois* draws out blood by its bite. By cutting the veins it sucks out through the blood stream whatever of life there is. The *prester* causes whatever it strikes to swell up to enormous size and die. Putrefaction often follows the swelling.

6. There are also *ammodytae*, the *cenchris*, *elephantiae*, *chersydri*, and *chamaedracontes*. Finally, whatever the name, there is a peculiar form of death caused by each of these serpents.

7. Scorpions, skinks, and *lacertae* are classed as worms, not as serpents. These foul creatures, if they hiss, are less dangerous. They scarcely have passions unless they are wandering off to their mates. There are also the *iaculi*, which strike whatever animal fortune brings in their way.

turns to Solinus' *Collectanea rerum memorabilium* for a discussion of mythical creatures (see chaps. xlviii–xlix) and ends by quoting the *Epistula Alexandri* (chap. xlix, 17, note 8). Again, as before, one can often tell what Fulcher, and Solinus, meant by referring to Pliny's *Historia Naturalis*, used by Solinus.
[2] Solin. *Col.* 27, 52–53.   [3] *Ibid.*, 27, 28–29.

8. The *scytale* gleams with such a variety of colors on its back that its beauty arrests the attention of those seeing it. The *dipsas* by its bite causes a lethal thirst. The *hypnale*, which kills by sleep, is used to induce death, as the experience of Cleopatra shows. The poison of other serpents, since it admits remedies, deserves less notice.[4]

9. These marvels are no less amazing than those seen by Alexander the Great in India. He confided to his master Aristotle and to his mother Olympias, "I would not have believed that there were so many wonders unless I had seen them with my own eyes."[5] Truly was this king a magnificent man in every respect, sagacious and circumspect in his affairs, vigorous in his vigor and powerful in power, and not like a flying feather or floating chaff.

LXI

The Arrival of Bohemond the Younger, the Son of Duke Bohemond, and His Reception in Antioch.   1. Since Bohemond had set out later in this year[1] than expected, we thought he would not come as had been announced and as popular expectation promised. But since according to the word of the prophet the way of man is not in his own hand, it is not from man but from the Lord that the progress of man is ordered [Jerem. 10:23], our imagination in great part deceived us in our hope. For that does not come to pass which human greed decides upon but which God justly judges proper for human deserts.

2. But when our king notified us at Jerusalem by letters that Bohemond had already landed at Antioch all of us were delighted.[2] We all praised God who had conducted Bohemond safely.

The sun had already set when Bohemond entered port by night.

[4] *Ibid.*, 27, 30–34.

[5] *Epistula Alexandri* in Rypins (ed.), *Three Old English Prose Texts*, 79, sec. 15.

[1] In mid-September, 1126 (chap. lvii, 3).

[2] Baldwin had been in the area of Antioch since his relief of al-Athārib in the latter part of the summer (chap. lv, 5). Hagenmeyer estimates that Bohemond arrived in the latter half of October (*HF* 820, note 2). Fulcher indicates that he, Fulcher, was then at Jerusalem.

3. Bohemond, on coming to Antioch, was joyfully welcomed by all. The king went out with a great procession and eagerly received him amidst the repeated cheers of the populace. The king and Bohemond had an immediate conference. Right after it the king turned over to Bohemond all his land and gave him one of his daughters in marriage.[3]

Behold father-in-law and son-in-law, father and son,
May the one esteem the other so that both be the stronger.

4. Then after the nuptials were arranged the wedding was carried out in lawful form. Bohemond while seated upon his throne was made prince and was vested in his very handsome robe of state. After his nobles were assembled they took the oath of fealty they owed to him as his men, swearing that they would serve him from that day forward. This was in the presence of the king and with his approval.[4]

5. After these things were done the king returned to Jerusalem.[5]

The Constellation of Scorpio was shining amidst the stars
of the sky
When Bohemond was welcomed as the ruler of Antioch.[6]
Now the orbit of the year has receded and stands ready to
begin the new.[7]

LXII

The Pestilence of Rats. 1. In the year eleven hundred twenty-seven of the birth of our Lord, in the fifth indiction, a multitude of rats appeared in the region of Palestine in such great number that some of them seized an ox by the hindquarters, suffocated him, and ate him along with seven wethers. Finally after having

[3] Alice, the second daughter of Baldwin II.
[4] Baldwin's determination to retain the alliance and support of Antioch is apparent here and in the betrothal of his daughter to Bohemond.
[5] Before Christmas, estimates Hagenmeyer (HF 822, note 14). See note 7.
[6] The period of the constellation of Scorpio ran from *ca.* October 23 to November 22. See HF 822, note 15.
[7] By "now" (*nunc*) it would seem that Fulcher wrote this passage about December 25, 1126, with which date he began reckoning the year 1127.

ravaged far into the land of the people of Acre they went up the mountain of Tyre, seeking water. From here they were driven back into the confines of the valleys in numberless thousands by a high wind and a savage and pestilential rainstorm. That area remained badly infected by the rotting of their dead bodies.[1]

Here Ends the *Historia Hierosolymitana*
of Master Fulcher of Chartres

[1] The account of the plague of rats in 1127 is original with Fulcher. Hagenmeyer suggests that it occurred in the summer when natural increase would have brought the rodents to the greatest number (*HF* 822, note 1). The abrupt ending seems to indicate that Fulcher stopped writing soon after this time. Presumably, he died or became incapacitated; otherwise, he would have mentioned such events as Baldwin's expedition into the Wādī Mūsâ in August or September, 1127 (Ibn-al-Qalānisī, *The Damascus Chronicle*, 182), the arrival of Baldwin's choice of son-in-law and heir, Count Fulk of Anjou, the next spring, or the death of Patriarch Gormond and the election of his successor, Stephen of Chartres, also in 1128 (William of Tyre, XIII, xxiv, xxv).

BIBLIOGRAPHY

†

PRIMARY SOURCES

Abu'l Faraj. *The Chronography of Gregory Abû'l Faraj, the Son of Aaron, the Hebrew Physician Commonly Known as Bar Hebraeus*, trans. Ernest A. Wallis Budge. Vol. I. London: Humphrey Milford, Oxford University Press, 1932.

Abulfedae tabulae Syriae, ed. Köhler. Lips., 1766.

Alberic of Trois-Fontaines. *Alberici mon. Trium Fontium Chronicon*, ed. G. G. Leibnitius. Hannov., 1698.

Albert of Aix. *Liber Christianae expeditionis pro ereptione, emundatione, restitutione sanctae Hierosolymitanae ecclesiae*, in *RHC, Occ.*, IV. Paris: Imprimerie Nationale, 1879. Pp. 265–713.

Alexander of Telese. *Alexandri Telesini coenobii abbatis de rebus gestis Rogerii II Siciliae libri IV*, in L. A. Muratori (ed.), *Rerum italicarum scriptores*, Vol. V. Mediolani: Ex typographia Societatis palatinae in regia curia, 1724. Pp. 607–45.

Anna Comnena. *Anne Comnène Alexiade: Règne de l'empereur Alexis I Comnène* (1081–1118), ed. and trans. Bernard Leib. ("Collection Byzantine pub. sous le patronage de l'Association Guillaume Budé.") 3 vols. Paris: Société d'édition *Les belles lettres*, 1937–45.

Anonymous Syriac Chronicle. "The First and Second Crusades from an Anonymous Syriac Chronicle," trans. A. S. Tritton, notes by H. A. R. Gibb, *Journal of the Royal Asiatic Society* (1933). Pp. 69–101.

Anselm of Ribemont. *Epistula I Anselmi de Ribodimonte ad Manassem archiepiscopum Remorum*, in *HEp*. Pp. 144–46.

————. *Epistula II Anselmi de Ribodimonte ad Manassem archiepiscopum Remorum*, in *HEp*. Pp. 156–60.

Baldric of Dol. *Historia de peregrinatione Jerosolimitana*, in *RHC, Occ.*, IV. Paris: Imprimerie Nationale, 1879. Pp. 1–111.

Bongars, Jacques (ed.). *Gesta Dei per Francos*. 2 vols. in 1. Hannov.: Typis Wechelianis, apud heredes Ioan. Aubii, 1611.

Bréhier, Louis (ed. and trans.). *Historie anonyme de la première croisade*. ("Les classiques de l'histoire de France au moyen age" pub. sous la direction de Louis Halphen.) Paris: Librairie ancienne Honoré Champion, éditeur. 1924.

Caffaro di Caschifellone. *Annales Genuenses*, in L. A. Muratori (ed.), *Rerum italicarum scriptores*, Vol. VI. Mediolani: Ex typographia Societatis palatinae in regia curia, 1725. Cols. 247–610.

————. *De liberatione civitatum orientis*, in *RHC, Occ.*, V. Paris: Imprimerie Nationale, 1895. Pp. 47–73.

Cerbani, Cerbanus. *Translatio mirifici Martyris Isidori a Chio insula in civitatem Venetam*, ed. Paul Riant in *RHC, Occ.*, V. Paris: Imprimerie Nationale, 1895. Pp. 321–34.

Dandulo, Andrea. *Chronicon*, in L. A. Muratori (ed.), *Rerum italicarum scriptores*. Vol. XII. Mediolani: Ex typographia Societatis palatinae in regia curia, 1778. Cols. 13–524.

Daniel, Abbot. *Vie et pèlerinage*, trans. B. de Khitrowo in *Itineraires Russes en Orient*. Vol. I. Genève: Fick, 1889. Pp. 1–83.

Descriptio sanctorum locorum Hierusalem (anonymous), ed. Rosalind Hill in *Gesta Francorum et aliorum Hierosolymitanorum: The Deeds of the Franks and the Other Pilgrims to Jerusalem*. ("Medieval Texts," ed. V. H. Galbraith *et al.*) London, Edinburgh, Paris, Melbourne, Toronto, and New York: Thomas Nelson and Sons, Ltd., 1962. Pp. 98–101.

Dietrich von Niem. *Vitae pontificum Romanorum*, excerpts in Alph. Fritz, *Zur Quellenkritik der Schriften Dietrichs von Niem*. Paderborn und Münster: Druck und Verlag von Ferdinand von Schöningh, 1886.

Duchesne, André (ed.). *Fulcherii Carnotensis historia Hierosolymitana* (1095–1127), in *Historiae Francorum scriptores*.

5 vols. Paris, 1636–49. Vol. IV (1641), 816–89. Reprinted in *MPL*, CLV (Paris, 1854), cols. 821–942; *ibid.* (Paris, 1880), cols. 821–940.

Ekkehard of Aura. *Hierosolymita*, in *RHC, Occ.*, V. Paris: Imprimerie Nationale, 1895. Pp. 1–40.

Epistula Alexandri regis magni ad Aristotelem magistrum suum, ed. Stanley Rypins in *Three Old English Prose Texts in MS Cotton Vitellius A xv*. ("Early English Text Society," CLXI.) London: Humphrey Milford, Oxford University Press, 1924. Pp. 79–100. Also ed. Alfons Hilka, "Zur Alexandersage. Zur Textkritik von Alexanders Brief über Wunder Indiens," *Jahresbericht über das königliche katholische St. Matthias-Gymnasium zu Breslau für das Schuljahr 1908–1909*. Breslau: Druck von R. Nischkowsky, 1909. Pp. i–xx.

Epistula cleri et populi Luccensis ad omnes fideles, in *HEp*. Pp. 165–67.

Gesta Francorum Iherusalem expugnantium, in *RHC, Occ.*, III. Paris: Imprimerie Impériale, 1866. Pp. 487–543. Sometimes attributed to Bartolf of Nangis, otherwise unknown.

Guibert of Nogent. *Historia quae dicitur Gesta Dei per Francos*, in *RHC, Occ.*, IV. Paris: Imprimerie Nationale, 1879. Pp. 113–263.

Guizot, F. P. G. (ed.). *Histoire des croisades par Foulcher de Chartres*, in *Collection des mémoires relatifs à l'histoire de France*. Vol. XXIV. Paris: Chez J. L. J. Brière, Libraire, 1825. Translations of original sources.

Hagenmeyer, Heinrich (ed.). *Anonymi gesta Francorum et aliorum Hierosolymitanorum*. Heidelberg: Carl Winter's Universitäts-Buchhandlung, 1890.

———. *Epistulae et chartae ad historiam primi belli sacri spectantes: Die Kreuzzugsbriefe aus den Jahren 1088–1100*. Innsbruck: Verlag der Wagner'schen Universitätsbuchhandlung, 1901.

———. *Fulcheri Carnotensis historia Hierosolymitana (1095–1127)*, mit Erläuterungen und einem Anhange. Heidelberg: Carl Winters Universitäts-Buchhandlung, 1913.

Hill, John Hugh, and Laurita L. Hill (eds. and trans.). *Raymond d'Aguilers Historia Francorum qui ceperunt Iherusalem*. Philadelphia: The American Philosophical Society, 1968.

Hill, Rosalind (ed. and trans.). *Gesta Francorum et aliorum Hierosolymitanorum: The Deeds of the Franks and the Other Pilgrims to Jerusalem*. ("Medieval Texts," ed. V. H. Galbraith *et al.*) London, Edinburgh, Paris, Melbourne, Toronto, and New York: Thomas Nelson and Sons, Ltd., 1962.

Hinschius, Paul (ed.). *Decretales pseudoisidorianae et capitula Angilrami*. Lips., 1863.

Historia ducum Veneticorum, ed. H. Simonsfeld in *Monumenta Germaniae historica*, G. H. Pertz (ed.), *Scriptores*. Vol. XIV. Hannov., 1883. Pp. 72–89, 94–97.

Ibn-al-Athīr. *Extrait de la chronique intitulée Kamel Altevarykh*, in *RHC, Or.*, I. Paris: Imprimerie Nationale, 1872. Pp. 187–744.

Ibn-al-Qalānisī. *The Damascus Chronicle of the Crusades*. Extracted and translated from the chronicle (*Dhail* or *Mudhayyal Ta'rīkh Dimashq*) by H. A. R. Gibb. ("University of London Historical Series," No. 5.) London: Luzac and Co., 1932.

Ibn Baṭṭūṭa. *The Travels of Ibn Baṭṭūṭa A.D. 1325–1354*. Translated, with revisions and notes from the Arabic text edited by Charles Defrémery and B. R. Sanguinetti, by H. A. R. Gibb. 2 vols. Ser. 2, Nos. 110, 117. Cambridge: Pub. for the Hakluyt Society at the University Press, 1958, 1962.

Ibn-Muyassar. *Extraits d'Ibn-Moyesser*, in *RHC, Or.*, III. Paris: Imprimerie Nationale, 1884. Pp. 461–73.

Jaffé, Philipp, and Samuel Löwenfeld (eds.). *Regesta pontificum Romanorum*. 2nd ed. 2 vols. Lipsiae: Veit et comp., 1885–88.

Jakut. *Reisen*, ed. Ferdinand Wüstenfeld in *Zeitschrift der deutsch. morgenländ. Gesellschaft*, XVIII, 397 ff.

Jerome, St. *Liber de situ et nominibus locorum Hebraicorum* (sometimes called the *Onomastikon*), in *MPL*, XXIII. Paris, 1883. Cols. 815–976.

Kamāl-ad-Dīn. *Extraits de la chronique d'Alep par Kamal ed-Dîn*, in *RHC, Or.*, III. Paris: Imprimerie Nationale, 1884. Pp. 571–690.

Kohler, Charles (ed.). "Un sermon commémoratif de la prise de Jérusalem par les croisés, attribué à Foucher de Chartres," *ROL*, VIII (1901), 158–64.

Krey, August C. (ed.). *The First Crusade: The Accounts of Eye-Witnesses and Participants.* Princeton: Princeton University Press; London: Humphrey Milford, Oxford University Press, 1921. Translations of original sources.

Le Bas, Philippe (ed.). *Gesta Francorum seu Tudebodus abbreviatus*, in *RHC, Occ.*, III. Paris: Imprimerie Impériale, 1866. Pp. 119–63.

Lees, Beatrice A. (ed.). *Anonymi gesta Francorum et aliorum Hierosolymitanorum.* Oxford: Clarendon Press, 1924.

Li Estoire de Jerusalem et d'Antioche, in *RHC, Occ.*, V. Paris: Imprimerie Nationale, 1895. Pp. 621–48.

McGinty, Martha Evelyn (trans.). *Fulcher of Chartres, Chronicle of the First Crusade (Fulcheri Carnotensis historia Hierosolymitana).* ("Translations and Reprints from the Original Sources of History," third series, ed. John L. La Monte, Vol. I.) Philadelphia: University of Pennsylvania Press; London: Humphrey Milford, Oxford University Press, 1941.

Mansi, G. D. (ed.). *Sacrorum concilium nova et amplissima collectio.* New ed. 53 vols. in 60. Paris: H. Welter, 1900–27.

Martène, Edmond, and Ursin Durand (eds.). *Thesaurus novus anecdotorum.* 5 vols. Paris: 1717 ff.

Matthew of Edessa. *Extraits de la Chronique de Matthieu d'Édesse*, ed. and trans. Édouard Dulaurier in *RHC, Arm.*, I. Paris: Imprimerie Impériale, 1869. Pp. 1–150.

Mommsen, Theodor (ed.). *C. Ivlii Solini Collectanea rervm memorabilivm.* Berolin apud Weidmannos, 1895.

Oliver the Scholasticus of Cologne. *Historia regum Terrae S. (1096–1217)*, in *Die Schriften des Kölner Domscholastikus Oliverus*, ausg. v. Hoogeveg. Tübingen, 1894. Pp. 80–158.

Ordericus Vitalis. *Historiae ecclesiasticae libri XIII*, in *MPL*,

CLXXXVIII. Paris: Garnier fratres, 1890.

Ralph of Caen. *Gesta Tancredi in expeditione Hierosolymitana*, in *RHC, Occ.*, III. Paris: Imprimerie Impériale, 1866. Pp. 587–716.

Raymond of Aguilers. *Historia Francorum qui ceperunt Iherusalem*, in *RHC, Occ.*, III. Paris: Imprimerie Impériale, 1866. Pp. 231–309.

Richard of Cluny. *Chronicon ab imperio Caroli magni sive ab anno Christi 800 usque ad annum 1162*, in L. A. Muratori (ed.), *Antiquitates italicae medii aevi*. 6 vols. Milan, 1738–42. Vol. IV, 1079–1104.

Robert de Torigni. *Chronique de Robert de Torigni*, ed. Léopold Delisle. 2 vols. Rouen: A. Le Brument, 1872–73.

Robert the Monk. *Historia Iherosolimitana*, in *RHC, Occ.*, III. Paris: Imprimerie Impériale, 1866. Pp. 717–882.

Röhricht, Reinhold (ed.). *Regesta regni Hierosolymitani* (MXCVII–MCCXCI). Oeniponti: Libraria academica Wagneriana, 1893.

Romuald of Salerno. *Chronicon*, in L. A. Muratori (ed.), *Rerum italicarum scriptores*. Vol. VII. Mediolani: Ex typographia Societatis palatinae in regia curia, 1725. Cols. 1–244.

Rozière, Eugène de (ed.). *Cartulaire de l'Église du Saint-Sépulcre de Jérusalem*. Paris: Imprimerie Nationale, 1849.

Rufinus. *Flavii Josephi Hebraei historiographi opera interprete Ruffino presbytero*. Colon., 1524.

Ryan, Sister Frances Rita (trans.). "History of the Expedition to Jerusalem by Fulcher of Chartres." Master's thesis, University of Minnesota, June, 1916. Pp. i–iii, 1–274.

Saewulf. *Relatio de peregrinatione ad Hierosolymam et Terram S. annis 1102 et 1103*, in *Recueil de voyages et de mém. pub. par la Société de Géographie*. Vol. IV. Paris, 1839. Pp. 818 ff.

Saumaise, Claude de (ed.). *Plinianae exercitationes in Caji Julii Solini Polyhistoria*. 2 vols. Trajecti ad Rhenum apud Johannem vande Water *et al.*, 1689.

Secunda pars Historiae Hierosolymitanae, in *RHC, Occ.*, III. Paris: Imprimerie Impériale, 1866. Pp. 545–85.

Sibt Ibn al-Jauzī. *Mir'at az-zamān. Extraits*, in *RHC, Or.*, III. Paris: Imprimerie Nationale, 1884.

Sicard of Cremona. *Chronicon*, in L. A. Muratori (ed.). *Rerum italicarum scriptores*. Vol. VII. Mediolani: Ex typographia Societatis palatinae in regia curia, 1725. Cols. 529–626.

Stephen of Chartres. *Epistula II Stephani comitis Carnotensis ad Adelam uxorem*, in *HEp*. Pp. 149–52.

Sturluson, Snorri. *Heimskringla*, in Finnur Jonsson (ed.), *Nóregs Konunga Sogur*. 4 vols. in 3. København: S. L. Mollers Bogtrykkeri, 1893–1901.

Theodore of Kloster Pöhde. *Theodori Palidensis narratio profectionis Godefridi ducis ad Jerusalem*, in *RHC, Occ.*, V. Paris: Imprimerie Nationale, 1895. Pp. 187–98.

Translations and Reprints from the Original Sources of European History. Philadelphia: History Department, University of Pennsylvania, 1894–99. Vol. I revised 1902.

Tudebode, Peter. *Historia de Hierosolymitano itinere*, in *RHC, Occ.*, III. Paris: Imprimerie Impériale, 1866. Pp. 1–117.

Urban II. *Epistula Urbani II papae ad omnes fideles in Flandria*, in *HEp*. Pp. 136–37.

Usāmah ibn-Munqidh. *An Arab-Syrian Gentleman and Warrior in the Period of the Crusades: Memoirs of Usāmah ibn-Munqidh (Kitāb al-I'tibār)*, trans. Philip K. Hitti. ("Records of Civilization: Sources and Studies," ed. Austin P. Evans.) New York: Columbia University Press, 1929.

Wallon, Henri (ed.). *Historia Iherosolymitana: Gesta Francorum Iherusalem peregrinantium* (MXCV–MCXXVII) *auctore Domno Fulcherio Carnotensi*, in *RHC, Occ.*, III. Paris: Imprimerie Impériale, 1866. Pp. 311–485.

Walter the Chancellor. *Galterii cancellarii Antiocheni bella Antiochena*, in *RHC, Occ.*, V. Paris: Imprimerie Nationale, 1895. Pp. 75–132.

———. *Galterii cancellarii bella Antiochena*, ed. Heinrich Hagenmeyer. Innsbruck: Verlag der Wagner'schen Universitäts-Buchhandlung, 1896.

William of Malmesbury. *De gestis regum Anglorum libri quinque*, ed. William Stubbs. (*Rolls Series*, No. 90.) 2 vols. London: Her Majesty's Stationery Office, 1887–89.

William of Tyre. *Historia rerum in partibus transmarinis gestarum*, in RHC, Occ., I. Paris: Imprimerie Royale, 1844.

———. *A History of Deeds Done Beyond the Sea*. Translated and annotated by Emily Atwater Babcock and August C. Krey. ("Records of Civilization: Sources and Studies," ed. Austin P. Evans, No. 35.) 2 vols. New York: Columbia University Press, 1943.

Secondary Works

Books

Andressohn, John C. *The Ancestry and Life of Godfrey of Bouillon*. ("Indiana University Publications, Social Science Series," No. 5.) Bloomington, Ind., 1947.

Baedeker, Karl. *Palestine and Syria*. 5th ed. Leipzig: Karl Baedeker; London: T. Fisher Unwin; New York: Charles Scribner's Sons, 1912.

Baramki, Dimitri. *Phoenicia and the Phoenicians*. Beirut: Khayat's College Book Cooperative, 1961.

Bartholomew, John (ed.). *The Times Atlas of the World*. 5 vols. London: Times Publishing Co., 1955–59.

Becker, Alfons. *Papst Urban II (1088–1099)*. Teil 1: *Herkunft und kirchliche Laufbahn. Der Papst und die lateinische Christenheit* ("Schriften der Monumenta Germaniae historica" 19/1). Stuttgart: Anton Hiersemann, 1964.

Besly, Jean. *Histoire des comtes de Poitou*. Paris, 1647.

Boulanger, Robert. *Lebanon*, trans. J. S. Hardman. ("Hachette World Guides" under the direction of Francis Ambière.) Paris: Hachette, 1965.

Breasted, James H. *A History of Egypt from the Earliest Times to the Persian Conquest*. 2nd ed. New York: Charles Scribner's Sons, 1937.

Cahen, Claude. *La Syrie du Nord à l'époque des croisades*. Paris:

Librairie orientaliste Paul Geuthner, 1940.

Chalandon, Ferdinand. *Histoire de la domination Normande en Italie et en Sicile.* 2 vols. Paris, 1907; reprinted in New York: Burt Franklin, 1960.

——. *Jean II Comnène (1118–43) et Manuel I Comnène (1143–80).* 2 vols. Paris: Picard, 1912; reprinted in New York: Burt Franklin, 1960.

Curtis, Edmund. *Roger of Sicily and the Normans in Lower Italy, 1016–1154.* New York and London: G. P. Putnam's Sons, The Knickerbocker Press, 1912.

David, Charles Wendell. *Robert Curthose, Duke of Normandy.* ("Harvard Historical Studies," Vol. XXV.) Cambridge: Harvard University Press, 1920.

Downey, Glanville. *A History of Antioch in Syria.* Princeton: Princeton University Press, 1961.

Du Cange, Charles Du Fresne. *Glossarium ad script. mediae et infimae latinitatis.* 6 vols. fol. Basil, 1762.

Dussaud, René. *Topographie historique de la Syrie antique et médiévale.* Paris: Librairie orientaliste Paul Geuthner, 1927.

Eiselen, Frederick C. *Sidon: A Study in Oriental History.* ("Columbia University Oriental Studies," Vol. IV.) New York: Columbia University Press, 1907.

Elgood, Percival G. *Later Dynasties of Egypt.* Oxford: Basil Blackwell, 1951.

Erdmann, Carl. *Die Entstehung des Kreuzzugsgedankens.* Stuttgart: W. Kohlhammer Verlag, 1965. (Unveränderter reprografischer Nachdruck der Ausgabe Stuttgart, 1935.)

Fabricius, Johann Albert. *Bibliotheca latina mediae et infimae aetatis.* 6 vols. Hamburg, 1734–46. Vol. II.

Fedden, Robin, and John Thompson. *Crusader Castles.* Beirut: Khayat's College Book Cooperative, 1957.

Fleming, Wallace B. *The History of Tyre.* ("Columbia University Oriental Studies," Vol. X.) New York: Columbia University Press, 1915.

Gindler, Paul. *Graf Baldwin I. von Edessa.* Halle A. S.: Hofbuchdruckerei von C. A. Kaemmerer & Co., 1901.

Giry, A. *Manuel de diplomatique*. Paris: Librairie Hachette et Cie, 1894.

Gjerset, Knut. *History of the Norwegian People*. 2 vols. New York: Macmillan and Co., 1915.

Green, D. H. *The Millstätter Exodus*. Cambridge: The University Press, 1966.

Grousset, René. *Histoire des croisades*. 3 vols. Paris: Librairie Plon, 1934–46.

Hagenmeyer, Heinrich. *Peter der Eremite*. Leipzig: Otto Harrasowitz, 1879.

Hansen, Joseph. *Das Problem eines Kirchenstaates in Jerusalem*. Luxemburg: Luxemburger Kunstdruckerei A. G. vorm. Dr. M. Huss, 1928.

Heyck, Eduard. *Genua und seine Marine in Zeitalter der Kreuzzüge*. Innsbruck, 1886.

Hill, John Hugh, and Laurita L. Hill. *Raymond IV, Count of Toulouse*. Syracuse: Syracuse University Press, 1962.

Hitti, Philip K. *History of Syria*. New York: The Macmillan Co., 1951.

———. *History of the Arabs*. London: Macmillan and Co., 1937.

———. *Lebanon in History*. London: The Macmillan Co.; New York: St. Martin's Press, 1957.

Iorga, Nicolas. *Les narrateurs de la première croisade*. Paris: J. Gamber, Éditeur, 1928. Pp. 38–61.

Iskenderian, Galust Ter-Grigorian. *Die Kreuzfahrer und ihre Beziehungen zu den Armenischen Nachbarfürsten bis zum Untergange der Grafschaft Edessa*. Weida i. Th.: Druck von Thomas und Hubert, 1915.

Join-Lambert, Michel. *Jerusalem*, trans. Charlotte Haldane. London: Elek Books; New York: G. P. Putnam's Sons, 1958.

Knoch, Peter. *Studien zu Albert von Aachen: Der erste Kreuzzug in der deutschen Chronistik*. ("Stuttgarten Beiträge zur Geschichte und Politik," Band I.) Stuttgart: Ernst Klett Verlag, 1966.

Lamb, Harold. *The Crusades: Iron Men and Saints*. New York:

Doubleday, Doran and Co., 1930.

La Monte, John L. *Feudal Monarchy in the Latin Kingdom of Jerusalem.* Cambridge, Mass.: Mediaeval Academy of America, 1932.

Mayer, Hans Eberhard. *Geschichte der Kreuzzüge.* Stuttgart: W. Kohlhammer Verlag, 1965.

Michaud, J. F. *Bibliographie des croisades.* 2 vols. Paris, 1822.

———. *Bibliothèque des croisades.* 2nd ed. 4 vols. in 5. Paris, 1829–30.

———. *Histoire des croisades.* 3 vols. Paris, 1812–17.

Molinier, Auguste. *Les sources de l'histoire de France.* 6 vols. Paris: A. Picard et fils, 1901–1906.

Munro, Dana Carleton. *The Kingdom of the Crusaders.* Student's Edition. New York, London: D. Appleton-Century Co., 1935.

Nicholson, Robert Lawrence. *Joscelyn I: Prince of Edessa.* Urbana: University of Illinois Press, 1954.

———. *Tancred: Crusading Leader and Lord of Galilee and Antioch.* Chicago: University of Chicago Libraries, 1940.

Olmstead, A. Ten Eyck. *History of Assyria.* Chicago: University of Chicago Press, 1951.

Paetow, Louis J. (ed.). *The Crusades and Other Historical Essays Presented to Dana C. Munro by His Former Students.* New York: F. S. Crofts and Co., 1928.

Pirenne, Henri. *Medieval Cities,* trans. F. D. Halsey. Princeton: Princeton University Press, 1939.

Prutz, Hans. *Kulturgeschichte der Kreuzzüge.* Hildesheim: Georg Olms Verlagsbuchhandlung, 1964; Reprografischer Nachdruck der Ausgabe Berlin, 1883.

Rey, E. G. *Les colonies franques de Syrie aux XIIe et XIIIe siècles.* Paris: Alphonse Picard, Éditeur, 1883.

——— (ed.). *Les Familles d'outremer de Du Cange.* Paris: Imprimerie Impériale, 1869.

Riant, Paul. *Expéditions et pèlerinages des Scandinaves en Terre Sainte au temps des croisades.* Paris: Ad. Laine et J. Havard, 1865.

Richard, Jean. *Le royaume latin de Jérusalem.* Paris: Presses

Universitaires de France, 1953.

Robert, Ulysse. *Histoire de pape Calixte II*. Paris: Alphonse Picard; Besançon: Paul Jacquin, 1891.

Röhricht, Reinhold. *Geschichte des Königreichs Jerusalem* (1100–1291). Innsbruck: Verlag der Wagner'schen Universitäts-Buchhandlung, 1898.

———. *Geschichte der Kreuzzüge im Umriss*. Innsbruck: Verlag der Wagner'schen Universitäts-Buchhandlung, 1898.

Runciman, Steven. *A History of the Crusades*. 3 vols. Cambridge: University Press, 1951–54.

Setton, Kenneth M. (editor-in-chief). *A History of the Crusades*: Vol. I, Marshall W. Baldwin (ed.), *The First Hundred Years*. 5 vols. projected. Philadelphia: University of Pennsylvania Press, 1955.

Shepherd, William R. *Historical Atlas*. 9th ed. New York: Barnes and Noble, Inc., 1964.

Stevenson, W. B. *The Crusaders in the East*. Cambridge: at the University Press, 1907.

Stieler, Adolf. *Handatlas über alle Theile du Erde und über das Weltgebaüde*. Gotha: Justus Perthes, 1881.

Sybel, Heinrich von. *Geschichte des ersten Kreuzzugs*. Dusseldorf, 1841; 2nd ed. Leipzig, 1881.

Tafel, Theophilus Luc. Fridericus. *De via militari Romanorum Egnatia, Dissertatio geographica*. Tubingae: Prostat apud H. Laupp., 1842.

———. *Via militaris Romanorum Egnatia*. Partes occidentalis et orientalis. Tubingae: Typis Hopferi de l'Orme, 1841.

Waas, Adolf. *Geschichte der Kreuzzüge*. 2 vols. Freiburg: Verlag Herder & Co., 1956.

Wilken, Friedrich. *Geschichte der Kreuzzüge nach morgenlänishchen und abendländischen Berichter*. 7 vols. in 8. Leipzig, 1807–32.

Wolff, Theodore. *Die Bauernkreuzzüge des Jahren 1096*. Tübingen, 1891.

Yewdale, Ralph Bailey. *Bohemond I, Prince of Antioch*. Princeton: Princeton University Press, n.d. [probably 1924].

Articles

Archer, Thomas Andrew. "Godric," *Dictionary of National Biography*, ed. Leslie Stephen and Sidney Lee. From the earliest times to 1900. Vol. VIII (n.d.; reprinted London: Humphrey Milford, Oxford University Press, 1921–22, 1937–38), 47–49.

Barker, Ernest. "The Crusades," *Encyclopaedia Britannica* (1910), VII, 524–52. Later reprinted as a separate volume entitled *The Crusades*. London: Humphrey Milford, Oxford University Press, 1923.

Barth, (Jo.) Kaspar von. "Animadversiones ad Bongarsianos scriptores historiae Palaestinae," in Petri a Ludewig, *Reliquiae manuscriptorum*, Vol. III. Lips., 1720.

Beaumont, André A. "Albert of Aachen and the County of Edessa," in *Crusades-Munro*. Pp. 101–38.

Brundage, James A. "An Errant Crusader: Stephen of Blois," *Traditio*, XVI (1960), 380–95.

———. "Fulcher of Chartres," *Catholic Encyclopedia* (1967), VI, 217.

———. "Recent Crusade Historiography: Some Observations and Suggestions," *Catholic Historical Review*, XLIX (1964), 493–507.

Cahen, Claude. "The Turkish Invasions: The Selchükids," in Setton (ed.), *Crusades*, I, 135–76.

Cate, James Lea. "The Crusade of 1101," in Setton (ed.), *Crusades*, I, 343–67.

———. "A Gay Crusader," *Byzantion*, XVI (1942–43), 503–26.

Crawford, Robert W. "Ridwān the Maligned," in James Kritzek and R. B. Winder (eds.), *The World of Islam*. London: Macmillan and Co., 1960.

Czajkowski, Anthony F. "The Siege of Antioch in the First Crusade," *Historical Bulletin*, XXVI (1948), 79–85.

Dehérain, Henri. "Les origines du *Recueil des historiens des croisades*," *Journal des Savants* (Nouvelle série, 17e année; Paris: Hachette et Cie, Libraires-Éditeurs, 1919). Pp. 260–66.

Duncalf, Frederic. "The Councils of Piacenza and Clermont," in Setton (ed.), *Crusades*, I, 220–52.

———. "The First Crusade: Clermont to Constantinople," in Setton (ed.), *Crusades*, I, 253–79.

———. "The Peasants' Crusade," *AHR*, XXVI (1921), 440–53.

Fink, Harold S. "The Foundation of the Latin States, 1099–1118," in Setton (ed.), *Crusades*, I, 368–409.

———. "Mawdūd of Mosul, Precursor of Saladin," *Muslim World*, XLIII (1953), 18–27.

———. "The Role of Damascus in the History of the Crusades," *Muslim World*, XLIX (1959), 41–53.

Ganshof, François-L. "Recherches sur le lien juridique qui unissait les chefs de la première croisade à l'empereur byzantin," in *Mélanges offerts à M. Paul-E. Martin*. ("Mémoires et documents publiés par la Société d'Histoire et d'Archéologie de Genève," XL.) Genève, 1961. Pp. 49–63.

Gibb, H. A. R. "The Caliphate and the Arab States," in Setton (ed.), *Crusades*, I, 81–98.

———. "Zengi and the Fall of Edessa," in Setton (ed.), *Crusades*, I, 449–62.

Hagenmeyer, Heinrich. "Chronologie de la première croisade (1094–1100)," *ROL*, VI–VIII (1898–1901).

———. "Chronologie de l'histoire du royaume de Jérusalem, règne de Baudouin I (1101–1118)," *ROL*, IX–XII (1902–11).

Hill, John Hugh, and Laurita L. Hill. "The Convention of Alexius Comnenus and Raymond of Saint-Gilles," *AHR*, LVIII (1953), 322–27.

Knapp, Joseph Arnim. "Reisen durch die Balkanhalbinsel während des Mittelalters nach der kroatischen Original-Abhandlung des Peter Matkovic," *Mittheilungen des kais. und kön. geographischen Gesellschaft in Wien*, XXIII, neuen Folge, XIII (1880).

Knappen, M. M. "Robert II of Flanders in the First Crusade," in *Crusades-Munro*. Pp. 79–100.

Kramers, J. H. "Kharput," *Encyclopaedia of Islam*, II (1927), 914–16.

Krey, August C. "Urban's Crusade—Success or Failure," *AHR*, LIII (1948), 235–50.

La Monte, John L. "The Lords of Le Puiset on the Crusades," *Speculum*, XVII (1942), 100–18.

———. "Some Problems in European Crusading Historiography," *Speculum*, XV (1940), 57–75.

Laurent, J. "Des Grecs aux croisés: Étude sur l'histoire d'Édesse," *Byzantion*, I (1924), 367–449.

"Lusignan," *Grand Dictionnaire universel du XIXe siècle*, ed. Pierre Larousse, X (1873), 795.

Moeller, Ch. "Godefroid de Bouillon et l'avouerie du Saint-Sépulchre," in *Mélanges Godefroid Kurth*, I. Liège, Paris, 1908. Pp. 75–79.

Munro, Dana Carleton. "A Crusader," *Speculum*, VII (1932), 321–35.

———. "Did the Emperor Alexius Ask for Aid at the Council of Piacenza?" *AHR*, XXVII (1922), 731–33.

———. "The Speech of Pope Urban II at Clermont, 1095," *AHR*, XI (1906), 231–42.

——— (ed.). "Urban and the Crusaders," *Translations and Reprints from the Original Sources of European History*, Vol. I, revised. Philadelphia: History Department, University of Pennsylvania, 1902.

Riant, Paul. "Inventaire critique des lettres historiques des croisades," *AOL*, I, 181–83.

Riant, Paul. "Inventaire des matériaux rassemblés par les Bénédictines au XVIIIe siècle pour le publication des *Historiens des croisades*," *AOL*, II, 105–30.

Richard, Jean B. "Fulcher of Chartres," *Encyclopaedia Britannica* (1966), IX, 994.

Runciman, Steven. "The First Crusade: Antioch to Ascalon," in Setton (ed.), *Crusades*, I, 308–41.

———. "The First Crusade: Constantinople to Antioch," in Setton (ed.), *Crusades*, I, 280–304.

———. "The Holy Lance at Antioch," *Analecta Bollandia*, LXVIII (1950), 197–205.

Sheffy, L. F. "The Use of the Holy Lance in the First Crusade." Master's thesis, University of Texas, 1915.

Sobernheim, M. "Ibn 'Ammār," *Encyclopaedia of Islam*, II (1927), 360–61.

Thatcher, Oliver J. "Critical Work on the Latin Sources of the First Crusade," *Annual Report of the American Historical Association for the Year 1900*. 2 vols. Washington, D.C.: Government Printing Office, 1901. Vol. I, 501–509.

Thompson, James Westfall. "The Latin Historians of the Crusades," chap. XVIII in *A History of Historical Writing*. 2 vols. New York: Macmillan Co., 1942. Vol. I, 310–23.

INDEX

†

Aaron, 147
Abel, murder of, 292
Abraham, Patriarch; Garden of, 128; sepulcher of, 145; at Harran, 273; sojourn near Aleppo, 273
Académie des Inscriptions et Belles-Lettres, 51
Accon, 114; *see also* Acre
Acharon, 114, 144, 176
Acre, futile siege of, 13; capture of, 29, 176, 223; also called Ptolemais, 114, 142, 174, 176, 200, 205; siege of, 174, 240; Baldwin I departs from, 200, 205; Adelaide of Sicily arrives at, 209; Adelaide departs from, 218; Baldwin II departs from, 235; supplies troops, 242; Venetians land at, 243; Franks return to, 245, 253; Franks gather to besiege Tyre, 255; situated in Lower Galilee, 262; troops of, in Damascan raid, 288; near Belus River, 293; Babylonian fleet passes by, 296; *see also* Accon, Ptolemais
Actipus, *see* Arce
Adalia, Bohemond II sails past, 298; Gulf of, dangers in, 299
Adelaide of Sicily, marries Baldwin I, 7n, 31; dismissed by Baldwin I, 14, 217; departure from Acre, 14, 218; Fulcher's disapproval of royal marriage, 40; death of, 221
Adhemar, Bishop of Le Puy, Fulcher's attitude toward, 37; apostolic vicar for crusade, 67; marches through Dalmatia, 72; at Dorylaeum, 85; believes story of Holy Lance false, 100; leader of Antioch, 104; sorties from Antioch, 105; death of, 107, 111; presides over Council of Antioch, 268
Aelia, 119
al-Afḍal Shāhānshah, vizier of Egypt,

al-Afḍal Shāhānshah (*cont.*)
125n, 163n; plans invasion of 1105, 182n; 186n; 200n; *see also* Lavedalius
Ager sanguinis, 227n
'Ain Mūsâ, spring, 147n
Alberic of Trois-Fontaines, 49
Albert of Aix, author of *Liber Christianae expeditionis*, 5; use of Fulcher, 47; published legend of Peter the Hermit, 49
Alemanni, 88
Aleppo, army of Maudūd moves to, 201; Il-Ghāzī retires toward, 233; lands devastated by Franks, 252; besieged by Baldwin II, 272, 273, 274; Abraham's sojourn at, 273
Alexander, King, captures Tyre, 260; received at Jerusalem, 260; in India, 288, 302
Alexius (I) Comnenus, Emperor, acquires Nicaea, 9, 82; defeats Bohemond I, 13; attacked by Bohemond I, 21; concern for his capital, 28; Fulcher's attitude toward, 37; 72; rewards princes at Constantinople, 80; rewards Franks at Nicaea, 83; accused of trickery and violence toward pilgrims, 192; makes treaty with Bohemond I, 193; death of, 221
Alice, Princess, married to Bohemond II, 32
Allobroges, 88
Ambrose, author of *Hexaemeron*, 45, 300
Ambushes laid for peasants of Jerusalem, 278
al-Āmir, Caliph of Cairo, 200n
Amircaradigum, 84
Amirdalis, advisor of Corbagath, 104–105
Amirsoliman, 104

· INDEX ·

Baldwin II (*cont.*)
Mesopotamia, 231; summons followers
from Sidon to Joppa, 234; crosses Jordan, 234; reconciled with Pons of
Tripoli, 236; relieves Sardanaium, 236;
appeals to Venice for aid, 238n; released from cell by Armenians, 246n;
counsels escape of Joscelin, 248; second
capture by Belek, 252; offered freedom
by Belek, 253; surrenders Kharput to
Belek, 254; spared by Belek, 254;
nephew of, spared by Belek, 254;
removed to Harran, 254; besieges Aleppo, 273; heads Frankish-Muslim coalition, 273n; retires to Antioch, 275;
returns to Jerusalem, 275; fails to relieve Cafarda, 278; relieves Hasar, 279;
builds castle of *Mons Glavianus*, 282;
raids lands of Damascus in 1125, 282;
in 1126, 288–91; departs for Lower
Syria, 294; returns to Antioch, 295
Banyas, 11, 260, 262; *see also* Caesarea
Philippi, Dan, Paneas
Bardarius River, 77
Bari, arrival of crusaders, 8, 75; desertion of faint-hearted, 36, 75–76
Barker, Ernest, 52, 53
Barra, capture of, 112
Barth, Kaspar von, 48, 50
Bartolf of Nangis, name given author of
*Gesta Francorum Iherusalem expug-
nantium*, 5, 21
Basilisk, 300, 301
Bavarians, 88
Beaked ships, 151n, 176, 194, 212, 238,
244n
Beersheba, 262
Beirut, ambush near, 11, 139; by-passed
in 1100, 11; capture of, 13, 29, 196;
by-passed in 1099, 114; Baldwin I
camps near, 142; defile near, passage
of crusaders of 1101, 166; Baldwin I
asks Genoese aid against, 195; plun-
dered, 197; visited by Titus, 293; citi-
zens of, defeat Egyptian fleet, 296
Belek, Nūr-ad-Daulah, captures Baldwin II, 16; recaptures Kharput, 16;
death of, 16, 262, 263, 264; attacks
Zardana, 236n; captures Joscelin and
Galeran, 237, 240; captures Baldwin
II, 240; holds Baldwin II and Joscelin
in captivity, 246; wife of, in citadel of

Belek, Nūr-ad-Daulah (*cont.*)
Kharput, 248; sees eyes torn out in
vision, 248; orders death of Joscelin,
248; imprisons Joscelin at Kharput,
250; recaptures Baldwin II, 252; captures Kharput, 252; acquires Aleppo,
252n; offers Baldwin II terms for Kharput, 253; recaptures Kharput, 253;
spares Baldwin II, 254; spares Galeran,
254; removes Baldwin II to Harran,
254
Belus, father of Dido of Carthage, 258
Belus River, 293
Benedict, Archbishop of Edessa, at defeat at Harran, 178; release of, 179
Bernard, Chancellor, Diocese of Chartres, 6
Bernard, Patriarch of Antioch, 175n,
230n; appeals to Venice for aid, 238n
Berthereau, Dom, 50; death of, 51
Bertrand, comes to Tripoli, 193; quar-
rels with William Jordan, 194; vassal
of Baldwin I, 195; assists in capture of
Beirut, 196; marches with Baldwin I to
Rugea, 201; father of Pons of Tripoli,
235
Bethlehem, 28; arrival of crusaders, 115;
seen by Fulcher in 1099, 132; Baldwin
I passes through, 147; scene of coro-
nation of Baldwin I, 148; scene of
coronation of Baldwin II, 232; 255
Bethsan, 262, 288; *see also* Scythopolis
Bira, burned by men of Ascalon, 265
Blessed Mary, Church of, at Antioch,
93; Basilica of, at Bethlehem, 116, 148
Blessed Nicholas, Church of, 75
Boëthius, *De consolatione philosophiae*,
45; quoted, 174
Bofinat, 77
Bohemond I, captured by Turks, vii, 27,
28, 29, 135; rules Antioch, 11, 38, 128;
pilgrimage to Jerusalem, 11, 19, 26,
129; war with Alexius, 13, 21, 30; de-
feated by Alexius, 22; proceeds to
France, 24, 181; calls for manpower,
24; letter of princes and, 26; visits Lake
Tiberias, 26; visits Baalbek, 27; effort
to control Antioch, 27; attempt of
Baldwin I to rescue, 27; released by
ibn-Dānishmend, 29, 175; defeated at
Harran, 29, 178; trip to Italy and
France, 29, 177, 181n; treaty with

Ethiopians (*cont.*)
125; at battle of Joppa, 158; infantry at Ascalon, 183; flight from battle at Ramla, 187, 188; in attack on Joppa, 241; ambushes by, 278

Euphrates River, crossed by Turks, 80; Baldwin I rules east of, 128; crossed by Bohemond I, 178; Baldwin I and Tancred mobilize at, 198; crossed by Maudūd, 201, 205; crossed by Bursuk ibn-Bursuk, 211; origin of, 217; crossed by Baldwin II, 225; crossed by Il-Ghāzī, 232n; crossed by Borsequinus, 274, 281

Eustace of Boulogne, listed in letter to Pope Urban II, 108; did not claim Jerusalem, 225n

Eustace Garnier, lord of Caesarea and Sidon, chosen defender of Jerusalem, 240; death of, 246

Eutropius, *Breviarium ab urbe condita*, 45

Evremar, Patriarch of Jerusalem, successor to Daimbert, 39; brings aid to Baldwin I at Ramla, 184, 185; journeys to Rome, 190, 191; ends career as Bishop of Caesarea, 228

Exameron, see Ambrose, *Hexaemeron*

Fabricius, Johann Albert, 50
al-Faramā', fatal journey of Baldwin I to, 15, 31, 221; Egyptian fleet cruises past, 296

Faramia, 221; *see also* al-Faramā'

Fernus River, at Antioch, 92, 93; Turks driven into, 97; Baldwin I joins Tancred at, 202; *see also* Orontes River

First Crusade, initiated by Pope Urban II, 3, 71

Firuz, betrayer of Antioch, 98n

Flemings, language of, 88

Foundering of ship at Brindisi, 76

France, customs of, 284

Frankish-Muslim coalition, headed by Baldwin II, 273n

Franks, first passage through Rome, 19, 70; second passage through Rome, 19, 164; transformation into Orientals, 35, 271; martyrdom of, 58; leave Nicaea, 83; destitution in Anatolia, 87; language of, 88; arrival at Antioch, 92; starve during siege of Antioch, 94;

Franks (*cont.*)
expel women during siege of Antioch, 95; starve outside of Antioch, 96; escape from Antioch by ropes, 102; starve within Antioch, 103; meet Arab band near Joppa, 161; besieged on hill west of Tiberias by Maudūd, 207

French pilgrims, arrival at Joppa, 149

Frisians, 88

Fulbert, Bishop of Chartres, 6

Fulcher of Chartres, author of *Historia Hierosolymitana*, vii; describes Council of Clermont, 3, 25, 61–69; starts crusade with Robert of Normandy and Stephen of Blois, 3, 6, 8, 26, 74–75; reports establishment of county of Edessa, 3, 88–92; chaplain of Baldwin I, 3, 92; time of writing, 4, 13, 18–24, 177–81, 252; mentions self by name, 5, 20, 71, 89, 92, 131, 145, 188; from area of Chartres or Orleans, 6, 11, 139; possibly once Prior of Mount of Olives, 6; priestly behavior, 7; age in 1123, 7, 252; age in 1125, 7, 281–82; familiar with *Templum Domini*, 7n, 118; audience with Pope Urban II, 8, 74–75; encounters partisans of anti-pope Guibert at Rome, 8, 75; reaches Bari, 8, 75; winters in southern Italy, 8, 75; sees ship founder at Brindisi, 8, 76; sails to Albania, 8, 77; travels on *Via Egnatia*, 8, 77n; admires Constantinople, 8, 79; reaches Nicomedia, 8, 80; sees bones of followers of Peter the Hermit, 8, 80; at siege of Nicaea, 8, 81–83; at Dorylaeum, 9, 84–87; at Antioch in Pisidia, 9, 87; at Iconium, 9, 87; at Heraclea, 9, 88; at Marash, 9, 89; joins Edessan expedition of Baldwin I, 9, 89; uses anonymous *Gesta*, 9, 18–20, 43; did not witness crusade from Antioch to Jerusalem, 9; uses Raymond of Aguilers, 9, 18, 19, 20, 43; sees Laodicea, Tripoli, Caesarea, Jerusalem, Bethlehem, Jordan Valley, Paneas, Lake Tiberias, Baalbek, Tortosa in winter of 1099–1100, 11, 130–34; in ambush near Beirut, 11, 138–42; travels via Antioch, Gibellum, Maraclea, Tortosa, Archas, Tripoli, Beirut, Tyre, Haifa, Caesarea, Arsuf, Joppa to Jerusalem, 11, 138, 142–43;

Marcisophar, reached by Baldwin II, 289; *see also* marj aṣ-Ṣuffar
Maria, Countess of Edessa, 251n
Marj aṣ-Ṣuffar, 289n; *see also* Marcisophar
Marra, cannibalism of Franks at, 112; destruction of, 113; *see also* Ma'arrat-an-Nu'man
Martene, Edmond, 50
Martyred knight, ascends to Paradise, 179
Massacre at Caesarea, 154
Massacre at Jerusalem, 122
Mathilda, Countess of Tuscany, ally of Urban II, 25, 70
Matthew of Edessa, Armenian chronicler, 5n, 48
Maudūd of Mosul, invades Palestine, 14, 22, 30, 204n, 205n, 207; campaigns of, 30; murder of, 30, 209, 211; Fulcher's tribute to, 36, 209; attacks Edessa, 197n; besieges Turbezel, 201n; *see also* Maledoctus, Mandulf
Mayer, Hans Eberhard, 55
Medan, 289
Medes, attack men of Antioch, 177
Media, land of, 58
Mediterranean Sea, 58n; part called Arm of St. George, 66; 146n; 216n; origin of, 299; *see also* Great Sea
Melitene, approached by Bohemond, 135; delivered to Baldwin I, 135; *see also* Malatya
Memnon, sepulcher of, 293
Menander, historian, 258
Mesopotamia, enemies from, 58, 149, 177; Edessa located in, 90, 197, 217; Turks from, 129; Turks cross, 201; Euphrates crosses, 217; Baldwin II rules as far as, 231; Kharput located in, 250
Messinopolis, 78
Meteors, 13
Methone, Venetians sail to, 239; devastated by Venetians, 276; Bohemond II arrives at, 298
Michaud, Joseph François, 51
Michiel, Domenico, Doge of Venice, commands fleet, 238n; 243n, 255n, 278n; *see also* Doge of Venice
Migne, J. P., 51
Millstatter Exodus, use of Fulcher, 47
Miracles, Fulcher's belief in, 41

Miriathos, 84
Moab, land of, 261
Modin, 115
Mohammed, termed an idol, 37, 118; termed an advocate, 94
Molinier, Auguste, 52
Mons Glavianus, castle near Beirut, 282
Montréal, castle built by Baldwin I, 14, 31, 215; return of King Baldwin I to, 216; *see also* ash-Shaubak
Moon, portent of, 219
Morphia, queen of Baldwin II, 232n
Moses, strikes rock, 147; speaks with God, 147
Mount Calvary, 22, 251
Mount Carmel, 114
Mount Gilead, 235, 253
Mount Hor, 147n
Mount Horeb, 215n
Mount Lebanon, above Archas, 113; source of Jordan River, 133; above Raphania, 293
Mount of Olives, ascended by Daimbert, 22; located outside of Jerusalem, 117; casket of Baldwin I met at, 222
Mount Pilgrim, castle of Raymond of Saint-Gilles, 181n, 194
Mount Sinai, 216
Mount Tabor, 288
Mount Zion, above Pool of Siloam, 116; in south Jerusalem, 117; attacked by Count Raymond, 120; residence of Daimbert, 143
Muḥammad, Selchükid Sultan, 211n
Munro, Dana C., thinks Fulcher was probably at Clermont, 8n; 53n; opinion of Fulcher's value, 54; on Urban's speeches at Clermont, 62n; 66n
al-Musta'lī, Faṭimid Caliph of Cairo, 125n, 163n
al-Muzeirib, 289n

Nabatanea, 262
Nablus, captured by Turks, 30, 207n; 288n; *see also* Neapolis, Sichem
Nahr al-'Awaj, see Pharpar River
Nahr al-Kalb, ambush at, 6, 27; Pass of, 138n, 167n
Nahr al-Kasimije, 259n
Nahr Na'man, 293n; *see also* Belus River
Napthali, territory of, 205; 260

Peter, Archbishop of Apamea, 236n
Peter the Apostle, Church of, at An-
tioch, 92; discovery of Holy Lance in,
100
Peter the Hermit, followers slain near
Nicomedia, 9, 73; legend of, 48, 49,
51; marches through Hungary, 72–73;
desertions among followers, 82n; legate
to Turks at Antioch, 103
Petra, area, Fulcher's journey to, 11,
147n
Pharpar River, 289n; see also Nahr al-
'Awaj
Philadelphia, city east of Jordan, 261
Philip I, King of France, death of, 22,
193; ruling in 1095, 61; father of Con-
stance, wife of Bohemond I, 181
Philippi, 78
Philistines, five cities of, 143, 144, 160,
242; land of, 226, 283, 296
Phoenicia, Turks cross, 205; invaded
by Assyrians, 258; named from Phoe-
nix, 261
Phoenicians, land of, contained Tyre
and Hazor, 257; furnish ships to As-
syrians, 259
Phoenix, 261
Pilgrims, arrive in 1113, 209
Pisans, assist in capture of Acre, 176n
Pisidia, 87
Pliny the Elder's Historia Naturalis,
used by Solinus, 41, 44, 285n, 300n
Plunder taken in battle of Ascalon, 127
Polyp, 300
Pompey, conquers Jerusalem, 261
Pons, Count of Tripoli, aids Baldwin I
in 1113, 30, 207n; denounces impu-
dence of Baldwin I, 207n; accompanies
Baldwin II, 228n; at battle of Tell
Dānīth, 229; refuses to submit to
Baldwin II, 235; reconciled with
Baldwin II, 236; knights squire of
Joscelin, 264; faithful ally of Jerusalem,
268; accompanies Baldwin II in at-
tempt to relieve Cafarda, 278; assists
Baldwin II relieve Hasar, 279; requests
aid of Baldwin II, 293; assists in siege
of Raphania, 294
Pontus, Straights of, 299
Praetoria, 78
Prester, 301
Princes return to native lands, 128

Privilegium, of Paschal II, 33; 269
Prologue of Fulcher, when written, 18,
24; 57
Provençals, followers of Count Ray-
mond, 105
Prutz, Hans, 52
Ptolemais, 114, 142, 174, 176, 200,
205; see also Acre
Pul, King of Assyrians, 259

al-Qawāmisī, Egyptian commander,
158n
Qinnasrīn, reached by Il-Ghāzī, 232n
Qubbat aṣ-Ṣakhrah, see Temple of the
Lord

Rachel, tomb of, 147
Ralph of Caen, Gesta Tancredi, used
by Fulcher, 46
Ramatha, 115; see also Arimathia
Ramla, twenty-four day vigil of Baldwin
I near, 12, 155; Baldwin I defeated
near, 12, 20, 29, 168; men of Ascalon
defeated near, 16, 191; Stephen of
Blois slain at, 20, 29, 169; Arabs defeated near, 20, 186; one of four cities
of Baldwin I, 28, 150; Baldwin I
escapes to, 29, 183; Syrian Christians
found at, 144, 163; Syrian Christians
threatened at, 163; bishop threatened
at, 163–64; Arabs encamp near, 167;
fugitives from battle shut up in, 169;
patriarch arrives at, 184, 185; number
of Franks in battle near, 185; Arabs
encamp near, 185; enemy defeated
near, 242; troops of, in Damascan raid,
288
Ranke, Leopold von, seminar of, 51
Raphania, capture of, 17, 294; Josephus
quoted on, 44; siege of, 291–92, 294;
Sabbaticus River located near, 293;
given to Count of Tripoli, 294
Raqqa, Bohemond I and Baldwin I defeated near, 178
Rats, plague of, 18, 303
Raven, 287
Raymond of Aguilers, author of Historia
Francorum qui ceperunt Iherusalem,
used by Fulcher of Chartres, 3, 18, 19,
20, 26, 43; uses anonymous Gesta, 19;
completes chronicle, 20; used by Wil-
liam of Tyre, 49; opinion of Harold
Lamb, 54

Vita of Frances Rita Ryan
(Sisters of St. Joseph)

✝

Mary Gertrude Ryan (later Sister Frances Rita Ryan) was born at Pipestone, Minnesota, on November 18, 1886, the fifth of the thirteen children of William H. and Mary Moriarty Ryan. She attended school at Pipestone, graduating from the high school in 1904 at which time she obtained a teacher's certificate by examination. She taught in rural schools, helped her parents at home, attended the Normal School at Mankato, Minnesota, taught at Okanogan, Washington, and spent the year 1910–11 teaching Eskimos in the area of Nome, Alaska. She then entered the novitiate of the Sisters of St. Joseph of Carondelet at St. Paul, Minnesota, on August 15, 1911, and made her final profession as a Sister of that Congregation on July 2, 1918.

Meanwhile, she attended the College of St. Catherine, St. Paul, Minnesota, in 1912–15, attaining the B. A. degree in 1915, and the University of Minnesota, acquiring the M. A. degree in June, 1916. This latter degree was awarded when she completed her thesis, "The History of the Expedition to Jerusalem by Fulcher of Chartres," under the direction of August Charles Krey. She later attended the University of Chicago, in 1925.

During her life Sister Frances taught history and Latin at St. Mary's Academy, Graceville, Minnesota, and in the secondary school of the College of St. Catherine until 1920. She was the principal of St. Anthony's High School, Minneapolis, in 1920–21, and probably in 1922–23. She taught at St. Margaret's Academy, Minneapolis, for the next ten years, was ill in 1933–34, and then taught at the Academy of the Holy Angels, also in Minneapolis, from 1935 to 1939. As a teacher she had a reputation for brilliance, wit, and a high standard of performance.

As a gifted scholar and expert Latinist, Sister Frances often assisted Professor Krey. She helped in the preparation of his volume, *The First Crusade* (Princeton, 1921), in which much of the translation of the first book of Fulcher was published. She also assisted Mrs. Willoughby M. Babcock and Dr. Krey in their translation and edition of A *History of Deeds Done Beyond the Seas, by William, Archbishop of Tyre* (New York, 1943). Unfortunately, a heart ailment cut short a promising career as teacher and scholar on June 13, 1939.

A HISTORY OF THE EXPEDITION TO JERUSALEM
1095–1127

has been set on the Linotype in eleven point Electra with two-point spacing between the lines. Perpetua capitals and italic were selected for display. The book was designed by Jim Billingsley, composed and printed by Heritage Printers, Charlotte, North Carolina, and bound by Kingsport Press, Kingsport, Tennessee. The paper on which the book is printed is designed for an effective life of at least three hundred years.

THE UNIVERSITY OF TENNESSEE PRESS
KNOXVILLE

DATE DUE

JAN 9 '78			
APR 1 5 1992			